Bernardo Cavallino of Naples

1616-1656

Bernardo Cavallino of Naples

1616-1656

INTRODUCTION

Ann Percy

ESSAYS

Nicola Spinosa and Giuseppe Galasso

CATALOGUE

Ann T. Lurie and Ann Percy

The Cleveland Museum of Art
The Kimbell Art Museum

Dabney Lancaster Library
Longwood College
Farmville, Virginia

ND
623
.C5
A4
1984

Exhibition Schedule

The Cleveland Museum of Art / Cleveland, Ohio
November 14 through December 30, 1984

Kimbell Art Museum / Fort Worth, Texas
January 26 through March 24, 1985

Museo Pignatelli Cortes / Naples, Italy
April 24 through June 26, 1985

The exhibition in the United States was made possible by a grant
from the National Endowment for the Arts, a federal agency,
and by a federal indemnity from the Federal Council
on the Arts and the Humanities.

Published in cooperation with Indiana University Press
Bloomington, Indiana 47405

©1984 by The Cleveland Museum of Art and Kimbell Art Museum
All rights reserved
Printed in the United States of America

Designed by Merald E. Wrolstad
Edited by Sally W. Goodfellow
Composition by Tecnicom Corporation, Solon, Ohio 44139
Printed by The Meriden Gravure Company, Meriden, Connecticut 06450

Library of Congress Catalogue Card Number: 84-072737
ISBN 0-910386-75-7

Contents

Color Plates
following pages 2, 34, and 42

Lenders to the Exhibition

Australia
Melbourne, National Gallery of Victoria

Austria
Schloss Rohrau, Graf Harrach'sche Familiensammlung
Vienna, Kunsthistorisches Museum

Canada
Ottawa, National Gallery of Canada

Czechoslovakia
Olomouc, Oblastní Galerie

England
London, I & G Fine Arts International Ltd.
London, Trafalgar Galleries

France
Caen, Musée des Beaux-Arts de Caen
Paris, Musée du Louvre

Germany
Brunswick, Herzog Anton Ulrich-Museum

Italy
Florence, Palazzo Vecchio
Milan, Museo d'Arte Antica, Castello Sforzesco
Milan, Museo Poldi Pezzoli
Milan, Pinacoteca di Brera
Milan, private collection
Molfetta, Pinacoteca del Seminario Vescovile Diocesano
Naples, Istituto Suor Orsola Benincasa
Naples, Museo e Gallerie Nazionali di Capodimonte
Naples, Collection Falanga
Naples, Collection Novelli
Naples, private collection
Rome, Gallerie Nazionale d'Arte Antica, Palazzo Corsini

Netherlands
Rotterdam, Museum Boymans-van Beuningen

Poland
Warsaw, Muzeum Narodowe

Scotland
Longniddry, East Lothian, Gosford House,
The Earl of Wemyss and March, K.T.

Spain
Madrid, Museo Lázaro Galdiano

Sweden
Stockholm, Nationalmuseum

Switzerland
Campione d'Italia, Silvano Lodi
Private collection

United States of America
Cleveland, The Cleveland Museum of Art
Fort Worth, Kimbell Art Museum
Hartford, Wadsworth Atheneum
Kansas City, The Nelson-Atkins Museum of Art
Malibu, California, The J. Paul Getty Museum
New York, Richard L. Feigen & Company
New York, Mario Modestini
Norfolk, Virginia, The Chrysler Museum
Private collection
Toledo, Ohio, The Toledo Museum of Art

Foreword

The great progress that has been made in understanding the complexities of Neapolitan painting between the death of Caravaggio in 1610 and the devastating plague of 1656 is one of the interesting achievements of recent art-historical studies. Much has been learned in a relatively short time through the energetic combing of church and civic records by local archivists, through the many discoveries by art dealers that have made available significant masterpieces of the period for public acquisition, through the gradual sifting of the material by scholars to further define individual personalities, and through the cleaning and restoration of great numbers of pictures—notably by the Soprintendenza per i Beni Artistici e Storici di Napoli. Indeed, the onslaught of the attack is not unlike the efforts of an earlier generation at the turn of the century in its definition of Quattrocento Florentine painting. The results to date have been impressive but, even so, much remains to be done. Today's understanding of a complicated achievement is made only more difficult because of the earlier disruption resulting from the grim plague of 1656, which in a few months' time wiped out half of the population of what had been Europe's second largest city.

A recent significant step in the broader recognition of the complexities—and the rewards—of seventeenth-century Neapolitan painting occurred with the exhibition Painting in Naples 1606–1705: From Caravaggio to Giordano shown in 1982–83 at London, Washington DC, Paris, and Turin. For many, the greatest single surprise of that exhibition was Bernardo Cavallino: it became, therefore, easily understood why Sherman E. Lee and Raffaello Causa were in the process of assembling an exhibition of this mysterious figure for their respective museums. The Kimbell Art Museum in Fort Worth, Texas, which had earlier organized the first major exhibition of Cavallino's great Neapolitan contemporary Jusepe de Ribera, subsequently joined the enterprise.

For Cavallino is indeed a mysterious figure: a creative life of little more than twenty years, only one dated work, and virtually no contemporary references. He was not unlike another anomaly of European painting some 300 years later, Vincent van Gogh, in that he assimilated the local influences and traditions of his time, and created a most original style, yet had no followers and little influence. He had a genius for treating the well-known stories of Biblical and classical history in a notably convincing manner. His personages—whether a young red-eyed Judith hovering somewhere between puzzlement and shock or a non-heroic Mucius Scaevola whose resolve has elements of the fanatic—were so representative of everyday persons that they become absolutely convincing. Repeatedly he dealt with disturbing tales, yet he painted them, almost ironically, with lyrical color effects that belied the horror of the scene. His skills in rendering form and his absolute ease in grasping unusual postures and movements led to seemingly effortless works. His intense manner was, for the most part, far removed from the flamboyance more usual in the work of his contemporaries.

An original and distinctive manner has made it possible essentially to establish the oeuvre of the master—although even as work on the exhibition was being completed important relevant works were appearing for the first time. The core group can be identified today, but given the dearth of precise facts, the matter of chronology, especially among the works of his middle years, remains a considerable puzzle. Attempting to make some inroads on this challenging problem became a justification for the exhibition. We hope, therefore, that further clarification may now occur once the pictures are seen together.

The acknowledgments published hereafter suggest the range of people who have contributed to the realization of this exhibition. Since the works associated with Cavallino's brief career are so few in number, every loan has been of the utmost importance. Owners have been remarkably generous; essentially half of Cavallino's known works are found in this exhibition. These works, when shown at the Museo Pignatelli Cortes in Naples, will be complemented by certain other works belonging to Capodimonte that could not come to the United States because of a previous commitment to the re-creation there of the Civiltà del Seicento a Napoli exhibition in the autumn of 1984.

The Museums were most fortunate that Ann Percy was prepared to pick up once again the various elements of her earlier unpublished research on Cavallino; she played a focal role in the planning and creation of the exhibition, and her sensitive introduction is an invaluable summary of the current understanding of this elusive painter. That the Philadelphia Museum of Art was prepared to free her for a considerable time from her duties as Curator of Drawings is most deeply appreciated.

Miss Percy worked closely with Ann Tzeutschler Lurie, Curator of Paintings at The Cleveland Museum of Art, and Nicola Spinosa at Capodimonte in choosing the paintings to be included. Mrs. Lurie carried the greatest part of the responsibility for working out the myriad details attendant on the creation of any major international loan exhibition. The catalogue is the result of the combined efforts of Miss Percy and Mrs. Lurie; the skill with which they have threaded their way through the problems of attribution and chronology should assure them a great debt of thanks on the part of many scholars. Those who have helped them with such good spirit are cited in the Preface, but particular thanks should be expressed to Renato Ruotolo for checking material in the Neapolitan archives.

Finally, it is most fitting that this exhibition be dedicated to the memory of the single person who has done most to bring awareness and understanding of the great splendors of seventeenth-century Neapolitan painting to his fellow citizens and to the larger world—Raffaello Causa. During his years as director of the fine gallery at Capodimonte, he used his authority to create a brilliant succession of exhibitions and to ferret out works lost or unknown even as he maintained an impressive life of scholarship. His sudden death as the final details of the exhibition were being completed was a tremendous shock, but the memory of his achievements has been a constant challenge to assure that in its final form the exhibition would be an appropriate reflection of his impressive standards.

Evan H. Turner
Director, The Cleveland Museum of Art
Cleveland, Ohio

Edmund P. Pillsbury
Director, Kimbell Art Museum
Fort Worth, Texas

Nicola Spinosa
Soprintendente Reggente per i Beni Artistici e Storici
di Napoli e Direttore di Museo e Gallerie Nazionali di Capodimonte
Naples, Italy

Preface

At a chance meeting in 1980 in Berlin, Raffaello Causa, Director of the Museo e Gallerie Nazionali di Capodimonte in Naples, and Sherman E. Lee, Director of The Cleveland Museum of Art, conceived the idea of a major exhibition of the paintings of Bernardo Cavallino as a pioneer tribute to one of the most original, appealing, and yet least-known painters of the early Neapolitan Seicento. The two museums enthusiastically proceeded with plans and were joined almost immediately by the Kimbell Art Museum, under its director, Edmund P. Pillsbury, as the third sponsor and exhibitor of Bernardo Cavallino of Naples, 1616–1656. By 1983 Evan H. Turner had succeeded Sherman Lee as Director of the Cleveland Museum and promptly lent his own enthusiasm and considerable energies in carrying the project forward. Sadly though, 1984 brought the untimely death of Professor Causa, even as the exhibition was taking final form; thus this great scholar and lifetime devotee of Cavallino was deprived of the fulfillment of his dream and the personal joy it would have brought.

The exhibition has been realized through the contributions and help of many, but in chief part, certainly, because of the generous consent of the Italian Government and its regional ministries of Naples to lend nearly all of Cavallino's major works in Italy to the United States exhibition. We join our Neapolitan colleagues in recognizing the following persons in Naples for their support of the exhibition and for their commitment to the arts: The Hon. Giulio Andreotti, Minister of Foreign Affairs; the Hon. Antonino Gullotti, Minister of Culture; The Hon. Giuseppe Galasso, Under Secretary of Cultural Affairs; The Hon. Vincenzo Scotti, Mayor of Naples; Dr. Riccardo Boccia, Prefect of Naples; The Hon. Antonio Fantini, President of the Regional Committee of Campania; The Hon. Giovanni Acocella, President of the Regional Council of Campania; Dr. Gianfranco Corrias, Chief Constable of Naples; The Hon. Amelia Cortese Ardias, Municipal Magistrate of Cultural Affairs of Campania; Prof. Mario Condorelli, Senator of the Republic of Italy; Dr. Guglielmo Triches, Director General of the Central Office of Architectural, Artistic, and Historical Monuments; Dr. Francesco Sisinni, Director General of the Central Office of Libraries and Cultural Institutions; Dr. Renato Grispc, Director General of the Central Office of Archives; Mr. Walter John Silva, Consul of The United States of America in Naples.

Nor could the exhibition have been possible without the United States Government's generous assistance, specifically, the support fom the Federal Council on the Arts and Humanities under the Arts and Artifacts Indemnity Act, and the National Endowment for the Arts.

Above all, we acknowledge with deep gratitude the generosity of the lenders, both individuals and public institutions — in Australia, Austria, Canada, France, the Federal Republic of Germany, Great Britain, Italy, the Netherlands, Poland, Spain, Sweden, and the United States—who so willingly parted with their important paintings for a period of many months. Theirs is a sacrifice of meaning and substance that has permitted the inclusion of more than half of Cavallino's works in the exhibition. Regrettably, the remaining works, no less important or desired, are missing because of conservation concerns, legal restrictions, conflicts in schedules, or because of limitations set on the exhibition budget. Among these are the two tondi, *Erminia among the Shepherds* and *Erminia and the Wounded Tancred*, from Munich; the *Finding of Moses* from Brunswick; the beautiful *Esther before Ahasuerus* in the Uffizi, Florence; the *Expulsion of Heliodorus from the Temple*, from Moscow; the single surviving original representation of the Tobias series, *The Curing of Tobit* in Kassel; and the exceptional *Saint Cecilia* at the Museum of Fine Arts, Boston, one of the few paintings by Cavallino in the United States.

We are deeply indebted to the Capodimonte and its staff; foremost is the late Raffaello Causa, whose deep understanding and love for Cavallino have remained a source of inspiration for all who have worked on the exhibition and its catalogue, and his successor, Nicola Spinosa, who has shared his knowledge, opinions, and research. Special thanks also go to Conservator Bruno Arciprete, who expeditiously restored paintings in time for the exhibition, and to Dr. Mariella Utili for her untiring and creative efforts to provide a smooth flow of communication across the Atlantic. Others, too, on the staff of the Capodimonte have contributed in countless ways—Denise Maria Pagano, Ernani Gambardella, Pierluigi Leone de Castris, Annachiara Alabiso, Ileana Creazzo, Roberto Middione, and Riccardo Lattuada—all have played a part in the common effort.

While many individuals at the Cleveland Museum have contributed in various ways to the realization of the exhibition and its catalogue—and sincere appreciation is extended to them all—some merit special thanks. Valuable assistance was given by the Registrar, Delbert Gutridge, and by Jacquelyn Casey of his staff, for handling the many complex details of insurance, transportation, customs, and couriers that are part of a loan exhibition. Martha Thomas, as administrative assistant and accountant for the exhibition, served with creativity and dedication. Hannelore Osborne, Assistant to the Curator of Paintings, helped with all aspects of research and accomplished the enormous task of compiling literary references and an extensive general bibliography. Another challenging assignment was that of drawing up an annotated inventory, based on Ann Percy's earlier research, listing 190 paintings published as by Cavallino but now lost, unidentified, or with doubted attributions; this work was carried out by Grace Fowler, Special Research Assistant, who contributed significantly to various aspects of the exhibition as well.

The catalogue, published jointly with the Kimbell Art Museum, contains an illustrated entry for each of the eighty-five works accepted as autograph by Ann Percy, Ann Lurie, and Nicola Spinosa. As such, it is the first catalogue raisonné of Cavallino's paintings, and it is hoped that it will serve as an important reference for future studies of this painter. (An Italian edition will accompany the Naples exhibition.)

The formidable task of editing a catalogue of multiple authorship fell to Sally W. Goodfellow, Associate Editor for Catalogues, who performed with dedication, perceptiveness, and infinite patience. Chief Editor Merald E. Wrolstad designed the handsome catalogue. Jandava D. Cattron undertook with diligence the complexities of translating Nicola Spinosa's essay, and Emilie P. Kadish provided help with revisions and editing—as did Pasquale Trisorio and George Nygren in like manner for Giuseppe Galasso's essay. Judith DeVere of the Conservation Department offered kind and able assistance with typing and proofreading. And in Philadelphia Kathy Gibbs deserves special thanks for typing Ann Percy's material for the catalogue.

The Museum Library, headed by Jack P. Brown, provided seemingly endless aid. Georgina Toth helped with bibliographical research and queries, as did Rena Hudgins, who also provided prompt translations of Italian letters and miscellaneous materials. Eleanor Scheifele, Photograph Librarian, enthusiastically and efficiently compiled the subject index for the catalogue. And others in the Library who served at varying times at the reference desk were helpful on many occasions. In the Art History and Education Department Mariana Carpinisan assisted with translations.

Finally, mention must be made of the host of friends throughout Europe and the United States—scholars; scouts; conservators; and staffs of museums, art archives, libraries, and universities—who have responded to requests and volunteered their expertise fully and freely, sharing their knowledge and discoveries. All are deserving of our warmest gratitude: Dr. Santiago Alcolea-Blanch; Manuel Gilberto Algranti; Prof. Diego Angulo Iniquez; Ian Appleby; Prof. Mercedes Agullo y Cobo; José Manuel Arnáiz; Angel Barrero Mandacén; Dr. Elisa Bermejo; Carmen Bernes; Prof. Jan Białostocki Bibliotheca Hertziana, Rome; Biblioteca Nacional, Madrid; Prof. E. Ward Bissell; John Brealey; Prof. Harvey Buchanan; Dr. Giuseppe De Vito; Lydia Dufour; Dr. Craig Felton; Prof. Oreste Ferrari; Freiberger Library of Case Western Reserve University, Cleveland; Frick Art Reference Library, New York; Enrique Garcia-Herraíz; Manuel Gonzales; Marco Grassi; Dr. Mina Gregori; Prof. José Gudiol; Claire Hendy; Hispanic Society of America, New York; Rupert C. Hodge; Insituto Diego Velazquez, Madrid; Dr. Sabine Jacob; Prof. Michael Jaffé; Dr. William Jordan; Dr. Rüdiger Klessmann; Dr. Robert Keyszelitz; Jaroslava Kopečná; Gabrielle Kopelman; Prof. José Labrador; Prof. Joseph L. Laurenti; Dr. Sherman E.

Lee; Library of the Metropolitan Museum of Art, New York; Library of the Museo del Prado, Madrid; Prof. Michael Liebmann; Clemens Linzen; Dr. Louise Lippincott; Prof. José López-Rey y Arrojo; Denis Mahon; Patrick Matthiesen; Museum of Fine Arts, Budapest; Dr. Manuela Mena Marqués; Maurizio Marini; Prof. José Milicua; Mario Modestini; Mary Newcome; Dr. Vincenzo Pacelli; Dr. D. Stephen Pepper; Prof. Alfonso E. Pérez Sánchez; Dr. Wolfgang Prohaska; Dr. Olga Pujmanová; Prof. Charles Reeves; The John and Mabel Ringling Museum of Art, Sarasota; Dr. Pierre Rosenberg; Dr. Renato Ruotolo; Dr. Eduard Safařík; Prof. Luigi Salerno; Helen Sanger; Dr. Erich Schleier; Dr. Lubomír Slavíček; Prof. Richard E. Spear; Dr. John Spike; Prof. Michael Stoughton; Prof. Bruce Wardropper; Witt Library, London; The Honorable Vice-Consul Stella Maria Zannoni, Cleveland; Prof. Angel Zorita.

Ann Tzeutschler Lurie
Coordinator for the Exhibition

Notes to the Reader

1. Of the eighty-five works in the catalogue, those that do not appear in any of the exhibitions carry the designation ''In catalogue only'' beneath their title in the entry.

2. Authorship of the catalogue entries is indicated by initials at the end of each entry:

ATL   Ann Tzeutschler Lurie

AP   Ann Percy

NS   Nicola Spinosa

3. Numbers in brackets—e.g. [21]—refer to catalogue entries. Numbers in parentheses with ''Inv.''—e.g. (Inv. no. 73)—refer to entries in the Inventory following the catalogue section. Likewise, numbers in parentheses with ''Appendix''—e.g. (Appendix, no. 9)—refer to items in the Appendix.

4. For all paintings the medium is understood to be oil.

5. Dimensions are given in centimeters; height precedes width. Seventeenth- and eighteenth-century measurements given in *palmi* are usually followed by the approximate equivalents in centimeters, based on 1 *palmi* = 26.4 centimeters.

6. References cited in abbreviated form are given in full in the Bibliography.

7. The usage of Annunciation(s) in singular or plural form when referring to the Master of the Annunciation to the Shepherds reflects the preference of the individual author.

Introduction

ANN PERCY

Naples, 5 March 1787
We have spent the second Sunday in Lent wandering from one church to another.
What is treated in Rome with the utmost solemnity is treated here with a lighthearted gaiety.
The Neapolitan school of painting, too, can only be properly understood in Naples.
Johann Wolfgang von Goethe

The chief problem confronting the student of Cavallino's art is that there are virtually no facts known concerning either his life or his work. We know that he was born in Naples in 1616 and that very likely he died there, aged forty, during the plague of 1656. Whether or not he ever traveled outside his native city is uncertain. Only eight of his eighty-odd known works are signed or initialed. One altarpiece bears a date of 1645, and he was paid for unidentified paintings in 1646 and 1649. Beyond this we have no information about his pictures dating from his own lifetime and very little from the two hundred and fifty years following.

So little contemporary evidence survives for Cavallino partly because the Neapolitans were not as fortunate as the Bolognese, Florentines, Romans, Venetians, or Genoese in having a seventeenth-century biographer of artists who knew his subjects personally or recorded anecdotes, oral traditions, and recollections of them relatively soon after their lifetimes. The first compendium of lives of the Neapolitan artists, Bernardo de Dominici's *Vite de'pittori, scultori, ed architetti napoletani*, appeared in 1742–43; in Cavallino's case the biographer was gathering information about his subject at least three-quarters of a century after the artist's death. Moreover, Cavallino worked almost exclusively within the cabinet-picture tradition, producing easel paintings and devotional pictures for private chapels and collections, a kind of art for which documentation rarely survives, or at least is difficult to retrieve. We

know of only one painting by him from a Neapolitan church [44]; an additional ten pictures in churches tentatively attributed to him, mainly in the late nineteenth century, are either lost or have been reassigned to other artists (see Inv. nos. 41, 44, 46, 59, 111, 130, 146, 148, 149, 151). He specialized in relatively small (approximately one by one and a half meters or less) canvases or coppers of scenes from the Old and New Testaments, the Apocrypha, Ovid, Tasso, Roman history, and mythology, and in single-figure images of saints. Such works were easily transportable, and de Dominici's contention that the pictures were sold outside the city, often under the names of other artists even during Cavallino's own lifetime, is probably correct. Because the paintings were mainly in private collections and were less readily accessible to visitors to Naples and to the authors of guidebooks and dictionaries of artists than were works in churches or public buildings, they rarely enter the eighteenth- and nineteenth-century literature. Cavallino, in effect, almost disappears after the mid-eighteenth century until his rediscovery from about 1910 onward in a number of articles and short studies. To a remarkable degree our conception of him is the creation of twentieth-century scholarship.

That so little early evidence survives concerning Cavallino must be in part due to certain circumstances in Naples itself that have compounded the difficulties of retrieving information about its seventeenth-century past.

1

Fig. 1. Cavallino. Detail of *The Meeting of Anna and Joachim at the Golden Gate of Jerusalem* [1].

"Wedged," in Goethe's phrase, "between God and the Devil," the city nourishes even today an ancient, dark, tragic, and primitive side. The same Fortuna—blind and deaf, dispensing bounty or distress according to her mood—who endows Naples with a natural situation of unsurpassable beauty, an irresistible climate, and an abundance of all growing things regularly turns the dark side of her face towards the city. Plagues, earthquakes, revolutions, volcanic eruptions, and world wars—violent and destructive events alternately orchestrated by nature and by man—have disrupted life continually since the seventeenth century. Much historical material has been destroyed in these circumstances, and much continues to be difficult of access.

Offsetting Cavallino's obscurity as an historical figure is his striking distinctiveness as a painter. At his maturity he surpasses all his Neapolitan contemporaries in the combination of a great virtuosity and refinement of brushwork with complex and dramatic compositions and an extraordinary originality of coloristic sense. He develops over rather a short career from an early academic, tenebrist grand manner heavily influenced by Riberesque naturalism, through an apparently calculated choice to produce easel pictures on a reduced scale infused by an intensely neo-Mannerist sense of elegance and drama, toward a late style novel for its emotionalism, its theatricality, and its brilliant palette. This development is difficult to explain, and we do not know whether it was nurtured solely by the artistic culture that Naples offered between about 1630 and 1656 or whether it was influenced in part by the artist's traveling to other cities in Italy. In any case, Cavallino was the kind of painter who rarely drew literally from his sources. What he derived from other artists was transformed immediately and intangibly into his own idiom. Spanish, French, Netherlandish, and native Italian elements commingle in his work in a unique fashion, so that we cannot even be sure who his first master was, only that he seems to have been trained in a thoroughgoing academic tradition. The still-undiscovered key to understanding this remarkable artist will no doubt

Fig. 2. Cavallino. Detail of presumed self-portrait in *The Martyrdom of Saint Bartholomew* [3].

Color Plate I. *Esther before Ahasuerus* [21].

Color Plate II. *The Curing of Tobit* [24].

Color Plate III. *Lot and His Daughters* [38].

Color Plate IV. *Saint Cecilia in Ecstasy* [43].

Color Plate V. *The Mystical Marriage of Saint Catherine of Alexandria* [50].

Color Plates VI and VII.
*The Virgin of the
Immaculate Conception* [51
Detail opposite.

Color Plate VIII. *Saint Anthony of Padua* [56].

be found in the particular circumstances of his patronage, in the commissioning and marketing of his highly personal works within the complex economic, political, and sociological situation of mid-Seicento Naples.

We can tally the contemporary mentions of Cavallino in sources and documents on the fingers of one hand, and those from the later seventeenth, eighteenth, and nineteenth centuries add little to the picture drawn by de Dominici and published in 1743. The date of his baptism, 25 August 1616, was published in the early 1950s.[1] By 1636, as we know through a document concerning the transferral of funds from his mother's estate, he had successfully entered a court petition to attain his majority.[2] He was then aged twenty, and we might risk a guess that this was a necessary formality for opening a workshop or otherwise establishing himself legally in his profession. From 1643 until 1646 he maintained a tiny bank account in the Banco del Sacro Monte dei Poveri in Naples,[3] and he inscribed the year 1645 along with his name on the spine of a book in his well-known painting of *Saint Cecilia in Ecstasy* [44]. In March of 1646 he received payment from an otherwise unidentified patron, Carlo Cioli, for large pictures of the *Annunication* and *Immaculate Conception*,[4] and in January of 1649 he was paid by the principe di Cardito for an unnamed "quatro grande" then in progress.[5] This is all we know about his life, and it is greatly to be hoped that additional archival evidence will eventually be discovered to flesh out these sparse facts. One would particularly like to know whether the artist died before, during, or after the great plague of 1656, the course of which was so horrific in terms of numbers of dead as to render impossible an accurate keeping of records.

From 1656 until the appearance of the first monograph on Cavallino in 1909 published notices of the artist, with but a few exceptions, are confined to brief mentions in dictionaries of artists or to listings of works in churches and private collections from the guidebooks and old inventories.[6] A list of 1673 and a manuscript note of 1675 dispatched from Naples by the Florentine correspondent of Cardinal Leopoldo de'Medici, Pietro Andrea Andreini, to the Florentine biographer of artists Filippo Baldinucci named Cavallino among those Neapolitan artists by whom drawings were owned by the Medici and as one of the celebrated painters working in Naples between 1640 and 1675.[7] The manuscript note seems to be the only biographical notice to fall between the year of the painter's death and that of de Dominici's *vita*,[8] and the latter is the single attempt at an extensive treatment of Cavallino's artistic personality before the twentieth century. While it should be used with care, it offers a certain amount of

biographical information and, more interestingly, a provocative assessment of the artist's formation and of the market situation within which his style matured.

Bernardo de Dominici (Naples 1683–1759) was himself a painter, of minor reputation, in Francesco Solimena's circle. Supposedly he labored for seventeen years on his lives of the Neapolitan artists in an effort to redress an unfortunate situation whereby his compatriots were ignored in the literature of art for lack of proper biographies.[9] Within thirty years of its publication in 1742–43 de Dominici's three-volume work came under fire for being uncritical, gossipy, full of inventions, and based on false manuscript sources;[10] later in the century another writer regretted that it did not contain "more information, better method, [and] fewer words."[11] In the late nineteenth and early twentieth centuries Neapolitan historians attacked it vigorously, and some of the biographer's anecdotes were, as a result, exposed as the tall tales they actually are.[12] In the case of Cavallino, de Dominici provides a patently wrong date of birth (10 December 1622) and such a bizarre account of his death that we are tempted to dismiss it out of hand, although there is no proof that the artist did not indeed die at the beginning of 1654, as de Dominici maintains, instead of in the plague of 1656, as modern scholarship assumes.[13] His story of Cavallino's discovery by Stanzione at the age of ten under the tutelage of a schoolmaster who encouraged his precocious talent in drawing at the expense of the rest of his studies may remind us of other similar stories, such as Vasari's account of Cimabue finding the child Giotto sketching sheep in the countryside; his description of Cavallino's death as an unfortunate consequence of the pleasures of love brings to mind as well Vasari's account of Raphael's last illness. All this is not to say, however, that the biography does not offer much of substance and interest.

De Dominici tells us that Cavallino studied with Massimo Stanzione for eight or so years from the age of ten.[14] Whether Stanzione was Cavallino's only master is problematic, and whether the younger artist actually joined his studio aged ten, or around 1626, is more so, especially as Stanzione is now thought to have been in Rome during at least part of the second half of the 1620s.[15] Moreover, virtually nothing is known about how Stanzione conducted the training of other artists in his studio. The idea is nevertheless reasonable that Cavallino began with a solid academic grounding in copying figural prints and drawings; in rendering the parts of the body separately and the whole figure in proportion; in copying bas-reliefs and antique statues; in studying the nude and *écorchés;* in learning chiaroscuro drawing and linear perspective; in

Fig. 3. Cavallino. Detail of *The Finding of Moses* [13].

studying the works of the old masters such as Raphael or Titian as well as those of the moderns like the Carracci, Guido Reni, and Domenichino; and in imitating nature and learning the rules of composition and *invenzione*—in short, in mastering the fundamentals of both *disegno* and *colore*.[16] Judging from the elegantly drawn contours of the artist's figures, their calculated placement, and their convincingly rendered flesh and musculature, wherever he trained a considerable amount of drawing from the model must have been involved in the process. In fact, the few drawings that bear reasonable attributions to him today are figure studies.

There was no academy of painting in Naples in Cavallino's lifetime where the practice—or the theory—of the profession could be learned,[17] and Stanzione's studio was presumably not the only place where an academic training could be obtained. Many Neapolitan painters active in the second quarter of the century trained with Jusepe de Ribera or Aniello Falcone, both of whom were noted for their figure drawings; Falcone, in fact, is known to have maintained a studio in his house for copying from the model.[18] It is possible also that Domenichino's studio offered opportunities for drawing from life; Nicolas Poussin is known to have trained in this manner with Domenichino in Rome before the latter's departure for Naples in 1631.[19] Both Ribera and Stanzione could have drawn from that great font of inspiration for the depiction of the nude, the Carracci's Galleria Farnese, during their stays in Rome,[20] and Cavallino himself is supposed to have copied figures from prints by Agostino Carracci with his childhood teacher before his entry into Stanzione's studio.[21] Unfortunately the paintings that can be isolated as the artist's earliest works [1-8] do not serve to clarify a precise source for his training on the basis of style. Whereas they show strong connections to the manner of Stanzione, especially in *The Meeting of Joachim and Anna at the Golden Gate* in Budapest [1], the influence of Ribera and of the still-unidentified Master of the Annunications to the Shepherds is apparent in equal measure [2-3]. Cavallino's works of the latter half of the 1630s also indicate a rapport with the work of Falcone [especially 3, 5-7, 9, 11, 15-17], who we know was at least a family friend, as the abovementioned document of 1636 names him as the intermediary through whom Cavallino's mother's legacy passed to the artist and his brother Tommaso.[22]

Although de Dominici's biography does not fully resolve the question of Cavallino's first master, his account of the direction of the artist's early development seems to be substantiated by the pictures themselves. Having said that Cavallino trained in an academic tradition—in that figure drawing, architecture, perspective, and a solid knowledge of literary sources were emphasized—he tells us that at the beginning of his career he participated in at least one large public decorative complex, the ceiling paintings for the church of San Giuseppe Maggiore dell' Ospedaletto, subsequently destroyed. These are generally attributed to Stanzione in collaboration with members of his school.[23] Then de Dominici provides us with what may be one of the major keys to understanding Cavallino's development: he says that on Vaccaro's advice the younger artist chose to depict figures on a smaller scale than "that of almost life size, on which scale Bernardo did not succeed with the same excellence that he did on a smaller one."[24] The early pictures themselves loosely suggest just such a sequence of events, in that a handful of very early canvases on the scale of public commissions [1-4] appears to be followed by groups of much smaller easel pictures in which the arrangements of figures are handled with increasing complexity and sophistication [5-13, 15-17].

De Dominici emphasizes the thoroughness of Massimo's teaching in the latter's insistence that his students master the Scriptures, Ovid, Tasso, and Flavius Josephus, so that they could make their own interpretations of subjects without merely parroting others' explanations of the stories or fables they were depicting. He tells us also that Cavallino, while still a pupil of Stanzione, was taken up by Andrea Vaccaro and set to copying figural scenes and effigies of saints; that he looked hard at Artemisia Gentileschi's paintings, especially in their coloring; that he copied works by Reni and Titian; that Massimo became jealous of his pupil's abilities; that Cavallino began to work on his own at about age eighteen; and that he was profoundly affected by Rubens's painting of *The Feast of Herod* in Gaspar Roomer's collection in Naples. The writer gives us, in addition, an evocative encapsulation of the artist's style, quoting praise of his "numerous works done in such a delicate manner and with such lifelike coloring, correctness, and naturalness that the figures seem not painted but alive; using a minimum of light sources, contrasts, and reflections, [and] manipulating light with such smoothness, he sweetly deceives the eye of anyone who looks at his pictures."[25] While recording his admiration of "the noble conceptions, the judicious compositions, the beauty of coloring, the refinement of design, and the great understanding of illumination . . ."[26] in Cavallino's works, the biographer regrets only "that he didn't give his women beautiful faces."[27] De Dominici's sources may be suspect or obscure, his facts occasionally wrong, and his anecdotes embellished, but his perception of Cavallino's art, when held up against the paintings themselves, works: he gives us an artist whose training includes the fundamentals of academic draughtsmanship; who begins in a more or less grand manner with public commissions and turns early on to cabinet-scaled pictures; who has a certain rapport with Andrea Vaccaro, Artemisia Gentileschi, and Massimo Stanzione, his works being occasionally confused with those by members of the latter's school; and who handles Caravaggesque tenebrism with a special and characteristic grace, combining naturalism with *soavità*.

Exactly thirty years after de Dominici's publication another Neapolitan artist-biographer, a pupil of Paolo de Matteis and Francesco Solimena named Onofrio Giannone (1698–after 1773), completed his own manuscript lives of local artists, a project undertaken because the writer felt that de Dominici's work was riddled with gossip and invention. Giannone's "additions," however, were not published until the twentieth century, and the account of Cavallino tells us nothing beyond that of de Dominici.[28]

The historian Luigi Lanzi, writing on the southern Italian schools of painting in 1792, praised Cavallino's specialty in compositions with small figures "alla pussinesca," full of spirit and expression and painted with a particular gracefulness; he commented that the artist's works are to be found in Neapolitan collections but are little known outside his own school.[29] Dictionaries of artists and other writers on the Neapolitan school up to the twentieth century drew largely from de Dominici's and Lanzi's accounts, listing Cavallino as a member of Stanzione's school.[30] Not until Carlo Tito Dalbono's assessment of the artist in his book of 1871 on Stanzione and his followers was an effort made to distinguish Cavallino's work from that of other members of Stanzione's school on the basis of style.[31] Six years later in Naples a large, general exhibition of the city's art from the Middle Ages to the present was mounted, which included manuscripts, incunabula, musical instruments, medals, sculpture, majolica, crèches, and paintings of the Neapolitan and foreign schools. Cavallino—together with a number of his contemporaries

Fig. 4. Cavallino. Detail of *The Payment of the Tribute* [16].

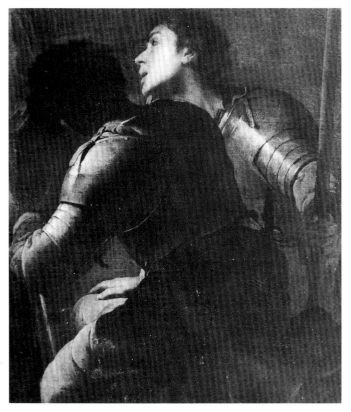

including Stanzione, Ribera, Vaccaro, Falcone, the Fracanzano, Agostino Beltrano, Giovanni Dò, Andrea de Leone, Domenico Gargiulo, Salvator Rosa, Pacecco di Rosa, and Francesco Guarino—was represented by six paintings and a drawing, all in private collections and only one of which is identifiable today [44].[32]

In the first quarter of the twentieth century the situation with regard to the previous two centuries' definition of Cavallino's oeuvre was reversed: whereas earlier his paintings were oftentimes presented under other artists' names, in the enthusiasm for his rediscovery from about 1910 onward many pictures now recognized as by his contemporaries were published as his. Cavallino's works were particularly confused with those of Vaccaro (Inv. no. 49) and Johann Heinrich Schönfeld (Inv. nos. 21, 32, 57), as well as with those of Giovanni Battista Spinelli (Inv. nos. 37, 120), Antonio de Bellis (Inv. nos. 10, 19), Francesco Guarino (Inv. nos. 56, 70), Paolo Finoglia (Inv. no. 44), and the Master of the Annunciations to the Shepherds (Inv. no. 25). In 1909, when Aldo de Rinaldis published his first small monograph on Cavallino, seventeen works by the artist were known and forty-four were listed as lost; today we would only accept nine of those original seventeen [3, 9, 12, 14, 36, 43, 45, 53, and Inv. no. 168]. In the teens and twenties well over forty new pictures were given to Cavallino in a number of articles;[33] only about half of these are still considered authentic. De Rinaldis's second monograph, published in 1921, provided a catalogue of fifty-one paintings, of which today we would judge twenty as autograph, five as copies, seventeen as wrong attributions, and nine are lost.

Twenty years ago only three signed works by Cavallino were known [44, 67, 82]. Today there are eight. In 1968 the Moscow *Expulsion of Heliodorus from the Temple* [83] was published as his; the following year the Cleveland *Adoration of the Shepherds* [79] joined the literature. Both of these pictures are late ones and help to illuminate the artist's style at his prime. The 1982–83 exhibition of Neapolitan Seicento painting included the London *Saint Peter* and *Saint Paul* [30-31], the only signed or initialed works known that are considered to predate the 1645 *Saint Cecilia*. Exhibited for the first time here is the initialed *Shade of Samuel Invoked by Saul* owned by the J. Paul Getty Museum [85], which adds a major new element to our knowledge of the artist's late works on copper. It is impossible to predict how many as yet unknown paintings may emerge to alter further our perception of Cavallino's style; in fact, around a dozen of the works in the present exhibition have surfaced on the market or have been identified in museum storerooms within the last decade.

In 1909 de Rinaldis perceptively linked Cavallino with the small-figure landscape and battle-scene specialists such as Salvator Rosa, Domenico Gargiulo, or Falcone rather than with the grand-manner painters such as Stanzione, Vaccaro, or Ribera.[34] Today we would no longer accept so rigid a separation between the academic artists and the small-figure painters; Falcone and Rosa, at least, worked in both modes.[35] However, we would certainly agree with de Rinaldis's suggestion that Stanzione and Vaccaro were for Cavallino merely points of departure and with his introduction of Ribera, Falcone, Gargiulo—and perhaps Rosa—as important elements in the artist's development, as well as with his characterization of Cavallino as a particularly independent figure among his contemporaries.[36] The publications of Roberto Longhi in 1915 and 1916 emphasized the significance of Battistello Caracciolo and Artemisia Gentileschi to Cavallino's work, as well the importance of Velázquez for Italian painting after Caravaggio,[37] and these figures—Velázquez and Gentileschi in particular—have been often mentioned as influences on Cavallino. Artemisia's approximately twenty-year stay in Naples virtually assures Cavallino's familiarity with her work; the likelihood of any considerable acquaintance on his part with Velázquez's paintings is not easily demonstrable, for the great Spanish painter did not visit Naples at any length, nor do his pictures seem to have existed in Neapolitan collections.

That we have today a clearer picture of Cavallino's oeuvre (as distinguished from numerous early copies and imitations and various misattributions), as well as a remarkably perceptive and poetic interpretation of his character as a painter, is above all due to the researches of the late Raffaello Causa during the past quarter century. In his 1972 survey of the artist's career Causa published for the first time a listing of original works, rejected attributions, and copies.[38] He emphasized the importance of the naturalist tradition of the Ribera school in Cavallino's formation, and especially of the Master of the Annunciations to the Shepherds, but also of Guarino, Falcone, Artemisia Gentileschi, Simon Vouet, Giovanni Benedetto Castiglione, and the Sicilian painter Pietro Novelli, who visited Naples in the early 1630s. In a few densely evocative paragraphs, he delineated the subtlety, complexity, and sophistication of Cavallino's personality, which for him was grounded in the naturalistic movement of the 1630s in Naples but was more refined and original, moving beyond Stanzione's vision toward a spirit of greater sentiment. Causa viewed Cavallino as aware of the small-scale realism of Aniello Falcone's work but totally indifferent to the factual, anecdotal approach of the Bamboc-

Fig. 5. Cavallino. Detail of *Esther before Abasuerus* [21].

Fig. 6. Cavallino. Detail of *Hercules and Omphale* [22].

cianti and as possessed of a sense of color that was at maturity "shrill, intense, clotted, saturated with light."[39] He saw the artist as an "evocative and anxious personality, tender, mournful, and sentimental: in effect, the only early-seventeenth-century Neapolitan painter who knew how to confront either sacred or secular subjects in an intimist key, divesting them of ecclesiastical, liturgical, or devotional baggage."[40] Causa related Cavallino's intellectual involvement to the literature and the theater of his day rather than to ecclesiastical issues.

In 1958 Ferdinando Bologna had associated Cavallino with a tendency in Neapolitan painting of the late 1630s away from Caravaggesque naturalism and toward a more painterly expression.[41] Oreste Ferrari, in his cogent 1979 summary of Cavallino's *fortuna critica,* rightly rejected the interpretation of the artist as a Caravaggesque painter and introduced a theory of an indirect acquaintance with Poussin and French classicism through Falcone and Andrea de Leone.[42] In 1982 Nicola Spinosa, in the most detailed chronological structuring to date of Cavallino's

development throughout the brief span of his career, suggested an early naturalistic phase closely related to the Master of the Annunciations to the Shepherds and Velázquez; followed by a more painterly manner in the late 1630s related to Rubens, van Dyck, and Ribera; succeeded by a period influenced by the Bambpccianti, Michel Sweerts, Falcone, and Castiglione, as well as Artemisia Gentileschi, Vouet, and Stanzione; then a renewed interest in van Dyck around 1645; and a late manner intensely affected by classicizing French painters working in Rome, such as Poussin, Charles Mellin, Sébastien Bourdon, and Jean Tassel.[43] It is difficult to confirm many of these comparisons through specific exchanges between individual paintings or between Cavallino and the other artists; in many cases—especially those of Velázquez, Novelli, Poussin, Bourdon, Tassel, and Sweerts—we do not even know for certain whether he knew the work of the painters by whom he is supposed to have been influenced. The present exhibition, by bringing together well over half of the artist's known oeuvre, offers a welcome

7

opportunity to make such assessments from the pictures themselves.

Cavallino's paintings, taken as a whole, indicate an artist of pronounced individuality. He does not derive from any obvious single source or tradition, and how he arrives where he eventually does with his work remains something of a mystery, despite all the suggestions we have summarized above. This was already seen as a problem in the eighteenth century. In 1773 Onofrio Giannone remarked that we do not really know where Cavallino studied or who his masters were; Luigi Lanzi, writing near the close of the century, said that no one in Stanzione's school, where he was supposed to have trained, was so formed by nature to paint as he was. Nearly a century later Carlo Tito Dalbono perceptively described him as following no single master directly but instead as generating his own manner from various elements "chemically" conjoined, forming something new and original, as gunpowder is created from saltpeter in combination with other ingredients.[44]

Fig. 7. Cavallino. Detail of *Christ Driving the Merchants from the Temple* [42].

Indeed, Cavallino combines a subtlety and intensity of coloring with a naturalistic rendering of surfaces, joining some of the Bolognese/Roman academic grand manner to an occasional close observation of genre detail similar to that of the low-life painters popular in his day (cf. Fig. 7). His lively multi-figure compositions are dramatically charged with a theatrical spirit of pose and expression at the same time that they must have been praised by his contemporaries for their grace and *tenerezza* (cf. Fig. 29).[45] In his hands flesh and materials are depicted with a naturalism of surface worthy of Ribera and the Master of the Annunciations to the Shepherds (cf. Fig. 30); at the same time he has a lightness of touch, a more delicate and finely tuned approach, that is very different from theirs (cf. Fig. 31). He often adopts a Caravaggesque intensity of contrasts of light and shade, of illumination striking one part of a head or body leaving the rest in shadow (cf. Fig. 4), but he seems psychologically more akin to Callot than he ever is to Caravaggio [13, 25]. He occasionally shows a certain grand manner and formality of composition that is related to that of Stanzione [2, 44, 50-52] but delivered on a smaller scale and with a more minute observation of surfaces (cf. Fig. 21). He renders physiognomy and genre detail with a closeness and accuracy that must relate to Falcone's work (cf. Fig. 13); yet he is dramatically more mannered and prettier than Falcone ever is (cf. Fig. 5). Without aspiring to the high seriousness of Poussin's art, which we cannot even be sure that he knew, Cavallino developed a certain approach to scale and to the relation of figures to format in his compositions that helps explain de Dominici's description of him as "a mixture of Guido, Rubens, and Titian, and also the Poussin of the Neapolitans."[46] Possibly the emotionally charged exchanges between figures so often encountered in Artemisia Gentileschi's work affected the artist [21]; but then, we ask, is it not instead—as Spinosa suggested—Vouet or some more classically French source that inspires his remarkable late female half-figures, such as the Stockholm *Judith with the Head of Holofernes* [82]? With Cavallino it is difficult to explore his sources as a means of reconstructing his development; we simply do not know enough at present about who painted what and when in his immediate circle from the mid-1630s to the mid-1650s, or about what was available to him of the work of non-Neapolitan artists, to discuss influences. In the end we are forced to rely on the evidence provided by the paintings themselves in an effort to sort out the artist's oeuvre and his chronology.

Fig. 8. Massimo Stanzione, Orta di Atella (?) 1585(?)–Naples 1656(?). *Saint John the Baptist Taking Leave of His Parents*. Canvas, 181 x 263 cm, ca. 1630–35(?). Museo del Prado, Madrid.

On turning to Cavallino's first pictures, we realize almost at once the physical fragility of our primary evidence concerning his work. His paintings have generally not survived in good condition into the twentieth century, and the earlier ones have proven particularly vulnerable to change, damage, or harsh cleanings. He typically uses a dark ground in these youthful works, toned with brown or red earth colors; on this he sets out shadowy background figures formed up from thin glazes and played against brightly illuminated foreground forms rendered opaquely and with more substantial impasto. The latter tend to survive rather well, whereas the figures not worked up with heavier impasto have frequently lost their glazes and appear as dark unmodulated shapes. This characteristic makes it extremely difficult to assess the authenticity of certain works from photographs and often distorts the artist's intentions in terms of composition and spatial depth, as well as adding yet a further element of uncertainty to the already difficult task of trying to date his pictures on stylistic grounds. The fact that many pictures have not been cleaned or restored in recent years further obscures our efforts to place them in chronological sequence, as many decisions about dating are based partly on the artist's handling of paint and use of color, and these characteristics may appear considerably altered by overpainting or discolored varnish.

Recent writers agree that the earliest paintings, which presumably date to Cavallino's late teens or early twenties and therefore around the mid-1630s, are the Budapest *Meeting of Joachim and Anna at the Golden Gate* [1], the Brunswick *Adoration of the Shepherds* [2], and the Naples *Martyrdom of Saint Bartholomew* [3];[47] to these I would add the recently rediscovered Milan *Communion of the Apostles* [4], the three small scenes from the life of Christ in private collections [5-7], and the Hartford *Flight into Egypt* [8]. Compared with others of his paintings, these works are distinguished by a tentative quality in the arrangement of stiff figures in flat rows against rather uninspired, conventional backgrounds and are unusually derivative from the grand manner of both Stanzione and Ribera, lacking the special dramatic character that informs the artist's more mature works. Although they are by no means huge, several are quite large canvases for Cavallino—who so far as we know adopted such a scale only four times more in his career—suggesting that some may have been altarpieces and thus lending credibility to de Dominici's story that Cavallino began with public commissions but turned early on to cabinet pictures.

Whereas the figures in the Budapest picture are very Stanzionesque (cf. Fig. 8)—it is interesting that this work has been attributed in the past to Stanzione as well as to various members of the Spanish school—and they are to a

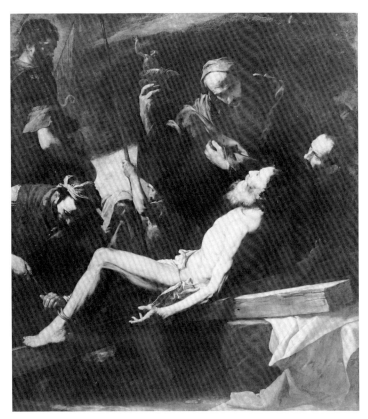

Fig. 9. Jusepe de Ribera, Játiva 1591–Naples 1652. *The Martyrdom of Saint Andrew*. Canvas, 285 x 183 cm, 1628. Szépmüvészeti Múzeum, Budapest.

Fig. 10. The Master of the Annunciations to the Shepherds, active in Naples 1630s–50s(?). *The Annunciation to the Shepherds*. Canvas, 180 x 261.5 cm. Museo di Capodimonte, Naples.

degree in the Brunswick, Naples, and Hartford pictures also, the handling of paint and the observation of surfaces in the Naples and Brunswick pictures are nearer the work of Ribera and the mysterious Master of the Annunciations to the Shepherds (cf. Figs. 9-10). The highly naturalistic [48] rendering of flesh, hair, fur, leather, wood, sheepskin, and feathers so obvious in these paintings—a characteristic also evident in the work of the Master of the Annunciations[49]—is fundamental to Cavallino's manner from his first pictures to his last ones. However, the naturalism of the artist's more mature works is not that of barnyard rusticity as the Master of the Annunciations' usually is, nor is it that of Ribera's wrinkled saints and hoary philosophers. Instead it conveys a sense of courtly luxury and elegance: with Cavallino the rough sheepskin that protects a shepherd's back [2] is soon abandoned for the rich fur that lines a king's robe [12].

The Milan *Communion of the Apostles* seems to mark Cavallino's turn from public commissions to more intimately scaled cabinet pictures. It links the large early paintings and a number of smaller canvases that are more Caravaggesque in composition and in their treatment of chiaroscuro [5-7, 9-11]. In the latter works dramatic illumination strikes foreheads, necks, shoulders, or elbows, with much of the rest of bodies falling away into shadow; occasionally the grouping of figures about tables [5-7, 9, 16-17] recalls the work of followers of Caravaggio of the previous generation, but Cavallino's own developing dramatic sense shares nothing fundamental with the stark, broad, reductive treatment and powerful tragic emotion of the late work of Caravaggio himself.[50] The rounded red-brown heads that have sunk into the shadow in so many of his paintings can be found earlier in the work of one of the first Neapolitan *Caravaggisti,* Carlo Sellitto, who died in 1614, two years before Cavallino was born (cf. Fig. 11). The minutely rendered observation of the surface qualities of flesh, metal, and other materials underscores the fact that the artist was by temperament best suited to work on a small scale.

At this point Cavallino seems closer in spirit to Aniello Falcone than to any other Neapolitan painter, although he never specialized in genre or battle scenes as Falcone did.[51] The latter was a versatile artist who worked in oil and in fresco on both church decorations and cabinet pictures; his *Rest on the Flight into Egypt* of 1641 belonging to the cathedral of Naples shows that he was capable of painting in an academic classical manner,[52] although he is best known for his battle pictures. By the time of the Naples *Finding of Moses* [13] or the Harrach *Banquet of Absalom* [17], Cavallino has mastered a more dramatic

Fig. 11. Carlo Sellitto, Naples 1581–1614. *Saint Cecilia*. Canvas, 250 x 183 cm, 1613. Museo di Capodimonte, Naples.

Fig. 13. Cavallino. Detail of *Saint Cecilia in Ecstasy* [44].

Fig. 12. Aniello Falcone, Naples 1607–1656(?). *A Battle between the Turks and the Christians*. Canvas, 136 x 168.5 cm, 1631. Musée du Louvre, Paris.

structuring of his earlier, rather conventional compositions into spatially complex and psychologically charged integrations of figures, in which each detail of face and clothing or armor is lovingly and minutely observed. Among the models he observed may have been those masterpieces of dramatic condensation, Falcone's battle scenes (cf. Fig. 12). Cavallino was in addition a virtuoso observer of still life (cf. Fig. 13), although he never seems to have painted it for its own sake, and Falcone seems to have been closely tied to the flourishing of that genre in Naples during the second quarter of the seventeenth century.[53] It appears that Falcone's and Cavallino's pictures may have appealed to the same collectors in Naples of the 1630s through the 1650s, as will be discussed below. And clearly the two individuals were acquainted, since the abovementioned document of 1636 cites Falcone as the intermediary through whom a legacy from Cavallino's mother was transferred to the artist and his brother.

Fig. 14. Ribera. *Pietà*. Canvas, 264 x 170 cm, 1637. Chiesa della Certosa di San Martino, Naples.

De Dominici credits the example of Falcone's most famous pupil, Salvator Rosa, with a role as exemplar in Cavallino's choice of cabinet-scaled pictures as his métier. Following his 1635 departure to pursue his career in Rome and Florence, Rosa—who was older than Cavallino by a year—returned only for a brief visit to Naples in 1637 or 1638;[54] nevertheless it is not at all unlikely that Cavallino and Rosa were close at some point, as both artists' beginnings refer to Bambocciantesque genre paintings and to the work of Ribera, as well as to that of Falcone, in their early progress toward their own individual styles.

Only in confronting certain paintings by Ribera, particularly of the mid- to late thirties, do we begin to understand many of the physical characteristics of Cavallino's handling of paint. In Ribera's *Saint Simon, A Duel between Women* (1636), and *Saint Paul the Hermit* (1640), all in the Prado,[55] we can see the source of Cavallino's richly impasted ridges of paint on the folds of draperies and of his extraordinary virtuosity in brushing out the transitions between transparent shadows and opaque lighted areas, or of eyebrows and hairlines into flesh. His fine observation of the surfaces of materials, and especially of white, with crisp impasto highlights and delicately brushed shadows, is also akin to that of the Spanish painter. Ribera's torso of Marsyas, in his *Apollo Flaying Marsyas* of 1637 in the Museo Nazionale di San Martino in Naples, and that of Christ, in his *Pietà* of the same year in the church of the Certosa di San Martino (Fig. 14),[56] have an intense physical presence conveyed through a combination of dense impasto and delicate brushwork; this, as well as their decidedly gray tonality, is very like Cavallino's Christ in his *Pietà* in Molfetta [67], which probably dates to the later 1640s. The head of the Fogg Art Museum's *Saint Jerome* of 1640 by Ribera,[57] with its half-open mouth clearly defined by warm transparent shadows and its carefully delineated, oddly formed eyes and subtly brushed-out eyebrows, is like many of Cavallino's early martyred saints [14, 27-28]. And the series of apostles that Cavallino produced probably in the late thirties and early forties [30-32, and Inv. no. 176] are so closely related to Ribera's philosophers and

Fig. 15. Ribera. *Elijah*. Canvas, 168 x 97 cm, 1638. Chiesa della Certosa di San Martino, Naples.

prophets of the late thirties—such as the Hartford *Philosopher* of 1637 and the Certosa di San Martino *Moses* and *Elijah* (Fig. 15) of 1638[58]—that Nicola Spinosa's suggestion (oral) that they may have been painted in *omaggio* to Ribera is persuasive.

One of the principal catalysts transforming Cavallino's early naturalistic and Caravaggesque manner into the very personal and idiosyncratic style of his maturity is a neo-Mannerism that seems to draw its inspiration at least in part from Netherlandish and French prints of the late sixteenth and early seventeenth centuries.[59] Cavallino's true arena is neither that of Falcone's raucous battlefields nor of Ribera's grim martyrdoms but is a rarified and courtly setting where elegantly garbed, regal figures flaunt the slenderest necks and ankles, where delicate heads bend gracefully forward and dancers' hands articulate, and where all is concentrated on the intensely emotional interchange between the dramatis personae. Many of his paintings [12-13, 19-21, 25, 45-46, 77-78, 80-81; cf. Figs. 16-19] show the same mannered figural types with swaying stances—often with one elbow elegantly akimbo—and the same spatially complex compositions that frequently feature a shadowed figure in the foreground seen from the back separating the observer from the illuminated central action that are seen in prints by artists like the brilliant Haarlem engraver Hendrik Goltzius (Mühlbracht 1558–Haarlem 1617) or members of his school or circle such as Jan Pietersz. Saenredam (Saerdam 1565–Assendelft 1607), Jan Harmensz. Muller (Amsterdam 1571–1628), and Jacob Matham (Haarlem 1571–1631),[60] or by the French printmaker Jacques Callot (Nancy 1592–1635).[61] Compare, for example, the arrangement of young women, some kneeling in front seen from the back, one seen from the side with her elbow crooked and one hand on her hip, in the Capodimonte *Finding of Moses* [13] to an anonymous print after Goltzius of *The Daughters of Cecrops Opening the Casket* (Fig. 16), to the anonymous *Mercury Enamoured of Herse* after Goltzius (Bartsch III. 107.67; *Illustrated Bartsch* 3:331), and to *Venus Presiding over Love and Pleasure* by Saenredam after Goltzius (Bartsch III. 245.77; *Illustrated Bartsch* 4:393). The complex composition of the Vienna *Adoration of the Magi* [19], with foreground figures—backs turned and leaning gracefully inward, silhouetted against the light in the center of the composition—was possibly inspired by prints like *Evening* from *The Times of Day* by Saenredam after Goltzius (Fig. 17), or *Diana's Nymphs Discovering Callisto's Pregnancy* by Matham (Bartsch III. 155.94; *Illustrated Bartsch* 4:84), or *The Adoration of the Shepherds* by Muller after Bartolomeus

Fig. 16. Anonymous artist. After Hendrik Goltzius, Mühlbracht 1558–Haarlem 1617. *The Daughters of Cecrops Opening the Casket Entrusted to Them by Minerva* (Bartsch III. 107.62). Engraving, 16.5 x 25 cm, 1589–90. The British Museum, London.

Fig. 17. Jan Pietersz. Saenredam, Saerdam 1565–Assendelft 1607. After Goltzius. *Evening*, from the *Times of the Day* (Bartsch III. 348.92). Engraving, 19.8 x 14.6 cm. The British Museum, London.

Fig. 18. Jacob Matham, Haarlem 1571–1631. After Goltzius. *Judith*, from *Old Testament Heroes* (Bartsch III. 195.254). Engraving, 25.4 x 16.2 cm. The British Museum, London.

Fig. 19. Jacques Callot, Nancy 1592–1635. *Cap. Ceremonia and Sig.ᵃ Lavinia*, from the *Balli di Sfessania* (Lieure 381 I/II). Etching, 7.2 x 9.3 cm, ca. 1622. National Gallery of Art, Washington, D.C., Rosenwald Collection.

Spranger (Bartsch III. 284.65; *Illustrated Bartsch* 4:498). The graceful pose of David in the Milan *David and Abigail* [25], hand on hip and one foot extended, can be compared to Matham's *Spring* from *The Four Seasons* after Goltzius (Bartsch III. 166.140; *Illustrated Bartsch* 4:130) or to the man at right in Saenredam's *Mars Presiding over War* (Bartsch III. 245.75; *Illustrated Bartsch* 4:391). A composition like that of Goltzius's *Judgment of Midas* of 1590 (Bartsch III.43.140; *Illustrated Bartsch* 3:133) may underlie the complex arrangement of figures in the Harrach *Esther before Ahasuerus* [61], and the figure of Judith in Cavallino's versions of *Judith with the Head of Holofernes* in London and Naples [45-46] are similar to Matham's Judith from *Old Testament Heroes* after Goltzius (Fig. 18). We are tempted to presuppose large studio holdings of such prints in Naples that an artist like Cavallino might have copied from, in whole or in part and over and over again until the elements thereof were part and parcel of his working vocabulary.

Callot—who spent the years 1614 to 1621 in Italy—has a specific connection to Naples, although he probably never went there,[62] in that a Neapolitan artist with whom he collaborated in Florence between about 1617 and 1621, Teodoro Filippo de Liagno—or Filippo Napoletano as he is usually called (Naples 1587/91–Rome ca. 1630)—returned to Naples around 1624–27 to play an important role in the developing genre of small figures painted in landscape settings furthered in Naples by Falcone and Rosa.[63] Cavallino was not the only painter of his generation to respond to a Mannerist stimulus that may have been nourished by a continuous tradition in Neapolitan painting through the early part of the seventeenth century. Domenico Gargiulo's gracefully posturing figures have often been compared to those of Callot, and one of Cavallino's most intriguing and little-understood contemporaries, the alchemist-painter Giovanni Battista Spinelli (active 1630s–ca. 1647)—whose work as a draughtman and painter has only been defined during the last two decades—shares with him in just these years the same kind of enthusiasm for northern Mannerist prints transformed into an idiosyncratically personal painting style of great dramatic intensity (cf. Fig. 20).[64]

Whereas about a dozen pictures can reasonably be isolated as Cavallino's earlier works and another ten or so clearly fall towards the end of his life, it is virtually impossible at this stage of research to establish a convincing linear development for all the eighty-odd works attributed to him. His style does appear, however, to go through a

Fig. 20. Giovanni Battista Spinelli, active in Naples, ca. 1630–ca. 1650. *David Playing the Harp before Saul.* Canvas, 253 x 309 cm. Galleria degli Uffizi, Florence.

succession of phases. For example, the Brera *Massacre of the Innocents* [34], the Liverpool *Rape of Europa* [35], the Kansas City *Rape of Europa* [36], the Warsaw *Dream of Saint Joseph* [37], the Paris *Lot and His Daughters* [38], and the Gosford *Drunkenness of Noah* [39] share a luminous quality in the treatment of flesh, with more transparent shadows than appear in earlier works, indicating a transition between the heavily tenebrist early pictures and the subtler palette of the artist's middle and late years. We know what Cavallino looked like at mid-career from the large *Saint Cecilia in Ecstasy* altarpiece [44] and its small *modello* [43], but without more firm dates it is futile to say which pictures closely precede or follow these works. Three works with rather elaborate and complex compositions, the Naples *Christ and the Adulteress* [40], the Norfolk *Procession to Calvary* [41], and the London *Christ Driving the Merchants from the Temple* [42], can be dated around 1640. Another group consisting of the Vienna and Rohrau *David* and *Esther* [60-61], the Florence *Esther* [62], and the Madrid *Martyrdom of Saint Stephen* [63], in which Cavallino's brushwork is more vibrant, fluid, and open and his coloring more brilliant, appears to date several years later. The splendid *Triumph of Galatea* [68], which probably dates to the end of the 1640s, shows the artist's total mastery of a subtly yet intensely naturalistic mode of figural painting that opens out into the remarkable complexity and individuality of his very late works [80-85].

It has often been remarked, as de Dominici was the first to comment, that Cavallino's work on a large scale appears somewhat different from his small-format pictures. If we separate the four accepted, mature large-scale works—the *Hercules and Omphale* [22], the *Saint Cecilia* [44], the New York *Triumph of Galatea* [68], and the Cleveland *Adoration of the Shepherds* [79], which, at approximately a meter and a quarter by two meters stand out from Cavallino's other pictures by virtue of size—we see that they seem to span the artist's maturity and thus form a kind of crude chronological framework. Because of its darker palette, greater chiaroscuro contrasts, denser handling of opaque impasto played against thinner, darker

Fig. 21. Cavallino. Detail of *Saint Cecilia in Ecstasy* [44].

15

Fig. 22. Cavallino. Detail of *Saint Anthony of Padua* [56].

to move from an early darker, more Riberesque and derivative style to a mature, highly individual manner marked by a neo-Mannerist dramatic intensity and a singularly brilliant coloristic sense [cf. 14 and 27-28 to 70-73 and 82].

One would guess that the three smallish coppers in Moscow, Fort Worth, and Malibu [83-85], as well as the Brunswick *David and Abigail* and *The Finding of Moses* [80-81], fall close to the end of the artist's life, as must the remarkable *Judith with the Head of Holofernes* in Stockholm [82]. These late compositions show Cavallino's amazing ability to articulate intense exchanges of glance and gesture among his balletically poised protagonists, the lyrical contours of whose figures and draperies are interrelated in the most ingenious manner. The last works are as much distinguished by their palette—clear sharp blues, acid pale greens, strong reds, silvery grays, yellow golds, and dull oranges—as they are by the theatrical spirit that infuses the compositions. The heavy dark shadows of the earlier works have gradually changed to luminous transparent ones, and the naturalism in rendering figures and materials is lighter and more fluent in touch but no less convincing. The choice of a copper support in some instances seems appropriate to the high, almost porcelain-like finish of the pictures themselves. In these carefully conceived and brilliantly executed vignettes no gesture is flatly rhetorical or banal, no stance miscalculated, and no facial expression dull or inappropriate. The artist has clearly arrived at an intensely individual mode of expression: we are left only to wonder exactly how he got there.

paint, and less sophisticated organization of figures in space, the *Hercules* seems the earliest of the four, dating perhaps around 1640. The *Saint Cecilia* of 1645 already shows a consistently thinner, more fluid paint facture, an abandonment of solid dark backgrounds for more opaque, tonally modulated ones, and a lighter, more transparent treatment of shadows; the *Galatea,* which one is tempted to associate with the abovementioned payment of 1649 by the principe di Cardito for an unnamed large painting, carries these characteristics yet further (cf. Fig. 30). The *Adoration of the Shepherds,* which may be dated to the early fifties, shows that Cavallino in his late work achieved a highly sophisticated organization in space of naturalistically observed figures, illuminated by ingeniously calculated light for great dramatic effect and rendered with a fine, fluid handling of paint and subtly calculated contrasts of bright opaque or primary colors against duller earth tones. In an effort to structure the artist's chronology, it is also helpful to isolate the twenty-six or so half-length figures and single-figure images, for they also seem

Besides the difficulty of establishing a chronology on the basis of a single dated painting, other problems remain unresolved concerning Cavallino's oeuvre and the development of his style. These include a number of pictures whose attributions are unclear, as well as the questions of why the artist's manner changed as it did in the 1640s, whether or not he ever traveled ouside Naples, and if he had a workshop or a close circle of imitators. Also puzzling is the almost total absence of known drawings by a painter who surely must have been an accomplished draughtsman.

That Cavallino's artistic personality still eludes clear definition is demonstrated by the fact that an important picture such as the *Lot and His Daughters* recently acquired by the Toledo Museum of Art [29], published for the first time here, has been accepted by some scholars and rejected by others since its appearance on the New York market in 1983. The handling of paint in the three figures' heads—compare Lot to the signed *Saint Peter* in London [30]—and in Lot's mauve shirt, with its delicately brushed transitions between light and shadow, as well as the landscape background, which relates to those in early pictures by Cavallino [1, 8], is convincing support of the attribution. However, in this writer's opinion, the bland and nerveless composition, languid poses, and rather wooden articulation of the contours of limbs and drapery are difficult to fit into Cavallino's manner of working at any period. Except for Lot's shirt, the painting of draperies lacks the fineness that always characterizes Cavallino's work.

Spinosa dates the picture to the late thirties or early forties, which would place it somewhat earlier than the smaller oval version of the subject in the Louvre, dated to the early forties [38]. Even considering the possible stylistic changes accompanying the great increase in scale this large picture would represent to an artist who usually worked within a smaller format, it is difficult to relate the unenergetic poses and composition of the Toledo *Lot* to the dynamic, tightly knit organization of the Louvre picture, with its subtle and lyrical orchestration of the contours of limbs and drapery—qualities that already appear in pictures by Cavallino dated to the late thirties [19-21]. This problem can be compared to that of the mysterious "Cain and Abel" master, whose painting of *The Death of Abel* in Capodimonte (Inv. no. 8), has many Cavallinesque aspects yet cannot be attributed to the artist himself. Other pictures in the present catalogue are contested attributions, such as the Milan *Communion of the Apostles* [4] and the three small scenes from the life of Christ [5-7]. Certain rejected attributions—such as the New York *Saint Catherine* (Inv. no. 54)—are difficult to explain away to other artists, all of which shows how hard it still is to separate Cavallino's work from that of his close contemporaries. His relation especially to Antonio de Bellis, Agostino Beltrano, Paolo Finoglia, Francesco Guarino, Bartolomeo Bassante, Andrea Vaccaro, Andrea de Leone, and Niccolò di Simone needs to be defined.

De Dominici suggests that the arrival of Rubens's *Feast of Herod* in Naples around 1640 had a catalytic effect on Cavallino's palette,[65] and it is true that the artist's use of color does change in the course of the forties from a darker tonality with jewellike contrasts of brilliant reds and blues to a more opaque quality with subtle interrelationships of acid greens, grays, dull oranges, bright and dull blues, and yellows. However, Cavallino's handling of paint and his palette are so distinctly non-Rubensian that we wonder if, were there a single catalytic event, it was not some other occasion, such as the arrival of Cardinal

Fig. 23. Simon Vouet, Paris 1590–1649. *The Angel with the Dice and Christ's Cloak*. Canvas, 102 x 78 cm. Museo di Capodimonte, Naples.

Filomarino's collection from Rome in 1642 (see below). There were contemporary examples in Naples of classicizing styles and non-tenebrist, more richly chromatic approaches to color from Bolognese, French, and Neapolitan sources: one thinks of Giovanni Lanfranco's frescoes in the church of Santi Apostoli;[66] of Domenichino's decorations in the Cappella del Tesoro of the Duomo;[67] of Simon Vouet's series of angels with the instruments of the Passion, recorded in the Filomarino collection, two of which are in Capodimonte (cf. Fig. 23);[68] of Charles Mellin's *Sacrifice of Abel* at Montecassino, recently rediscovered by Spinosa;[69] of the fact that a few pictures by Nicolas Poussin existed in Neapolitan collections;[70] of Ribera's splendid copper of *Saint Januarius Leaving the Furnace Unharmed* from the Cappella del Tesoro, presently undergoing a cleaning at Capodimonte that reveals its brilliant palette;[71] and of Stanzione's, Falcone's, Vaccaro's, and de Leone's classicizing decorative cycles in the church of San Paolo Maggiore, now considerably ruined. It is difficult to say whether any

Fig. 24. Cavallino. *Study of a Male Nude Half-Figure (Saint Sebastian?)*, recto. Red chalk on paper, 21 x 21.4 cm. Gabinetto Disegni e Stampe, Museo di Capodimonte, Naples.

Fig. 25. Cavallino. *Study of Legs*, verso of sheet reproduced in Fig. 24. Red chalk on paper, 21 x 21.4 cm. Gabinetto Disegni e Stampe, Museo di Capodimonte, Naples.

Fig. 26. Cavallino. *Study of a Male Nude Half-Figure*. Black chalk on paper, 32.5 x 26.8 cm. Museo Nazionale di San Martino, Naples.

Fig. 27. Cavallino. *Study of Saint Sebastian*. Black and red chalks on paper, 39.9 x 25.2 cm. Ashmolean Museum, University of Oxford, Oxford.

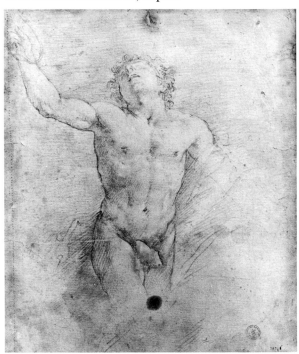

Fig. 28. Cavallino. *Study for the Virgin of the Immaculate Conception*. Black and white chalks on paper, 37.9 x 27.9 cm. The Pierpont Morgan Library, New York, János Scholz Collection.

or all of these affected the maturation of Cavallino's style, or whether he drew on a broader range of stimuli through travel, especially to Rome. In any case, his sources of inspiration are so transformed into his own late manner as to be individually unrecognizable.

The question of whether Cavallino had a workshop has also not been answered. He seems to have had no pupils, and no close followers can be identified. A painter who worked mostly on a rather intimate scale probably did not need much studio assistance. However, the odd phenomenon of the numerous Tobit scenes that derive from probable lost originals by Cavallino (Inv. nos. 2, 4, 9, 14) raise the question of a close imitator or follower and possibly of a limited workshop situation.

Finally, there is the puzzling circumstance of why only four drawings are known bearing reasonable attributions to an artist whose every picture proclaims that he must have drawn and redrawn heads, hands, limbs, and drap-

eries to arrive at the precisely calculated and highly sophisticated interrelationships of contours that characterize his works. Giovanni Battista Passeri in his life of Salvator Rosa comments that the Neapolitan artists as students were not given to long application to drawing but early on turned to their brushes and colors,[72] and we know from a letter of 1675 from the Florentine Pietro Andrea Andreini to Leopoldo de'Medici that draughtsmanship and drawings were not highly prized in Naples at that time.[73] Moreover, frequent pentimenti in Cavallino's pictures [3, 21-22, 36, 67-68] indicate that he often changed his mind after compositions were started on his canvases. All this notwithstanding, it is likely that many more drawings by the artist once existed. Possibly some are still unidentified in private collections or in the anonymous boxes of print rooms, but it is rather more probable that the bulk of them perished. Perhaps it is worth mentioning in this context that at about the mid-point of the year the plague raged in Naples a deputation was set up to mark with a cross and close the houses of the pestilence's victims, which probably included Cavallino, after everything belonging to the contagious person had been burned.[74]

Over twenty years ago the late Walter Vitzthum established the picture of Cavallino as draughtsman that obtains today. Two chalk drawings of male torsos—one with an old inscription to Cavallino—at Capodimonte (Figs. 24-25)[75] and at the Museo Nazionale di San Martino (Fig. 26),[76] together with a third torso that can be identified as a Saint Sebastian at the Ashmolean Museum (Fig. 27)[77] and a study for the Virgin of the Immaculate Conception at the Pierpont Morgan Library (Fig. 28),[78] form the basis of his graphic oeuvre. All four sheets are figure drawings, and the latter two can be related to lost paintings (Inv. nos. 153, 180). The draughtsmanship is tight and rather finicky, with a great emphasis on contours and on working up shadowed areas with shading or crosshatching in a manner similar to the styles of drawing of Aniello Falcone and Andrea de Leone. No ink drawings are known. An additional sheet in Toronto attributed by Vitzthum to Cavallino, which is closely related in composition to the Moscow *Expulsion of Heliodorus from the Temple* [83], is so difficult to relate in terms of draughtsmanship to the abovementioned four drawings—even if we suppose that it could be fifteen to twenty years later in date—that it should be rejected as an attribution to the artist.[79] Four drawings in Florence and Leningrad published as by Cavallino and rejected by Vitzthum should be excluded, and three sheets mentioned in old collections are lost.[80]

19

Fig. 29. Cavallino. Detail of *Esther before Ahasuerus* [62].

In a period when gestures, facial expressions, and the movement of bodies were vital means to painters' most fundamental end, the expression of human emotions,[81] Cavallino's work has been noted for the high pitch to which it brings the transmission of emotive experience that characterizes much of baroque art.[82] Over and over he depicts subjects (of his own or patrons' choosing)—such as David playing the harp before Saul [18, 20, 60], Esther kneeling before Ahasuerus [12, 21, 61-62] and Abigail before David [25, 80], Lot and his daughters [38, 74], Christ and the adulteress [40], Hercules and Omphale [22], Saul summoning the shade of Samuel [85], Mucius Scaevola standing accused before Porsenna [84], or the wounded Tancred discovered by Erminia [78]—where individuals engage in violent emotional confrontation and where erotic sentiment and sensuality of color and richness of materials can be given full play. Causa relates his "diffuse Tassesque sentiment, between the idyllic and the elegiac" to contemporary poetry and theater,[83] and there is, indeed, a strong theatrical element about Cav-

allino's paintings. They often appear, in fact, like vignettes from plays caught in mid-action.

P. A. Tomory has suggested that the dramatic situations of open-air plays in seventeenth-century Italy "must have exerted, at least, a visual influence in the grouping and positioning of the characters on the passing artist, thus providing him with additional 'real' evidence for the themes suggested to him by his intellectual patrons."[84] Thanks to the researches of Benedetto Croce, Giuseppe Ceci, and Ulisse Prota-Giurleo on the early baroque theater in Naples, we know that Cavallino's own lifetime saw a flourishing of comic theater and musical drama in the city that permeated all social levels, from the popular to the noble to the courtly.[85] The first stable public theater existed from the late sixteenth century at the church of San Giorgio dei Genovesi (known as San Giorgio alla Commedia Vecchia); it was here, apparently, that the characteristically Neapolitan *commedia* figure Pulcinella first appeared around 1609 or 1610, played by the famous comic actor Silvio Fiorillo.[86] The viceroys were often protectors of the theater and encouraged Spanish companies of *commedia* players to come to Naples: the conde de Lemos (viceroy 1610–16) composed comedies recited before the major literary academy in Naples, the Accademia degli Oziosi, as did many of the Neapolitan *letterati,* including the poet Giambattista Marino's father;[87] the conde de Monterrey (viceroy 1631–37) was so enthusiastic about dramatics that he broke with tradition by attending the public theater; and the conde de Oñate (viceroy 1648–53) introduced musical drama to Naples in 1651 with a performance of Monteverdi's *L'Incoronazione di Poppea.* Between 1653 and 1655 seven musical dramas were presented at the Teatro di San Bartolomeo, built about 1620 at the expense of the Casa Santa degli Incurabili.[88] Performances throughout the seventeenth century took place at the viceregal court and in private houses for a select few, acted by dilettanti or by professional troupes; at the public theaters, which included the Teatro dei Fiorentini ("della Commedia Nuova"), where the Spanish companies especially performed, and the Teatro di San Bartolomeo, where Italian companies held forth; and in local dialect in improvised theaters or in the open air at Largo del Castello. Neapolitan comics were famous from the late sixteenth century onward. Ties between Neapolitan artists and the local theater are not lacking: besides the well-known examples of Gianlorenzo Bernini and Salvator Rosa—who, admittedly, had left Naples by the time they are recorded as dramatic writers or comic performers—Michele (or Michelangelo) Fracanzano—the son of Cavallino's contemporary Francesco Fracanzano, who married Rosa's sister Giovanna—became a famous Pulcinella in the latter half of the seventeenth century.[89]

Any demonstration of a specific connection between Cavallino's painting and contemporary local theater must await further evidence, either through a visual record of performances or through stylistic characteristics apparent within the plays themselves that can be associated with the pictures, but the direction is one that should be pursued in attempting to come to a fuller understanding of Cavallino's art. The contemporary theater, poetry and prose, the *letterati* of Naples's numerous literary academies, the collectors of paintings, the patrons of art, the dealers, the agents, and the middlemen—these would seem to be the areas to explore in order to understand why Cavallino painted the subjects that he did in the manner in which he presented them.

Possibly the most provocative subject treated by de Dominici in his life of Cavallino is that of the artist's patronage. The biographer believed that Cavallino's father died when the artist was young, and in order to help support his family Bernardo was forced to paint for various *artefici di pittura* and second-hand dealers at miserable daily wages. Although it was not unusual at the time for young, unknown artists to start out working for dealers, in Cavallino's case his works are supposed to have often been sold outside the city under the names of other, sometimes foreign, painters at considerably greater sums than he was paid for them. The cabinet pictures in which he specialized were sold by one dealer in particular, Giuseppe di Felice, to local collectors and in various parts of Europe, especially England, at good prices. Stanzione is supposed to have obtained for Cavallino a commission to do some paintings for the very wealthy Flemish merchant and collector residing in Naples, Gaspar Roomer (Antwerp ca. 1590–Naples 1674), who is said to have exported Cavallino's pictures to Flanders as the work of other artists. De Dominici maintains that, though Cavallino knew others were profiting at his expense, he was too good-natured and too humble to object, and that he was so poor when he died that he had to be buried at the expense of his parish church of San Nicola alla Carità.[90]

It is indeed true that Cavallino's paintings are widely scattered today, as the present catalogue demonstrates, and the idea that they were misattributed early on is supported by the fact that almost without exception his works are to be found under other names in eighteenth- and nineteenth-century museum catalogues and inventories. For example, the Harrach copy (Inv. no. 30) of the Bologna *Denial of Saint Peter* [9] was attributed to Domenico Fetti

in 1745 and 1749, although it had very likely been bought in Naples less than twenty years previously. The Kassel *Healing of Tobit* [24] appears as Guercino in a 1749 inventory, and the Munich *Erminia* scenes [77-78] were given to Fetti in an inventory of 1885. The Brunswick *David and Abigail* and *The Finding of Moses* [80-81] were early on called Jean Baptiste Mole or Jean Boulanger, with the recently published *Adoration of the Shepherds* [2], which entered the collection before 1737, misidentified as a copy after Caravaggio. In the nineteenth century the Liverpool *Rape of Europa* [35] was attributed to Francesco Romanelli; the Stockholm *Judith with the Head of Holofernes* [82]—which bears a "BC" monogram—to Giovanni Battista Coriolano or to Giovanni Benedetto Castiglione; the Vienna *David before Saul* [60] to Bartolomeo Manfredi; and the Harrach *Banquet of Absalom* [17], which with the abovementioned *David before Saul* was probably acquired in Naples around 1730, to the Spanish school. Even the Capodimonte *Cantatrice* [70], which may well never have left Naples, appears in an 1870 inventory as school of Pacecco di Rosa.

Cavallino's works may actually have been exported during his lifetime under other names, but the account of his spending his entire career in the service of second-hand dealers seems romanticized. We know that he was paid directly by patrons for pictures in 1646 and 1649. Moreover, rather than his having to work throughout his life to support his family, it seems possible that only Bernardo and his older brother Tommaso were left alive by 1636. The document of transferral of funds from his mother's estate dated that year mentions only Bernardo and Tommaso (born 1614) as heirs: their father, Giovanni Maria, and brothers Onofrio (born 1618), Leonardo Francesco (born 1619), and Giovanni Sabato (1621) are not mentioned at all; presumably Giovanni Maria was dead, as Tommaso, the eldest son, is mentioned as guardian of his two minor siblings, Bernardo and Leonardo, by 1632. A sixth brother, Leonardo (born 1623), is mentioned as one of the heirs at the time of Cavallino's mother's death in 1632 but is referred to as having died by 1636.[91] In addition, the fact that the artist caused himself to be declared legally of age between 1632 and 1636 may have something to do with the start of his independent working life, perhaps even the establishment of a workshop, if indeed he had one.

By the second quarter of the eighteenth century de Dominici ranked Cavallino with Stanzione, Vaccaro, Luca Giordano, and Francesco Solimena as among the finest painters Naples had produced. This is despite the fact that, so far as we know, the artist never did frescoes, produced

Fig. 30. Cavallino. Detail of *The Triumph of Galatea* [68].

no large extant church or palace decorations, and enjoyed almost no ecclesiastical patronage. De Dominici listed a number of Cavallino's pictures in important local private collections, and the artist's work must by this time have been highly regarded in his native city.[92] However, not enough is known about Neapolitan collections and patrons before the mid-seventeenth century to judge whether this was the case during the artist's lifetime. Most of the published collection inventories are from the eighteenth century, and the earlier guidebooks to the city do not give detailed descriptions of private collections.[93] We do not understand exactly how the process of buying and selling cabinet pictures in the city was effected, nor do we know to what extent there might have been knowledgeable and enthusiastic individuals who patronized certain artists in the way Ferrante Spinelli, principe di Tarsia, for example, favored Aniello Falcone. It seems clear that Naples had no Cassiano dal Pozzo, the well-known intellectual, collector, and member of the Barberini circle in Rome whose patronage was so important to Poussin, or don Antonio Ruffo, the Messinese collector who through agents commissioned work from painters as far afield as Guercino and Rembrandt.[94]

The most important private galleries in early-seventeenth-century Naples were apparently those of Gaspar Roomer, his associates and compatriots Jan and Ferdinand Vandeneynden (father and son), and Cardinal Ascanio Filomarino, archbishop of Naples. Roomer had a great many pictures—a substantial holding already was recorded in 1634—and he patronized local artists like Ribera, Stanzione, Caracciolo, and Falcone, as well as procured works by Frenchmen (Vouet, Valentin) and Northerners, many of them Flemings, including van Dyck, Rubens, Paul Brill, Cornelis Poelenburgh, Abraham Brueghel, and others.[95] The Vandeneynden collection, as we know from an inventory of 1688 by Luca Giordano when it was divided between Ferdinand Vandeneynden's three daughters, contained works by many of the Neapolitans (for example, Stanzione, Ribera, Vaccaro, Falcone, Cavallino, Gargiulo, Mattia Preti, Luca Giordano, Paolo Porpora, Giacomo Recco, and Giovanni Battista Ruoppolo), as well as by outsiders, both Northern and Italian, such as Poussin, Jan Miel, Pieter van Laer, Castiglione, Lanfranco, and

Fig. 31. Cavallino. Detail of *The Singer* [70].

22

Salvator Rosa.[96] Cardinal Filomarino (Naples 1580/83–1666), a member ot the Barberini circle in Rome, was named archbishop of Naples in 1641 and brought from Rome a collection of pictures in 1642. His gallery at that time may have included works by Titian, Raphael, Annibale Carracci, Lanfranco, Poussin, Domenichino, Francesco Albani, Guido Reni, the Cavaliere d'Arpino, Pietro da Cortona, Vouet, and Valentin; of Neapolitan artists he seems mainly to have patronized the Fracanzano.[97] These collectors were all influential as patrons in Naples, but it is interesting that two were Flemish-born and dealers as well as collectors, and the third, while a native Neapolitan, had formed his artistic taste and much of his gallery in Rome. We know that literary academies flourished in Naples during the period, but there is no indication that a comparable activity in the private commissioning of pictures, the patronage of individual artists, and the informed assembling of picture collections by the nobility and professional classes existed.[98] As Oreste Ferrari, Renato Ruotolo, and Gérard Labrot have pointed out, private collecting in Naples, especially as compared to Rome,

seems for the most part to have been more a question of "show" than of knowledgeable and selective support of particular artists.[99] It seems that only in the cases of the abovementioned galleries were the tastes of collectors and the presence of the collections themselves of real influence in the development of Neapolitan Seicento painting.[100]

In Cavallino's case we can attempt only a few guesses about his patronage at this point. Unfortunately we know nothing about the collections of the two individuals by whom he was paid for works in the 1640s, Carlo Cioli and the principe di Cardito (see notes 4 and 5 below), and we have no contemporary proof that he was actually patronized by the two better-known collectors who later evidence suggests bought his pictures, Gaspar Roomer and Ferrante Spinelli, principe di Tarsia. De Dominici says that Roomer patronized Cavallino, and, indeed, a work by the artist is listed in the 1688 inventory of the collection of one of the daughters of Roomer's close associate and heir, Ferdinand Vandeneynden, which could have derived from the Roomer collection (Appendix, no. 4). In addition, we know that the "principe di Bransvich" bought some choice pieces at stiff prices from Roomer's collection when it was being dispersed shortly after his death,[101] and it is interesting that three pictures by Cavallino today are in the Herzog Anton Ulrich-Museum in Brunswick, which are traceable in inventories from the early eighteenth century [2, 80-81]. Celano lists Cavallino's works in the collection of the principe di Tarsia in 1692,[102] and a 1734 inventory of the collection lists two paintings, now lost (Appendix, nos. 5, 9). It is interesting to compare a certain pattern of taste in these collections: Roomer owned battle scenes by Aniello Falcone already by 1634,[103] and Ferrante Spinelli, principe di Tarsia, was a major patron of Falcone's; his collection contained about fifty of the artist's works and he provided Falcone with a residence in his palace in 1651.[104] Spinelli's gallery also included other cabinet-picture specialists—a tradition with which Cavallino's work was obviously associated—such as Salvator Rosa and Domenico Gargiulo.[105] Another Neapolitan collection in which Cavallino's pictures are listed by the end of the century is that of Domenico di Martino, who also owned paintings by Falcone, Rosa, and Gargiulo (as well as by Vaccaro, Bartolomeo Bassante, and Paolo Finoglia).[106] It is indeed likely that the contemporary taste for Cavallino's pictures was closely bound up with that for the best-known small-figure specialists, including that for another associate of Falcone and battle-scene painter, Andrea de Leone, who—like Falcone—was able to combine the approach of the cabinet-picture

Fig. 32. Cavallino. Detail of *Erminia among the Shepherds* [76].

23

Fig. 33. Cavallino. Detail of *The Adoration of the Shepherds* [79].

painter with an academic and classicizing grand manner. This particular combination of elements also describes the work of Nicolas Poussin and perhaps helps explain why, in the critical view of the eighteenth century, de Dominici took such pains to characterize Cavallino as "the Poussin of the Neapolitans."

Another aspect of Cavallino's oeuvre that suggests that he had a specific source or type of patronage is the way in which his pictures are often produced in thematic series with probable allegorical and rhetorical associations or intentions. As Louise Lippincott has pointed out, the subjects of the three paintings on copper that recently emerged from Spain, Cavallino's *Mucius Scaevola before Porsenna* [84] and *The Shade of Samuel Invoked by Saul* [85] and Andrea Vaccaro's *Jonah Preaching at Nineveh*—the combination of which would seem to denote unlikely companions—share a common theme in that in each a king is warned that his course of action will lead to his death and the destruction of his people unless he repents and averts disaster.[107] It seems improbable that such a message is unintentional and unrelated to a commission for a particular recipient, although it is difficult to assess whether or not such a series of themes might be associated with a particular military or political event. Others of Cavallino's subjects are conjoined as pendants or in series: the drunkenness of Lot and Noah are paired twice [38-39, 74-75], as are David playing the harp to soothe Saul, and Esther interceding before Ahasuerus to spare her people [60-61, possibly 20-21]; Abigail interceding with David to spare her husband's flocks appears as a pendant to Pharaoh's daughter finding the infant Moses [80-81]; and de Dominici lists a series of four Old Testament subjects sent to Spain by don Pedro Antonio de Aragón (viceroy 1666–72) that represent Judith with the head of Holofernes, Jael and Sisera, Samson and the Philistines, and Deborah and Barak (Inv. nos. 79, 83, 86, 105). The latter are all themes of the weak triumphing over the strong through God's intervention. These various series likely had an allergorical, topical, or rhetorical intent, no doubt a common practice of the time but one that suggests a specific set of commissions and special patrons rather than a situation in which an artist worked at the behest of dealers.

Fig. 34. Cavallino. Detail of *The Expulsion of Heliodorus from the Temple* [83].

Returning, in conclusion, to Cavallino's paintings and to the attempts to sketch out his place in the Neapolitan school between about 1630 and 1656, we can see that the eighteenth-century view of his art has been considerably revised in the light of modern scholarship. As Nicola Spinosa points out in his essay in the present catalogue, the contemporary local situation within which Cavallino's style matured was rich and complex. De Dominici gave us Stanzione, Vaccaro, Artemisia Gentileschi, Rubens, Titian, and Guido Reni as the fundamental influences on the artist's development. In reality, we find a much more complicated picture in which Caravaggesque tenebrism and the naturalistic traditions of Ribera, the Master of the Annunciations, and Falcone are taken up, refined, and rendered more elegant, mannered, luminous, and coloristically subtle and intense. The influences of Rubens and Titian emphasized by de Dominici should be reinterpreted in the light of the tendency toward seeing a greater painterly quality and chromatic richness in Neapolitan painting of the thirties and forties, noted by scholars in recent years

Fig. 35. Cavallino. Detail of *Mucius Scaevola before King Porsenna* [84].

and described at length by Spinosa below. And, as Stephen Pepper has perceptively stated (in correspondence, 1984) regarding the suggested influence of Reni on Cavallino, it is difficult to imagine two painters whose approaches to the depiction of sacred imagery are more different: in his words, Reni is always concerned with the grandeur and universality of his images, eschewing any ingredient that would tend to bind form to its sensuous existence; Cavallino, on the other hand, starts from the very premise that Reni wishes to avoid, namely, that the conviction of an image lies first in its sensuous quality.

To reach a fuller understanding of its character, Cavallino's art needs to be examined further in relation to that of a number of other painters of the period, both Neapolitan and foreign. For example, Cavallino likely had some rapport or connection with local still-life specialists, such as the Recco or Paolo Porpora; with the Genoese painter Castiglione, who arrived in Naples for a stay of undetermined length in 1635, bringing a style that combined influences of Rubens, van Dyck, and Poussin;[108] with two of Castiglione's Neapolitan followers, Andrea de Leone and Niccolò di Simone; with certain Frenchmen who either visited Naples or whose works were there by the 1630s or 1640s (i.e., Poussin, Vouet, and Charles Mellin, again discussed by Spinosa below); and possibly with van Dyck and Velázquez, because van Dyck's portraits seem so clearly reflected in certain of Cavallino's elegant figures [53, 64] and because the virtuosity of brushwork in the mature work of Velázquez, who was briefly in Naples in 1630 and 1649, seems so comparable to that in certain late pictures by Cavallino [63, 79].[109]

The personalities of many artists whose styles are related to Cavallino's are not yet defined, and the chronologies of many key figures—especially of Stanzione, Vaccaro, Falcone, Gargiulo, Finoglia, Guarino, and the Master of the Annunciations—are not established. It is clear, for example, that Vaccaro's and Cavallino's styles are at some points close (cf. cat. nos. 84-85; Inv. no. 49; Fig. 36), but it is not easy to say in which direction the influence went, and one rather suspects that it was that of the younger painter upon the elder. In some cases—such as those of Giovanni Dò and Bartolomeo Bassante (or Passante)—we know very few works by the artists in question; yet Bassante's signed *Adoration* in the Prado (Fig. 37) shows a strong connection between Cavallino and this little-known painter who was probably his near contemporary. Several artists with whose works Cavallino's manner shares certain stylistic affinities are beginning to emerge from obscurity: thanks to recent articles, Nunzio Rossi, Agostino Beltrano, Giovanni Battista

Fig. 36. Andrea Vaccaro, Naples 1605–1670. *The Meeting of Jacob and Rachel at the Well*. Museo di Palazzo Reale, Naples.

Quagliata, Niccolò di Simone, and, in particular, Antonio de Bellis are now better defined as artistic personalities.[110] Giuseppe De Vito's researches on Antonio de Bellis (cf. Fig. 38) have resulted in a separation of his hand from Cavallino's, and we may hope eventually to define the nature of the two artists' relationship.[111]

We do not know at this point whether Cavallino had students or a workshop, but an extraordinary number of contemporary pictures, often known only through photographs, have been attributed to him for which we lack either artists' names or explanations of their connections with Cavallino or both.[112] Perhaps an understanding of certain mysterious figures such as the Tobit master or masters (Inv. nos. 1, 3, 5-6, 15-18; Figs. 24b-c), the Cain and Abel Master (Inv. nos. 8, 34, 63; Fig. 39), and the authors of the Metropolitan Museum's *Saint Catherine* (Inv. no. 54), the Colnaghi *Saint John the Evangelist* (Inv.

Fig. 37. Bartolomeo Passante (or Bassante), Brindisi 1614(?)–Naples 1656(?). *The Adoration of the Shepherds*. Canvas, 99 x 131 cm. Museo del Prado, Madrid.

Fig. 38. Attributed to Antonio de Bellis, active in Naples 1630s–50s. *The Finding of Moses*. The National Gallery, London (see Inv. no. 10).

Fig. 40. Anonymous Neapolitan artist, follower of Cavallino. *Saint John the Evangelist*. P & D Colnaghi & Co., London (see Inv. no. 58).

Fig. 39. Anonymous Neapolitan artist, follower of Cavallino. *The Death of Abel*. Museo di Capodimonte, Naples (see Inv. no. 8).

no. 58; Fig. 40), and the *Judith with the Head of Holofernes* at Capodimonte that has been rejected as Cavallino's work (Inv. no. 12) will eventually clear up questions of close imitators or a studio. The exact nature of Cavallino's contemporary influence in his native city eludes us as much as do the sources of his formation. Judging from the presumed self-portraits [3, 11, 20, 40, 41, 53, 59, 84] recurring throughout his career—each of which confronts the viewer with an intensely self-conscious, even melancholic, gaze—we are tempted to speculate that the enigmatic quality that has surrounded this artist for over three hundred years might well have been his own intention.

My *ringraziamenti* date back over twenty years: to Robert Enggass for leading me to the topic of Cavallino a long time ago; to Raffaello Causa, Ferdinando Bologna, Eugenio Battisti, and Arnold Noach for helpful criticism; and to the late Anthony Blunt, the late Vitale Bloch, Francis Haskell, Jennifer Montagu, the late Benedict Nicolson, Pierre Rosenberg, and Sir Ellis Waterhouse for being examples of what art historians are all about. Oreste Ferrari, Giuliano Brigand, and Stephen Pepper have given assistance, stimulation, leads, criticism, advice, and challenge. Michael Stoughton has pursued Cavallino in the bank archives of Naples and consulted on myriad questions; we share the memory of a quixotic and fruitless pursuit of Cavallino's bones in the parish of San Nicola alla Carità. I owe a major debt of gratitude to the Bibliotheca Hertziana in Rome and to its staff, as well as to the Witt Library in London and to Rupert Hodge. In addition, Albert Albano, Jack Baer, Arnauld Brejon de Lavergnée, the late Antonio de Mata, Giuseppe De Vito, Craig Felton, Mlles Grassi and Labbra, Gabrielle Kopelman, Suzanne Lindsay, Louise Lippincott, Michael Mahoney, Maurizio Marini, Patrick Matthiesen, Vincenzo Pacelli, Alfonso E. Pérez Sánchez, Frans Pijnenburg, Wolfgang Prohaska, Eduard Safařík, Barbara Sevy and Carol Homan, Walter Strauss, Stefano Susinno and Carlo Virgilio, Peter Sutton, Agnes Szigethi, Mark Tucker, Susan Urbach, Clovis Whitfield, and Federico Zeri deserve my special thanks. Anne d'Harnoncourt, director of the Philadelphia Museum of Art, has borne with characteristic grace and understanding the inconvenience of having one of her staff heavily involved in a project for another institution. My friend Renato Ruotolo, besides providing invaluable assistance in the archives of Naples, has opened my eyes, mind, and heart to the city in a way that no one else could. Three others of my friends have, over the past two years, been more than helpful, they have been heroic: my deepest gratitude to Elizabeth Cropper, Carl Strehlke, and Joseph Rishel. AP

The passage quoted at the beginning is from Goethe's *Italian Journey (1786-1788),* trans. W. H. Auden and Elizabeth Mayer (San Francisco: North Point Press, 1982), p. 181.

1. Prota-Giurleo 1953, p. 158 (first published in a Neapolitan daily paper, *Roma,* 13 July 1950). I am grateful to Renato Ruotolo for providing a full transcription of the baptismal documents for the Cavallino children from the parish archive of the church of Santa Maria della Carità (now San Liborio alla Carità) in Naples:

Libri dei Battezzati, vol. 1

fol. 141: "A 10 [aprile 1614] battezzato per me D. Giuseppe De Matteis Thomase, figlio di Gio: Maria Cavallino, et Beatrice Lopes, lo tenne Aniello Basso, et Vittoria di Fiore"

fol. 159: "A 25 [agosto 1616] da D. Gio: Batta Cece battezzato Bernardo, figlio di Gio: Maria Cavallino et Beatrice Lopes, lo tenne Filippo Billi, et Camilla Fatizzo"

fol. 169: "A di detto [14 gennaro 1618] battezzato per me Honophrio figlio di Gio: Maria Cavallino, et Beatrice Lopes, lo tenne Francesco Mosane, et Diana Porpora"

fol. 181: "A 17 [novembre 1619] battezzato per me Lonardo Francesco figlio di Gio: Maria Cavallini, et Beatrice Lopes, lo tennero Giulio Baiardi, et la Sig.ra Giulia Spinola"

fol. 197: "A 27 [ottobre 1621] battezzato per me Gio: Sapato figlio di Gio: Maria Cavallino, e Beatrice Lopes, lo tenne Gerolamo Pica, et Catherina Morello"

fol. 212: "A 29 detto [giugno 1623] battezzato per me Leonardo figlio di Gio: Marino Cavallino, et Beatrice Lopes, lo tenne il sig. Gio: Batta Caracciolo, et la sig.ra Giulia d'Alessio"

The date of birth of Bernardo's brother Onofrio (1618) can thus be corrected from Prota-Giurleo's erroneous transcription (1613). Battistello Caracciolo was godfather to Cavallino's brother Leonardo (born 1623), leading Prota-Giurleo to suggest that Cavallino's father himself may have been a painter, but this is not demonstrable. Many artists lived in this parish at the time (see Naples 1977, pp. 30-31).

Unfortunately the death registers are missing for the period in question, but the indexes to them survive, showing that unspecified members of the Cavallino family died in 1649, 1672, and 1677. No members of the family appear in the marriage registers, suggesting that Giovanni Maria's was the only family by the name in the parish at the time, as Renato Ruotolo kindly informs me.

2. Archivio Storico del Banco di Napoli, Banco dello Spirito Santo, matr. 272:

"D. 197-14-xi-1636

Ad Aniello Falcone D. 197. E per lui a Tomase e Bernardo Cavallini come figli ed eredi della q. Beatrice Lopes etiam per intermediam personam del q. Leonardo Cavallino loro fratello ex testamentum e dichiarati per la Vicaria mediante decreto di preambolo in banca a comp. di D. 250, atteso l'altri D. 53 - li detti Tomaso e Bernardo l'hanno ricevuti da esso di contanti et detti per la retrovendita che li detti fratelli detto nomine questo di li han fatto d'annui D. 15, 6, 2-1/2 restanti di maggior summa l'anni passati tanto per essi quanto per la quondam Costanta de Mandatis sua madre, e altri suoi fratelli iurum renduti a Marcantonio Lopez et per detto Marcantonio alla detta q. Beatrice mediante cautele per mano di notare Tomaso Aniello d'ysea di Napoli con le quietanta di capitale e terze, atteso sibbene li detti D. 250 a tempo di detta ricompra si dovevano depositare per farcene altra compra conforme la conditione opposta nel patto di retrovendendo non di meno a beneficio suo di detti suoi fratelli e dell'heredità della q. loro madre è stata fatta ampia indennità tanto per detto Marcantonio e Beatrice Turino sua moglie insolidum quanto per detti fratelli Cavallini anco insieme respettive mediante altri istr. rogato in curia di Tomaso Aniello per mano di notar. F.co Ricciardo notato alla margine di detto istrumento di vendita alla quale se habbia relatione.

"Si fa fede per l'attuario Tomaso Merolla attuario della Gran Corte della Vicaria qualmente mediante decreto di preambolo di detta Gran Corte interposto a 31 gennaio 1632 Tomaso, Bernardo e Lonardo Cav-

allini furono decretati figli legittimi e naturali, et heredi universali ex testamento della q. Beatrice Lopes loro madre cum 6-1-9 (6-4[?]) ognuno di loro per uguali parti et portione e che l'uno riceva [?] all'altro servata la forma del testamento et la tutela delle persone e beni delli predetti Bernardo e Leonardo Cavallini minori fu data in persona di Tomase loro fratello et altro decreto interposto per detta Gran Corte il predetto Bernardo Cavallino fu declarato maggiore.
Conditionati a Tomase e Bernardo Cavallino heredi ut supra."

Vincenzo Pacelli very kindly provided this unpublished document from the archives.

3. Information courtesy of Michael Stoughton, who discovered that Cavallino deposited the small sum of three ducats and three *tari* during the first half of 1643, which was withdrawn during the first six months of 1646.

4. On 16 March 1646 Cavallino was paid forty-seven ducats by Carlo Cioli toward seventy ducats owed for an *Annunciation* and an *Immaculate Conception,* each nine *palmi* high and seven wide (ca. 237 × 186 cm). The document, from the Archivio Storico del Banco di Napoli, Banco del Salvatore, giornale di cassa 19, will be published by V. Rizzo in an article entitled "Documenti inediti sui pittori napoletani del Seicento" in the forthcoming *Civiltà del '600.* Renato Ruotolo kindly provided this information.

5. D'Addosio 1912-13, p. 42. I am grateful to Renato Ruotolo for providing a full transcription from the Archivio Storico del Banco di Napoli, Banco dell'Annunziata, giornale di cassa 270 (pages not numbered): "23 gennaio 1649: Al Ecc.mo signor Principe di Cardito D.Quaranta, et per esso a bernardo cavallino disse a complimento di D.ti Cinquanta, atteso li altri D.10 li ha ricevuti di contanti, quali sono per conto di uno quatro grande li fà jn piede della quale polisa vi è la firma del sudetto bernardo cavallino a lui D.40." Unfortunately the receipt referred to above as signed by Cavallino is lost.

6. See below, note 30 and Appendix. Cavallino's works rarely are mentioned in the eighteenth- and nineteenth-century guidebooks to Naples, except for the well-known *Saint Cecilia,* and some unnamed pictures mentioned early on in the collections of Domenico di Martino and the principe di Tarsia (Celano [1692] 1970, 3:1616-17; Parrino 1714, pp. 156, 342; Sigismondo 1788-89, 1:233). A number of paintings are attributed to him in old inventories and descriptions of collections, primarily in Naples and dating before 1800, but for the most part these works are lost or are not securely identifiable with any known today (see Appendix). His name was not associated with an intertwined "BC" monogram in the old dictionaries of artists' signatures, so that anyone trying to identify a painting on the basis of this monogram would find other artists with the same initials, such as Castiglione, Bernardino Curti, and Bartolomeo or Giovanni Battista Coriolano, listed under the designation "BC" (Brulliot 1832, p. 100, nos. 794-95; Nagler 1858-79, 1:758-59, nos. 1723, 1725-26). It is probable that few works appear under his name in eighteenth- and nineteenth-century auction catalogues, although these have not yet been studied thoroughly. And to date no engravings after his pictures are known to this writer. If such exist, they are most likely to be found under the names of other artists.

7. In the 1673 "Listra [sic] de' nomi de' pittori di mano de' quali si hanno disegni" unfortunately the subject of the drawing by Cavallino that is included is not given. The artist is listed in Andreini's "Nota de' pittori, scultori et architettori che dall' anno 1640 sino al presente giorno hanno operato lodevolmente nella città e Regno di Napoli" sent to Baldinucci as "Bernardo Cavallino, morì da 20 anni in circa" (Baldinucci [1845−47] 1974-75, 6:185, 366).
Renato Ruotolo recently identified the compiler of the "nota" of 1675 as Andreini (Ruotolo 1982, pp. 10, 22 n. 29). The "nota" is not precise for artists who died two or three decades previously, so it cannot be used to pin down Cavallino's death date to around 1655, but it does reinforce the idea that the artist died in the plague of 1656. Baldinucci unfortunately never worked up his notes on the Neapolitan artists into biographies before his death in 1697. Had he done so, we would presumably know more about Massimo Stanzione, Battistello Caracciolo, Belisario Corenzio, Andrea Vaccaro, the Fracanzano,

Andrea de Leone, Jusepe de Ribera, Pacecco di Rosa, Artemisia Gentileschi, Anella di Rosa, the Recco, Domenico Gargiulo, Aniello Falcone, Carlo Coppola, and Bartolomeo Bassante, among others. See also Ceci 1899, pp. 163-65; Schlosser 1967, pp. 474-75.

8. Cavallino does not appear in one of the few sources on Neapolitan painting written prior to de Dominici, the manuscript by Camillo Tutini (ca. 1600−1667; see Croce 1898b), or in the 1734 Naples edition of Pellegrino Antonio Orlandi's *Abecedario pittorico.*

9. One cannot help but wonder whether the well-known prejudice against local Neapolitan painters in the first part of the Seicento, as demonstrated by the circumstances of the commissioning of the decoration for the Cappella del Tesoro in the Duomo in the early 1620s (see Schleier in London and Washington 1982−83, p. 45), was one of the reasons for this neglect. Only those artists who were active outside Naples, such as Rosa or Bernini, are well recorded in contemporary biographies. As Thomas Willette has pointed out (orally), the plague of 1656, which took the lives of nearly half the city's population and of many painters as well, did much to break the continuity of oral traditions passed down in artists' workshops.

10. Giannone [1773] 1941, pp. 1-2.

11. ". . . più cose, migliore metodo, meno parole" (Galanti 1792, p. 253 n. 1); see also Comolli 1788−92, 2:245-53, for censure of de Dominici's accuracy, methodology, and critical integrity.

12. Faraglia 1882−83, 1892; Croce 1892; Ceci 1902, 1905, 1908, 1913. Concerning the possibility of de Dominici's forging his own sources, see especially Prota-Giurleo 1955, pp. 25-32.

13. De Dominici says that Cavallino died of gonorrhea maltreated because he was too bashful and ashamed to admit to his ailment. The account, however, brings in Cavallino's mother and his "sorrowing sisters," whereas the documents of the artist's family's baptisms show that he had five brothers, four surviving infancy, with no mention of any sisters (see above, note 1). We know from the document of 1636 (see above, note 2) that his mother had died by 1632.

14. De Dominici 1742-43, 3:33-35.

15. Novelli Radice 1974, p. 100.

16. Grossi 1813, unpaginated, provides this outline of typical academic training as Stanzione's method of instruction. It should be noted, however, that Giovanni Battista Passeri in his life of Salvator Rosa comments that the Neapolitans traditionally avoided a long application to the study of drawing and turned early to their brushes and colors (Passeri in Baglione 1733, p. 290). An interesting insight into the apprenticing of painters and the emphasis on draughtsmanship in Naples in the 1630s is given by a document of 1632 whereby Paolo Porpora's mother places him at age fifteen in the service of Giacomo Recco, aged twenty-nine, for three years. According to the terms of the agreement Recco was obliged to keep the boy during the day, providing meals and instruction "secondo la capacità del suo ingegno," sending him home at night; however, the student was to draw every night at home, and if he didn't keep up this exercise he was to be forced to sleep at his master's house and be made to draw (Prota-Giurleo 1953, pp. 12-13).

17. An organization of painters and miniaturists, playing-card decorators, gilders, and "rotellari" existed from the sixteenth century in Naples for the benefit and protection of those who followed these professions. By about 1641 the painters and miniaturists had split off from the rest, and in 1665 a Congregazione dei Pittori, which met at the Gesù Nuovo, was established, with Andrea Vaccaro elected as its first head in 1666. This existed for religious and charitable purposes rather than didactic or theoretical ones. However, associated with it was an "accademia del nudo" founded by Vaccaro for training young artists as well as for the use of established professionals. See de Dominici 1742−43, 3:139; Giannone [1773] 1941, pp. 127-30; Ceci 1898b; Commodo Izzo 1951, pp. 36-37; Strazzullo 1962a; Naples 1977, pp. 44-46.

18. De Dominici 1742-43, 3:73; Giannone [1773] 1941, p. 111. Ribera's ability as an academic draughtsman has often been emphasized (see especially Jonathan Brown in Princeton and Cambridge 1973-74, esp. pp. 119-22; Jonathan Brown in Fort Worth 1982, pp. 79, 81). The

29

academic quality of Falcone's draughtsmanship is demonstrated by sheets at the Pierpont Morgan Library and the Metropolitan Museum of Art; his drawings have been confused from the eighteenth century with those of contemporaries working in Rome such as Andrea Sacchi and Andrea Camassei (New York 1967a, nos. 74-75; Bean in New York 1979, pp. 50, 130). Saxl cites a document of 23 January 1636 whereby Falcone contracts for a nude model for three sittings a week at his house for three months (Saxl 1939–40, p. 86 n. 3).

19. Blunt 1966-67, 1:57.

20. Ribera in 1615–16 (Fort Worth 1982, p. 29), Stanzione in 1617–18 (Borsook 1954, pp. 271-72) and ca. 1625–30 (Novelli Radice 1974, p. 100).

21. De Dominici 1742–43, 3:33.

22. See above, note 2.

23. According to de Dominici, the commission was obtained through Andrea Vaccaro. He says that Cavallino's painting for the ceiling was mistaken for the work of older or better established members of Stanzione's school, such as Pacecco de Rosa, Agostino Beltrano, or Francesco Guarino, or for that of Vaccaro or even of some non-Neapolitan painter. (One notices how over and over again the work of outside painters is valued above that of the local Neapolitans, a prime example being the well-known 1621 resolution of the Deputati del Tesoro that Neapolitan artists should be excluded from the decoration of the Cappella del Tesoro in the Duomo, one of the premier commissions of the period; see above, note 9). Unfortunately the ceiling of the Ospedaletto was destroyed in the earthquake of 1784, so no conclusion can be drawn regarding Cavallino's collaboration; before its destruction it was described as decorated with pictures by "various good artists," with a scene by Stanzione in the center flanked by works by Vaccaro, Antonio de Bellis, Michele Fracanzano, Scipione da Salerno, and others" (Sarnelli 1697, p. 265).

24. ". . . quasi della grandezza del Naturale, nella qual misura non riesce Bernardo di quella eccellenza che nella picciola" (de Dominici 1742–43, 3:36). De Dominici is comparing the *Saint Cecilia* altarpiece [44] with the small oil study for it [43] and is finding the latter more successful. It is interesting that de Dominici has Vaccaro citing to Cavallino the example of Salvator Rosa, who misguidedly judged his own grand and heroic compositions to be more successful than his small-figure scenes of brigands, soldiers, etc. As Rosa and Cavallino were nearly the same age, and as Rosa left Naples at just about the same time Cavallino began to work independently, it is difficult to see that this critical assessment of Rosa's work could have been made early enough to affect Cavallino's change in scale, which must have occurred not long after the mid-1630s.

25. ". . . molte opere di così delicato stile, e di vivo colore, proprietà, e naturalezza, che non sembrano dipinte, ma vive le sue figure; servendosi di pochissimi lumi, sbattimenti, e riflessi, riverberando la luce con tal soavità, che dolcemente inganna la vista di chiunque li guarda" (ibid., p. 42). The writer is ostensibly quoting from one of his manuscript sources, now lost, some notes by the Neapolitan painter Paolo de Matteis (1662–1728).

26. ". . . le nobili idee, i giudiziosi componimenti, la bellezza del colorito, la squisitezza del disegno, ed il grande intendimento nel lumeggiare . . ." (ibid., p. 43).

27. ". . . che alle Donne non diede bellezza di volto . . ." (ibid.).

28. Giannone [1773] 1941, pp. 107-8. The self-portrait he publishes as representing Cavallino (fig. 20) seems idealized, as do many of his other portraits of Neapolitan artists.

29. Lanzi 1792, 2:463.

30. Orlandi 1753, p. 102; Fiorillo 1801, 2:813; Ticozzi 1818, 1:108; Zani 1819–24, 6:104; Pilkington 1824, 1:186; Galanti 1829, p. 254; Nagler 1835–52, 2:450; Rosini 1839–47, 6:203; Minieri Riccio 1844, p. 92; Ranalli 1845, p. 1125; Siret 1848, p. 421; Müller and Singer 1895–1901, 1:240; *Bryan's Dictionary* 1903–5, 1:273.

31. Dalbono 1871, pp. 33, 53, 94, 107-10, 119.

32. Naples 1877, p. 133, nos. 117-22, p. 169, no. 33.

33. See especially Hermanin 1910, 1911, 1912; Voss 1911; de Rinaldis

1917, 1920a; Sestieri 1920, 1921; Venturi 1921; Ortolani 1922.

34. De Rinaldis 1909, pp. 7-8.

35. For example, as early as 1773 Giannone noted that although Falcone was a specialist in battle scenes he never abandoned the academic mode of emphasis on good draughtsmanship or the production of public church commissions (Giannone [1773] 1941, p. 111; see also note 18 above).

36. De Rinaldis 1909, pp. 4, 7-8, 52, 54, 57-58, 62.

37. Longhi 1915, pp. 59, 130-35; 1916a, pp. 248-49, 304, 308-10; see also Lurie 1969, pp. 145-47.

38. Causa 1972, pp. 941-44. The first attempt at a catalogue raisonné of Cavallino's works was this writer's unpublished master's thesis (Percy 1965).

39. ". . . squillante, intenso, grumoso, impastato di luce" (Causa 1972, p. 944).

40. "Suggestiva ed inquietante figura, tenero, elegiaco, sentimentale: in effetti l'unico pittore del primo Seicento napoletano che sapesse affrontare in chiave intimista la rappresentazione, sacra o profana che fosse, e sempre spogliandola da ogni remora chiesastica, da ogni complicazione di liturgia e di impegno devozionale" (ibid., p. 941).

41. Bologna 1958, p. 18; see also Bologna 1952, p. 52.

42. Ferrari in *Dizionario biografico* 22 (1979):787.

43. Spinosa in Turin 1983, pp. 158-68.

44. See above, notes 28-29; Dalbono 1871, p. 109.

45. For a modern definition of *tenerezza* as used in a seventeenth-century source, see Scaramuccia [1674] 1965, p. 41; the word connotes fluency and softness (as in Correggio), or the opposite of *durezza,* the lack of ability to render the formal quality of substances.

46. ". . . un misto di Guido, del Rubens, e di Tiziano, ed ancora il Pussino de'Napolitani" (de Dominici 1742–43, 3:42). A literal interpretation of Guido Reni, Rubens, and Titian as the primary influences on Cavallino is less rewarding than applying de Dominici's statement in an analogical sense. As early as 1920, de Rinaldis advocated restricting the idea of Guido's influence to Cavallino's rapport with Vaccaro, of Rubens's to a certain "ruddy impasto" seen in the Neapolitan painter's work, and of Titian's to the Venetian element of Francesco Fracanzano's and Giuseppe de Ribera's styles (de Rinaldis 1920a, p. 7). It should always be borne in mind that de Dominici's definition of Cavallino's style was based on an acquaintance with far fewer paintings by the artist than are known to us today.

47. Causa 1972, p. 943; Ferrari in *Dizionario biografico* 22 (1979):787; Spinosa in London and Washington 1982–83, p. 135.

48. In describing this stylistic quality as naturalism, which here refers to the realistic depiction of surfaces and materials especially as associated with the school of Ribera in Naples, we should be careful to distinguish our use of the term from the seventeenth-century connotations of the words *naturalezza* or *verità*. In Cavallino's time the latter would no doubt have had overtones of contemporary theoretical arguments over the Caravaggesque method of direct observation from nature and non-idealized depiction of often humble types as models versus the classical-idealist position that the artist's challenge is to render human figures with a more perfect beauty than nature provides through a process of selection and idealization (cf. Mahon 1947, pp. 62-66).

49. On the complicated question of establishing the oeuvre of this master, whose dates, origins, and chronology are as obscure as his identity, see especially Bologna 1952, p. 52 (where his work is associated with an anti-Caravaggesque, painterly trend in Neapolitan painting of the 1630s); Milicua 1954, p. 72 (where a connection to Cavallino is drawn); Hernández Perera 1955 and 1957; Bologna 1958, p. 31 n. 7; Pérez Sánchez 1961, and 1965, pp. 372-75 (where the prior attribution of many of his works to Spanish painters is brought out), pls. 122-24; Longhi 1969, pp. 50-52, figs. 36-48; De Vito in London and Washington 1982–83, pp. 190-91; De Vito 1983.

50. Significantly, Cavallino is not included in Benedict Nicolson's posthumously published survey (1979) of the international Caravagges-

que movement. See also Spear in Cleveland 1971, pp. 17-25.

51. A connection between Falcone and Cavallino, and the possibility that Cavallino should be placed in Falcone's school, has long been suggested. See Vaccaro 1838, p. 10; Saxl 1939–40, pp. 82-83 n. 6, p. 86 n. 2; Causa 1957, p. 40; Percy 1965, pp. 15, 23-24, 39-40; Spinosa in London and Washington 1982–83, p. 135.

52. See London and Washington 1982–83, no. 43, repr. p. 77.

53. Ibid., pp. 153, 160, 195.

54. Kitson in London, 1973b, p. 9. According to Prota-Giurleo (1929, p. 15), Rosa was in Naples in May and October of 1638.

55. Repr. in Pérez Sánchez and Spinosa 1978, pp. 99, 108, 116, figs. 45, 100, 157, pls. XII and XXIII.

56. Repr. in London and Washington 1982–83, pp. 86, 90, nos. 122-23.

57. Repr. in Fort Worth 1982, no. 32.

58. Repr. in Fort Worth 1982, no. 17, and in London and Washington 1982–83, pp. 88-89, nos. 124-25.

59. A neo-Mannerist strain in Cavallino's work has been noticed for some time (see Benesch 1926, pp. 248, 250, who mentions Bellange's prints in this connection; Juynboll 1960, p. 87, compares Buytewech, Muller, and Callot).

60. See Illustrated Bartsch 3:107, 123, 133, 328, 331; 4:84, 121, 130, 163, 177, 220-24, 228, 230-31, 248, 357, 391, 393, 408, 470, 498.

61. See Washington 1975, esp. nos. 64-65, 90, 93.

62. See Diane Russell in Washington 1975, pp. 76, 83 n. 79.

63. On Callot, Filippo Napoletano, and Naples, see Paris 1967b, pp. 9-12; Florence 1967, p. 25; Vitzthum 1968; Chiarini 1972, p. 20; Putatoro Murano 1976, p. 194; Rome 1981, nos. 2-28.

64. See Naples 1966–67, no. 14, pl. 9; Florence 1967, nos. 9-26, pls. 8-13; Longhi 1969; Abbate 1970; Causa 1972, pp. 925-26; London and Washington 1982–83, pp. 254-56.

65. De Dominici 1742–43, 3:35.

66. Schleier in Florence and Rome 1983, pp. 201-15, figs. 198, 201, 206, 212-13.

67. Spear 1982, 1:68-71.

68. Crelly 1962, pp. 184-85, no. 80 A-B, repr. figs. 3-4. The Filomarino inventory published by Ruotolo 1977, p. 80, lists the dimensions of the twelve Vouets as about three by four palmi, or about 79 × 95 centimeters, near the pictures' published dimensions of 78 × 102 centimeters.

69. Spinosa 1982.

70. Costello 1950, p. 275 (documents the existence of paintings by Poussin in the collection of Geronimo Guzman in Naples in 1630); Blunt 1958; Ruotolo 1977, pp. 77, 80.

71. Pérez Sánchez and Spinosa 1978, pp. 120-21, no. 189, repr.

72. Passeri in Baglione 1733, p. 290.

73. Ruotolo 1982, p. 22 n. 27.

74. Nappi 1980, p. 16.

75. Gabinetto Disegni e Stampe, Museo e Gallerie Nazionali di Capodimonte, Naples. Recto: Study of a Male Nude Half-Figure (Saint Sebastian?). Verso: Study of Legs. Inv. no. 139. Ex. coll. Firmian (inv. no. 103201). Red chalk on paper, 210 × 214 mm. Inscribed on recto: 61/Bernardo Cavallini; on verso: 22/103201/Ber Caval/ [illegible] or Napolitano. Exh. Naples 1966–67, no. 19; Rome 1969–70, no. 19; Paris (Dessins) 1983, no. 23. See Vitzthum 1961, p. 314.

76. Museo Nazionale di San Martino, Naples. Study of a Male Nude Half-Figure. Inv. no. 20746. Ex. coll. Ferrara Dentice, Naples. Black chalk on paper, 325 × 268 mm. Inscribed on recto: 20746. Exh. Naples 1966–67, no. 20; Rome 1969–70, no. 20; Paris (Dessins) 1983, no. 24. See Vitzthum 1961, p. 314.

77. Ashmolean Museum, University of Oxford, Oxford. Saint Sebastian. Inv. no. 816. Purchased 1952; ex. coll. Piancastelli? (see Ellis in Barnard Castle 1962, no. 39). Black and red chalks on paper, 399 × 252 mm. Inscribed on recto: Bernardo Cavallini. Exh. Barnard Castle 1962, no. 39 (as a tentative attribution to Cavallino). See Parker 1956, 2:426-27, no. 816, repr. pl. CLXXVIII; Ivanoff 1959, p. 147, repr. pl. 81; Vitzthum 1961, p. 314.

This drawing appears to be a preparatory study for a lost painting, known only from a reproduction (see Inv. no. 180).

78. The Pierpont Morgan Library, New York. Study for the Virgin of the Immaculate Conception. Inv. no. 1975.32. Ex. coll. Giovanni Piancastelli (L. suppl. 2078a); Mr. and Mrs. Edward Brandegee (L. suppl. 1860c); Janos Scholz (L. suppl. 2933b). Black chalk, traces of white chalk, on paper, 379 × 279 mm. Inscribed on recto: Bernardo Cavallino. Selected exhibitions: Sarasota 1961, no. 62; New York 1967a, no. 109; New York 1969, no. 23; Santa Barbara 1974, no. 29. Selected bibliography: Scholz 1960, p. 62, repr. fig. 10; Vitzthum 1961, p. 314; Ferrari 1962, p. 236; Vitzthum 1971, p. 82, repr. pl. IX; Scholz 1976, p. xix, no. 101, repr.

This often published and frequently exhibited drawing was first identified as the study for a lost Immaculate Conception once in Palermo (Inv. no. 153) by Oreste Ferrari (1962).

79. The Art Gallery of Ontario, Toronto, Ontario. The Expulsion of Heliodorus from the Temple. Inv. no. 69/35. Ex. coll. John Tetlow (L. 2868); Michael Jaffé. Black chalk on paper, 264 × 410 mm. Exh. Regina and Montreal 1970, no. 43; Toronto 1981–82, no. 75 (full bibliography).

On the London market in the mid-1960s with an attribution to Giovanni Bilivert (Florence 1576–1644), the sheet was attributed to Cavallino by Vitzthum, who related it to the Moscow Expulsion of Heliodorus (Vitzthum 1971, p. 89, fig. 15). Catherine Johnston kindly brought to my attention another painting of the subject, a work by Bertholet Flémalle (Liège 1614-1675), that is also closely related in composition to the Toronto drawing (repr. Musées royaux des Beaux-Arts de Belgique, Brussels, Le Siècle de Rubens, 15 October – 12 December 1965, p. 81, no. 82; also repr., as Prud'hon, in The Burlington Magazine 115 [April 1973]:1ii).

80. In the Gabinetto Disegni e Stampe degli Uffizi, Florence, a Liberation of Saint Peter (11994F; Refice 1951, p. 270, repr. p. 266, fig. 8; reattributed to Schönfeld by Carpegna in Rome 1958, p. 35; Vitzthum 1971, p. 82, lists as not by Cavallino) and a Virgin Adoring the Christ Child (11995F; Refice 1951, p. 270, repr. p. 266, fig. 7; attribution rejected by Vitzthum 1971, p. 82). In the Hermitage Museum, Leningrad, two sheets with a Martyrdom of Saint Agatha and a Martyrdom of a Female Saint attributed to Cavallino in a 1961 Hermitage collection catalogue (pp. 93-94, nos. 835-36, no. 835 repr. pl. L) have been rejected by Pierre Rosenberg (1968, p. 155 n. 10) and Walter Vitzthum (1971, p. 82). Other sheets on the borderline of Cavallino's graphic oeuvre—possibly copies of his lost originals—are a Saint Barbara in the Pushkin Museum, Moscow, which Causa has (orally) called a copy after Stanzione (6525; red chalk, 369 × 264 mm; Vitzthum 1971, p. 82) and the Maidservant of Judith with the Head of Holofernes in the Hessisches Landesmuseum, Darmstadt (AE 1749; red chalk, 230 × 180 mm; Vitzthum 1971, p. 81, pl. II, as Massimo Stanzione). An eighteenth-century chalk and wash study of the Galleria Corsini, Rome, copy after Cavallino's Departure of Tobit (Inv. no. 9) was sold at Sotheby's, London, 4 July 1977, lot 135. The lost sheets are the two pen and ink David scenes listed as in Mariette's collection (Appendix, no. 18) and a study of a young woman—possibly identifiable with the Pierpont Morgan's drawing—exhibited in Naples in 1877 (no. 169) as in the Persichetti collection.

81. Lee [1940] 1967, p. 25.

82. As expressed by Tomory 1967, pp. 182-85. See also Costantini 1930, 1:224-56, 361; 2:74-75, on the question of sentiment and sensuality in Cavallino's work.

83. ". . . un diffuso sentimento tassesco, tra idillio e elegia" (Causa 1972, p. 942).

84. Tomory 1967, p. 185.

85. Croce 1889-90, 1898c, [1891] 1926; Ceci 1893; Prota-Giurleo 1952, 1962.

86. Prota-Giurleo 1962, p. 20.

87. Croce 1889–90, p. 631; [1891] 1926, p. 57.

88. Ibid., p. 640; p. 83.

89. Croce 1898c, p. 650; Prota-Giurleo 1929, pp. 15, 48; 1953, p. 89. Michele Fracanzano was listed as a painter in Naples in 1659 and was

still there in 1681; in 1685 he went to Paris as a comic actor, where he still was in 1697.

90. De Dominici 1742-43, 3:37-40, 42-43. On Italian seventeenth-century artists working for dealers, see de Dominici 1742–43, 3:72, and Haskell 1963 ed., p. 120. In this context one recalls Passeri's account that Salvator Rosa had his first start in Naples when Lanfranco bought a picture by him displayed anonymously in a shop in via della Carità (Passeri in Baglione 1733, pp. 290-91).

Other instances of the early dispersal of Cavallino's paintings are mentioned by de Dominici. Vaccaro is said to have paid the artist while the latter was still a student of Stanzione to copy certain works, including half-length figures of female saints by Guido Reni in the collection of the principe di Conca, and then sent some of these pictures to Spain. De Dominici also says that the Spanish viceroy don Pedro Antonio de Aragón (viceroy 1666–72) sent four pictures back to Spain—but as many of the viceroys to Naples returned home with quantities of paintings, this would hardly have been unusual—and that Cavallino's works were sold to Venice and Germany. A Giovanni Sciarpin is said to have bought four half-figures of female saints or martyrs from the collection of Gennaro Marotta in 1722 for export to England (Appendix, no. 15); Sciarpin is probably identifiable with a Jean Charpin who belonged to London artists' academies in 1711 and 1720 *(Vertue Note Books* vi, *The Walpole Society* 30 (1951–52):168, 170; Michael Levey, *The Later Italian Pictures in the Collection of Her Majesty the Queen,* London: Phaidon Press, 1964, pp. 83-84).

91. See note 2 above.

92. De Dominici 1742-43, 3:37-40, 42-43. De Dominici makes a point of quoting praises of Cavallino by foreign visitors to Naples knowledgeable in art. Cavallino's pictures are listed in the collections of Francesco Valletta, the marchese di Grazia, Nicola Salerno, and a family named Caputi. The Valletta collection is especially interesting, as Francesco was the grandson of a well-known lawyer and intellectual, Giuseppe Valletta (1636–1714), whose house was the center of a literary circle that included the philosopher and historian Giambattista Vico (1668–1774), whose library was one of the most famous in Europe at the time, and whose collection included pictures and objects of antiquarian interest (Parrino 1714, p. 129; Schipa 1901; Consoli Fiego 1922). De Dominici may have had access to material on seventeenth-century artists in the Valletta circle or collections. It has been suggested that Vico, who had an interest in painting and the figurative arts, aided de Dominici in the compilation of his lives of the artists (Destito 1925, pp. 290-91).

93. Ferrari in Ferrari and Scavizzi 1966, 1:12-13. On Neapolitan collections, see especially Capaccio 1634; Celano [1692] 1970; Parrino 1714; Celano 1724; Colonna di Stigliano 1895; Rogadeo di Torrequadra 1898; Colombo 1900; de la Ville sur-Yllon 1904; Fastidio 1906; Ceci 1920; Saxl 1939–40; Blunt 1958; Bologna 1958; Caracciolo 1959; Mormone 1961-62; Haskell 1963 ed.; Ruotolo 1973, 1974, 1977; Labrot 1979; Pacelli 1979a; Ruotolo 1979, 1982; Labrot and Ruotolo 1980. See especially the recent researches of Renato Ruotolo, Vincenzo Pacelli, and Gérard Labrot on the patterns of seventeenth-century Neapolitan collecting.

94. Haskell 1963 ed., pp. 98-114, 209-10; Ruffo 1916–19.

95. Capaccio 1634, p. 864; Vaes 1925, pp. 184-202; Burchard 1953; Haskell 1963 ed., pp. 205-8; Ruotolo 1982.

96. Ruotolo 1982, pp. 27-39.

97. Ruotolo 1977.

98. On Neapolitan poets, writers, and men of letters, see, for example, de' Pietri 1634, pp. 66-68, and 1642; Minieri Riccio 1879–80. Naples claimed Torquato Tasso, Giambattista della Porta, and Giambattista Marino as native sons; Marino was *principe* of the most important literary academy in Naples, the Accademia degli Oziosi, at the time of his death in Naples in March of 1625. One of the first members of this academy, founded in 1611, was Vespasiano Spinelli, principe di Tarsia (Minieri Riccio 1879–80, p. 148), whose family were later patrons of Falcone and probably Cavallino. It is revealing that the account of 1632 of a French visitor to Naples, Jean-Jacques Bouchard—a member of the Barberini circle in Rome and friend of Cassiano del Pozzo who was received into the Accademia degli Oziosi in Naples—leaves the impression that Neapolitan intellectuals were more interested in theater and in archaeology, history, theology, and mathematics than in the visual arts (Marcheix [1897], pp. 27-28, 91-101).

99. Ferrari in Ferrari and Scavizzi 1966, 1:12-13; Labrot and Ruotolo 1980, pp. 27-29, 37, 44.

100. Ruotolo 1982, p. 5.

101. Ibid., pp. 9, 21 n. 23.

102. Celano [1692] 1970, 3:1616 (Celano calls the artist Francesco Cavallino).

103. Capaccio 1634, p. 864. See also Blunt 1969.

104. Saxl 1939–40, pp. 81-83.

105. Celano [1692] 1970, 3:1616.

106. Ibid., p. 1617.

107. See discussion in "New Acquisitions: 1983," *J. Paul Getty Museum Journal* 12 (1984).

108. See Blunt 1939-40, esp. pp. 146-47; Philadelphia 1971, pp. 26, 28, 51-52; Newcome 1978; Brigstocke 1980; Standring 1982, 1:113-17. Brigstocke publishes a painting by Castiglione dated 1633, two years before we know he visited Naples, which clearly shows the influence of Poussin on the manner of Castiglione that had such an effect on Andrea de Leone.

Perhaps it is worth noting that on 18 March 1637 a "Giovanni Castiglietti"—a name not found in Thieme-Becker—was paid in that city for a painting of *Christ Washing the Feet of the Apostles* (Strazzullo 1955, p. 20).

109. Van Dyck's putative stopover in Naples (Mariette 1853–62, 2:175; *L'Arte* 1899, p. 502) could have occurred following his flight from the plague in Palermo in 1624, but scholars generally reject the probability of this visit (Vaes 1924, p. 217). However, the artist's time is not so closely accounted for during his years in Italy (late 1621 to late 1627) that a trip to Naples can be definitely ruled out. On the question of van Dyck and Naples, I am grateful for the comments of Susan J. Barnes, who is preparing a dissertation on van Dyck in Italy at New York University.

Velázquez spent an unknown number of weeks in Naples between August and December of 1630 on his return to Spain from his first trip to Italy, which lasted from mid-1629 to early 1631 (Harris 1982, p. 17; see also Garrard 1980, p. 109, n. 53). During his second stay in Italy (spring 1649 to summer 1651) he is known to have made only short trips to Naples and Gaeta in June/July of 1649 and March of 1650; however, for the last six months of this Italian stay his whereabouts are more or less unaccounted for (Harris 1982, pp. 26, 28, 146).

110. Novelli [Radice] 1974; Volpe 1974; Novelli Radice 1978, 1980; De Vito 1982; De Vito in De Vito et al. 1983, pp. 7-38; Ruotolo in De Vito et al. 1983, pp. 57-71.

111. To De Vito's illustrations in his 1982 article on de Bellis, I would add the following works that have borne attributions to Cavallino: Private collection, Naples, *Saint Martyr* (Capodimonte photo 3343); sale, Sotheby's, London, 1 June 1977, lot 93, repr., *Saint Catherine;* and Piero Corsini Gallery, New York, *Christ and the Woman of Samaria at the Well.*

112. Some interesting works known at present, mainly through photographs, that seem to represent various followers of Cavallino are: (1) *Lot and His Daughters,* octagonal, ex. coll. Briganti (cf. Vaccaro 1838, pp. 21-22), apparently the same hand as (2) *Lot and His Daughters,* circular, Silvano Lodi, Campione d'Italia, Switzerland, in 1983; (3) *The Meeting of David and Abigail* (Fig. 25a), apparently the same hand as (4) *The Rape of Europa,* Museo Nazionale Pepoli, Trapani (Inv. no. 72), (5) *The Resurrection of Lazarus,* Museo Nazionale Pepoli, Trapani, and (6) *Moses Striking Water from the Rock,* Art Center Company S. A., Panama, in 1982; (7) *The Sacrifice of Noah,* Museo Nazionale Pepoli, Trapani; (8) *Rebecca and Eleazer at the Well,* sale, Christie's, London, 26 March 1971, lot 13.

Painting in Naples During Bernardo Cavallino's Lifetime

NICOLA SPINOSA

The span of Bernardo Cavallino's artistic career corresponds almost exactly to one of the most complex and fertile periods, given the variety of circumstances and richness of consequences, in the entire history of Seicento painting in Naples: the twenty odd years between the early 1630s and the end of the dramatic events which, though situated in the line of recent local tradition, saw the waning of earlier techniques and trends and the rise of a new age of Neapolitan painting and art.

It was in these years, to use a formula affected by critics that is nonetheless too summary and superficial, that the foundations were laid and circumstances matured for the transition of Neapolitan painting from naturalism to the baroque. In reality, even if the formula can give some idea of the immense importance of that moment in the process of transformation undergone by Neapolitan painting in the middle of the Seicento, the situation, both at the outset and in its developments and immediate consequences, seems to be far more complex and difficult to define.

On the other hand, while various equivocal examples of a prolonged period of late Mannerism were still flourishing among artists such as Belisario Corenzio, Fabrizio Santafede, Giovanni Bernardo Azzolino, and Giovanni Vincenzo Forli, the Neapolitan scene had for some time already participated in the long but inevitable decline of the early naturalist trends that matured after Caravaggio's two sojourns in Naples at the end of the first decade and the beginning of the second. The premature death in 1614 of Carlo Sellitto, one of the earliest Neapolitan followers of Caravaggio, brought to an end on an ambiguous note the brief career of a painter vacillating between a timid, albeit precocious, attraction to Caravaggesque luminism and a persistent fascination with the styles of Azzolino and late Mannerism. Filippo Vitale, who in rare instances during the second decade had paid more attention to Caravaggesque trends in Naples than Sellitto, had already begun to experiment after 1620 with new approaches to naturalism arising from a different source and divested of the lucidity and rigor displayed in his early efforts. Then Battistello Caracciolo, although the first Neapolitan to adhere with conviction and steadfastness to the tenets of Caravaggism, developing from them consequences of exceptional naturalistic vigor in a long series of works completed around the middle of the second decade, gradually committed himself—after a trip to Rome, Florence, and Genoa in 1618—to an inevitable revision of earlier experiments. As a result, he alone of all the Neapolitan painters came to create images of sustained monumentality, abstract formal beauty, and an overtly neo-Mannerist cast.

It must, however, also be noted that the crisis that had developed in Naples in the 1620s within the early naturalist movement was compounded by manifestations of other figurative trends in the work of Guido Reni, Antiveduto Grammatica, Simon Vouet, and especially the Valencian Jusepe de Ribera. Ribera, in Naples uninterruptedly from 1616, had been evolving his own highly individualistic interpretation of the Caravaggio canon as early as his youthful sojourn in Rome.

Ribera's career throughout the whole of the third decade was marked at times by periods of implacable realism or harsh naturalism in which converged echoes of various examples of Northern Caravaggesque painting in Rome and, most particularly, indications of a sensibility shaped by the substance and style of Iberian Counter-Reformation spirituality. But it represents, in fact, a real step forward in a new naturalistic direction for the Neapolitan artistic scene—a direction that encouraged the neo-Mannerist inclinations of Battistello and the sensitive but controlled Caravaggesque efforts of the young Paolo Finoglia at the Certosa di San Martino.

Another notable painter committed to a vigorously naturalistic approach emerged alongside Ribera perhaps as early as the mid-1620s: that anonymous personality once incorrectly identified as Bartolomeo Bassante, who executed the *Nativity* now in the Prado, Madrid, and whom Causa hypothetically identified as the Spaniard Juan Dò (active in Naples prior to 1626). Although art historians agree at least on his Iberian origin, they prefer to identify this painter now as the "Master of the Annunciation to the Shepherds."

Following the example set by Ribera and more recently by the Master of the Annunciation to the Shepherds, various painters of the younger generation and of differing extractions—Francesco Fracanzano, Agostino Beltrano, the young Francesco Guarino, Juan Dò (the author of two *Adorations of the Shepherds*, one at the Pietà dei Turchini, the other at the Escorial), the Dutch artist Matthias Stomer (in Naples since 1624), and the young Aniello Falcone—brought about, between the late 1620s and the early 1630s, a sustained recovery of the naturalist movement. Their style, however, was more vigorous and their figures more corporeal. They focused on the investigation, with respect to the earlier naturalist traditions of Sellitto and Battistello, of previously ignored aspects of popular and rural daily life; their goal was to achieve, dryly and tersely, an extraordinary depth and warmth of human sentiment.

The results of this revival parallel, after a fashion, those attained by Velázquez during the period called "Roman" (even though he worked for a short time in Naples, between 1630 and 1631, possibly as a guest of Ribera).

Meanwhile, around 1629, Massimo Stanzione returned from Rome, shortly thereafter to become, along with Ribera, the major force in Neapolitan painting until the middle of the century. But unlike Ribera, the Master of the Annunciation to the Shepherds, or the other painters who had recently reaffirmed the topicality and value of naturalism, Stanzione seemed to reject every option that might make him appear bound to a particular trend, even in his initial efforts following his return to Naples (e.g., *The Sacrifice of Moses* at Capodimonte, the *Life of the Baptist* in the Prado, the first canvases of *Saint Bruno* painted for the chapel at San Martino, or the *Bacchanal* in the Prado—all dating successively from 1629 to 1633).

In Rome, where he also demonstrated his awareness of Battistellian Caravaggism, Stanzione had obviously studied the works of the great artists of the Renaissance, as well as those of Annibale. But what is most important, he had succeeded in grasping, with a modern sensitivity and a persistently open mind, the positive value so inherent in both the classicist paintings of the Emilians (the early works of Lanfranco, Domenichino, and Reni in particular) and the efforts of "reformed" Caravaggesque artists such as Vouet.

Stanzione returned to Naples, therefore, with a varied and complex cultural baggage whose diverse contents had been harmoniously blended. The result was images of sustained formal elegance and manifest expressive clarity within vast compositions, both sacred and profane, in which the pictorial narrative always assumes the accents of sentiments associated with everyday life.

The sophisticated, highly refined painterliness of Stanzione's approach, though far from the increasingly harsh abstractions in the late works of Battistello or the full-bodied naturalism of a Ribera or a Master of the Annunciation to the Shepherds, would seem to have quickly found a considerable following among the other Neapolitan painters. The strong bond established by Massimo with Artemisia Gentileschi appears also to have contributed substantially to the definition of Stanzione's approach. Artemisia was in Naples at the very beginning of the period 1629–30. During her productive stay there she collaborated with Massimo on the *Life of the Baptist* now in the Prado. Her presence was to prove of great significance, not only for painters associated with Massimo's style during the 1630s but also for masters of the earlier naturalism, like Paolo Finoglia, a follower of Battistello who had moved to the province of Apulia at the end of the decade to continue working in the style of vigorous naturalism (the erroneous attribution of *Joseph with the Wife of Potiphar* in the Kress Collection, Fogg Art Museum, Cambridge, Massachusetts, to Gentileschi is not without cause), or following the manner recently arrived at by Ribera and the Master of the Annunciation to the Shepherds (as the very young Bernardo Cavallino was doing).

So it was that at the start of the fourth decade, perhaps just as Bernardo Cavallino was about to embark on his precocious painterly career, the situation in Naples, though indeed varied and complex, appeared to have substantially stabilized. On one side there were the naturalists associated with Ribera or the Master of the Annunciation to the Shepherds, and on the other, Massimo Stanzione and many others who were gradually moving toward his tempered narrative classicism. The mature Battistello, however, was now completely isolated. At most, he exerted some influence during that time on the bizarre and tormented Giovanni Battista Spinelli, although more through mental affinity and choice of subject matter than similarity of style. For Spinelli had already been grappling for several years with his frantic studies of prints and Northern models and had produced the first of his paintings to be marked by an exaggerated anti-naturalism—the *Saint Stephen* now in a private collection in Florence.

But it is precisely at this point, when the major trends emerging within painting between the end of the 1620s

Color Plate IX. *Saint Lawrence* [58].

Color Plate XI. *"La Pittura": An Allegory of Painting* [66].

Opposite: Color Plate X. Detail of *Mattathias Slaying the Officer of King Antiochus on the Altar at Modin* [59].

Color Plates XII and XIII. *The Triumph of Galatea* [68]. Detail opposite.

Color Plate XIV. *Lot and His Daughters* [74].

Color Plate XV. *The Drunkenness of Noah* [75].

Color Plate XVI. *Erminia among the Shepherds* [77].

and the beginning of the next decade were firmly reconciled, that one can already discern the first signs of the gradual, broadly based disintegration of the qualities inherent both in recent contemporary works in the naturalist vein and products of the trend dominated by the works Stanzione had completed after his return from Rome.

Moreover, Jusepe de Ribera—very soon to become the major protagonist in the process of revising recent local tradition—who revealed, in various paintings that may be dated from 1632 on (particularly in *Jacob with the Flock* [Escorial], which, in fact, bears just that date), an increasingly pronounced rejection of his former preference for an accentuated realism. He now embraced a painting style characterized by a brighter, more luminous color spectrum and, above all, by a greater human warmth and expressiveness.

The process reached full maturity in some of Ribera's paintings executed from 1634–35 on, then rapidly spread to the entire group of painters who had been leaning toward naturalism for some time, following precisely the example of the Valencian painter and the Master of the Annunciation to the Shepherds. In particular, from the mid-1630s one can see within the naturalist movement a progressive decline in the motifs and characteristics that had marked the recent figurative trend: harshness of form and expressive energy lose their hold; chromatic substance and sentimental notes soften; sparkling tones and bold chiaroscuro contrasts fade; and images once rendered by the skillful juxtaposition of pure, jewellike colors and enhanced by a fluid luminosity now communicate deeply felt emotions by the power of painterly evocation alone.

But this new emphasis on pictorial enrichment and on rendering objects and feelings in a moderately natural way while at the same time maintaining, and even giving priority to, the most basic tenets of painting—light and color—was not a phenomenon involving only the exploration of the naturalistic approach that had been carried out up to that point. Nor was it limited to Ribera or the Master of the Annunciation to the Shepherds or whoever else had absorbed the earlier tradition of vigorous naturalism. Very quickly, in fact, painters of other extractions or of different orientations (e.g., Stanzione, Vaccaro, Pacecco de Rosa) became involved—artists who had until then deferred to the notion of painting as sentimental storytelling rather than as the result of freshly perceived, tangible reality. The giving way to a broader sense of beauty in painting among artists of various backgrounds does not imply denial of or opposition to the trends and characteristics of the earlier figurative tradition. Rather, it stemmed from a common, already widespread, need for a more genial, more compelling mode of interpretation, and was now resolved, above all, by means of luministic enhancement and a softened color palette.

This expansion of painterliness introduced in the mid-1630s—which, moreover, reflected the secular and religious spirituality then at work in vast sectors of Neapolitan society—was nourished for a while by the repeated contacts maintained by the Neapolitan artistic community, especially from 1633–34 on, with some of the most advanced proponents of the figurative trend in Rome after 1630. But possible contact with the young Velázquez of the Roman period (which somehow made itself felt among the naturalist painters in Naples shortly after 1630) was not the most decisive factor for those Neapolitan painters committed to the manner of the naturalist tradition (and, therefore, especially to Ribera, the Master of the Annunciation to the Shepherds, Francesco Fracanzano, or to Aniello Falcone). For them, rather, it was the awareness that grew out of the recent investigations carried out in Rome by painters of the neo-Venetian movement that inspired them to broaden their acceptance of the painterly style. These neo-Venetians had been able to extract from their sensitive reevaluation of various works, of Titian in particular, but also those of Paolo Veronese, invaluable ideas for a painting style of extraordinary chromatic beauty and radiant luminosity.

Art historians have yet to ascertain and define with precision the details of the complex relationships established by those Neapolitans in the naturalist camp with the Roman neo-Venetianism of Poussin, Mola, Sacchi, and the young Pietro da Cortona. Furthermore, these relationships were also very quickly complicated by the participation of other painters working in Naples in the manner developed recently by Massimo Stanzione, painters who made different choices and produced different results. These individuals were equally interested in establishing new ties with other aspects of the various movements of painting in Rome. In addition, the openness of the Neapolitans towards luminous painterliness over the years had found exact parallels in Genoa, Rome, and Palermo, tending in the direction indicated by Rubens during his first Italian sojourn and seen in the resplendently rich paintings by van Dyck. Together with Roman neo-Venetianism, these provided further attractive alternatives to an affirmation of painting being valued as the unbridled exaltation of light and color.

At the center of this second movement characterizing Neapolitan painting after the mid-1630s was Giovanni

Benedetto Castiglione, who is documented as having been in the Naples area in 1635, even though some of his paintings had already been circulating between Rome and Naples for some time.

The name of Castiglione (called Il Grechetto) conjures up that of another important exponent of Vandyckism in the Mediterranean area, Pietro Novelli (called Il Monrealese). Novelli established and maintained a relationship of significant reciprocal exchange, which lasted well beyond his brief stay in Naples (sometime between 1631 and 1633), with the artists influenced by Ribera, and he exerted considerable influence on the style of various local painters, especially Andrea Vaccaro.

Nor should it be forgotten that some of the most important Neapolitan collections came in time to include works by Rubens and van Dyck themselves, a fact that had certainly not escaped the attention of local artists, given the numerous copies painted in Naples and the record of sources that has survived.

The results of these contacts with various exponents of Roman neo-Venetianism and Mediterranean Vandyckism coalesced rather quickly in increasingly evident ways. From 1634 on, the work of Ribera in particular began to display solutions of great painterly beauty: striking rendering of light and an exquisite chromatic texture characterize compositions such as the *Saint Zacharias* in the Musée des Beaux-Arts in Rouen, the *Holy Family Appearing to Saint Bruno and Other Saints* in the Palazzo Reale in Naples, and the *Immaculate Conception* (with its wealth of strong Vandyckian overtones) and other canvases executed for Las Augustinas Descalzas in Salamanca. The renewal of expressive intensity achieved solely by means of an extraordinary expansion of the painting medium's potential can be seen especially in the various compositions of 1637: two versions of *Apollo Flaying Marsyas,* in the Musées Royaux des Beaux-Arts de Belgique in Brussels and the Certosa di San Martino in Naples, respectively; the *Venus Discovering the Dead Adonis* in the Galleria Corsini, Rome; *Isaac Blessing Jacob* in the Prado, Madrid; and the *Pietà* in the Certosa di San Martino, Naples.

One perceives in the Master of the Annunciation to the Shepherds—who provided a brilliant alternative, within the compass of naturalist explorations, to Ribera's harshly realistc style in the 1620s—an increasing acceptance of a painterly style, albeit less substantial, in various works dating from the mid-1630s on: *The Return of the Prodigal Son* at Capodimonte (once attributed to Francesco Fracanzano), the fragment of an *Adoration of the Magi* once in the Ruffo collection in Rome, the extraordinary *Adoration of the Shepherds* in the Longhi collection in Florence, and the *Birth of the Virgin* in the church of Santa Maria della Pace in Castellammare di Stabia.

Francesco Fracanzano, on the other hand, denounced more visible ties with the style of some of the painters associated with the neo-Venetian trend, especially with the young Pietro da Cortona. Abruptly distancing himself from the still-vigorously-naturalist tendencies apparent in the *Saint Anthony Abbot with Saint Paul the Hermit* painted in 1634 for the Neapolitan church of Sant'Onofrio dei Ciechi, Francanzo produced barely a year later canvases for San Gregorio Armeno that displayed a sweeping, gilded style. He then went on to the rich luminous effects of the *Saint Catherine of Alexandria* now in the offices of the Previdenza Sociale in Rome, in which the paint almost melts from the "heat" of a luminosity ever more fluid and radiant.

The paintings of Francesco Guarino after 1635 also began to show with equal clarity the retreat of vigorous naturalism's original characteristics before the painterly style. This is especially apparent in the *Annunciation to Zacharias* in the Collegiata di Solofra and the *Immaculate Conception* in the Congrega dei Bianchi, also in Solofra. In these compositions, both executed in 1637, the artist's recourse to a greater pictorial intensity is impressive and implies a close connection with Stanzione's style (an implication that later proves to be quite misleading).

It is difficult to determine—in Ribera's case especially, but also with regard to the Master of the Annunciation to the Shepherds, Francesco Fracanzano, and Guarino—exactly what kinds of affiliations were established from time to time with the neo-Venetian trends and the various manifestations of Italian Vandyckism. But for Aniello Falcone it seems clear that the contacts already established in Rome and later renewed in Naples with the early Roman works of Poussin, together with the outstanding examples of Grechetto's seductive chromatic sensuality, were decisive factors, even though his increasing interest in the young Poussin—an interest to be taken up by various Neapolitan painters later on in the mid-1640s—was already taking on implications in a classicizing direction that were to become more clearly defined in the years to come. Thus Falcone moved away from the naturalist style (closer to Velázquez) of his early *Schoolmistress* (formerly in the Lord Spencer collection) or of his *Battle Scene* of 1631 (in the Louvre; Fig. 12) toward the warmly radiant luminosity seen in his *Battle between the Hebrews and the Amalekites* (dated to ca. 1635) in Capodimonte, and four paintings now in the Prado: *The Gladiators, The Entrance into the Arena, The Concert* (outstanding for its treatment of color and light), and *The Expulsion of the Merchants from the Temple*, the latter works datable ca. 1640.

After completing his *Pietà* at San Martino in 1638, even Massimo Stanzione began to appear attentive to the painterly style. In fact, everything he painted during the following decade demonstrates its effect. But for Massimo, as for other artists who had for some years applied themselves to copying and refining ideas emerging from his polished, elegant narrative painting style (which shortly thereafter was to be enriched by his search for subtler solutions of moderated classicism), contact with the various manifestations of the trend toward the painterly style began to produce conflict. The situation was made even more complex by the great interest surrounding other artistic experiments that were under way in both Rome and Naples after 1630. (Since the consequences of these diverse stylistic tendencies within the group of painters variously influenced by Stanzione were not to be felt before 1640, it will be appropriate to return to this point in greater detail below.) For several years thereafter, these same inclinations were to affect in different ways some artists of the younger generation who had started out in the mid-1630s from premises and pressures quite different from those nurturing the preferences of the group connected with Stanzione. These younger painters Ferdinando Bologna aptly dubbed "pittori di 'valore.'"

In the meantime, it must be noted that around 1640 even a painter as bizarre as Spinelli, whose works had displayed from the first an exaggerated anti-naturalist approach, was unable to escape the fascination of certain subtle compromises between naturalism and painterliness attempted by the Master of the Annunciation to the Shepherds and others within the naturalist circle in Naples. In paintings such as *Christ and the Woman of Samaria at the Well* in the Romano collection in Florence, *Jacob's Dream* in a private Roman collection, and the *Nativity* in the National Gallery in London, Spinelli's concessions are quite apparent.

But the efficacy of solutions mediating between applications of naturalism and new demands for a broader, more compelling painterly approach (already set forth by Ribera and the Master of the Annunciation to the Shepherds) finds more definitive confirmation and develops hitherto unforeseen possibilities for subsequent expressive developments, above all, in the first paintings by the very young Bernardo Cavallino, along with those of Antonio de Bellis depicting *Episodes from the Life of Saint Charles Borromeo* (at least those canvases securely by his hand) at San Carlo alle Mortelle and now correctly dated from 1636 to 1638, and *The Adoration of the Shepherds* by Bartolomeo Bassante (a signed work, now in the Prado; Fig. 37).

Cavallino demonstrated a remarkable sensitivity and intelligence, particularly in his ability to imitate the style of the Master of the Annunciation to the Shepherds. And he was the first to launch a series of successful probes into the various developments sustained up to that time by the naturalist tradition that were distantly though discernibly Caravaggesque in origin. Shortly after 1640 he added to this vision a more extensive and determined revival of emotional qualities beyond the range of verbal articulation that had stimulated and accompanied the Neapolitans' growing interest in the various painterly solutions worked out by both the neo-Venetian and the Vandyckian movements.

There is, in fact, no other explanation for the aesthetic efforts made by the still-quite-youthful painter between the end of the 1630s and the beginning of the following decade, when he worked somewhat in the manner of Battistello Caracciolo in *The Liberation of Saint Peter* in Pio Monte della Misericordia, or in that of the various examples of "reformed" Caravaggism developed in Rome after 1610, particularly by numerous transalpine artists. In no other way can one understand the reflexes of this intelligent return to the tempered naturalism of Vouet in his large painting of *The Circumcision* in Sant'Arcangelo in Segno (Fig. 41) or of Artemisia in the first canvases she painted in Naples. These are works that can be singled out for their unique formal elegance (closest to Stanzione), for their luminous colors, and for their controlled expressiveness—especially in large-sized canvases painted after 1640.

Likewise, the subsequent emotional participation of the young artist in the smallest details of the work of Castiglione and, later on, of other exponents of neo-Venetianism and Vandyckism in the Mediterranean area cannot be properly understood without reference to Cavallino's formative years spent in the shadow of Ribera, the Master of the Annunciation to the Shepherds, and the other Neapolitan naturalists who had recently embraced the painterly style.

Other painters, meanwhile, in part following the example of Falcone but more often inspired by the paintings of Castiglione they had seen in Rome or Naples, revealed—from the early 1640s and, therefore, in anticipation of or concurrently with Cavallino's recent tendencies—a new, expanded capacity to understand fully and assimilate the extraordinary potential for evocation and the communication of emotion inherent in the style of Grechetto after 1630.

Most particularly, after 1640 it was Andrea de Leone who proved to be one of the most attentive and sensitive

Fig. 41. Simon Vouet, Paris 1590–1649. *The Circumcision*.
Canvas, 293 x 193.5 cm, signed and dated. Chiesa di S.
Arcangelo a Segno, Naples (on deposit, Museo di Capodimonte).

a brilliant alternative to Falcone's compositions of the
same subject. The numerous biblical or mythological
scenes Leone painted around the mid-1640s (before his
initial affinities for Castiglione led to the development of
new insights in the Poussinesque manner of his first
experiments with the painterly style) also speak to his
profound interest in Castiglione.

Working at about the same time as Leone, Niccolò di
Simone followed roughly the same path. His two versions
of *The Martyrdom of Saint Januarius*, in the Pio Monte
della Misericordia and the Museo Nazionale di San Martino
in Naples, reveal Grechettian tendencies. In the 1643 canvases and frescoes at Santa Teresa agli Studi he showed
himself quite attentive also to the style of Domenico Fias-
ella. Then there followed a brief period of interest in
Poussin, an interest clearly evident later on in *The Sacrifice
of Noah* now in the Prado (where it is incorrectly
attributed to Andrea de Leone) and as passed through the
filter of de Leone in the *Homage to Bacchus*, in the Pagano
collection in Genoa). Ultimately, he regressed into painting a series of unassuming reinterpretations in the manner
of Stanzione as early as the end of the 1640s.

To the Neapolitan naturalists influenced around 1634–
35 by the painterly style must be added also the artist of
The Last Supper painted in 1641 for Santa Maria della
Sapienza, even though he is better known for his numerous sacred and profance compositions featuring *terzine*
figures. Domenico Gargiulo began his artistic career following the ideas of Filippo Napoletano and Jacques Callot.
In the 1640s he established a fruitful bond with Schönfeld
(who was in Naples from 1643 to 1649, during which time
he, too, was attracted by Cavallino's work, particularly
the rendering of figures and the elegantly rich use of light
and color) and also drew nearer to Cavallino's manner,
resulting in a style in which Gargiulo espoused a rhapsodic
revival of Castiglionesque and Poussinesque techniques.

Carlo Coppola, a follower of Falcone, also demonstrated more than just a marginal interest in painterly
methods of Grechettian origin. His style exhibits obvious
affinities for Niccolò di Simone whose abovementioned
Martyrdom of Saint Januarius is reflected in his own
Martyrdom of Saint Januarius executed in the same year
(and now in a private collection in London), and in his
Saint Peter with the Fish (formerly in the collection of
Vitale Bloch in The Hague). In his few compositions of the
1650s he became a mediocre imitator of Gargiulo's style.

From this diffuse yet broad participation of the Neapolitan artistic community in the development and assim-
ilation of the styles articulated by the painterly trends of
the 1630s (whether of neo-Venetian or of Vandyckian

revivers of Castiglione's rich handling of light and color.
Leone even went so far as to reproduce to the letter some
of Castiglione's Roman compositions (for example, *The
Journey of Jacob* in the Kunsthistorisches Museum,
Vienna, which is a copy of Grechetto's work on the same
subject that is now in Marco Grassi's collection in New
York). Equally revealing is his long series of *Battle Scenes*
(from the earliest, painted in 1641, and which is now in the
Louvre, to the Neapolitan group at Capodimonte, and in
two private collections in Naples, to which must be added
the versions of a similar subject in the frescoes at Villa
Bisignano in Barra, formerly attributed to Falcone). These
Battle Scenes present, within the limits of the genre,

origin), it would also have been logical to expect certain developments in the direction of the baroque to take root in Naples, as they already had in Rome, especially when one considers that by 1634 Giovanni Lanfranco was already active in the Gesù Nuovo, where he began a long succession of decorations of illusionistic, baroque expansion that were finally completed—after interruptions at San Martino, Santi Apostoli, the Palazzo Arcivescovile, and the Cappella del Tesoro di San Gennaro—in 1646. Meanwhile, Pietro da Cortona from Rome, who executed a work for the church of the Gerolamini in 1638, was yet another emmisary of the pronounced baroque style. Moreover, some of the Neapolitan collections could also have served as sources of inspiration to the local painters for the new trends in Roman painting. But for the baroque overtures of a Lanfranco or a Pietro da Cortona to be fully recognized and appreciated in Naples, one must wait until the second half of the century, when the mature baroque works of Mattia Preti and the early works first of Luca Giordano and later of Francesco Solimena unfold on the ceilings, domes, and altars of the city.

This is not the place to examine why the Neapolitans resisted for so long a baroque development of their fertile painterly premises. Such reasons are eminently cultural and tied to religion, as well as being political and intensely social in nature. Here, instead, it will be noted that alongside the intense experimentation with painterly styles carried out with renewed vigor—after the initial steps in the mid-1630s—by artists of the younger generation (those reaching maturity after 1640), the Neapolitan community witnessed, from the very beginning of the 1640s, a growing diffusion of the classicist trend rather than renewing contacts with some of the specific aspects of that trend, which, with subtly differentiated premises and resolutions, had for some time already found a considerable audience and following in Rome.

In Naples, as has been mentioned above, the classicist movement had already found expression in the controlled, elegant formulae and the charming discursive painting Massimo Stanzione produced after the conclusion of his stay in Rome in 1629. Even in the 1640s Stanzione still dominated the complicated series of events that drew many local painters closer to classicism, even those who had initially made considerable efforts in behalf of naturalist experimentation. In an interminable series of canvases and frescoes executed for the Certosa di San Martino (Cappella del Battista), San Paolo Maggiore (Cappella di Sant'Agata), the Gesù Nuovo, and Santa Maria Regina Coeli (in which his monumental *Saint Januarius Healing the Woman Possessed*, painted for the sacristy of

the Tesoro di San Gennaro, must also be included), Stanzione accentuated his earlier inclination to purge his sophisticated, refined vocabulary of every hint of naturalism by reinterpreting more carefully and more ambitiously the ''classical'' works of Guido Reni and Domenichino in Naples. But he did not renounce any of the effects of sensitizing the pigment and elegantly articulating the imagery within an ever-expanding space; and, with the *Annunciation* (dated to 1655) in Marcianise and the *Visitation* in the Gesù Nuovo (Fig. 42), he concluded a long and brilliant career on a note of extraordinary protobaroque intensity.

Fig. 42. Massimo Stanzione, Orta di Atella (?) 1585(?)–Naples 1656. *The Visitation*. Chiesa del Gesù Nuovo, Naples.

Quite different was the outcome of experiments begun along the very same lines by other Neapolitan artists in the classicist circle. Pacecco de Rosa, for example, after a moderately naturalist beginning, had already drawn nearer to Massimo Stanzione's style in 1636 with his *Saint Nicholas of Bari* in the Certosa di San Martino. At the beginning of the following decade, he painted a long series of sacred and profane pieces consciously developed from direct models in Stanzionian classicism (from Reni to Domenichino in particular). But for a short time he also incorporated in his painting certain aspects of the classicist movement in Rome. The paintings in this mode are highly refined and outstanding for their rich tonal gradation. In *The Judgment of Paris* (in the Akademie, Vienna) and the *Venus and Mars* in the Capodimonte collection at Montecitorio but also in well-known compositions such as the *Annunciation* of 1644 in San Gregorio Armeno, the *Massacre of the Innocents* at the Philadelphia Museum, the *Madonna and Child* in Santa Marta, and the 1652 *Vision of Saint Thomas Aquinas* in Santa Maria della Sanità, classicist balance surpasses the Stanzionesque style itself in achieving effects of sustained formal purity and schematic chromatic intensity.

A further example would be that of Filippo Vitale, Pacecco de Rosa's former teacher. Vitale's earlier intense involvement with naturalism notwithstanding, he too adopted a deliberately classicist style after 1640 in the *Pietà* in Santa Maria Regina Coeli.

Again in the same circle, Beltrano likewise accepted in the end the growing influence of Stanzione's work in the Naples of the 1640s. Paintings such as *The Last Supper of the Apostles, Saint Martin and the Beggar,* and *The Martyrdom of Saint Alexander*—all painted at the end of the decade and once in the cathedral of Pozzuoli—illustrate the results: images of sustained monumentality and quiet elegance. His subsequent works at the Sanità and Santi Apostoli seem, by comparison, increasingly sluggish and involuted.

Finally, even Francesco Guarino looked to Stanzione's Renian and classicist-oriented works for guidance. However, his ability to keep intact, in all of his paintings dating from the 1640s, material vigor and expressive immediacy, as well as his skill in handling both vibrant colors and light set him apart from the similar abilities. The best evidence is provided by Guarino's altarpiece of 1643, *The Miracle of Saint Benedict,* at Sant'Antonio Abate in Campobasso, followed by works that display an increasingly robust sense of classicism: *The Madonna of the Rosary with Saints and Female Donors* painted for San Domenico in Solofra and the two versions of *The Death of Saint Joseph* at San Sossio di Serino and the Collegiata in Solofra, both derived from a prototype by Stanzione.

The eclectic artist Andrea Vaccaro also worked in styles vacillating between Massimo's approach and the muted, expressive chromatics of Cavallino's late works. (Massimo had already served as a filter for Vaccaro's earlier Renian propensities, followed by his striking awareness of van Dyck exhibited in the 1636 painting of *Saint Mary Magdalene* at the Certosa di Martino.) Vaccaro's *Jonah Preaching to the People at Nineveh* (now in a private collection in London and belonging to a series of paintings on copper by Cavallino [see 83-85])—and the *Abraham and the Angels* in a private collection in Naples provide fine examples of his eclecticism.

Even an artist like Spinelli was affected by the style of Stanzione and certain formal techniques worked out by Pacecco. His *Madonna and Child with Saints Augustine and Charles Borromeo* at San Severo alla Sanità in Naples and his *Saint Nicholas of Bari Freeing the Young Cup-Bearer* in the cathedral at Castellammare di Stabia, both painted after 1640–42, bear witness to the fact. The point is of particular interest since Spinelli had been working for some time in the Neapolitan area independently of both the distinctly naturalist and the moderately classicist movements, following instead his own completely intellectual and neo-Mannerist (albeit anti-naturalist and anti-classicist) concept of reality.

Moreover, not even Aniello Falcone could resist Stanzione's influence, as he demonstrates in the 1641 painting of *The Rest on the Flight into Egypt* in the Duomo in Naples and the frescoes in the Cappella Firrao in San Paolo Maggiore. And yet Falcone had in fact been among the very first to enter into contact with other trends of a classicist persuasion, which were later to find considerable following in the Neapolitan area as an alternative to Domenichino's purism. These trends, which preceded the particular painterly style initiated by the young Nicolas Poussin in Rome at the end of the 1620s from within the neo-Venetian movement while simultaneously forging links with Sacchi on the one hand and Castiglione and Pietro Testa on the other, had been at the root of the deliberately classicist naturalism of some *Battle Scenes,* as well as of the two compositions *The Gladiators* and *The Entrance into the Arena* (all painted by Falcone at the end of the 1630s and all now in the Prado).

Paintings by Poussin, furthermore, had already reached Naples before 1630—the *Adoration of the Golden Calf* cited by Felibién, for example, of which only a fragment remains today in a private collection in London, and other compositions mentioned by Valguernera as being in the collection of Signor Guzman. The Frenchman's work in Rome had thus begun to be studied and appreciated, alongside that of Grechetto, within the framework of the painterly trend of Roman neo-Venetianism.

But it was above all after 1640, in conjunction with the more extensive diffusion of instances of renewed classicism throughout the Neapolitan area, that local painters' interest in Poussin increased. That interest was enhanced by new implications: the Poussinesque manner offered an alternative to the expansion of purist solutions that had been executed, for the most part, in very strict observance of the classicist Romano-Bolognese sources of Massimo Stanzione.

From Andrea de Leone, whose *Adoration of the Golden Calf* in the De Young Museum of San Francisco bears mentioning (though the work is clearly a replica by the Neapolitan of the original, partially destroyed, version by Poussin; however, it still carries the false signature of Poussin), to Niccolò di Simone, and from Bernardo Cavallino to Antonio de Bellis and Domenico Gargiulo, one sees a steady growth during the second half of the fifth decade in figurative techniques that recall the young Poussin at the peak of neo-Venetianism. It is almost as if by preferring the academic anti-naturalist interpretations of a Pacecco de Rosa or a Beltrano, and even in the face of Massimo Stanzione's formal elegance, one could still safeguard the aims of painting. The key was to reconcile these aims with the new demands of moderate classicism expressed by a heightened perception of the culture of the day while retaining the still-valid lessons of painterliness preserved in the sharply defined imagery of the neo-Venetian Sacchi, the young Pietro da Cortona and, above all, Nicolas Poussin.

Poussin, on the other hand, had strongly influenced another Frenchman drawn to Rome from his native Lorraine at the end of the 1620s: Charles Mellin. Mellin's affinities for Poussin and neo-Venetianism are clearly demonstrated in the fresco decoration painted in 1631 for a chapel in San Luigi dei Francesi and most likely also in the now-destroyed frescoes painted between 1636 and 1637 in Montecassino, to judge by the recent discovery, also in Montecassino, of *Abel Making Offerings to the Eternal Father* (dated 1634), and the reassignment to his hand of various paintings once attributed, interestingly enough, to Poussin's neo-Venetian phase. Mellin was definitely in Naples from 1643 to 1647; while there, he created a series of compositions that were somewhat weakened, however, by his contact with the group of painters working in the tradition of Stanzione's classicism, and especially with Pacecco. The two surviving canvases at Donnaregina

Nuova (the *Immaculate Conception* completed in 1646 and the *Annunciation* dated to 1647) constitute, in fact, a clear example of the ultimate decline of purism.

One cannot dismiss the possibility that Poussin also may have spent some time in Naples in 1647. Still, apart from the fact that the Neapolitans continued to maintain contact with the artistic community in Rome throughout the remainder of 1630s, and the 1640s (even though principally interested in the exquisite painterly and neo-Venetian aspects of Poussin's work there), it must not be forgotten that in 1641 Cardinal Ascanio Filomarino had been transferred to Naples from Rome to assume the responsibilities of archbishop. The cardinal is generally viewed as having been the chief supporter of classicism in Naples. However, in the collection of this man—who had been closely associated in Rome with the house of Barberini and the principal artists connected with that great patrician family's history—along with paintings by various artists active in Rome in very different circles, it was precisely Poussin's works of the neo-Venetian phase and Mellin's of the San Luigi dei Francesi period that proved to be amply represented. These paintings by Poussin and Mellin could not have escaped the attention of those Neapolitans involved in developing compromises between the painterly style and classicism, offering a valid alternative to the recent purist trend while at the same time preserving the most personal and fruitful elements of the local tradition that evolved from a naturalist matrix: solely through the use of certain combinations of rich, warm color, unlimited expansion of light, and refined formal elegance could the artists express in a clear and natural way the profound stirrings of the heart more than of the mind, the cares of everyday life, and the joys of the ephemeral.

Such was the synthesis attained by Bernardo Cavallino at the height of his rather brief career at the end of the 1640s and the beginning of the following decade. At the same time, Jusepe di Ribera, recently recovered from a long illness, was reaffirming—with works like *The Mystical Marriage of Saint Catherine* (at the Metropolitan Museum of Art, New York), *Saint Januarius Emerging from the Furnace Unscathed* (in the Tesoro del Duomo, Naples), or, again, *The Apostles' Last Supper* (at San Martino)—the value of robust, luminous painting in the manner of a tradition that went from Titian and Veronese to the mature Velázquez, to be taken up again by Giordano, and continued on through to Goya.

A rapid succession of small and medium-sized paintings by Cavallino—from the biblical scenes in Brunswick [80-81] to the two tondi in Munich [77-78] illustrating

41

episodes from *Jerusalem Delivered* to the *Adoration of the Shepherds* in Cleveland [79], to the series of related compositions representing Biblical and Roman history now scattered among museums in Moscow, Fort Worth, and Malibu [83-85]—gives testimony not only to an incredibly wide range of extreme tonal beauty but also to a skillful compositional buoyancy and measured, formal elegance in which the images are endowed with convincing plasticity, yet are delicate and fragile like polychrome soft-paste porcelain figurines of the eighteenth century.

Bernardo Cavallino was not alone in this difficult attempt to safeguard the canons of the pictorial tradition recently evolved in Naples by reconciling them with contemporary requirements of formal grace and an equilibrium in composition and sentiment. Right alongside him (in fact, progressing at about the same rate) in this intelligent, lucid, and sensitive but still-cautious revival of the more emotional aspects of Poussin in his neo-Venetian phase and of other French and Roman artists working in the 1630s in an exquisitely painterly fashion was Antonio de Bellis. De Bellis, it will be remembered, had begun his career at the end of the 1630s precisely in the same way as the very young Cavallino: in terms of a renewed naturalist commitment. A group of canvases based on the Bible— *Samson and Delilah* (in a private collection in Naples), *The Sacrifice of Noah* (in Houston; Fig. 43), *Moses Striking the Rock* (in the Museum of Fine Arts, Budapest), *The Finding of Moses* (in The National Gallery, London; Fig. 38), and two tondi illustrating *The Drunkenness of Noah* and *Lot and His Daughters* (in two private collections in Milan)— all formerly assigned to Cavallino, and four paintings of *Saint Joachim, Saint Anne, The Immaculate Conception*, and *The Assumption* in one of the lateral chapels of San Carlo alle Mortelle, consistently show signs of earlier naturalist preferences. But they also stand as the clearest testimony of an affinity that links de Bellis to the exquisite and diaphanous Cavallino of the latter's final Poussinesque and proto-eighteenth-century compositions.

Fig. 43. Antonio de Bellis, active in Naples 1630s–50s.
The Sacrifice of Noah. Canvas, 101.6 x 128.6 cm. The Museum of Fine Arts, Houston (Samuel H. Kress Collection).

Color Plate XVII. *The Adoration of the Shepherds* [79].

Color Plates XVIII and XIX. *The Meeting of David and Abigail* [80]. Detail opposite.

Color Plate XX. *The Finding of Moses* [81].

Color Plate XXI. *Mucius Scaevola before King Porsenna* [84].

Color Plates XXII and XXIII. *Judith with the Head of Holofernes* [82]. Detail opposite.

Color Plate XXIV. *The Shade of Samuel Invoked by Saul* [85].

A Capital and Its Kingdom

GIUSEPPE GALASSO

The Naples that was the capital of the Kingdom of the Two Sicilies was a typical example of the propulsive events connected with the development of a modern state power in all fields of social life. In the seventeenth century its political-administrative function was at its peak. The monarchy under the Spanish Hapsburgs concentrated offices and tribunals in the capital. The growth of the capital was both a symbol and an instrument of the royal power: *a symbol* because it gave physically the idea of the king's superiority above any other power, in particular above the feudal one, present within the state; *an instrument* because with the offices and the tribunals as well as with its military forces, the monarchy organized in the capital its strategic and material base to exercise its power, at the time stronger than that of all other authorities within the Kingdom.

To this end the monarchy aimed at securing privileges for the capital, in some ways, exceptional ones. In the particular case of Naples they granted, on one hand, a partial but consistent fiscal immunity, exempting the people from paying the state taxes and obliging them to pay only the city ones; on the other hand, they ensured to the city a quite constant food supply, in particular, wheat supplies even during periods of scarcity. The price of bread was set politically, below the market price.

The concentration of the monarchy's power in the capital induced the feudal aristocracy to move into the city. The barons left their provinces and their castles. They had to show tangibly their loyalty to the king by abandoning all aspects of persistence of "particolarismo." New demands on culture and on social habits were taking place in the capital; the aristocracy could no longer confine itself within the traditional life of its castles.

The new *politesse* could be attained only in the shadow of the king's viceregal court in Naples, which became more and more dominant and despotic, even over fashions and customs. But, above all, the capital was the seat of the ruling power; it was necessary to be near the government itself to obtain its offices and benefits (which now more than ever before could be granted) and also to influence its trends and activities. These elements made the capital rich and feverish. It was the place where the wealth of the Kingdom was concentrated through royal grants and through revenues from the feudal aristocracy and other classes of the provinces. Thus, the capital became the center of business affairs—of contracting, public works, concession of services, of public and private loans. The feudal aristocracy as well as the professional and merchant classes chose the capital as their headquarters. The king and both aristocrats and the rich demanded sumptuous living quarters, no less than even the clergy. The city underwent an almost complete renovation; handicraft and services expanded in proportion. The most important manufacturers in Naples, particularly those engaged in the luxury goods of silk, gold, and silver received the greatest impetus. The silk group, the grain merchants, and the financiers (the latter two groups being nearly identical) often became very powerful pressure groups. Cardinal de Grenelle's comment that the people in Naples, or, in this case, the manufacturing and trading Third State, were richer than the nobility is not unfounded.

These circumstances, and the attendant growth of such a rich market, drew into the city people from everywhere — above all, foreigners. One of the most informed men of the Naples of those times, Giulio Cesare Capaccio, recognized the importance of their presence. "It's not the destiny, nor the stars," he writes, "which make the greatness of the cities; rather, the trade and the people's concourse, as one can see looking at Antwerp, Amsterdam, Lisbon,

Seville, or Paris." Thus, Naples was above all the place where the flood of immigration from the provinces ended. The city offered—with its privileges, its development, its revenues, and its concentration of power—unlimited possibilities for work, for business, for wealth, and for subsistence even at the lowest levels of society. In addition, it allowed its inhabitants escape from the excessive taxation of the crown and from feudal and patriarchal arrogance, not to mention irregular food supplies—all problems that troubled the provinces. The new advantages, however, were offset by a myriad of problems that arose: poor people accepting the most precarious and unlikely jobs; and a lack of housing that forced people to sleep in the open, under porticoes, on the steps of churches and mansions, in caves and emergency shelters, by the sides of the streets, in the rooms where they worked, or under the tables used for selling merchandise. Out of such circumstances, one can easily comprehend the emergence of an urban mob, dressed in rags and going about barefoot. The expressions describing this mob—*lazzaroni, mascalzoni*—symbolized their miserable conditions, which stood as a colorful background to the magnificence of the court and the luxurious life of aristocrats and the wealthy. But if life in Naples was wretched, these mobs knew that they would have it worse in the provinces.

Capaccio commented: "Naples became so large due to the high concentration of population living in it." As a matter of fact, it became, from the second half of the sixteenth century, the second largest city after Paris: it stayed such until the beginning of the eighteenth century. The rate of its growth was indeed impressive: 100,000 people at the beginning of the sixteenth century to about 250,000 at the end of the same century; and more than 350,000, very likely, before the devastating plague of 1656. The very large population and the economic growth that characterized sixteenth-century Europe certainly hastened such expansion. The more the provinces grew in population, the more the people moved into the capital. The more the capital expanded, the more it attracted other human waves into it.

At the beginning, during the 1560s, the crown attempted (uselessly) to control the overcrowding of the city. Its efforts were concentrated in limiting the construction of new buildings. But such restrictions were easily avoided by Neapolitan contractors. It seems evident that the governmental restrictions not only contradicted the peoples' prospects of a more certain existence with fewer vexations than they faced by living in the provinces, but also contradicted the government's own policy that gave fiscal and food privileges to the people living in the capital, even as it tried to limit their moving in. In 1615 it was ascertained that the prohibitions against intensified building construction had been widely violated, and that there had been a considerable increase in construction in the small villages surrounding the city; according to some writers of the seventeenth century, these "villages" had become large towns. Opportunities in the building trade were so attractive that some merchants from Genoa, around 1630, offered to raise new walls in order to enlarge the city limits; these would include all of a series of areas already urbanized and very close to the old walls. In exchange, the merchants asked that they be granted permission to build on any available space within the new walls and that they became the owners of such spaces. For various reasons, nothing came of it; therefore, Naples in the middle of the seventeenth century had reached a state of great congestion.

Some of the characteristics of a congested urban center are important to note. The need for space indicated taller buildings. In Naples, reports Capaccio in the 1630s, the houses are five or six floors tall, twice as high as those in Paris. It is possible to build so high, adds the same author, because the building material (the Neapolitan "tufa" stone) is quite light and bonds well with the local mortar. The same exigency to exploit to the maximum extent the availability of space within the city left unchanged the ancient plan of the Greek and Roman town, which was imposed on new housing projects. Naples, during this period, looked like a kind of city of skyscrapers that rose up from the long and very narrow alleys. The open spaces and the wide perspectives of the Renaissance urban architecture did not "take" here at all. Its palaces are imposing, but they are not as monumental and beautiful as those of Rome, Florence, or Venice. And sanitary conditions were even worse than the bad conditions common to all cities of pre-industrial and proto-industrial Europe.

All felt a latent but constant and deep sensation of social tension. The impression of such a huge human presence was matched by an intense social degradation. People said, when they referred to the beauty of places admired by all, that Naples was "a paradise inhabited by devils." As a matter of fact, one could experience there exceptional incidents of human rejection and violence. People feared the "serra-serra" (shut down-shut down—i.e., the extemporaneous urban jacquerie whose sole purpose is pillage), an event when everyone hastened to shut down the doors of shops and houses. Given such circumstances, Naples is indeed the place to be chosen for whoever wishes to study one of the most typical examples of a great *lumpen-proletariat* of the pre-industrial era.

An important historical fact is that despite its large human aggregation, Naples did not succeed in crossing the threshold of a decisive economic transformation. Its function as a consumers' market prevailed over that of a great production center. Although it was the demographic, administrative, political, and civil metropolis of the Kingdom, it did not retain its leadership in southern Mediterranean economic affairs, as it had over the previous four to five centuries. From this point of view, the Neapolitan megalopolis of the seventeenth century was no more successful than the much smaller Naples of the Angevins and Aragonese of roughly three centuries earlier. The situation lasted a long time, however, and by the end of the eighteenth century Galanti observed that out of the twenty international businesses present in Naples, nineteen were run by foreigners and only one by a Neapolitan.

By contrast, it should be noted that during the growth of metropolitan Naples in the sixteenth century, its bureaucratic and professional characteristics were far more accentuated, marked by a "tertiary" bond to public services and to the comforts of the aristocrats and the bourgeoisie. At that time Naples was the economic heart of the Kingdom: its large, international harbor promoted the city's growth as a mercantile and financial center. Exports of the Kingdom could be loaded at any of the many minor ports, but all imports had to be unloaded in Naples and from there transported to the provinces (usually by sea since the road network, centered mostly in the capital, was partial, discontinuous, and long). As the center of mercantile speculation, and with a monopoly over the Kingdom's financial resources (at the beginning of the sixteenth century there had still been some provincial banks—by the end of the century, there were none), Naples centralized the political and administrative power within its boundaries but it did not achieve a corresponding economic centralization.

In fact, the Kingdom was composed, from an economic point of view, of an aggregate of diverse areas that were only partially unified. The transfer of sheep from Abbruzzi and Molise constituted a large, interregional system with the plains of Capitanata. The Adriatic and Ionian coasts of Puglie were important export centers for products such as wheat, oil, and wine. The Calabrian provinces were throughout two centuries the heart of the southern silk culture before diminishing to a purely survival level. The same economic isolation, with the exception of a few areas, affected Basilicata and the inner provinces of Campania. Only the maritime areas closer to Naples formed a relatively strong organic relationship with the capital.

Within a Kingdom so little consolidated, Naples' mercantile leadership and financial monopoly were only fragile connective tissues. The real economic power, more organic and specific, rested on the city's position both as the capital of the Kingdom and as the center of money movements administered by the crown itself. The difference in the rate of growth between the metropolis and the many provincial centers is, therefore, not surprising. For example, in 1861, Bari, the second largest city in the Kingdom, had a population of only 34,000 people compared to the 450,000 inhabitants of Naples. The major towns and cities of the Kingdom patterned themselves after Naples, but as many "small Naples," they remained disparate entities rather than becoming integrated urban systems—particularly in the South.

Naples owed to all these developments, which were already clear and determined by the middle of the seventeenth century, the particular intensity and physiognomy with which it lived, in comparison with other European cities, its role of a modern capital. The rebellion led by Masaniello in 1647–48 echoed the situation: it grew out of the internal tensions of the city as well as those that were peculiar to the provinces. These tensions were linked by a dominant—although not exclusive—motive: the crown's fiscal policy. But the rebellion did not attain anything, except to reinforce the capital's lack of urban directives for the rest of the Kingdom; in fact, the rebels from Naples could not even establish effective relations with the rebels from the provinces. The revolts that sprang up seemed not to grow out of a strong desire for a better future, but were merely an expression of the classes; as such, they lacked a political-social perspective within the context of the country and its system. If indeed the rebellion of 1647–48 marked a memorable date for the country, it marked a more relevant one for the capital.

In the year 1656 Naples experienced a pestilence that killed sixty percent of its population. But once again a large immigration and the heavy post-epidemic demographic growth quickly repopulated the city. At the beginning of the eighteenth century Naples registered a population of twenty-five percent less than in 1656. By that time other European cities, starting from London, had left it far behind. Its economic and social recovery after the plague was very slow, more than confirming the limits imposed on its growth and its relative modernization, for which the city had been a principal initiator up to the first half of the seventeenth century.

In the meantime, the major trade routes had totally moved from the Mediterranean to the Atlantic Ocean. The withdrawal from the Italo-Spanish area in favor of the

English-French-Rhine ones was by now completely clear; it had developed, in all of its effects, into the so-called general crisis of the seventeenth century. Southern Italy, which in the sixteenth century still represented an important area within the productive and mercantile geography of the Euro-Mediterranean economy, was forced to concede its position because of the shift in trade routes and the emergence of the new international economy, which was anticipating the industrial revolution. Naples suffered similar consequences and found itself facing the new era with many of the same basic problems shared only by a few other Italian and European cities.

By now, even the Neapolitan cultural elite became aware of the city's declining position. The events taking place in the "great" capital, as reported in concurrent writings in the sixteenth and seventeenth centuries, were attributed to the undisputed material growth of the city, and to the fact that Naples seemed to be moving toward the same "trends" of the major European cities. It passed unnoticed at the time that the growth of Naples exceeded the effective capacity of the city's real resources and energies. It further went unnoticed how much that growth had been due both to the privileges the captial granted as compared to the provinces, and to the sacrifice of provincial undertakings that were less pressed by the demands of the monarchy and by the capital itself as embodying the crown's powers. This changed in the eighteenth century. The sense of security, grandeur, future, and alignment with the most advanced currents of European history was now lost, never to be restored after the middle of the seventeenth century, except for Naples' pledge to rise from its state of historical inferiority. The Illuministic culture made charges against the capital, defining it as an enormous head on the top of a thin, weak body from which it absorbed, as a parasite, its life blood. At the same time, the backwardness of the South was being discovered, even though it was still considered, in comparison to the most advanced European civilizations and economies, a rich country.

Professionals, tax contractors, financiers, merchants, feudatories, clergy, speculators, and the royal retinue appeared in the eyes of the Neapolitan Illuminists to constitute the vehicle of the parasitic life in Naples. In opposition, they pressed for a return to agriculture, land reforms, promotion of trades and manufacturing relevant to the needs of the country, improved financial support for agriculture and trade, and measures to improve the quality of life in the provinces.

Reformative Illuminism had partial and tardy success; the knot between southern backwardness and the "Nea-politan question" would not be untied until 1860, with the reunification of Italy. Then Naples would have to face the problem that it has been a victim of its own history (a problem that has not been solved even now), and seek to recover an identity more congenial and suitable to its unique possibilities; to transform itself from a privileged capital, one overcrowded and similar to "a giant with feet of clay," into a modern regional town. This difficult process of transformation, which gave rise to important industrial and modern economic phenomena (reported both properly and improperly as a period of decadence after 1860), gave impetus to the southern provinces and its towns and was therefore viewed as proof of the validity of the Illuministic criticisms. As one example, Bari increased it population, between 1860 and 1980, from 34,000 to 450,000, while the population of Naples rose from 450,000 to 1,200,000. The southern regions, paralleling these developments, found different ways and modes of growth and affirmation; they initiated relations with other Italian cities that were far better focused than the traditional ones with Naples. Today, therefore, only scattered fragments remain of the historic role of Naples both in the South and over the South.

Nonetheless, to strike a balance in this way would be neither precise, complete, nor even just. The negative side of relations between Naples and the rest of the Kingdom, corresponded, as a matter of fact, to the positive side that is identified with the services rendered by Naples to the entire Kingdom. Certainly Naples, as an instrument of the crown, had triumphed over feudalism and thereby enabled the South to become a notable example of a modern state. And the capital in other instances effected modernization in the country, although limits were, of course, necessary. Furthermore, Naples paid the price, as a social and cultural urban center, for exercising its role of capital and for supporting its growth, which in turn derived from that role. But above all, the most positive aspect of Naples was its intellectual and moral role in the Kingdom: it was not a dominating city like Venice, Genoa, or Florence. The flow of aristocrats and the people from the provinces made the capital a true synthesis, as well as the entire southern region (at least from an ethnic and social standpoint). The special-interest and power groups that at times controlled the life and the activities of the city were a projection of the whole country.

The city continued to remain a municipality without a municipal spirit, and largely identified itself as a state and national structure; it was extremely proud of its titles and of its functions, and cultivated and even amplified its privileges. This thread tied together through the centuries the groups that succeeded in wielding power, and through those groups Naples realized itself as a great capital. For centuries it was the seat of the only southern university, in which many generations of southerners grew up. With Humanism, the baroque, and Illuminism it guided the Kingdom in its contacts with the modern culture, breaking the provincial limitations and making possible an important contribution to the European culture and spirit. It offered the solid base that gave the South its connotation of an historical, anthropological, and cultural unity. By this time the autonomous political unity of the South that motivated the supremacy of Naples had ended, but the unitary connotation of the South lived on at certain other levels. Such an image applies to Naples as well, and reflects the sadness inherent in the transitoriness of life and history: *fecisti patriam diversis gentibus unam*.

The Catalogue

Early Works
Numbers 1 through 29

Mature Works
Numbers 30 through 66

Late Works
Numbers 67 through 85

The attempt to establish a relative chronology for Bernardo Cavallino's paintings has been a major justification for this exhibition. The Museums have, therefore, departed from normal practice in making this a catalogue raisonné of all the paintings presently accepted as autograph works by Cavallino. As a result, those works that have been generously lent to the exhibitions are assured of being seen in a broader context.

1

1

The Meeting of Anna and Joachim at the Golden Gate of Jerusalem

Canvas, 229 x 178.5 cm.
Szépmüvészeti Múzeum, Budapest

In catalogue only

The painting combines two episodes from the life of Anna and Joachim, parents of the Virgin Mary—in the foreground, their encounter and embrace at the Golden Gate of Jerusalem, and in the background, in small scale, the angel's announcement to Joachim of Mary's birth. The subject is from the thirteenth-century Golden Legend of Jacobus de Voragine, which recounts how Joachim, scorned for his childlessness, went to live among the shepherds. An angel appeared to him announcing that his wife, Anna, would bear a daughter and that, as a sign, he was to go to the Golden Gate of Jerusalem where Anna would meet him.[1] In medieval and Renaissance art the scene of Joachim's and Anna's tender embrace came to symbolize both the birth of Mary and her Immaculate Conception. After the Council of Trent, however, scenes of the Meeting were gradually replaced by the image of Mary alone—as the Virgin of the Immaculate Conception—which Cavallino painted several times [26, 51; see also Inventory]. Those Seicento artists, including Cavallino, who represented the Meeting, continued to employ the older pictorial device of the continuous narrative that had been kept alive by engravers such as Adriaen Collaert. Collaert's engraving after Stradanus, based on an engraved silver altar (Museo degli Argenti, Florence), illustrates this (Fig. 1a).

Because of the close compositional ties between representations of the Meeting of Anna and Joachim and The Visitation of Mary and Elizabeth—both picturing two figures tenderly greeting each other—artists often used original elements from each in the depiction of both subjects, which resulted in a "family resemblance" between paintings of the two subjects—particularly if artists shared an artistic milieu. For example, Guarino's *Visitation* in Berlin-Dahlem bears a certain resemblance to Cavallino's Budapest painting (or vice versa), while both compositions resemble a much earlier *Visitation* by Mariotto Albertinelli (1503; in the Uffizi, Florence), a painting which either artist could have known through an engraving. Another example of particular interest in connection with Cavallino's *Meeting at the Golden Gate* is a late-eighteenth-century engraving illustrating the Visitation in a book of the *Ufficio della SS Vergine de' Sette Dolori* (Fig. 1b).[2] The image seems to recall a lost painting by a member of Cavallino's circle that is close

Fig. 1a. Adriaen Collaert, Antwerp ca. 1560–1618. After Johann Stradanus (1523–1605). *The Meeting of Anna and Joachim at the Golden Gate of Jerusalem*. Engraving, 18.6 x 13.3 cm. Staatliche Graphische Sammlung, Munich.

Fig. 1b. Anonymous artist. *The Visitation*. Engraving. (After S. Bonaventura, *Ufficio della S. S. Vergine de'Sette Dolori* (Naples, 1816 edition).

to the Budapest painting in the disposition of the two main figures and in the artist's handling of drapery. Other points of comparison are the two gesticulating males—probably Joseph and Zacharias—who are very close to those in Cavallino's *Saint Bartholomew* [3], *Mattathias* [59], and *Esther before Ahasuerus* [62], and Mary's graceful gait with the tender joining of hands between Mary and Elizabeth. It is this rhythmical grace, which the engraver has captured so well, that is lacking in the two rather statuesque central figures of the Budapest painting and that no doubt contributed to the problem of its attribution.

The *fortuna critica* of this picture reflects the complex association of Spanish and Neapolitan elements in Cavallino's formation, just as visually the work itself shows connections to both Jusepe de Ribera and Massimo Stanzione. Its history of attributions has been overwhelmingly to Spanish artists, for example, to Francisco Ribalta (Esterházy cat. 1835), Francisco Pacheco (Budapest 1904, 1906; Cook 1907-8), Alonso Cano (Mayer 1908), and Pablo Legote (Mayer 1910, 1911; Budapest 1913, 1916; Mayer [1913] 1922; Pevsner and Grautoff 1928; Ortolani in Naples 1938; Gaya Nuño 1958). However, as early as 1914 Longhi suggested Stanzione as the artist. Pigler (1931), although agreeing with Longhi's attribution to Stanzione, suggested that the two side figures were painted by Cavallino. Finally, Causa in 1966 attributed the entire foreground group to Cavallino and suggested that the background was the work of Scipione Compagno, an approximate contemporary of Cavallino who specialized in landscapes with small figures and who was described by de Dominici as a fellow pupil with Salvator Rosa in the school of Aniello Falcone.[3] Causa pointed to a similar landscape background in an *Adoration of the Shepherds* in the National Gallery, London (currently ascribed to Bartolomé Murillo).[4]

Spinosa (letter of 28 May 1982) agreed with Causa's attribution to Cavallino but remarked on the stylistic closeness to both Stanzione and the Master of the Annunciation to the Shepherds. A comparison of Cavallino's two main figures with Stanzione's Elizabeth and Zacharias in the *St. John the Baptist Taking Leave of His Parents*, in the Prado, Madrid (Fig. 8), supports Spinosa's observation that Cavallino was directly influenced by Stanzione. In this writer's opinion, Cavallino may have painted the foreground

Fig. 1c. Copy after Cavallino. *The Meeting of Anna and Joachim at the Golden Gate of Jerusalem*. Canvas, 89 x 58.4 cm. Duke of Wellington Collection, London.

Fig. 1d. Attributed to Bartolomé Esteban Murillo, Seville 1617−1682. *The Meeting of Anna and Joachim at the Golden Gate of Jerusalem*. Canvas, 82.5 x 62.5 cm. State Hermitage Museum, Leningrad.

composition as a young painter when still under the tutelage of Stanzione, possibly copying a model provided by Stanzione. Cavallino may then have been allowed to add the two side figures—one, his own invention, and the other a tribute to Ribera. The smiling boy on the right is obviously borrowed from Ribera's young satyr in the *Drunken Silenus*, and a similar young boy also appears in Ribera's etching of the *Martyrdom of Saint Bartholomew* as well as in the *Preparation for the Crucifixion* (Palazzo Pitti, Florence). The latter example is especially interesting because Cavallino himself may have represented the subject in a work that is now lost (Inv. no. 138). Judging from the description of a painting attributed to Cavallino in an early inventory of the Spanish Royal collection,[5] the work was undoubtedly inspired by Ribera's painting of that subject, and it is tempting to speculate whether it might also have included a laughing boy. There exist at least four related versions of Ribera's *Preparation for the Crucifixion*.[6] One additional copy, apparently by a competent painter, was mentioned and illustrated under the name of "Carracci" in a list of paintings of the "Puerto Seguro, Malaga," preserved in the library of the Museo del Prado.

The derivative quality of the Budapest painting places it at the beginning of Cavallino's career. Its large scale, relative to most of the artist's oeuvre, suggests that it may have been painted for a church originally, reminding us of de Dominici's comment that among Cavallino's early works as Stanzione's pupil were church commissions.[7] Reasons for supporting the attribution of this work to Cavallino may be found in the similarity of the broad, sculpturesque drapery of Joachim to that of Joseph in the early *Flight into Egypt* in Hartford [8]; in the likeness of the delicate face of Anna's attendant to other faces by Cavallino, such as that of the Virgin in the Brunswick *Adoration* [2]; and in the similarity of the landscape—assuming that the landscape was painted by Cavallino—to early pictures by him in Hartford and at Capodimonte [8, 10, 13]. These early landscape backgrounds or portions of landscapes are close to the work of Domenico Gargiulo in the rosy-blond, opaque tonality and in the tiny figures that usually inhabit them. Causa's opinion that the background in the Budapest painting is by Scipione Compagno would suggest that there may have been a connection between the early work of Cavallino and the circle of Falcone.

Two copies, or variants, of the Budapest painting are extant. The lesser known, which was discovered recently through a photograph (Fig. 1c) in the "Weitzner file" preserved in the J. Paul Getty Museum Library, was listed in the collection of the Duke of Wellington, Apsley House, London, under the title "Joseph Visiting Elizabeth." It measures 89 x 58.5 cm. The painting duplicates the entire foreground figure group but it does not include the angel's announcement to Joachim in the background. Without the figures, the landscape in the Weitzner version resembles that in the *Flight into Egypt* in Hartford [8]. The second variant, in the Hermitage, Leningrad, measuring 82.5 x 62.5 cm, lacks the young woman on the left (Fig. 1d). Like the work it copies, it has been assigned to various Spanish painters: first to Juan Battista del Mazo, then to Francisco de Ribalta, and finally to Murillo, by E. de Liphart (1910). ATL

1. *The Golden Legend* 1969, pp. 522-23.
2. This engraving was brought to my attention by Giuseppe De Vito.
3. De Dominici 1742–43, 3:252-53; see also Nappi in London 1982, pp. 269-70.
4. The London picture has at varying times since the eighteenth century borne attributions to Velázquez, Francisco de Zurbarán, Francisco Pacheco, Pablo Legote, Antonio del Castillo, Pedro Orrente, the school of Seville, Francesco Fracanzano, and Giovanni Dò (London 1952, p. 61, and 1970, p. 75).
5. Pérez Sánchez 1965, p. 384. See Inv. no. 138.
6. Pérez Sánchez and Spinosa 1978, p. 98, no. 37, a-c.
7. De Dominci 1742–43, 3:36.

Collections
Edmund Burke, London (sale, 1821, Paris); Esterházy.

Exhibitions
None.

Literature
Esterházy cat. 1835. De Térey in Budapest 1904, no. 766; in Budapest 1906, p. 65, no. 301. Cook 1907-8, p. 300, pl. 2. Mayer 1908, pp. 519-20, fig. 3. De Liphart 1910, p. 45. Mayer 1910, p. 398; 1911, pp. 136-37, pl. xxviii, fig. 33; [1913], p. 301. De Térey in Budapest 1913, pp. 116, 349, no. 301. Longhi 1914, p. 319; 1916a, pp. 245, 248 n. 2, 314. De Térey in Budapest 1916, pp. 350-51, no. 301. Mayer 1922, p. 301. Von Loga 1923, p. 212. Mayer 1923, p. 183. Pevsner in Pevsner and Grautoff 1928, p. 235. Pigler 1931, p. 160. Pigler in Budapest 1937, no. 766, repr. p. 98. Ortolani in Naples 1938, p. 45. Ceci in Thieme-Becker 31 (1939):473. MacLaren 1952, pp. 61-62 n. 5 [1970 ed., pp. 75-76 n. 6]. Pigler in Budapest 1954, 1:543, no. 766, and 2: 114, repr. Gaya Nuño 1958, pp. 58, 218. Longhi 1961, 1:173. Pérez Sánchez 1965, p. 477. Pigler in Budapest 1968, 1: 663, no. 766, and 2: fig. 127. Causa 1972, pp. 943, 983 n. 115, fig. 312. Schleier 1975, pp. 30-31, 33 n. 6, fig. 6. Ferrari in *Dizionario biografico* 22 (1979):787. Causa in *Larousse Dictionary* 1981, p. 56. Spinosa in London and Washington 1982–83, p. 135. Paris 1983, p. 188. Turin 1983, p. 158.

2

The Adoration
of the Shepherds

Canvas, 191 x 141 cm.
Herzog Anton Ulrich-Museum, Brunswick

Exhibited in USA only

Presumably one of Cavallino's earliest pictures and thus dating around the mid-1630s or possibly before, this canvas has been in the Museum collection since before 1737, first ascribed to Caravaggio (Brunswick 1776), then listed as "Anonymous" (Brunswick 1867), and later as seventeenth-century Italian, possibly Neapolitan (Brunswick 1969), and seventeenth-century Italian, Neapolitan school (Brunswick 1976).[1] It was first published as Cavallino in 1982.[2] It is painted on the coarsely woven canvas often used by Cavallino in his early works and, like many of them, has suffered some damage, especially in the background figures.

The painting's tonality is dark, with a brilliant red accent in the dress of the Virgin. Its comparatively large-scale, restricted palette, summarily rendered architectural background, surface naturalism, and generally Stanzionesque figure type of the Virgin suggest a logical placement of the work near in time to the early Budapest [1] and Naples [3] pictures. The subject was represented again by Cavallino in one of his finest late paintings, the canvas in the Cleveland Museum [79].

In this early version the artist seems to exploit every opportunity to introduce a variety of rustic, carefully observed surfaces, such as sheepskin, fur, and feathers; in fact, the closeness of Cavallino's early manner to the naturalism of the Master of the Annunciations to the Shepherds is particularly apparent here in the rendering of the shepherd's leather garment, the sheep, the cock, and the wooden and leather saddle (cf. Fig. 10). Spinosa (in London and Washington 1982–83) has also compared the picture to Aniello Falcone's somewhat later *Rest on the Flight into Egypt*, in the sacristy of the Duomo in Naples, dated 1641.   AP

1. Information courtesy of Gert Adriani, Herzog Anton Ulrich-Museum, and Ann T. Lurie.
    2. It was first identified as an early Cavallino by the present writer in the late 1960s and was independently recognized and published as such by Giuseppe De Vito in 1982.

Collections
Dukes of Brunswick, in the ducal gallery at Salzdahlum, near Brunswick, before 1737.

Exhibitions
London and Washington 1982–83, cat. no. 24, repr.; Paris 1983, cat. no. 11, repr.

Literature
Brunswick 1776, p. 47; 1867, no. 303; 1868, no. 322; 1969, p. 81, no. 1028; 1976, p. 34, no. 1028. De Vito 1982, pp. 37-39, fig. 22. Turin 1983, pp. 158, 160.

2

3

3

The Martyrdom of Saint Bartholomew

Canvas, 205 x 158 cm.
Museo di Capodimonte, Naples

Ascribed to the school of Andrea Vaccaro in the Quintavalle Capodimonte inventory of about 1930,[1] this work is apparently the same picture attributed to Cavallino from the 1870s (Dalbono 1871, 1876; Naples 1877) but occasionally mistitled as the *Martyrdom of Saint Andrew*. It was listed in de Rinaldis's first monograph on Cavallino (1909); the attribution was confirmed by Ferdinando Bologna in 1953 (Causa 1972).

The work is very dark in tonality, with accents of red in the drapery at front left, white in the saint's loincloth and executioner's sleeves, and bright blue and beige in the sky. Recently restored, it has suffered considerably in the past, with an especially large loss between the third and fourth heads from left and to the more thinly painted row of background figures.

This is apparently the first of a series of paintings produced throughout Cavallino's career that each contain, ostensibly, a self-portrait. The stylish, handsome, attendant soldier in the large hat at left whose features are so specifically recorded as to seem portraitlike appears in such a number of works, visibly growing older, that it does not seem unreasonable to propose that these are Cavallino's own features [see also 11, 20, 40, 41, 53, 59, 84]. In virtually every appearance of the self-portrait, Cavallino appears as a so-called conduit figure making eye contact with the spectator and presenting, as it were, the action of the event on stage.[2] He almost always appears in the elegant pose seen here, so often found in Mannerist prints,[3] body in profile and face turned to the viewer, one elbow akimbo with his hand behind his back. The exact pose is to be found in the latest of the presumed self-portraits, in the *Mucius Scaevola before King Porsenna* at Fort Worth [84].

The picture, which seems close in date to the Brunswick *Adoration* [2], is somewhat similar in the types of figures to Ribera's *Martyrdom of Saint Andrew* of 1628 in Budapest, although the composition is arranged rather differently (Fig. 9).[4] One might also compare Ribera's *Saint Bartholomew* of 1634 (sale: Sotheby's, London, 6 July 1983, lot 39) to Cavallino's saint. The play of opaque impasto against luminous dark ground on Saint Bartholomew's torso and legs and the arms of the attendant figure who ties his feet, as well as the observation of materials in the white loincloth and shirtsleeves of the two figures, seems to reflect as well Ribera's treatment of surfaces, in the manner in which the older artist develops through a particular and characteristic brushwork an impasto that gives texture and definition to the forms. Whereas Cavallino represents the actual moment of the saint's martyrdom, in which the executioner begins to strip the skin from his arm, he does not dwell on the agonizing aspect of the situation in the way that Ribera does in his *Martyrdom of Saint Bartholomew* in the Palazzo Pitti or his *Apollo Flaying Marsyas* in the Museo Nazionale di San Martino and in the Musées royaux des Beaux-Arts, Brussels.[5] The bespectacled, bearded, priestlike figure fourth from left closely resembles a face repeated by Aniello Falcone in two paintings now in the Prado, a *Christ Driving the Merchants from the Temple* and a *Concert*, the latter of which bore an old attribution to Cavallino.[6]

Saint Bartholomew's story is found in *The Golden Legend* of Jacobus de Voragine.[7] One of the twelve apostles, Bartholomew overthrew idols in the temples of India and converted one of the rulers of the region. In Cavallino's picture the feet and eagle of a pagan idol appear on the plinth at upper right; the idolatrous priests are presumably the third and fourth figures from left. Bartholomew was flayed alive, and his bones are supposed to have been transported in the ninth century to Benevento, an ancient small city in Campania where Naples's patron saint, Saint Januarius, was bishop in the third century.   AP

1. Information courtesy of Pierluigi Leone de Castris, Museo di Capodimonte.
2. In the manner of the Quattrocento *festaiuolo* tradition described by Michael Baxandall in *Painting and Experience in Fifteenth-Century Italy: A Primer in the Social History of Pictorial Style* (London, Oxford, & New York: Oxford University Press, 1972), pp. 71-74.
3. See, for example, Hendrik Goltzius's *Great Standard Bearer* and *Standard Bearer* (Bartsch 39.125 and 70.218), repr. in *Illustrated Bartsch* 3:123, 190.
4. Pérez Sánchez and Spinosa 1978 , pp. 96-97, no. 32, repr. p. 97 and pl. IX.
5. Pérez Sánchez and Spinosa 1978, pp. 97, 109, nos. 34, 103-4, repr. pp. 97, 109, and pls. XI, XXIX, XXXI.
6. Pérez Sánchez 1965, pp. 289-90, pl. 134.
7. *Golden Legend* 1969, pp. 479-85.

Collections

In the Museum's collection by 1870; previous location unknown.

Exhibitions

Naples 1953–54, cat. no. 17, fig. 24.

Literature

Dalbono 1871, p. 109; 1876, pp. 470-71. Naples 1877, p. 133. De Rinaldis 1909, p. 19, cat. no. 6; 1911, p. 416. Hermanin in Thieme-Becker 6 (1912):225. Corna 1930, 1:227. Causa 1957, p. 42. Molajoli in Naples 1957, p. 73; in Naples 1958, p. 56; in Naples 1960, p. 111; in Naples 1964, p. 54. Percy 1965, p. 69, no. 103. Causa 1972, pp. 943, 984 n. 115. Ferrari in *Dizionario biografico* 22(1979):787. Causa in *Larousse Dictionary* 1981, p. 56; in Naples 1982 , p. 147, repr. p. 100. De Vito 1982, p. 38. London and Washington 1982-83, pp. 135, 137, 147. Paris 1983, pp. 188, 190. Turin 1983, pp. 158, 160, 168.

4

The Communion
of the Apostles

Canvas, 153 x 115 cm.
Private collection, Milan

Exhibited in the great seventeenth- and eighteenth- century Italian painting exhibition at the Palazzo Pitti in 1922, at which time the attribution to Cavallino was doubted (Nugent 1925–30), this interesting picture dropped out of sight for a number of years and is still not universally accepted today. Spinosa rejects it (in conversation,1984), whereas in the opinions of Causa (in conversation, 1983) and the present writer it is an early work by Cavallino. Large enough in scale to have been a church commission, it appears to be a key picture in the artist's turning from public commissions such as the Capodimonte *Saint Bartholomew* [3] to smaller cabinet pictures such as the series of scenes from the life of Christ in private collections in Italy and Sicily [5-7].

The dark tonality with accents of red, blue, grayish white, and dull gold is typical of early Cavallino, as is the delicate handling of paint in the more densely impastoed foreground figures as compared to the thinly painted rows of dark heads in back. The dramatic tenebrism of the scene, illuminated partly by candles and partly by mystical sources of light, is more Caravaggesque than others of Cavallino's early works and links the painting to certain youthful pictures by the artist that are especially Caravaggesque in lighting and composition [5-7, 9]. In the shadowy heads in the background we can also see the possible influence of the work of one of the first-generation Neapolitan followers of Caravaggio, Carlo Sellitto (cf. Fig. 11).

The ground is dark and the support is the typical coarsely woven canvas of Cavallino's early years. Christ's head has suffered some damage and possibly some repainting, as has his blue robe at the left edge.

The rather unusual subject, the Communion of the Apostles—all twelve are present, although it is difficult to make out some of the heads in the reproduction—differs from a Last Supper in that here Christ in the guise of a priest offers the mystically illuminated Host to the apostles. The real presence of Christ in the Blessed Sacrament was reaffirmed by the Council of Trent after the Eucharistic controversies of the Reformation and was given special emphasis in adorations of the sacrament, such as the Forty Hours' Devotion, a practice established in Italy before the mid-sixteenth century. It is interesting that Ribera also represented the Institution of the Eucharist as a Communion of the Apostles in a huge and important picture commissioned for the church of the Certosa di San Martino at the beginning of 1638 but still not finished in February 1651 and not displayed *in situ* until 6 October 1651, just under a year before the artist's death.[1] Although Ribera's expansive composition, set in the open air before a loggia, little resembles the less ambitious effort of his young contemporary, the shared subject possibly reinforces a connection between Cavallino and Ribera's work of the mid- to late 1630s [see 1, 3, 30, 31].   AP

1. Pérez Sánchez and Spinosa 1978, pp. 124-25, no. 207, pl. LX-LXI.

Collections
Ettore Zoccoli, Rome.

Exhibitions
Florence 1922, cat. no. 258.

Literature
Nugent 1925–30, 2:571. Longhi 1961, 1:499, and 2:fig. 229.

4

5

5, 6 & 7

Christ
Washing the Feet
of the Apostles

Canvas, 57 x 74.5 cm.
Private collection, Palermo

In catalogue only

The Payment
of the Tribute

Canvas, 54 x 74.5 cm.
Private collection, Palermo

In catalogue only

The Last Supper

Canvas, 56 x 75 cm.
Private collection, Italy

In catalogue only

Published in the 1920s as in a private collection in London, these small pictures recently reappeared in London auctions and have since been separated. They seem to represent an early moment of Cavallino's adoption of an intimate, cabinet-sized type of picture, tenebrist in nature but rendered on a very small scale and with a minutely careful observation of faces and still-life elements that may derive from a close acquaintance with the work of Aniello Falcone (cf. Fig. 12). In these works more of Cavallino's typical facial types emerge, such as the round-faced, open-mouthed youth at the far right of *The Payment of the Tribute*, an inhabitant of others of Cavallino's compositions [42, 53]. The tendency to produce small-scale multi-figure history or religious compositions in series that is seen here continues throughout the artist's career and can be seen in some of his latest works [80, 81, 83-85]. In fact, these three pieces, which show Christ washing the apostles' feet (John 13:5-10), Peter retrieving the temple tax from the mouth of a fish (Matthew 17:24-27), and the Last Supper (Matthew 26:26-28; Mark 14:22-24; Luke 22:19-20), may once have formed part of a larger series of scenes from the life of Christ.

In Causa's opinion these works were not by Cavallino but by another artist working in his manner. They are not in prime condition, the more thinly painted background figures having especially suffered considerable loss of surface.   AP

Collections
Farina, London; principe di Gerace, Naples (all three paintings); sales: Sotheby's, London, 10 December 1980, lot 274 (*The Payment of the Tribute* and *Christ Washing the Feet of the Apostles*), and 18 February 1981, lot 21 (*The Last Supper*).

Exhibitions
None.

Literature
Sestieri 1920, p. 269, figs. 19 (*The Payment of the Tribute*), 20 (*Christ Washing the Feet of the Apostles*), 21 (*The Last Supper*). Musto 1920, p. 180. De Rinaldis 1921, p. 18. Ortolani 1922, p. 194. Percy 1965, p. 65, nos. 82 (*Christ Washing the Feet of the Apostles*), 83 (*The Last Supper*), 84 (*The Payment of the Tribute*).

6

7

8

The Flight into Egypt

Canvas, 102.5 x 126.6 cm.
Wadsworth Atheneum, Hartford,
The Ella Gallup Sumner
and Mary Catlin Sumner Collection

Attributed to "Bassano" when it was sold on the London market in 1931, the picture was identified as by Cavallino at least by 1938. It is dark in tonality, with accents of white and gray in the foremost angel's garments and of dull purple in Joseph's robe and dark yellow in his cloak. The strong contrasts of light and shade, the Stanzionesque types of figures and the straightforward arrangement of the figures in a row suggest an early dating. Indeed, the painting can be described as summarizing most of the problems associated with defining the artist's early manner in that, instead of clearly depending on a single master, it combines characteristics that seem to derive from several artists older than Cavallino. The observation of surfaces with a high degree of naturalism relates the picture to the work of Ribera and the Master of the Annunciations to the Shepherds. The realistically depicted saddle can be compared with that in Cavallino's *Adoration of the Shepherds* in Brunswick [2], a work very close to the Master of the Annunciations, and the less densely and opaquely rendered faces of the two background attendant angels that, in effect, dissolve into the luminous reddish-brown shadows can be related to similar figures by the unnamed master (compare especially his *Birth of the Virgin* in the church of Santa Maria della Pace in Castellamare di Stabia).[1] The figures of Mary and Joseph are Stanzionesque in type, if not in scale: compare that of Joseph to the lefthand figure in Stanzione's *Saint John the Baptist Taking Leave of His Parents* in the Prado (Fig. 8) and that of Mary to Mary in Stanzione's *Annunciation* in the church of Santa Maria Regina Coeli in Naples, documented early in 1640.[2] The leftmost angel shows the elegantly mannered grace combined with an intense and precise naturalism that distinguishes Cavallino's work from that of his contemporaries. The background in the distance at right is quite different in character from the lefthand part of the painting: its rolling hills, distinctive feathery foliage, and romantic small huts are rendered in opaque blue-green, beige, and pink tones rather like the landscapes of Cavallino's contemporary Domenico Gargiulo. It can be compared to the righthand portion of landscape background in the Budapest *Meeting of Joachim and Anna* [1], which Causa has suggested was actually painted by Scipione Compagno.　　　　　　AP

1. Repr. in London and Washington 1982-83, no. 85, p. 83.
2. Gabinetto Fotografico della Soprintendenza alle Gallerie di Napoli, neg. no. 10638; see Causa 1972, p. 937.

Collections
Anonymous sale, London, 8 May 1931, lot 102; Kenneth Clark, London; acquired by the Atheneum in 1942.

Exhibitions
London 1938, cat. no. 312. Northampton 1947, cat. no. 6. Sarasota and Hartford 1958, cat. no. 16a, repr. Bridgeport 1962, cat. no. 1. Detroit 1965, cat. no. 161, repr.

Literature
Fredericksen and Zeri 1972, p. 50.

8

9

9

The Denial of Saint Peter

Canvas, 63 x 103 cm.
Private Collection, Bologna

In catalogue only

This painting was first published by de Rinaldis in 1909 in a private collection near Naples. A copy in the Harrach collection (Inv. no. 30) has occasionally been published as the original; however, the Bolognese picture is surely the autograph version and must date quite early, to the latter half of the 1630s. It shows a palette typical of the early Cavallino, with a dark ground; dramatic chiaroscuro; and strong accents of red, blue, dull orange, and gray. Many of the glazes have been lost, especially on the background figures and the *repoussoir* form at left, leaving them flat, undefined shapes. In the better-preserved central group in the foreground, Cavallino's characteristic delicate handling of paint is easier to discern. The picture also shows Cavallino's rapport with the precise observation of faces, elements of armor, and still life that is found in Aniello Falcone's work (cf. Fig. 12).

This is as close in manner as Cavallino ever comes to the Bamboccianti, or northern low-life genre painters active in Italy and especially in Rome in the 1620s through the 1640s, who have often been mentioned as influences on his work. As Causa pointed out, however, his refined, poetic approach has nothing in common with the anecdotal recording of picturesque low-life subjects in which the Bamboccianti specialized.[1] Instead, the minutely realized and luminously refined observation of this guardroom scene—in which soldiers are gaming at a table and Peter, retiring into the background, is pointed out by a serving maid—is closer in spirit, although certainly not in technique, to Dutch high-life interiors or guardroom pictures of 1620s or 1630s, which one wonders if the artist might have known through engravings or through original works in Neapolitan collections.[2]   AP

1. Causa 1972, p. 941.
2. On these Dutch traditions, see Peter C. Sutton, et al., *Masters of Seventeenth-Century Dutch Genre Painting* (Philadelphia: Philadelphia Museum of Art, 1984), pp. xxxii-xxxviii.

Collections
Medici d'Ottajano, Naples; marchese di Campolattaro, Torre del Greco; Conte Paolo Gaetani d'Aragona, Torre del Greco.

Exhibitions
None.

Literature
De Rinaldis 1909, p. 33, cat. no. 11. Hermanin in Thieme-Becker 6 (1912):225. De Rinaldis 1917, pp. 179, 182, repr.; 1920a, p. 4; 1921, p. 17, pl. X. Sestieri 1921, p. 184. A. Venturi 1921, p. 211 n.1. Musto 1921b, p. 160. Consoli Fiego 1922, p. 108. Ortolani 1922, pp. 191, 198. A. Venturi 1925, p. 74. Benesch 1926, p. 250. Pevsner in Pevsner and Grautoff 1928, p. 185. Ortolani in Naples 1938, p. 65. Percy 1965, p. 58, no. 46.

10

10

The Soldiers
Quarreling over
the Seamless Cloak
of Christ (?)

Canvas, 101 x 129 cm.
Museo di Capodimonte, Naples
(Banco di Napoli)

Exhibited in Naples only

This early, dark, difficult-to-read painting can be dated to the second half of the 1630s on the basis of the palette of dull orange, mauve, dull green, red, gray, and blue played against a warm dark red-brown ground; the tawny blue and beige landscape, like others of Cavallino's early pictures set outdoors [8, 13], is closely related to the work of Domenico Gargiulo. There is an ambiguity in the arrangement of the figural group at left, which can best be explained by suggesting that the canvas is cut at the left edge and has lost part of the furthermost figure; otherwise the various arms, hands, heads, and legs do not fit logically together. The subject has been called "Saint Paul and the Centurion" from the time of the picture's first publication, but it is difficult to identify with Paul's various imprisonments at the hands of centurions as described in The Acts of the Apostles. The scene may depict the subject of the soldiers quarreling over the seamless cloak of Christ when he was crucified (John 19:23-24), with one drawing his knife to cut the garment while others restrain him.   AP

Collections
Private collection; Banco di Napoli, Naples, acquired 1942.

Exhibitions
None.

Literature
Molajoli in Naples 1948, p. 103. Refice 1951, pp. 263, 270 n. 4, fig. 2. Molajoli in Naples 1953, pp. 27, 45, pl. 44. Chiarelli 1954, p. 220. Molajoli in Naples 1961, p. 53; in Naples 1964, p. 59. Percy 1965, p. 55, no. 35. Causa 1972, p. 943.

11

11

The Return
of the Prodigal Son

Canvas, 65 x 128 cm.
Museo di Capodimonte, Naples

As often happens with Cavallino's early works, the sophisticated composition in this painting—with a figure at left seen from the back in dark shadow leaning toward the illuminated central part of the composition, and a rather complicated interplay of attendant figures—is difficult to grasp because of the picture's condition. The lefthand *repoussoir* figure has lost most of its surface color, as have its nearby companions, and appears as a dark unmodulated shape. On the other hand, the delicate use of impasto and strong chiaroscuro contrasts that are hallmarks of Cavallino's early style characterize the group with the father and son.

In its greater complexity of composition, this picture seems somewhat more mature than the earliest tenebrist works, such as the three scenes from the life of Christ in Italian private collections [5-7] or the Capodimonte *Soldiers Quarreling* [10]. The face second from left that is partly obscured by the figure seen from behind appears to be one of the presumed self-portraits [cf. 3].

The parable of the prodigal son is recounted in Luke 15:11-32.   AP

Collections
Principe di Sirignano; Rodolfo Wenner, Naples; acquired by the Museum in 1955.

Exhibitions
None.

Literature
De Rinaldis 1921, p. 16. Santangelo 1955, p. 374, repr. Causa 1957, p. 42. Molajoli in Naples 1957, p. 73; in Naples 1958, p. 56; in Naples 1961, p. 52; in Naples 1964, p. 54, fig. 75. *Kindlers Malerei Lexikon* 1 (1964), unpaginated. Percy 1965, p. 54, no. 30. Moir 1967, 1:175-76, 2:66, fig. 220. Pée 1971, p. 122, fig. 300. Minicuci in *Dizionario Enciclopedico Bolaffi* 3 (1972):207. Lehmann in Kassel 1980, p. 88. Causa 1982, pp. 101, 147, repr.

12

Esther
before Ahasuerus

Canvas, 71 x 97 cm.
Istituto Suor Orsola Benincasa,
Naples

This picture, one of Cavallino's most exquisite early works, was included in de Rinaldis's 1909 catalogue when it was in the Rocco–Pagliara collection in Naples. Executed on the coarsely woven canvas typical of the artist's early pictures, it has undergone restoration for the present exhibition, which has revealed the ravishing quality of the coloring and the handling of paint. Ahasuerus is in a brilliant red robe and yellow tunic; the glazes rendering the fur collar of his robe are remarkably fine. The background figures wear brown, pale orange, dull yellow green, and grayish brown. Esther's dress is a brownish olive green shot with fine blue impasto highlights; a similar coloring can be found in the somewhat later painting of the same subject currently in a Swiss collection [21], and in the Capodimonte *Finding of Moses* [13], which probably can be dated near this picture. Esther's train is silvery gray. Faces and materials are rendered with the finest and most delicate brushwork. The rather tight handling of paint, the distribution of figures in a flat row in front of an architectural background, and the predominantly dark tonality with accents of red, yellow, gold, dull orange, and gray green all indicate a dating early in Cavallino's career, in the second half of the 1630s.

The subject was obviously a favorite one with the artist, as he represented it several times more [21, 61, 62]. Esther, a Jewess and consort of the Persian king Ahasuerus, used her influence at court to save her fellow countrymen from destruction at the hands of their enemy Haman. Like David playing before Saul, the subject of Esther, dressed in royal apparel and bowing a supplicant before Ahasuerus to receive the touch of his golden scepter (Esther 5:2), offered Cavallino a chance to indulge his love of depicting elegant and richly garbed figures in a courtly setting. The drama and emotionalism of Cavallino's depiction suggests that his source was the additions to the Book of Esther in the Apocrypha:

> And it came to pass on the third day, when she had ceased to pray, that she took off the clothes in which she had worshiped, and dressed herself in splendor. When she was magnificently clad, she invoked the aid of the all-seeing God and Savior, and took with her her two maids; on one she leaned languishingly, while the other followed her, carrying her train. She was radiant with her perfect beauty, and her face

> was happy as it was lovely, but her heart was in an agony of fear. When she had gone through all the doors, she stood before the king. He was seated on his royal throne, clad in all his magnificence, and covered with gold and precious stones; he was an awe-inspiring sight. And he raised his face, burning with splendor, and looked at her with the fiercest anger; and the queen fell down and turned pale and fainted, and she collapsed upon the head of the maid who went before her.

> Then God changed the king's spirit to mildness, and in great anxiety he sprang from his throne and caught her in his arms, until she came to herself, and he reassured her with soothing words, and said to her, "What is it, Esther? I am your brother. Courage, you shall not die, for our command is only for the people; come near." Then he lifted the gold scepter and laid it upon her neck, and he embraced her and said, "Tell me!"[1]

AP

1. *The Apocrypha* 1959, pp. 171-72.

Collections
Pagliara, Naples.

Exhibitions
None.

Literature
De Rinaldis 1909, p. 30, cat. no. 10. Hermanin in Thieme-Becker 6 (1912):225. De Rinaldis 1917, pp. 180, 183, repr.; 1920a, pp. 4, 6. Longhi 1920b, p. 91. De Rinaldis 1921, pp. 15-16, pl. VIII. Sestieri 1921, p. 184. Ortolani 1922, p. 194. Consoli Fiego 1922, p. 107. Benesch 1926, p. 250. Pevsner in Pevsner and Grautoff 1928, p. 185. De Rinaldis 1929, p. 30. Nugent 1925–30, 2:564. Costantini 1930, 1:254. Ortolani in Naples 1938, p. 66. Juynboll 1960, p. 90. Percy 1965, p. 56, no. 38 . Pée 1971, p. 174. Causa 1972, pp. 942, 944, 982 n. 108. Florence 1979, p. 212.

12

13

The Finding of Moses

Canvas, 76 x 102 cm.
Museo di Capodimonte, Naples
(Banco di Napoli)

This charming painting is one of the most attractive of Cavallino's works that are datable on stylistic grounds to the latter half of the 1630s. In it he has already arrived at his characteristic graceful, round-faced figure types and his subtly organized compositions where a number of figures interact, here in a circle, around a central focal point. The picture, in rather good condition , shows a Gargiulo-like blond and blue background on the right with a generally dark ground on the left. The figures are dressed in dull gold, blue, dull green, reddish orange, yellow green, and grayish white. Many of the elements that make up Cavallino's characteristic style are evident in this work: it combines a Riberesque naturalism in the observation of surfaces, rendered on a small scale and showing a minute observation of faces and a delicate handling of impasto typical of Falcone, with dramatic tenebrist lighting, a Callot-like Mannerist elegance in the figures (cf. Fig. 19), and a female figure type that is rather like those of Artemisia Gentileschi or Massimo Stanzione on a small scale. The strong Mannerist element that is so important a part of Cavallino's style is evident here; compare, for example, an anonymous print after Goltzius of *The Daughters of Cecrops Opening the Casket Entrusted to Them by Minerva* (Fig. 16) in both figures and composition.

This subject brought out the best of Cavallino's talents, as he represented it again in a work now in Brunswick [81] that is indisputably one of his finest late paintings, just as this is one of his most attractive earlier works.

The preparation of the canvas introduces an interesting technical note. Cavallino used a variety of canvases, ranging from finely to very coarsely woven examples. Early works such as this one are often on coarsely woven canvases with large interstices between the threads. In the case of this picture—as well as of the Capodimonte *Saint Bartholomew* [3]— the back of the canvas was prepared as well as the front, possibly to provide greater stability to the painted surface.   AP

Collections
Paolo Wenner, Naples; private collection, Naples, by 1938.

Exhibitions
Florence 1922, cat. no. 262; São Paulo 1954, no. 32.

Literature
Rolfs 1910, pp. 277-78. Longhi 1920b, p. 91. Sestieri 1920, pp. 251, 262-64, 267-68, fig. 17. De Rinaldis 1920a, p. 6, fig. 7; 1921, p. 16, pl. VII. Sestieri 1921, pp. 184-89, repr. p. 194. Ortolani 1922, p. 192. [Ceci] 1923, p. 24. De Rinaldis 1929, pl. 40. Nugent 1925-30, 2:560-61, repr. Costantini 1930, 1:254. Ortolani in Naples 1938, p. 65. Molajoli 1948, p. 103. *Emporium* 114 (1951):87, repr. Molajoli in Naples 1953, pp. 27, 45, pls. 47-49. Chiarelli 1954, p. 220. Rivosecchi 1959, pp. 24, 26, repr. Molajoli in Naples 1961, p. 53. *Gazette des Beaux-Arts* ser. 6, 57 (1961), suppl. 65, no. 181. Scavizzi in Naples 1963, p. 28. Molajoli in Naples 1964, p. 59, fig. 76. Percy 1965, p. 55, no. 34. De Filippis 1970, pl. 19.

13

14

A Saint Martyr
(Saint Agatha?)

Canvas, 118 x 87 cm.
Museo di Capodimonte, Naples
(Gift of Maria Proto Pallavicino,
duchessa di Albaneta)

Exhibited in Naples only

This picture has been recognized as by Cavallino from the early years of this century, when it belonged to the Proto d'Albaneta collection; it was included in de Rinaldis's 1909 catalogue of Cavallino's work.

Most of the artist's images of saints, apostles, heroines, or allegorical figures are half-length or three-quarters-length. This is one of the few full-length and seems to be the earliest in date, dating probably somewhat after the mid-1630s, not far from the early *Saint Bartholomew* [3], the small scenes from the life of Christ in private collections [5-7], and the Hartford *Flight into Egypt* [8]. A characteristic of early works that this painting shares with the youthful Brunswick, Naples, Milan, and Hartford pictures [2, 3, 4, 8] is a rather generalized and simplified structure of the hands; by the early forties Cavallino renders hands with much greater naturalistic detail and three-dimensionality [30-31].

The picture is painted on coarsely woven canvas and has suffered considerable losses, with the more opaquely rendered portions, as usual, the better preserved. The overall effect is very dark: the saint wears a gray robe, dark blue sash, and mauve mantle. The rendering of surfaces derives from the naturalistic tradition of Ribera. The figure of the saint is generally Stanzionesque; compare, for example, Stanzione's *Saint Agatha in Prison*, at Capodimonte, which has been dated on stylistic grounds to the early 1630s.[1] The sufferings of Saint Agatha, a third-century Sicilian martyr, are described by Jacobus de Voragine (see text of [28]).   AP

1. Repr. in London and Washington 1982-83, p. 257.

Collections
Proto d'Albaneta, Naples; gift to the Museum in 1960.

Exhibitions
Florence 1922, cat. no. 265; London 1930, cat. no. 770; Naples 1975, repr.

Literature
De Rinaldis 1909, p. 36, cat. no. 12. Hermanin in Thieme-Becker 6 (1912):225. De Rinaldis 1917, p. 181; 1920a, p. 4 n. 2; 1921, p. 16, pl. ix. Sestieri 1921, pp. 188, 195. Ortolani 1922, p. 194. [Ceci] 1923, pp. 24-26. Ojetti, Dami, and Tarchiani 1924, pl. 87. De Rinaldis 1929, pl. 44. Nugent 1925–30, 2:572-73, repr. London 1931, 1:167, no.491 (770). Carli 1938, p. 269. Ortolani in Naples 1938, pp. 65-66. Masciotta 1942, p. 147. Betti 1960, p. 17. Molajoli in Naples 1961, p. 52. *Gazette des Beaux-Arts* ser. 6, 59 (1962), suppl., p. 55, fig. 201*bis*. Molajoli in Naples 1964, p. 54. Percy 1965, p. 54, no. 31. Pée 1971, p. 167, fig. 317. Causa in Naples 1982, p. 147, repr. p. 101. London and Washington 1982–83, p. 135. Paris 1983, p. 189. Turin 1983, p. 158.

14

15

15

The Flagellation
of Christ

Canvas, 67 x 64 cm.

Galleria Falanga, Naples

Exhibited in Naples only

This small picture may or may not have originally been conceived as an octagon; it has usually been considered a pendant to its present companion piece, an *Annunciation to the Shepherds* by the Master of the Annunciations to the Shepherds (Fig. 15a), and thereby to indicate an early collaboration on Cavallino's part with the mysteriously anonymous master whose work is so close to his own work of the 1630s. However, although the two pictures have been together since at least before 1920, they do not fit well together compositionally and the figures are of noticeably different scale. It seems more likely that they were conjoined at a later date rather than originally produced as pendants. Both works were attributed to Cavallino until Hernández Perera published the *Annunciation* as by the Master of the Annunciations in 1957. In 1972 Causa rejected the attribution of the *Flagellation* as well to Cavallino, giving it to the Master of the Annunciations.

Painted on coarsely woven canvas, the picture is generally typical of Cavallino's early dark manner, although the two small heads at right are uncharacteristic of his faces and handling of paint. Since the canvas appears to have been enlarged at both sides, possibly to conform to the octagonal shape, these may be additions by another hand. The pose of Christ, with drooping head and crossed hands, is similar to a half-length *Flagellation* in the Quadreria dei Gerolamini in Naples, once considered as from the workshop of Ribera but recently restored to the master and dated very early (ca. 1615–16).[1] A comparison to the grand prototype in Naples, Caravaggio's *Flagellation*—

Fig. 15a. The Master of the Annunciations to the Shepherds. *The Annunciation to the Shepherds.* Galleria Falanga, Naples (see Inv. no. 25).

Fig. 15b. Attributed to Cavallino. *The Flagellation of Christ.* Canvas, 110 x 130 cm. Present location unknown; formerly private collection, Naples.

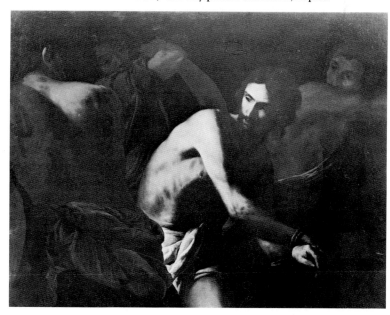

painted in 1607 for the de Franchis Chapel in the church of San Domenico Maggiore but not, apparently, *in situ* until near the end of Cavallino's life—only underlines the vast difference in approach between the two painters. The small scale, seductiveness of surface, and mannered grace of Cavallino's picture has little connection to the monumental size, austerity, and profound seriousness of Caravaggio's version.

A possible autograph, later, lost, version of the subject was recently in a Neapolitan private collection (Fig. 15b).   AP

1. Pérez Sánchez and Spinosa 1978, p. 93, no. 20, repr. p. 94.
2. Mina Gregori in London and Washington 1982-83, no. 15, repr.
3. Marini 1974, p. 103, no. 8, repr. (as Giovanni Dò). In Marini's opinion (in correspondence, 1984), the work may actually be by Cavallino.

Collections
Ospedale abbruzzese pro orfani dei contadini morti in guerra, Naples; A. Gualtieri, Naples; Baronessa Maria de Biase, Naples, by 1938.

Exhibitions
Naples 1938, pp. 66, 319.

Literature
Longhi 1920b, p. 153. De Rinaldis 1920a, pp. 58-59, repr; 1921, p. 16, pl. xxiv. Sestieri 1921, p. 184. Ortolani 1922, p. 193; in Naples 1938, p. 64. Percy 1965, pp. 50-51, no. 20. Causa 1972, p. 982 n. 110. London and Washington 1982–83, pp. 135, 194. Paris 1983, p. 188. Turin 1983, p. 214.

16

The Payment of the Tribute

Canvas, 71 x 98 cm.
Museo di Capodimonte, Naples,
Gift of Giuseppe Cenzato

Exhibited in Naples only

Cleaning has rendered this painting more legible but exposes a certain unevenness of condition; the gray background seems oddly flat, Peter's sleeve appears to have lost all its glazes, and the *repoussoir* figure at left has little surface modeling. The two figures at right, painted in thicker impasto, have survived in better condition; the brilliant blue of the sleeve and trousers of the second soldier from right is especially noteworthy. The picture can be dated to the latter years of the thirties; it seems to fall between the early tenebrist works [especially 4-11] and a group of pictures of greater sophistication of composition and refinement in the lifelike observation of surfaces [especially 19-22].

The subject of Christ instructing Peter to fish at Capernaum—in the mouth of the first fish he would catch would be found the money to pay the temple tax—is found in Matthew 17:24-27.   AP

Collections
Giuseppe Cenzato; gift to the Museum in 1957.

Exhibitions
None.

Literature
Ortolani in Naples 1938, p. 178. Molajoli in Naples 1948, p. 104. Causa 1957, p. 42. Molajoli in Naples 1957, p. 73; in Naples 1958, p. 56. Brugnoli 1959, p. 199, detail repr. *Gazette des Beaux-Arts* ser. 6, 55 (1960), suppl. p. 45, fig. 154. Molajoli in Naples 1961, p. 52, fig. 35; in Naples 1964, p. 54. Percy 1965, p. 53, no. 29. De Fillipis 1970, pl. 17. Pée 1971, p. 122, under no. 45. Causa in Naples 1982, pp. 101, 147, repr.

16

17

The Banquet of Absalom

Canvas, 103 x 121 cm.
Graf Harrach'sche Familiensammlung,
Schloss Rohrau, Austria

Presumably purchased in Naples by Alois Thomas Raimund, Count Harrach (1699–1742), viceroy to Naples between 1728 and 1733, the painting was formerly attributed to the Spanish school (Vienna 1856), to Mattia Preti (Mitidieri 1913; Chimirri and Frangipane 1914), and to Gioacchino Assereto (Longhi 1916b); Venturi first gave it to Cavallino in 1921, and his attribution was immediately contested by Musto (1921b). Executed on coarsely woven canvas, it seems to be in good condition and, like the Vienna *Adoration of the Magi* [19] and the *Esther before Abasuerus* [21] in Switzerland, can be used as a touchstone to explore the various phases of Cavallino's style before 1645. It is one of his most Caravaggesque pictures in its treatment of illumination: a harsh light strikes across the stagelike setting, bringing some figures into strong relief, with others dropping away into shadow. The extreme virtuosity with which the still-life elements—gold and silver dishes, basins, jars, tankards, and platters—are rendered underlines Cavallino's skill in this specialty, which, however, he never seems to have practiced for its own sake. Instead of the arrangement of figures in a flat row parallel to the plane of the picture, as generally prevails in his earliest paintings, Cavallino has here developed a diagonal recession into the background space emphasized by the figure at the right.

So far as we know, this is the artist's only depiction of this subject, which comes from 2 Samuel 13:28-29 and recounts how one of King David's sons, Absalom, causes another, Amnon, to be murdered at a banquet in revenge for ravishing their sister Tamar.   AP

Collections

Probably acquired in Naples by Alois Thomas Raimund, Count Harrach, viceroy to Naples (1728–33).

Exhibitions

London 1930, cat. no. 765. Naples 1938. London and Washington 1982-83, cat. no. 25, repr.

Literature

Vienna 1856, p. 40, no. 197; Vienna 1897, unnumbered. Mitidieri 1913, p. 446. Chimirri and Frangipane 1914, pl. xvii. Longhi 1916b, pp. 370, 371. Musto 1921b, p. 160. A. Venturi 1921, pp. 211-12, 214, fig. 3. Ortolani 1922, p. 190. Venturi 1925, pp. 74, 77, fig. 25. Benesch 1926, pp. 253-54, 256, fig. 181. Vienna 1926, p. 90, no. 233. London 1931, p. 167, no. 490 (765). Delogu 1937, pp. 404, 409-10, repr. Masciotta 1942, p. 147. Refice 1951, pp. 260, 263, fig. 1. Heinz in Harrach cat. 1960, p. 26, no. 71, fig. 9. Juynboll 1960, p. 90. Longhi 1961, 1:322. Percy 1965, p. 58, no. 49. Causa 1972, p. 943, fig. 313. Paris 1983, p. 188. Turin 1983, pp. 158-61, repr.

17

18

David Playing
the Harp
before Saul

Canvas, 94.5 x 130 cm.
Museum Boymans-van Beuningen,
Rotterdam

In catalogue only

In the friezelike arrangement of figures, the flatly observed architectural background, and the strong tenebrism combined with a handling of paint that is both dense and delicate in the two principal figures, this picture relates to works such as the Bologna *Denial of Saint Peter* [9], the London *David before Saul* [20], and the Paris *Esther before Ahasuerus* [21]. However, the worn condition of the more thinly painted figures attendant on the two main protagonists makes dating the picture somewhat difficult, and Causa (1972) has called the work a seventeenth-century copy. Saul wears a gray-white brocaded cloak with gold trim, David a reddish robe with gray-white sleeves. The background figures are dressed in dull green, brown, and yellow brown. The intensely dramatic, mannered gestures that are characteristic of Cavallino's mature work are evident here in the figure of Saul.

The story of the shepherd youth David, summoned to the court of the Israelite king Saul because of his ability to soothe the king's troubled mind with his skill as a harpist, is given in 1 Samuel 16:14-23. It was represented by Cavallino in two other pictures in London and Vienna [20, 60]; the more mature version in Vienna is paired with a scene of *Esther before Ahasuerus*, another Old Testament subject that Cavallino seems particularly to have favored for its potential to represent scenes of courtly magnificence.   AP

Collections

Sale, Van Marle en Bignell, The Hague, 1951, no. 1207; W. R. Juynboll, Leiden; acquired by the Museum in 1961.

Exhibitions

None.

Literature

Juynboll 1960, pp. 82, 84, repr. *Emporium* 134, no. 800 (1961):95, repr. *Gazette des Beaux-Arts* ser. 6, 59 (1962), suppl., p. 57, fig. 209. Percy 1965, p. 63, no. 75. Causa 1972, p. 983 n. 111. Wright 1980, p. 74.

18

19

The Adoration
of the Magi

Canvas, 101.5 x 127 cm.
Kunsthistorisches Museum, Vienna

Exhibited in Naples only

Sold at auction in Vienna in 1918 as Bartolomeo Biscaino,[1] the work was acquired by the museum in 1928, with an attribution to Cavallino by Johannes Wilde and Roberto Longhi (Vienna 1928) and by Gustav Glück (Benesch 1928). Painted on coarsely woven canvas, it is in unusually good condition for an early picture by Cavallino. The composition is complex, with lighting falling across the middle between shadowed *repoussoir* figures at the far left and those in the background. The artist's strong naturalistic bent is evident in the fur hat of the attendant figure at far left and in the saddle upon which the Virgin is seated, as well as in the carefully observed chains, crowns, vessel, and censer. It seems that the model for the Virgin was the same as that for one of the attendants at the far left in the *Esther before Ahasuerus* in a Swiss private collection [21] and for Omphale in the *Hercules and Omphale* [22], also in a Swiss collection, as all these female figures have the same long, rather distinctive face.

Because of its well-preserved state, this picture provides a sort of summation of the qualities of Cavallino's early manner. Chiaroscuro contrasts are sharp and abrupt, but the brushwork that forms up the figures and renders the surfaces of materials in a very naturalistic handling of paint is delicate and subtle. The palette, in which accents of blue, gray white, and rich red contrast with a predominantly dark tonality, also includes subtler mauve pinks, greens, and pale browns. The influence of Northern late Mannerist prints on the swaying stances of Cavallino's figures, their emphasized gestures, and the *repoussoir* figures shown partly in shadow is fully evident here.[2] Compared to the *Adoration of the Shepherds* in Brunswick [2], datable some years earlier, to Cavallino's earliest moments, this work shows a Mannerist complexity of composition and elegance of pose that was to be developed to an ever higher pitch as the artist matured. It can tentatively be dated around 1640, and de Dominici's evocative summation of Cavallino's early style may be aptly applied to it:

> Combining, therefore, [the impression made by Rubens's *Feast of Herod*] with the style of Massimo Stanzione, Cavallino created his own beautiful and erudite manner, which at the same time appears tender, gentle, and delicate but with great technical skill in the use of chiaroscuro and a dramatic striking of

brightness against dark, strong shadows, which, as he used a single light source, usually terminate at the center of the principal figures, bestowing on them a gravity and an indescribable decorum in addition to the natural gracefulness in the distribution of the light itself, a quality in which Cavallino was singular, as we have described above.[3]

AP

1. Information courtesy of Wolfgang Prohaska, Kunsthistorisches Museum. A note in the Museum's curatorial files indicates that the work appeared in the 1918 sale, as Biscaino, but the catalogue has not been traceable.

2. Compare, for example, prints by Jan Saenredam after Hendrik Goltzius (*Evening*; Bartsch 92.248), and Jan Muller after Bartolomeus Spranger (*The Adoration of the Shepherds*; Bartsch 65.284), repr. in *Illustrated Bartsch* 4:408, 498.

3. "Unendo perciò a quella [the impression made by Rubens's *Feast of Herod*] la maniera di Massimo, venne a comporre la sua bella, ed erudita maniera, che ad un tempo istesso sembra dolce, gentile, e delicata, ma con grande arteficio di chiaro scuro, e con grandi sbattimenti di lumi, e di ombre, grave, e robuste, servendosi egli di un sol lume, che terminando per lo più nel mezzo e sulle principali figure, viene a dar loro una gravità, ed un decoro indicibile, oltre alla grazia naturale nella distribuzione di esso, nella qual parte fu il Cavallino singolare, come abbiam detto di sopra" (de Dominici 1742-43, 3:35).

Collections
Sale, Kunst-Auktions Salon Kende-Schidlof, Vienna, 21-22 October 1918, lot 6; Alfred Wassermann, Vienna; acquired by the Museum in 1928.

Exhibitions
Naples 1938.

Literature
Vienna 1928, p. 44, no. 509A. Benesch 1928, pp. 49, 51. *Art News* 36 (May 1938): 10, repr. Vienna 1938, p. 34, no. 509A. Causa 1949, p. 278 n. 15. Vienna 1965, p. 37, no. 495. Percy 1965, p. 72, no. 113. *Kindlers Malerei Lexikon* 1 (1964), unpaginated. Causa 1972, p. 943. Marini 1974, no. 63, repr. Ferrari in *Dizionario biografico* 22 (1979):787. London and Washington 1982−83, pp. 135, 147, 194. Paris 1983, p. 188. Turin 1983, p. 158.

19

20

20

David
Playing the Harp
before Saul

Canvas 74.5 x 102 cm.
Heim Gallery, London

In catalogue only

This rather early picture, which recently appeared on the London market and presumably dates around 1640, has been so extensively damaged and repainted that the only relatively intact areas are the figures of Saul and his attendant, and of David and the man next to him. The figure at far left is the third example we have encountered of the apparent inclusion of a self-portrait in a painting by Cavallino [see 3, 11]; the elegant pose—arm akimbo and eyes staring straight at the viewer—reminds one of similar figures in Dutch high-life genre scenes of the first third of the seventeenth century. One wonders if Cavallino somehow knew "merry company" scenes by artists such as Willem Buytewech (Rotterdam 1591/92-1624) or Dirck Hals (Haarlem 1591-1656), although such similarities might of course derive from common sources in prints.

The subject was treated by Cavallino in two other paintings [18, 60].   AP

Collections
Family of Lopez y Royo, duca di Taurisano; private collection, London.

Exhibitions
None.

Literature
London and Washington 1982−83, p. 147.

21

Esther
before Ahasuerus

Canvas, 76 x 102 cm.
Private collection, Switzerland

Painted on coarsely woven canvas and datable to around 1640, this picture seems to be in unusually fine condition, with the delicate glazes on faces and materials better preserved than in many of Cavallino's relatively early works. The ground is a dark red brown, and the background is dark green, gray, and olive gray. The left-hand figures are dressed in dark mauve red, dull yellow, and brown. Esther's dress is dark brown with delicate pale blue impasto highlights; her brocade cloak is silvery gray. Ahasuerus wears a red robe, a gray blouse with yellow sleeves, and dark yellow stockings with gray-white tops; his attendants are dressed primarily in gray. The chiaroscuro contrasts are rather startling, almost harsh, whereas the impasto highlights on the king's scepter and crown are remarkably delicate.

The rendering of the fur lining of the king's robe and of the red hat of the second attendant figure from the right is very fine and well preserved, showing the extremely personal level of refinement to which Cavallino was able to bring the Neapolitan naturalist tradition of the second quarter of the Seicento. It is interesting that the same face—that of the female attendant fourth from the left— is found in the Virgin of the Vienna *Adoration* [19] and in the Omphale of the *Hercules and Omphale* in a Swiss private collection [22]. Perhaps the model was a member of Cavallino's family, redepicted in the same manner that he repeated his self-portraits.

X radiographs show a first trial in which Ahasuerus's head was much further to the left, almost directly in front of where Esther's now is, with his profile coinciding with the left cheekbone of the present attendant female supporting Esther by the elbow. Therefore, it is clear that Cavallino altered the arrangement of figures after beginning the composition, shifting Ahasuerus several centimeters to the right. Whether this evidence suggests that the artist worked *alla prima* (or directly on the canvas) without preliminary drawings in the manner of Caravaggio is difficult to assess, as so few drawings attributed to Cavallino survive. The great sophistication of his figures' poses and the complexity of their interrelationships in his compositions suggests the opposite—i. e., that the pictures and the individual figures therein were composed on the basis of carefully finished preparatory drawings. Nevertheless, pentimenti appear in other works throughout the artist's career [e. g., 3, 22, 67, 68, 76].

It is quite possible that this is the picture recorded by de Dominici in the Francesco Valletta collection in Naples:

> In the house of the learned D [on] Francesco Valletta, worthy nephew of the famous lawyer mentioned above, are seven pictures by Cavallino; one, measuring five *palmi* wide and three high, [depicts] Esther who kneeling before Ahasuerus faints, and the king rising from his throne seeks to assist her, while her ladies-in-waiting also rush to her aid; other principal figures are in the painting who represent the king's courtiers, and receiving the shadow [that falls upon them] they form a counterpoint to the primary illumination that is spread upon Esther, the principal figure of the action, in which a golden robe that wonderfully adorns her and renders her majestic makes a great display, and in this painting one sees imitated in large measure the beautiful and marvelous coloring of Peter Paul Rubens.[1]

The canvas seen by the biographer was apparently about 30 centimeters wider than this picture (3 by 5 *palmi*, or ca. 79 x 132 cm), and the composition differs slightly in several respects. De Dominici describes Esther as kneeling, fainting before Ahasuerus, who rises from his throne to aid her while her handmaidens hasten to do likewise. Nevertheless, his description fits this version of the subject better than the Orsola Benincasa, Harrach, or Uffizi versions [12, 61, 62], although Esther is not kneeling. In addition, de Dominici describes a picture in which the light falls primarily on the central figure of Esther, who wears a gold robe, whereas here the light strikes virtually all the figures, and Esther's robe is more silver than gold. It is also difficult to see the connection with Rubens's palette that de Dominici associates with this picture, especially as we know from the biographer that the most important work by Rubens in Naples was the *Feast of Herod* now in Edinburgh, which, in its bright, ruddy tonality, could hardly be more different from this dark, tenebrist painting. Cavallino's handling of paint is not in the slightest Rubensian; if it can be said to have a Northern quality, this is instead a luminous precision of surface naturalism akin to the work of Dutch or Flemish genre painters of the first half of the seventeenth century, such as Michel Sweerts or David Teniers the Younger, although we do not know for certain if Cavallino might have known works by these artists.

A copy of this work has been published as in a private collection in Milan (Inv. no. 82). AP

1. "Nella Casa dell'eruditissimo Sig. D. Francesco Valletta, degno nipote del celebre Avvocato mentovato di sopra, sono sette quadri del nostro Cavallino; Uno della misura di palmi cinque per traverso, e tre per altezza, nel quale è dipinta Ester che postasi inginocchione avanti Assuero vien meno; e'l Re levatosi dalla Sedia cerca soccorrerla, nel mentre che le Damigelle altresì accorrono in ajuto di lei; sono in questo quadro altre figure principali, che i cortegiani del Re rappresentano, e ricevendo l'accidente dell'ombra, fan contraposti al lume principale, che si diffonde su l'Ester, principal figura dell'azione, nella quale fa pompa un drappo dorato, che mirabilmente l'adorna, e maestosa la rende, e in questo quadro si osserva in gran parte imitata la bella, e maravigliosa tinta di Pietro Paolo Rubens" (de Dominici 1742–43, 3:37-38).

Collections
Possibly Francesco Valletta, Naples, by 1743; private collection, Sweden; François Heim, Paris, 1983-84.

Exhibitions
None.

Literature
De Dominici 1742–43, 3:37-38.

21

22

22

_____

Hercules and Omphale

Canvas, 128 x 187 cm.
The Property of a Swiss Collector

In catalogue only

Probably datable around 1640, this important picture appears to be the earliest of four large-scale compositions by Cavallino [44, 68, 79] that at intervals punctuate the sequence of smaller-scale easel paintings of the forties and fifties. Executed on coarsely woven canvas and in generally good condition despite some abrasion throughout, the work shows a pentimento indicating that Omphale's face was once rendered in profile turned to the left instead of in three-quarters front view. It is dark in tonality, with the relatively undifferentiated dark background that characterizes Cavallino's earlier works; the technique of depicting flesh with crisply brushed transitions from dark shadows to opaque impasto highlights is in the naturalistic tradition of Ribera, as are the upturned grinning faces of attendant figures in the background. Omphale wears an olive green-brownish dress with pale blue highlights—an unusual tonality seen in two other early works by Cavallino [12, 21]—and grayish-white slashed sleeves and gold trim. Other figures wear mauve, gray, white, blue, and dull orange, reflecting the restricted palette of Cavallino's earlier work.

The sudden appearance of a large-scale mythological subject in an oeuvre largely comprised of scenes from the Old and New Testaments, the Apocrypha, and the Golden Legend is surprising. Omphale, in mythology, was a Lydian queen who bought Hercules—the Greek hero renowned for his strength and courage—as a slave and set him to woman's work as an act of purification for Hercules' having killed the son of Eurytus. Hercules is here endowed with women's spinning implements, Omphale with his club and lion skin. Besides the relatively unusual subject matter, the work is remarkable for Cavallino in its scale and in the heavy naturalism of the body of Hercules and the grinning Riberesque attendants, later to be tempered toward greater refinement in comparable figures in paintings in New York [68] and Brunswick [81]. Surely a relatively youthful and not quite successfully resolved effort at depicting such a theme in such a format, it is a work whose place in Cavallino's development will not be understood until further research clarifies the question of his patrons and the manner of commissioning of his works.

A seventeenth-century copy of the picture, in ruined condition, is in the Real Santa Casa dell' Annunziata, Naples.[1]   AP

1. Causa 1972, p. 982 n. 108.

Collections
Allomello, Rome, 1957.

Exhibitions
None.

Literature
Causa 1957, p. 42. Percy 1965, p. 74, no. 142. Causa 1972, pp. 942, 982 n. 108.

23

23

The Angel
Liberating Saint Peter
from Prison

Canvas, 33 x 42 cm.
Mario Modestini, New York

Exhibited in USA only

This charming picture proves Cavallino's ability to render scenes of considerable dramatic impact on quite a small scale—so small, in fact, that one wonders whether the present work may not have served as *modello* for a lost, larger composition of the subject.[1] It can be dated with the Kassel *Curing of Tobit* [24] to a moment in which the sophisticated and lyrical articulation of the contours of draperies that is so remarkable a characteristic of Cavallino's maturity is becoming evident. The brushwork with which the angel's rich red cloak and dull green tunic is rendered is typical of Cavallino's calculated and refined delicacy of touch.

The subject (from The Acts of the Apostles 12:6-8) was apparently represented by the artist in a similar but reversed composition that included the two sleeping soldiers guarding Peter, known only through a copy until a few years ago in the church of the Gerolamini, Naples (Inv. no. 111; Fig. 23b). Companion piece to the latter was a *Denial of Saint Peter*, also a copy (Inv. no. 130; Fig. 23a). Another version of this subject close to Cavallino's manner but clearly by another hand is in a private collection in Switzerland (Inv. no. 24). AP

1. The canvas—which is the coarsely woven type used often by the artist—may have originally been somewhat more ample in height, as it is difficult to imagine an artist who loved to render elegantly shaped and dramatically high-lit angels' wings as much as Cavallino did interrupting such a wing so abruptly as here.

Fig. 23a. Copy after Cavallino. *The Denial of Saint Peter*. Present location unknown; formerly Chiesa dei Gerolamini, Naples (see Inv. no. 130).

Fig. 23b. Copy after Cavallino. *The Angel Liberating Saint Peter from Prison*. Present location unknown; formerly Chiesa dei Gerolamini, Naples (see Inv. no. 111).

24

24

The Curing of Tobit

Canvas, 70 x 77.2 cm
(all four corners cut and replaced).
Gemäldegalerie Alte Meister,
Staatliche Kunstsammlungen, Kassel

In catalogue only

According to Museum records, this painting was acquired before 1749 by Landgraf Wilhelm VIII of Hesse (reigned 1730–60), whose collection became state property in 1866. A 1749 inventory (no. 231: "Guerchin da Cento: Der Junge Tobias, wie er seinen Vater sehend macht; in verguldem Rahmen, Höhe 2 Schuh 11 Zoll, Breite 2 Schuh 5-1/2 Zoll [ca. 92 x 75 cm]") and old catalogues and inventories up to 1878 attribute it to Guercino;[1] Eisenmann (in Kassel 1888) and Gronau (in Kassel 1913) call it seventeenth-century Spanish. The attribution to Cavallino was made by Hermann Voss around 1913 (Gronau in Kassel 1913).

Datable to the early 1640s, the work is executed on coarsely woven canvas and shows some later retouches on the bottom foreground; the dog; and the angel's shoulder, arm, and face. The two background faces have lost some of their definition. The painting has an overall dark tonality with accents of gray, dull green, and blue. One is struck, as in the earlier *Communion of the Apostles* in Milan [4], with Cavallino's ability to depict the dramatic lighting of angels' wings.

This picture raises an interesting question concerning Cavallino's contemporary reputation and the possible existence of a workshop. Whereas his pictures are occasionally copied early on [1, 9, 22, 26, 37, 40, 62, 82], they do not seem to be systematically imitated, except in the case of the Immaculate Conceptions (Inv. nos. 42-43, 45-47, 152) and the stories of Tobit (Inv. nos. 1-6, 9, 14-18). The latter generated a series of versions, the authorship of which is difficult to sort out. The Kassel

picture seems to be the only known original of all the Tobit scenes.

Scenes from the Book of Tobit were noted early on as important for Cavallino. De Dominici describes three of them: two were on copper, apparently pendants, showing the *Departure of Tobias* and *Marriage of Tobias* in the Francesco Valletta and marchese di Grazia collections, respectively (Appendix, nos. 13-14); the third was on canvas, also in the Valletta collection, showing the *Marriage of Tobias* (Appendix, no. 13). From de Dominici's detailed description we can conclude that the *Departure of Tobias* today in the Palazzo Corsini in Rome (Inv. no. 9; Fig. 24a) is a copy on canvas, presumably from the eighteenth century, of the lost oil on copper by Cavallino in the Valletta collection. His description of the pendant to this copper, the *Marriage of Tobias* in the collection of the marchese di Grazia, could fit either of two series of versions of this subject, none of which is on copper and none of which seems to be original (Inv. nos. 14-18). In the same way, de Dominici's description of the third Tobit scene known to him by Cavallino, the canvas of the *Marriage* in the Valletta collection, could fit any of the above versions, although the dimensions are closest to that in the Prado.

De Dominici's detailed descriptions of the pairing of Tobit scenes suggest that these subjects might have been frequent companions in Cavallino's oeuvre. Indeed, today we have a number of paired Tobits that seem to derive from originals by Cavallino but that depict stocky, thick-limbed figures that are far from his usual slender proportions and that lead us to suspect that we are concerned with a still-nameless contemporary imitator or follower. The known pairs of curings of Tobit and marriages of Tobias are in the Prado (Inv. nos. 6, 18; Figs. 24b, c), the Museo Correale in Sorrento (Inv. nos. 1, 16), the Museo Nazionale d'Abruzzo in L'Aquila (Inv. nos. 5, 17), and formerly in the Gualtieri collection, Naples (Inv. no. 15; possibly only the *Marriage*). An additional version of the healing of Tobit is in the collection of David Rust, Washington, D.C. (Inv. no. 3), and a similar version, known through a photograph, was on the market at Montecarlo.

Whereas the abovementioned pairs all seem to derive from a follower of Cavallino, there are three canvases that appear to be copies of original representations of

Tobit scenes by Cavallino himself: the Norfolk *Marriage of Tobias* (Inv. no. 14; Fig. 24d); the formerly Buffardi, now Rebuffat, collection, Naples, *Curing of Tobit* (Inv. no. 2; Fig. 24e); and the Seattle *Curing of Tobit* (Inv. no. 4; Fig. 24f). The latter appears to be a copy of a close variant of the Kassel picture, with the figures slightly differently arranged. The complex interrelationship of all these copies, versions, variants, and imitations suggests that this was one of Cavallino's most popular themes. Strangely, only one original, the Kassel picture, survives. One wonders if the many closely related versions point to a workshop imitator.

The book of Tobit is part of the Apocrypha and recounts how Tobit, a pious Jew of the captivity of Nineveh, was cured of blindness in his old age by his son Tobias, using the gall of a fish miraculously retrieved with the aid of the archangel Raphael. Andrea Vaccaro also depicted a series of Tobit scenes, now in the Prado.[2]   AP

1. Information courtesy of F. Lahusen, Staatliche Kunstsammlungen, Kassel.
    2. Pérez Sánchez 1965, p. 462, pls. 174-77.

Collections
Acquired by Landgraf Wilhelm VIII of Hesse, before 1749.

Exhibitions
None.

Literature
Kassel 1783, p. 45, no. 39; 1819, p. 36, no. 216; 1830, p. 42, no. 249. Parthey 1863, 1:61. Kassel 1888, p. 283, no. 440 (249); 1913, p. 64, no. 477; 1929, p. 15. Carli 1938, pp. 262-63. Pigler 1956, 1:188. Vogel in Kassel 1958, p. 42, no. 477, repr. Percy 1965, pp. 48, 49, no. 11. Liebmann 1968, p. 459. Herzog in Kassel 1969, p. 91, no. 477, fig. 78. Lehmann in Kassel 1975, fig. 95; in Kassel 1980, pp. 88-89, repr.

Fig. 24a. Copy after Cavallino. *The Departure of Tobias*. Galleria Nazionale d'Arte Antica, Palazzo Corsini, Rome (see Inv. no. 9).

Fig. 24b. Imitator of Cavallino. *The Marriage of Tobias*. Museo del Prado, Madrid (see Inv. no. 18).

Fig. 24c. Imitator of Cavallino. *The Curing of Tobit*. Museo del Prado, Madrid (see Inv. no. 6).

Fig. 24d. Copy after Cavallino. *The Marriage of Tobias*. The Chrysler Museum, Norfolk, Virginia (see Inv. no. 14).

Fig. 24e. Copy after Cavallino (?). *The Curing of Tobit*. Rebuffat Collection, Naples (see Inv. no. 2).

Fig. 24f. Copy after Cavallino. *The Curing of Tobit*. Seattle Art Museum, Seattle, Washington (see Inv. no. 4).

25

25

The Meeting of David and Abigail

Canvas, 75 x 102 cm.
Civica Pinacoteca del Castello
Sforzesco, Milan,
Bequest of Count Gian Giacomo
Attendolo Bolognini, 1856

The subject was treated by Cavallino in a more elaborate composition later in his career (see [80] and discussion under same). This version, which dates from the first half of the 1640s, is comparable in the handling of paint to the Kassel *Curing of Tobit* [24] and the Kansas City *Abduction of Europa* [36]. And it represents a more intimate encounter between Abigail and David than the Brunswick scene, revealing Cavallino's tender whimsicality and his affinity for expressive color. The servant, who leads David's horse[1] by a twisted red rein (Cavallino used smilar red cords for Galatea's dolphins [68]), wears a golden-ochre shirt covered by a breastplate with a blue sash tied loosely around his waist. The imposing figure of David stands out in the scene. He is dressed in a blue blouse with slashed sleeves exposing a white shirt, and a brilliant red cloak is draped over one shoulder. His leggings are moss green with strings of golden yellow. Abigail's colors, befitting her humble supplicant's role, are somber. Her muted green dress blends into the gray-brown background, enlivened by the gleaming highlights of her trailing robes. The sky is salmon pink.

The figure of Abigail, with minor changes, appears in a painting (Fig. 25a) by an unknown artist who must have seen both this painting and the elaborate Brunswick version, if not a third version—as yet undiscovered—by Cavallino himself. The kneeling woman in the painting *Moses Striking the Rock*, which was once attributed to Cavallino (see Inv. no. 101) but which Causa later attributed to Micco Spadaro or Agostino Beltrano, has a similarity to the Abigail in this painting, which may have served as the original model.   ATL

1. There is some damage and restoration to the left side and head of the horse.

Collections
Count Gian Giacomo Attendolo Bolognini, Milan.

Exhibitions
Naples 1938, p. 319; Leningrad 1978.

Literature
Percy 1965, p. 50, no. 18. Causa 1972, pp. 942, 944, 982 n. 108. Causa in *Larousse Dictionary* 1981, p. 56. London and Washington 1982-83, p. 145. Paris 1983, p. 196. Turin 1983, p. 166.

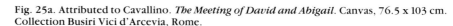

Fig. 25a. Attributed to Cavallino. *The Meeting of David and Abigail*. Canvas, 76.5 x 103 cm. Collection Busiri Vici d'Arcevia, Rome.

26

The Virgin
of the Immaculate
Conception

Canvas (oval), 67.5 x 43.5 cm.
Musée des Beaux-Arts de Caen,
France

*Exhibited in Fort Worth
and Naples only*

The subject of the Immaculate Conception must have been popular for Cavallino, judging from the number of early copies and imitations it generated. Copies of this composition, published here as an original but in Causa's opinion also a copy (in conversation, 1983), are in the Bowes Museum, Barnard Castle (Inv. no. 43), formerly with Adolph Loewi, Los Angeles (Inv. no. 47), formerly in the Sestieri collection, Rome (Inv. no. 152), and in the archbishop's house in Caserta (Inv. no. 42).[1] Another copy in storage at Capodimonte records the same figure in reverse, with slight alterations in the pose and in the arrangement of draperies. A version showing a variant pose, formerly in a private collection in Palermo but now lost (Inv. no. 153; Fig. 26b), is interesting in that one of the few surviving drawings by Cavallino is a study for it (Fig. 28; see Introduction, note 78). From an old reproduction this appears to be an original picture, not very large but of great charm. Another variant of the subject from a Neapolitan church, long considered a possible original, has after a recent cleaning been revealed to be an early copy or imitation of Cavallino (Inv. no. 46; Fig. 26a).

An interesting characteristic of these pictures is their extremely small dimensions, varying from around sixty to seventy-five centimeters high; they were obviously produced as small private devotional images. On the other hand, Cavallino may at some point have executed the subject for a public or church commission: the splendid *Immaculate Conception* belonging to the Brera [51] is of a scale that could denote a painting removed from a church. As in the case of

Fig. 26a. Copy after, or imitator of, Cavallino. *The Virgin of the Immaculate Conception*. Museo di Capodimonte (on deposit); formerly Chiesa di San Giovanni Battista delle Monache, Naples (see Inv. no. 46).

Fig. 26b. Attributed to Cavallino. *The Virgin of the Immaculate Conception*. Present location unknown; formerly private collection, Palermo (see Inv. no. 153).

Cavallino's Tobit scenes [see 24], it is puzzling that so few originals survive among such a profusion of copies and imitations.

The Caen picture is painted on coarsely woven canvas and shows repairs to the left of the Virgin's head in the upper left background and in several places on her robe. Her robe is gray, her mantle blue; the background is an opaque blue and beige over a brown ground. The painting appears to be fairly early, perhaps dating around 1640.

The subject of the immunity of the Virgin from original sin at the moment of her conception was the object of a feast in the church from at least the seventh century but did not become dogma until 1854; there were controversies over the doctrine from the eleventh century onward, and three seventeenth-century popes—Paul V (1617), Gregory V (1622), and Alexander VII (1661)—took stands on the question. The scriptural source for the image of the Virgin crowned by stars and standing on a crescent moon is from Revelation 12:1 ("And there appeared a great wonder in heaven; a woman clothed with the sun, and the moon under her feet, and upon her head a crown of twelve stars"). Two large and important depictions of the Immaculate Conception similar in arrangement to Cavallino's tiny canvas were painted by Ribera in 1635 and 1637, both apparently for the convent of Las Agustinas Descalzas in Salamanca.[2]   AP

1. The latter two known from photographs from Loewi and Capodimonte (LFSG 7552-nlx), respectively.
2. Fort Worth 1982, pp. 167-75.

Collections
Art market, Paris, 1974.

Exhibitions
Caen 1980, cat. no. 10, repr.

Literature
Gazette des Beaux-Arts ser. 6, 85 (1975): suppl., pp. 4-5, no. 16, repr. Ponnau 1976, p. 343, no. 20. Brejon de Lavergnée and Dorival 1979, p. 92. Paris 1983, p. 195.

27

A Saint Martyr (Saint Catherine of Alexandria?)

Canvas, 155 x 125 cm.
Palazzo Doria, Genoa

In catalogue only

As the picture is set into an eighteenth- or nineteenth-century stucco enframement high up on the wall of a room on the *piano nobile* of the Palazzo Doria, its quality and condition are difficult to assess. It appears to be a relatively early original, and it is apparent that only the central rectangle that encompasses the figure of the saint down to about mid-thigh was actually painted by Cavallino; the format has been considerably enlarged on all sides to fit the architectural enframement. Reducing the image to its original proportions greatly enhances its dramatic impact.

The picture is painted on coarsely woven canvas and is dark in tone. The saint wears a gray robe and a blue and red mantle, with an almost transparent, light brown veil across her chest. Red ribbons are threaded in her hair. The clarity of the shadows, the three-dimensionality of the hands, especially the one that holds the sword, and the relative complexity of the contours of drapery suggest a dating around 1640, after the earliest period of the mid- to late thirties but before the *Saint Cecilia* of 1645. The crown, palm, and sword may identify the saint as Catherine of Alexandria. Either this picture or an almost identical version was in the Enrico Frascione collection, Naples, in the early 1920s (Inv. no. 175).   AP

Exhibitions
None.

Literature
De Rinaldis 1920a, pp. 5, 6, fig. 6; 1921, p. 17, pl. xi [see Inv. no. 175]. Percy 1965, p. 48, no. 7. Zampetti 1967, pp. 13, 26 n. 10, repr. p. 53, fig. 29.

27

28

28

Saint Agatha

Canvas, 64.1 x 50.8 cm.

City Art Gallery,
York, England

In catalogue only

Painted on coarsely woven canvas, this work was apparently once on a slightly smaller stretcher, and the damages all around the edges of the very dark background are crudely filled in in places. The shadows on the face and hands are transparent brown; the saint's blouse is white, her veil pale brown, and her mantle dark blue. A trace of blood above her right breast identifies the subject as Saint Agatha, whose story is recounted in the Golden Legend: a third-century martyr from Catania, unshakable in her faith and chastity, she endured various tortures, including having her breasts torn off.[1] Again we see a combination of a Stanzionesque figure type with a Riberesque naturalism in the depiction of surfaces. The saint's face is, in fact, remarkably like that of Ribera's *Saint Jerome* in the Fogg Art Museum, Cambridge, Massachusetts, in the odd shape of the eyes, the fine brushwork used to merge eyebrows with flesh, and the half-open mouth crisply laid in against transparent shadows. Ribera's painting is dated 1640,[2] and the work by Cavallino seems near it in date, judging from the clarity of the shadows and the artist's ability to suggest the three-dimensionality of the figure's head and hands. Other versions of the subject by Cavallino are in Capodimonte [14], and The Detroit Institute of Arts [48]. AP

1. *Golden Legend* 1969, pp. 157-61.
   2. Forth Worth 1983, p. 209, no. 32, repr. p. 208.

Collections
Arcade Gallery, London, 1955; gift to the City Art Gallery by F. D. Lycett-Green, 1955.

Exhibitions
York 1955, cat. no. 136; Barnard Castle 1962, cat. no. 35.

Literature
City of York Art Gallery *Preview* 11, no. 41 (1958):400-401, repr. York 1961, p. 13, no. 853, pl. 27. Crombie 1962, pp. 396-97, fig. 3. Nicolson 1962, p. 317. New York 1962, under no. 14. Percy 1965, p. 59, no. 51. Neumann 1969, p. 41, no. 77; 1971, p. 241 n. 27. Causa 1972, p. 984 n. 116. London and Washington 1982−83, p. 135. Turin 1983, p. 158.

29

Lot
and His Daughters

Canvas, 230.5 x 183 cm.

The Toledo (Ohio) Museum of Art,
Clarence Brown Fund

This painting illustrates a well-known episode from the Old Testament (Genesis 19:30-35); Lot, the nephew of Abraham, fled Sodom with his two daughters, who reduced him to a state of drunkenness and then seduced him; Moab, founder of the Moabite race, was begotten from the incestuous union with the eldest daughter, and from that with the second daughter, Ben-ammi, the founder of the Ammonites, was born. The episode is recounted in the Scriptures to underline the common origin of the Israelites with the two neighboring populations, the Moabites and the Ammonites. The painting depicts the moment in which Lot is convinced by his daughters to drink wine; in the left background the houses of Sodom are in flames and, in the distance, the image of Lot's wife, who was reduced to a pillar of salt for having disobeyed Divine Will by turning back to look at the city, is visible.

This theme was frequently treated in the first half of the Seicento by various Neapolitan painters like Battistello Caracciolo, Massimo Stanzione, Giovanni Battista Spinelli, and Antonio de Bellis, in addition to Cavallino himself, but the paintings, or ones of similar subjects, were meant for private residences rather than churches or private chapels.

The painting exhibited here was attributed to Cavallino even before entering the collections of the Toledo Museum. However, doubts about the attribution were expressed orally by Wolfgang Prohaska and the late Raffaello Causa, who was inclined to assign it to Antonio de Bellis or Francesco Guarino. Lurie and Percy likewise reject the attribution to Cavallino. The hypothesis

29

has also been suggested that the painting may be a work from Artemisia Gentileschi's second Neapolitan period.

In the current state of knowledge, the attribution to Cavallino still remains the most convincing. More specifically, we are dealing here with one of the Neapolitan painter's very rare, extant, large-scale compositions. Its date should be placed between the end of the 1630s and the beginning of the next decade because of its apparent stylistic affinities with the manner of Artemisia Gentileschi at the time of her first Neapolitan sojourn (1629/30–38).

Cavallino's rapprochement with Gentileschi, and especially with some of her manner of rendering figures and light in her well-known compositions such as the *Esther before Ahasuerus* in the Metropolitan Museum of Art in New York and the *David and Bathsheba* in the Columbus (Ohio) Museum of Art, is primarily suggested by the specific formal qualities and application of color in the two female figures. Even if one ignores the fact that the same characteristics are also evident in various early paintings by Cavallino of both small and medium scale (for example, the Capodimonte *Soldiers Casting Lots for the Cloak of Christ* [10]), it is above all the chromatic and expressive harmony of the pictorial surface throughout the composition that confirms the validity of the attribution to the Neapolitan painter.

Undeniably by Cavallino are: the preciousness of Lot's costume, especially the velvet jacket highlighted by subtle passages of light; the capturing of intense suffering that defines the old man's features, also apparent in many of the half-figures of young saints and prophets painted by the artist; and the skillful handling of warm colors to convey through slight chiaroscuro transitions the natural features of the rocky cave that serves as the background to the scene. This last technique is also seen in other well-known early compositons by Cavallino.

The painting is in any case one of the notable testimonies to the heights that Neapolitan painting reached between the end of the fourth decade and the beginning of the next, by which time the mid-thirties crisis over traditional naturalistic values had given way to a total acceptance of a manner of rich painterly intensity. The present work also documents with

extreme clarity Cavallino's orientation in those years when, after his training had brought him into contact with the recent experiments of Ribera and the Master of the Annunciation to the Shepherds that vacillated between naturalism and pictorialism, he widened his research to other aspects of the past figurative tradition at Naples. It was the period in which he knew how to graft onto his former experiences the results of a careful study of possibilities still to be found in paintings like the great *Circumcision* painted in 1626 by Simon Vouet for Sant'Arcangelo a Segno (now at Capodimonte) or in several compositions by Artemisia, in contact with Massimo Stanzione, at the time of her first stay in Naples (from *The Birth of the Baptist* at the Prado to the first canvases for the cathedral of Pozzuoli, now in the museum of the Certosa di San Martino).

It is therefore quite probable that, as in other large-scale paintings by Cavallino, the supposed differences that are here evident with respect to his small- and medium-scale compositions—besides being aggravated by the consequences of an old, ill-advised cleaning—can be explained as the result of an even more marked dependence, in works with life-sized figures, on Stanzione and Gentileschi in particular.

That which has been discussed above is also valid, for example, for a painting securely by Cavallino's hand (even if dated at the end of the forties)—the New York *Triumph of Galatea* [68]. Galatea's facial type, which is very similar to the face of Lot's daughter on the righthand side of the Toledo canvas, goes back clearly to Gentileschian models.

Even if one did not wish to accept any evidence in the present painting that a collaboration existed between the young Cavallino and the Roman paintress—a rapport that did, in fact, exist between the latter and Massimo Stanzione on other occasions—and even if at this time such a hypothesis seems highly improbable, one might find it more broadly justified in the light of a better knowledge of Gentileschi's relationships with other painters active in Naples during her long stay there.

NS

Collections
Private collection, Switzerland; acquired by the Museum in 1983.

Technical Note

This painting of *Lot and His Daughters* exemplifies Cavallino's very individual and sensitive technique. There is a constant juxtaposition not only of lights and darks and of contrasting colors but also of varying densities of paint. Solidly, heavily painted colors—such as the white, yellow, and blue—are set off by thinly painted ones, like the salmon-pink robe across Lot's knees, and the cool pink lining of the skirt of the daughter on the left.

The thinly painted areas are very rich in medium in proportion to pigment. This overabundance of medium makes it possible to apply the paint fluidly and delicately, but it represents an inherent flaw in Cavallino's handling of oil paint that can be seen in many of his works. All oil paint, when thinly applied, tends to become somewhat translucent with the passage of time, but when the proportion of medium to pigment is exaggerated, this tendency becomes pronounced. The pigment is lost—almost drowned—in a sea of medium. The delicate paint layer, opaque when applied, turns in time into a glaze, allowing the ground—in this case a dark one—to shimmer through and darken the color. This technical malaise is also apparent in the skirt of the daughter on the left, and in the sky.

Gabrielle Kopelman, New York, NY

30 & 31

Saint Peter and Saint Paul

Canvas (octagonal), each 127 x 94 cm.
Saint Peter signed on book at right
(see below). *Saint Paul* signed on sword
blade: BERN [rest is illegible].
Trafalgar Galleries, London

This pair of half-figure apostles, first published in 1982, are the earliest signed works by Cavallino to have come to light. They are dated here to the early years of the 1640s, although Causa considered them to date somewhat earlier, around 1635. The virtuosity with which the artist captures the three-dimensional quality of the hands and faces suggests a more mature phase than the earliest single-figure saints [14, 26, 27], where hands and faces are more summarily defined in terms of muscles and skin surfaces. The heavy tenebrism, nevertheless, suggests a dating before 1645. The pictures' apparent relationship to Ribera's series of "prophets" of 1638–43 in the church of the Certosa di San Martino in Naples, and especially to the canvases of *Moses* and *Elijah* (Fig. 15) dated 1638,[1] reinforces a dating to the early forties; Nicola Spinosa has suggested (in conversation, 1983) that Cavallino's pictures may even have been conceived as a sort of *omaggio* to Ribera, possibly with the older artist's paired versions of the two saints of the early 1630s, in Madrid and New York, in mind.[2] In the isolation of the dramatically illuminated , naturalistically observed bearded male figures against simple backgrounds Cavallino's *Peter* and *Paul* are very like Ribera's *Peter* and *Paul* or *Moses* and *Elijah*, and the Trafalgar pictures once bore traditional attributions to Ribera. An emphasis on the manipulation of impasto against luminous dark shadows through virtuoso brushwork is also shared by the two painters. Yet, typically, Cavallino's approach is softer and smoother than Ribera's: he adds an element of sinuousness and delicacy to a theme that in Ribera's hands is aggressively tough and straightforward.

To find Peter and Paul conjoined in pendant canvases is in no way unusual in Roman Catholic imagery. The two saints have long been associated as apostles of special authority in the founding of the Catholic church. They share a feast day (29 June), the anniversary either of their deaths or the translation of their relics (some accounts have them martyred on the same day, and there are old traditions that their bodies were once buried together). Cavallino represented the two saints together in a single painting now in a Bolognese private collection [33]. In the London pictures Saint Peter is dressed in blue and gold and holds the keys of the kingdom of heaven (Matthew 16:19); Saint Paul, in green and red, bears the sword of his martyrdom.

Like Ribera,[3] Cavallino seems to have produced single half-figure apostles in series, although most of these are presently unlocatable and are known only through photographs (Figs. 30-31a-d).   AP

1. Pérez Sánchez and Spinosa 1978, pp. 114-15, nos. 135-48, repr.
    2. Ibid., pp. 102-3, nos. 67-68, repr.
    3. Ibid., pp. 100-1, nos. 50-60, repr.

Collections
Farnborough Abbey, Hampshire, England.

Exhibitions
London 1982, cat. nos. 22 and 23, repr.

Literature
The Burlington Magazine 124 (November 1982):xxiii. London and Washington 1982–83, p. 136, repr. p. 146. Spear 1983, p. 135. Turin 1983, pp. 158-60, 167, repr.

30

Fig. 30-31a. Cavallino (?). *Saint Paul*. Present location unknown; formerly conde de Muguiro, Madrid (see Inv. no. 176).

Fig. 30-31b. Cavallino (?). *A Praying Saint*. Present location unknown (see Inv. no. 163).

Fig. 30-31c. Cavallino (?). *Saint Bartholomew*. Present location unknown.

Fig. 30-31d. Cavallino (?). *Saint John the Evangelist*. Present location unknown.

112

31

32

Saint Simon

Canvas (oval), 99 x 86.8 cm.
I. and G. Fine Arts International,
London

According to the *Golden Legend* (p. 633), Simon, the name of the apostle and martyr, is interpreted as "one who obeys or one who bears sadness." He had two surnames—Simon Zelotes and Simon the Cananean, after Cana of Galilee. He suffered a martyr's death, but its mode has been disputed; he was either crucified or sawn in half. Cavallino portrays him with a book and a saw;[1] the teeth of the saw, which Simon touches, are brought into subtle focus at the lower right. The curved outlines of the figure fit perfectly into the oval format. Lost in thought, the saint is dressed in a golden-yellow garment described with numerous highlights that provide rich tonal variation.

In style and composition the oval is closely linked with the paintings of the apostles *Peter* [30] and *Paul* [31], although the last-named works are larger (127 x 94 cm) and octagonal in shape. In all three works each apostle is caught in a moment of deep reflection, each is depicted with pronounced chiaroscuro, and the focus in each study is on the face and hands. The treatment of drapery, rendered in voluminous broad folds, in each case stresses monumentality rather than surface realism. Percy and Spinosa [see 30-31] point to obvious reflections in these paintings of Ribera's figures of 1638–43 in the church of the Certosa di San Martino in Naples, especially those of *Moses* and *Elijah*, dating from 1638. For that reason, Percy suggests a date of the early 1640s for Cavallino's *Peter* and *Paul*, which also seems convincing for the *Saint Simon*.

A third octagonal painting of an unidentified apostle that is like the *Saint Simon* in composition and size (95 x 75 cm) appeared on the Italian art market in 1968 (see Inv. no. 163). Causa (in letter of January 5, 1984) referred to it as a "praying Saint Joseph" and believed it to be a fine original by Cavallino (Fig. 30-31b).

The fact that there are at least three other paintings of apostles that have been identified as Cavallino's works would seem to suggest that there may have existed a series of the twelve apostles.[2] Two more octagonal paintings of apostles—to our knowledge unpublished—that are believed to be by Cavallino are a *Saint Bartholomew* (Fig. 30-31c) and *Saint John the Evangelist* (Fig. 30-31d), which in 1973 were with Francesco Romano.[3]   ATL

1. Hall 1979, p. 283, states that the cult of Saint Simon was revived in the eleventh century by the Holy Roman emperor, Henry III, a patron of art and learning, to which the book Saint Simon is holding may allude.

2. One of these (Inv. no. xxx), which at the time of publication (Milicua 1954, p. 72) was in the collection of the conde de Muguiro, Madrid, is another octagonal *Saint Paul*, closely related to the canvas in London (Fig. 30-31a).

3. The existence of the Romano paintings was brought to Ann Percy's attention by Pierre Rosenberg.

Collections

Unidentified private collection; Ponce Museum, San Juan, Puerto Rico; Central Picture Galleries, New York.

Literature

Fredericksen and Zeri 1972, p. 50.

33

33

Saints Peter and Paul

Canvas, 39 x 32 cm.
Private collection, Bologna

In catalogue only

This small, private-devotional picture probably dates to the first half of the 1640s. It is damaged around the edges but withal in good condition. Saint Peter is, traditionally, in blue and dull yellow, Saint Paul in green and red. Concerning the pairing of the two saints in Cavallino's oeuvre, see [30-31].   AP

Collections
Max Bondi, Rome, by 1920, through 1938;
Ettore Viancini Antiquario, Venice, 1968.

Exhibitions
None.

Literature
Sestieri 1920, pp. 261, 267, fig. 16; 1921, p. 184.
Ortolani 1922, p. 193. Ortolani in Naples 1938,
p. 65. Percy 1965, p. 70, no. 106. *Apollo* n. s.
87 (May 1968):civ, repr.

34

The Massacre of the Innocents

Canvas, 144 x 199 cm.

Pinacoteca di Brera, Milan

In catalogue only

The painting was exhibited in Naples in 1938 as a work by Cavallino (Ortolani in Naples 1938, p. 65). According to Professor Carlo Bertelli, superintendent of the Brera (orally, 1982), it appears that it had been overcleaned before it was acquired in 1948. The overcleaning led to disturbing losses in the background and scattered blemishes over the entire surface; thus, the condition of the painting makes dating difficult.

Cavallino's pronounced chiaroscuro in the *Massacre* is typical of his early style, as is the blue and blond Gargiulesque tonality of the background, as pointed out by Percy to this author. A date shortly after 1640 was suggested in D'Ossat's announcement of the aquisition by the Galleria Brera in 1949.

The slaughter of male infants at Bethlehem (Matthew 2:1-18)—ordered by Herod the king when he learned of Jesus' birth—was an event of such dramatic intensity that it inspired representations by nearly all the great masters, from Raphael to Poussin. Its special appeal to Neapolitan painters at the time of Cavallino may have been inspired by Giovanni Battista Marino, a famous Neapolitan poet, who made it the subject of one of his poems, contrasting ''the violence of the soldiers to the impotent despair of the mothers.''[1] Massimo Stanzione's strong focus on the brutal foreground scene in his painting of ca. 1640, no doubt inspired by the two powerful examples of Nicolas Poussin (Musée Condé, Chantilly) and Guido Reni (Pinacoteca Nazionale, Bologna), is reflected in Cavallino's central two figures. The background, with mothers—one of them likely Elizabeth, with the infant Saint John[2]—fleeing up the steps, is similar to compositions of the sixteenth century, such as the drawing by Jacopo Ligozzi (Verona ca. 1547–Florence 1626) in the Woodner Collection.[3]

There are several copies of similar versions of the *Massacre* that have been attributed to Cavallino in recent years, but to date this painting is the only autograph one known. In the 1960s Causa (orally) mentioned that a copy of it was in the collection of Baronessa Felicita Romano Avezzano; efforts to trace it have been unsuccessful. Two paintings of the subject were published with Cavallino attributions, one, by Milicua in 1954 (p. 71) (see Inv. no. 137), and another, sold in 1973 at Sotheby's in London (Fig. 34a). The first of these is a frieze-like composition that reveals some convincing Cavallinesque elements but is closer to Vaccaro's *Massacre of the Innocents* (Capodimonte); its background is Spadaresque. The second painting appears to be a strange pastiche of various elements from several of Cavallino's late works (see under [79], [83]), unless it is a copy after a lost original considerably later than the Brera version.

ATL

1. Lilia Rocco (in London 1982, pp. 201-2) suggests this influence from G. B. Marino's poem in her discussion of the *Massacre of the Innocents* by Francesco de Rosa, called Pacecco, in the Philadelphia Museum of Art.

2. Elizabeth's escape into the hills with the infant Baptist is told in the Apocryphal Book of Saint James (14:2). Other paintings with the steps in the background and fleeing figures are: one attributed to Mattia Preti by Maurizio Marini (1974, frontispiece and p. 135), likely featuring the plague of 1656; and *The Massacre of the Innocents* by Alonzo Rodriguez in the Museo Regionale in Messina.

3. George R. Goldner, *Master Drawings from the Woodner Collection*, exh. cat. (Malibu, Calif.: The J. Paul Getty Museum, 1983), pp. 72-73, no. 27, repr.

Fig. 34a. Attributed to Cavallino. *The Massacre of the Innocents*. Canvas, 122 x 149 cm. Present location unknown; formerly, sale, Sotheby's, London, 11 July 1973, lot 80.

34

Collections

Perrino, Naples, until 1935; acquired by the
Museum in 1949.

Exhibitions

None.

Literature

Ortolani 1938, p. 178; in Naples 1938, p. 65,
repr. *Bollettino d'Arte* 34 (1949):192, repr.
Percy 1965, p. 50, no. 17. Modigliani in Milan
1977, p. 109, no. 969.

35

35

The Rape of Europa

Canvas, 101 x 133.7 cm.
Walker Art Gallery, Liverpool

In catalogue only

In the nineteenth century this picture bore an attribution to Francesco Romanelli; it was first identified as by Cavallino by Denis Mahon in 1954 (in correspondence; see also Liverpool 1977). It survives in rather poor condition, with particular damages to the left edge and to the figural group at the left. The sky is heavily repainted, and there are numerous losses on all the figures. Europa's face is perhaps the best preserved portion. The tonality of the picture is dark, with yellow-gold, purplish-pink, blue, dark green, and gray accents. It can be dated to the early 1640s. The subject is from Ovid's *Metamorphoses*:

> . . . Jove
> Put down his heavy sceptre: the great
>   father,
> Great ruler of the gods, whose right
>   hand wields
> Triple-forked lightning, and whose
>   awful nod
> Makes the world tremble, put aside his
>   might
> His majesty, and took upon himself
> The form of a bull, went lowing with
>   the heifers
> Over the tender grass, showy and
>   handsome,
> The color of snow, which never a foot
>   has trodden,
> Never a raindrop sullied. The great
>   muscles
> Bulged on the neck, the dewlaps hung
>   to the chest,
> The horns were small, but every bit as
>   perfect
> As if a sculptor made them, and as
>   shining
> As any jewel, and the eyes and fore-
>   head
> Offered no threat, and the great gaze
>   was peaceful.
> And the king's daughter looked at him
>   in wonder,
> So calm, so beautiful, and feared to
>   touch him,
> At first, however mild, and little by
>   little
> Got over her fear, and soon was bring-
>   ing flowers
> To hold toward that white face, and he,
>   the lover,
> Gave kisses to the hands held out,
>   rejoicing
> In hope of later, more exciting kisses.[1]

Another, somewhat later, version is in Kansas City [36]. De Dominici records a painting of the subject in the Caputi collection, Naples, but it seems to have been smaller and vertical in format (Appendix, no. 10).   AP

1. Ovid, *Metamorphoses*, trans. Rolfe Humphries (Bloomington: Indiana University Press, 1961), p. 55.

Collections
Alexander Nowell, Underley Park, Westmorland; sale, Winstanley's, Liverpool, 12 July 1842; T. A. Hope; gift to the Gallery in 1882.

Exhibitions
Liverpool 1955, cat. no. 28, pl. VII; Barnard Castle 1962, cat. no. 34.

Literature
Liverpool 1885, no. 288, p. 63. Causa 1957, p. 42. Nicolson 1962, p. 317. Percy 1965, p. 49, no. 12. Causa 1972, p. 944. Liverpool 1977, 1:42, and 2:pl. 47. Ferrari in *Dizionario biografico* 22 (1979):788. Causa in *Larousse Dictionary* 1981, p. 56.

36

36

The Abduction of Europa

Canvas, 61 x 81.7 cm.
Nelson Gallery–Atkins Museum of Art
Kansas City

Published in de Rinaldis's 1909 monograph as in the Romano collection, Naples, this painting is unusual in that only the central figural group—Europa, attendants, and bull—appears to be by Cavallino's hand. The landscape background, and especially the two small figures at left, are by another artist, suggesting perhaps that Cavallino finished only the major figures or that the canvas was badly damaged to the point of having the background entirely repainted. X radiographs show the presence of a second attendant with bent head and upraised arm between Europa and the attendant at the right. This addition appears surely to be autograph, although more summarily rendered than the central group.

The figures share a luminous quality in the depiction of flesh with numbers 37-42 of the present catalogue, pictures that are datable to the first half of the 1640s, probably nearer 1645 than 1640. The very dark shadows of the early tenebrist works have here become lighter and more transparent. The tonality is generally dark, with the red-brown ground of the preparation often evident. Europa wears a dull green skirt and a blue drapery, her attendant dark green.

Cavallino depicted the subject in a canvas in Liverpool [35], perhaps datable slightly earlier than this version. AP

Collections

Salvatore Romano, Florence and Naples, by 1909; acquired by the Museum in 1931, as *The Rape of Europa.*

Exhibitions

San Francisco 1941, cat. no. 20, repr.; New York 1946, cat. no. 5; Seattle 1954; Sarasota 1961, cat. no. 28, repr.

Literature

De Rinaldis 1909, p. 16, cat. no. 5. Hermanin 1911, p. 185, pl. 41, fig. 3. Hermanin in Thieme-Becker 6 (1912):225. De Rinaldis 1917, p. 179; 1920a, pp. 3-4 n. 2, 6; 1921, p. 17. Sestieri 1921, p. 184. Corna 1930, 1:227. Refice 1951, p. 262. Juynboll 1960, p. 86. Ferrari 1961–62, pp. 236, 238 n. 28. Percy 1965, p. 48, no. 10. Causa 1972, p. 983 n. 111. Fredericksen and Zeri 1972, p. 50. Minicuci in *Dizionario enciclopedico Bolaffi* 3 (1972):207. Ferrari in *Dizionario biografico* 22 (1979):788.

37

The Dream
of Saint Joseph
with the Virgin
and Child Asleep

Canvas, 102 x 75 cm.
Muzeum Narodowe, Warsaw

Acquired by the Museum in 1937, the painting was formerly attributed to the Cavaliere d'Arpino. It must have been highly regarded, as we know of at least two early copies (Inv. nos. 31, 133).

Complex and sophisticated in composition, the Warsaw picture presumably dates to the first half of the 1640s, not long before the *Saint Cecilia* of 1645 [44]. The sleeping Joseph is a shadowy, silhouetted form in the left foreground, a bit of his neck and the angel behind him dramatically illuminated against the dark red-brown ground. In the right middleground the Virgin wears a red dress, and the Christ Child is on gray-white bedding under a dark blue drapery. These accents of red, blue, gray white, and flesh tones relate to the limited palette of Cavallino's early works, but the virtuosity with which the figures are depicted and the luminous shadows denote his more mature style, although the fluid quality of his post-1645 manner is not yet apparent here. Also well advanced are the extremely beautiful and lyrical contours of the angel's fluttering drapery and gesticulating arms, of Joseph's seated form, of the curtain that is draped above the Virgin and Child, and of the brightly illuminated central group of figures. At his maturity Cavallino was a master of subtly interrelated contours, and this work shows a highly sophisticated handling of the connections between the figures.

So far as we know, this is Cavallino's only depiction of the angel appearing to Joseph in a dream, warning him to flee to Egypt to avoid Herod's massacre of the innocents in Bethlehem (Matthew 2:13-21).

AP

Collections
Gift of Bishop A. Jełowicki, 1937.

Exhibitions
Warsaw 1901, cat. no. 18; Lublin 1921, cat. no. 22; Warsaw 1956, cat. no. 22, repr. Bordeaux 1959, cat. no. 57.

Literature
Warsaw 1938, cat. no. 16, fig. 9. *Emporium* 124 (1956):repr. p. 237. Białostocki and Walicki 1957, p. 511, pl. 179. *The Burlington Magazine* 104 (June 1962), suppl. 1, text under pl. IV. Percy 1965, p. 59, no. 50. Zampetti 1967, pp. 14, 55, fig. 31. Causa 1972, p. 983 n. 111; in *Larousse Dictionary* 1981, p. 56. Warsaw [n. d.], cat. no. 204.

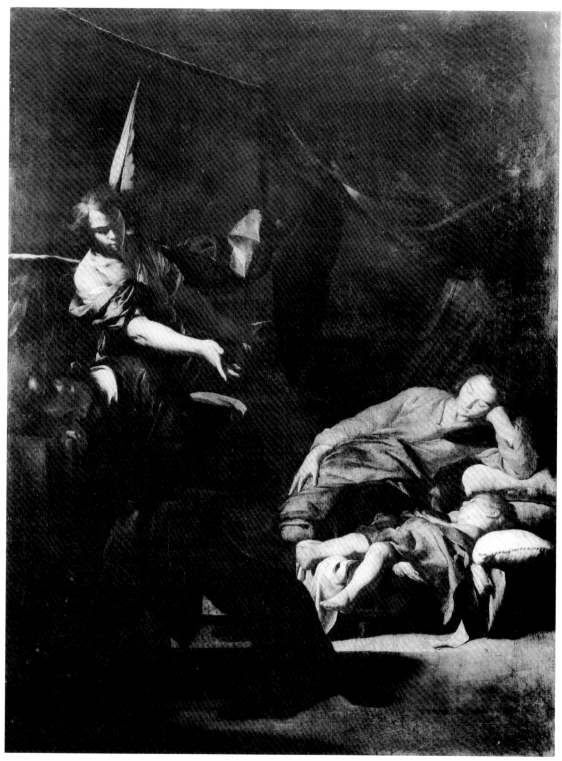

37

38

Lot
and His Daughters

Canvas (oval), 101 x 76 cm.
Musée du Louvre, Paris

*Exhibited in Fort Worth
and Naples only*

Old photographs show that the composition was originally extended to a rectangular shape. Nevertheless, there seems no reason to doubt that this canvas and the Gosford *Drunkenness of Noah* [39] are pendants, although the Paris picture is first recorded as passing through the London sale rooms in the late 1960s, and the Gosford picture was in Scotland before 1914. The two paintings share the same restricted palette of greens, grays, dull oranges, and blue played against a warm, dark, red-brown ground. Riberesque naturalism and emphasized tenebrist contrasts are still dominant in Cavallino's style, but the high-pitched sensuality of the two scenes is peculiarly his own.

De Dominici refers to a pair of oval scenes of *Lot Fleeing Sodom* and *Lot and His Daughters* by Cavallino, of about the same size, sold to Germany, whether in Cavallino's time or his own is not clear.[1] Despite the difference in subject between *Lot Fleeing Sodom* and this picture's pendant, *The Drunkenness of Noah* [39], it is tempting to identify the pair with de Dominici's mention.   AP

1. "In Alemagna due ovati, quasi della medesima misura [4 *palmi*; ca. 106 cm.], ma per alto, ed in uno era Lot, che fugge dalla Città di Sodoma con le figliuole, e la moglie, cambiata in statua di Sale, e nell'altro lo stesso Lot ubbriaco in mezzo alle figliuole suddette" (de Dominici 1742–43, 3:37). It is interesting, if perhaps irrelevant, to note that a "Lot and His Daughters, an upright oval" was sold as Ribera ("Spagnoletto") at Christie's in April 1799, lot 84, from Sir William Chambers's estate (John Harris, *Sir William Chambers; Knight of the Polar Star* [University Park and London: Pennsylvania State University Press, 1970], p. 184).

Collections

Sale, Christie's, London, 21 April 1967, lot 33, repr.; Julius Weitzner, London; Othon Kaufmann and François Schlageter, Strasbourg, 1967; gift to the Museum in 1983.

Exhibitions

London and Washington 1982–83, cat. no. 26, repr.; Paris 1983, cat. no. 12, repr.; Turin 1983, cat. no. 26, repr.; Paris 1984, cat. no. 28, repr.

Literature

De Dominici 1742–43, 3:37(?). Rosenberg 1972, pp. 343, 345 n. 3, fig. 10. Brejon de Lavergnée and Dorival 1979, p. 92, color pl. on reverse. *La Revue du Louvre et des Musées de France* no. 5-6 (1983):446. Paris 1984, pp. 20, 88.

38

39

The Drunkenness
of Noah

Canvas (oval), 103.5 x 78.7 cm.
The Earl of Wemyss and March, K. T.,
Gosford House,
Longniddry, Scotland

Presumably a pendant to [38], this painting was attributed to Velázquez in Gosford House inventories of 1914 and 1948; the attribution to Cavallino was made by Ellis Waterhouse (orally).[1] It is tempting to identify the two pictures with de Dominici's mention of a pair of ovals about a meter high of *Lot Fleeing Sodom* and *Lot and His Daughters* exported to Germany, although the former subject differs from that of the present canvas (see [38]). Nicola Spinosa's dating of these works to a couple of years before the 1645 *Saint Cecilia* seems perfectly correct (in London and Washington 1982–83). They share a lightening of the intense chiaroscuro contrasts of the earlier pictures toward more transparent shadows on flesh with numbers 37, 38, 40-42 of the present catalogue. Cavallino's special *poesia* in the lyrical play and interrelation of contours of limbs and draperies within his compositions, dramatized by his manipulation of light and shade, is evident in these canvases. One is constantly aware of the artist's masterful ability to depict the human figure. All of these qualities are carried to a graceful and striking conclusion in the remarkable later pendant versions of the subjects [74-75], where the sensual side of Cavallino's personality triumphs in his pure pleasure in the handling of paint and color harmonies.

The drunkenness of Noah, who was covered in his nakedness by his sons Shem and Japheth, is described in Genesis 9:20-23; Lot's seduction by his two daughters is told in Genesis 19:30-35.   AP

1. Information courtesy of the Earl of Wemyss and March.

Collections
Probably bought by the 10th Earl of Wemyss (1818–1914).

Exhibitions
Edinburgh 1957, cat. no. 19.

Literature
Carritt 1957, p. 343, fig. 16. Percy 1965, p. 48, no. 8. Causa 1972, pp. 942, 982 n. 108. Brejon de Lavergnée and Dorival 1979, p. 92. London and Washington 1982–83, p. 139. Paris 1983, pp. 183, 191. Turin 1983, pp. 158, 162. Paris 1984, p. 88, repr.

39

40

40

Christ
and the Adulteress

Canvas, 92 x 127 cm.
Museo di Capodimonte, Naples
(Banco di Napoli)

This picture, painted on coarsely woven canvas, is particularly difficult to date because it has suffered a good deal of wear. Spinosa (in conversation, 1983) places it in the latter half of the 1640s; here a dating of a few years earlier is suggested. Although the leftmost figure is barely legible, it may be one of the self-portraits the artist inserted periodically into his compositions throughout his career [see also 3, 11, 20, 41, 53, 59, 84].

It is very possible that this is the canvas mentioned by de Dominici as in the Francesco Valletta collection in Naples; the dimensions and composition are very close to de Dominici's description:

One sees in another [painting in the Valletta collection] of four *palmi* and five across [ca. 106 x 132 cm] the woman taken in adultery brought before Christ, who is seen stooping down to write on the ground the words noted in John 8:[1-8]. Christ is in the center, and the light diffuses itself all over his figure and on the ground where he bends down, passing as if by accident over the adulteress and those who hold her bound, so that it terminates in Christ; the apostles therefore stay behind him with little illumination and partly in dramatically contrasting light and shadow; from whence the painting derives a great decorum.[1]

AP

1. ''Vedesi in un altro [painting in the Valletta collection] di palmi quattro, e cinque per traverso la Donna adultera, presentata dinanzi al Cospetto del Salvatore, il quale si vede chinato a scrivere sul terreno le parole notate nel Cap. 8 del Vangelo di S. Giovanni: E situato il Cristo nel mezzo, ed il lume si diffonde tutto sopra la sua figura, e sopra il terreno dove ella posa, passando accidentalmente sopra la Donna, e sopra quei che la tengon ligata, sicchè viene a terminare nel Cristo; restano perciò gli Appostoli dietro a lui con poco lume, e parte sbattimentati; onde viene un gran decoro alla pittura'' (de Dominici 1742–43, 3:38).

Collections

Possibly Francesco Valletta, Naples, by 1743; Paolo Wenner, Naples, by 1921, through 1930.

Exhibitions

Florence 1922, cat. no. 261.

Literature

De Dominici 1742–43, 3:38. De Rinaldis 1921, p. 16, pl. xxv. Ortolani 1922, pp. 194, 198. Consoli Fiego 1922, pp. 107, 109, repr. [Ceci] 1923, p. 24. De Rinaldis 1929, pl. 46. Nugent 1925–30, 2:569-70, repr. Ortolani in Naples 1938, p. 66. Masciotta 1942, p. 147. Molajoli 1948, pp. 103-4. Commodo Izzo 1951, p. 172, no. 67. Montini 1952, p. 35. Molajoli in Naples 1953, pp. 27, 45, pls. 45, 46. Chiarelli 1954, pp. 220-21, repr. Milicua 1954, p. 72. Molajoli in Naples 1961, p. 53, pl. xlix; in Naples 1964, p. 59, fig. 77. Percy 1965, p. 54, no. 32. De Filippis 1970, pl. 18. Lehmann in Kassel 1980, p. 88.

41

41

The Procession to Calvary (Via Dolorosa)

Canvas, 101.6 x 132.1 cm.
The Chrysler Museum, Norfolk, Virginia,
Gift of Walter P. Chrysler, Jr.

Although the attribution of this picture to Cavallino has been rejected in the past (Enggass 1961; Ferrari 1961–62), it seems indubitably to be a work from his hand. In fact, one of the eight so-called self-portraits appears in the painting—the head of a dark-haired youth just to the left of the shorter arm of the cross, toward whom the old man on a horse (further left) appears to point.

The possibility that Cavallino portrayed his own head in some cases and full figure in others in a number of pictures that span his entire career is worth suggesting: in six of the eight cases the figure is in virtually the same position, standing with his right side in profile to the viewer, usually with his right elbow akimbo and his hand resting on the back of his hip, his head turned in three-quarters view. This elegant and mannered pose recurs from very early works like the Naples *Saint Bartholomew* [3] to very late ones like the Fort Worth *Mucius Scaevola before King Porsenna* [84]; the self-conscious, mannered stance and the figure's direct eye contact with the viewer in each case distinguish him from other protagonists in the scene. This same individual appears as well in the Naples *Return of the Prodigal Son* [11] and *Christ and the Adulteress* [40]—although the lower part of the face is blocked out by another figure in the former picture—in the London *David before Saul* [20], the Norfolk picture, and *Mattathias Slaying the Officer of King Antiochus* [59]. The same person appears to be portrayed in a different pose, three-quarters frontal, in the Rome *Saint Peter and the Centurion Cornelius* [53]. In numbers 3 and 84 he wears elaborate hats, and in all but 3, 11, and perhaps 40, he has a mustache. In 3 and 11 his hair is about chin length; in 20, 41, 53, 59, and 84 it falls to his shoulders. The face perceptibly ages: in the *Saint Bartholomew* [3] it is the smooth visage of a youth around twenty; in the *Mucius Scaevola* [84], the tense and puckered features of a man in his late thirties.

The tonality of *The Procession to Calvary* is much brighter and more opaque than the London *Christ Driving the Merchants* [42], although a dating of around 1645 may be suggested for both pictures. (Concerning the slight possibility that they may be pendants, see number 42.) One wonders whether the opaque impastoed figures in the upper right background of this picture reflect the influence of Giovanni Benedetto Castiglione's pic-tures, in which much smaller background figures are often opaquely rendered in pale greens, grays, and beiges in contrast to larger, more richly colored foreground ones. Castiglione is recorded in Naples for a stay of undetermined length in 1635.   AP

Collections
A. H. Kleiweg de Zwan, Amsterdam; Newhouse Galleries, New York, NY, 1957; Walter P. Chrysler, Jr.

Exhibitions
Provincetown 1958, cat. no. 54; Sarasota 1961, cat. no. 26; Fort Worth 1962; Austin 1963, cat. p. 37; Norfolk 1967–68, cat no. 41.

Literature
Chamberlain 1956, p. 46. Enggass 1961, p. 200 n. 3. Ferrari 1961-62, pp. 237-38, no. 26. Percy 1965, p. 62, no. 73. Minicuci in *Dizionario enciclopedico Bolaffi* 3 (1972):207. Zafran 1978, p. 246, fig. 6. Norfolk 1982, p. 31, repr.

42

42

Christ Driving the Merchants from the Temple

Canvas, 101 x 128 cm.
The National Gallery, London

In catalogue only

The tonality of this picture is very dark: Christ is dressed in mauve and blue; other figures wear dull red, orange, gray brown, dark green, blue, and gray white. The ground is a warm red-brown. Some damaged areas are apparent: for example, on Christ's upraised right arm, at the far left on the upraised arm and sleeve of the fleeing woman, on the seated *repoussoir* figure at left, and to the eye of the old man in profile at right.

The picture probably dates not far from the 1645 *Saint Cecilia*. The means of illumination is complex, with dark, silhouetted *repoussoir* figures in the foreground and with the light falling from the left across the central figures, picking out others in the distant background. Caravaggesque contrasts of light and shadow are enlivened, diffused, and transformed into a dramatic use of chiaroscuro that is more complex and fragmented than Caravaggio's and entirely personal to Cavallino's own mode of expression. Here again it is easy to see why Cavallino's compositions are often compared to theatrical scenes: the architectural elements that serve as the background function almost like stage sets, and the positioning of figures resembles a dramatically arranged *tableau vivant*.

It is tempting to speculate that this work may have been a pendant to the Chrysler Museum's *Procession to Calvary* [41], as the two canvases are almost exactly the same size, and in each case *repoussoir* figures at right and left lead diagonally inward to the main action, which is developed through dramatically swirling elements focusing on a center that in this picture is empty space and in the other is filled with the main protagonist, Christ. Cavallino pairs empty with action-filled centers in other pendant compositions [38-39, 74-75, 77-78, 80-81]. However, the difference in tonality—the London picture darker, the Norfolk picture blonder—makes it difficult to say securely that these works are companion pieces.

AP

Collections

Ettore Sestieri, Rome, by 1921; gift of Count Alessandro Contini-Bonacossi to the Gallery, 1935.

Exhibitions

Florence 1922, cat. no. 256; London 1950–51, cat. no. 317.

Literature

Sestieri 1921, pp. 185, 187-88, 190, repr. Ortolani 1922, p. 194. Ojetti, Dami, and Tarchiani 1924, pl. 83. Nugent 1925–30, 2:557-58, repr. Pevsner in Pevsner and Grautoff 1928, p. 186. Delogu 1931, p. 44, repr. C.K.J. 1935, p. 370. Note in *Pantheon* 16 (July-December 1935):319, repr. London 1937, repr. p. 95. Ortolani in Naples 1938, p. 65. Masciotta 1942, p. 147. Nebbia 1946, pls. 77-78 (details). Pigler 1956, 1:327-28. London 1958, p. 39, no. 4778. Juynboll 1960, pp. 85, 88, fig. 3. Zampetti 1960, p. 57. *Kindlers Malerei Lexikon* 1 (1964), unpaginated. Percy 1965, p. 49, no. 14. Levey in London 1971, pp. 84-85, no. 4778. Minicuci in *Dizionario enciclopedico Bolaffi* 3 (1972):208, fig. 187. Causa 1972, p. 943. London 1973a, p. 112, no. 4778. Ferrari in *Dizionario biografico* 22 (1979):787.

43

Saint Cecilia
in Ecstasy

Canvas, 61 x 48 cm.
Museo di Capodimonte, Naples

This picture and the altarpiece for which it apparently served as *modello* [44] are Cavallino's best known paintings, as well as being the only works for which we can trace a more or less continuous history from the seventeenth century onward.[1] The artist's work on a small scale has consistently been regarded more highly than his larger compositions, and Cavallino's first critic, de Dominici, held this exquisite *modello* in greater esteem than he did the full-scale altarpiece. Painted on coarsely woven canvas, it has suffered minor losses, especially around the edges and in an area between the extended hands of the saint, but is essentially in good condition. The background is rendered in tones of gray over a warm red-brown ground, with a dark green curtain. The angel with the floral crown wears gray and the saint a yellow-gold blouse with white slashed sleeves and a blue brocade mantle trimmed with gold.

Between the execution of the *modello* and that of the finished altarpiece, Cavallino slightly shifted the position of the music-making angel in the background and changed the angle of its head; by altering the position of Cecilia's head he gave her a more earthbound, less ethereal quality, and the angel bearing the crown likewise becomes a more static and heavier being through a change of pose. If a certain quality of weightless grace and rapt emotional interchange of glances was lost between the *modello* and the altarpiece, the lack is redeemed by the dramatic light that breaks over the face of the saint and the uplifted arm of the angel in the finished work. By 1645 we can see that Cavallino's handling of paint is beginning to take on the more fluid, thinly painted, somewhat impressionistic quality of his late works.

According to the *Golden Legend*, Saint Cecilia, a second- or third-century Roman martyr and the patroness of church music, was crowned by an angel with an unfading garland of lilies and roses.[2]   AP

1. This picture is apparently first noted by de Dominici, whereas the larger altarpiece is mentioned by Celano in 1692. The Naples picture is listed in Capodimonte manuscript inventories of about 1870 (Salazar) and 1930 (Quintavalle; information courtesy of Pierluigi Leone de Castris, Museo di Capodimonte).
   2. *Golden Legend* 1969, p. 691.

Collections
Chiesa di Sant'Antonio da Padova, Naples (sacristy); Domenico Barbaia, Naples; purchased by the Museo Reale Borbonico in 1841.

Exhibitions
Florence 1922, cat. no. 251, pl. 30; Paris 1935, no. 101; Naples 1938; San Francisco 1939, no. 25, repr.; New York 1940, no. 25, repr.; São Paulo 1954, cat. no. 31; New York 1967b, cat. no. 20.

Literature
Celano [1692] 1970, 3:1839; de Dominici 1742–43, 3:36. Giannone [1773] 1941, p. 107. Catalani 1845–53, 2:12 n. 1. Quaranta in Naples 1846, p. 238, no. 159. Nobile 1855–57, 1:631, no. 155. Dalbono 1871, pp. 108-9; 1876, p. 471. Naples 1877, p. 133. Filiangieri di Candida 1902, p. 254. De Rinaldis 1909, p. 23, cat. no. 8. Rolfs 1910, p. 277 and n. 2. De Rinaldis 1911, pp. 415-16, no. 393, pl. XLVII. Hermanin in Thieme-Becker 6 (1912): 225. De Rinaldis 1917, p. 183; 1920b, p. 46; 1921, p. 16, pl. XII. Sestieri 1921, pp. 193-94, 196, 198, detail repr. Ortolani 1922, pp. 191, 193-94. [Ceci] 1923, pp. 24-25, repr. Ojetti, Dami, and Tarchiani 1924, pl. 85. Benesch 1926, p. 250. De Rinaldis 1927, pp. 59-61, no. 285, pl. 51; in Naples 1928, pp. 59-61, cat. no. 285, pl. 51; 1929, pp. 32, 42, pl. 41. Corna 1930, 1:227. Costantini 1930, 1:255. Nugent 1935–30, 2:573, 575-76, repr. Delogu 1931, pl. 43. Mâle 1932, p. 189, fig. 99. Quintavalle in Naples 1932, p. 22, no. 285, pl. 55. Rome 1932, repr. opp. p. 325. McComb 1934, p. 51, fig. 48. Ortolani in Naples 1938, pp. 32, 65. Serra 1937–38, p. 527. Quintavalle in Naples 1940, pp. 15, 23, no. 285, repr. Salinger 1943, p. 298. Nebbia 1946, pl. 80. Camesaca and Galetti 1951, 1:617. Montini 1952, p. 35. Golzio 1955, 1:541-42. L. Venturi 1956–57, 3:repr. p. 41. Molajoli in Naples 1958, pp. 56, 58, repr. Betti 1960, p. 17. Juynboll 1960, p. 86. Zampetti 1960, p. 56, pl. 34. Molajoli in Naples 1961, p. 51, pl. L; in Naples 1964, p. 54, fig. 79. *Kindlers Malerei Lexikon* 1 (1964), unpaginated. Percy 1965, p. 52, no. 26. Moir 1967, 1:175 n. 74, 176, 306-7, and 2:66, fig. 222. De Filippis 1970, pl. V. Minicuci in *Dizionario enciclopedico Bolaffi* 3 (1972):207. Causa in Naples 1975, p. 256. Brejon de Lavergnée and Dorival 1979, p. 92. Ferrari in *Dizionario biografico* 22 (1979):788. London and Washington 1982–83, pp. 140-42. Paris 1983, pp. 191-93. Turin, Paris, pp. 162-63.

43

44

Saint Cecilia
in Ecstasy

Canvas, 183 x 129 cm,
signed and dated on binding
of book (lower right):
BC no. P. 1645
Palazzo Vecchio, Florence

First mentioned in the Neapolitan literature on Cavallino by Celano (1692) as in the church of Sant'Antonio da Padova, this painting has had a rather lively subsequent history. Sometime between 1788 and 1845 it was removed from the church, possibly during the Napoleonic suppression of Neapolitan churches, convents, and monasteries, which led to the taking of numerous pictures from ecclesiastical institutions in the years 1809–14.[1] By 1847 it was in the collection of the marchese di Sant'Angelo, and at some point during the first decades of the twentieth century it entered an important Neapolitan collection, that of Paolo Wenner, through which a number of other paintings by Cavallino also passed. In March of 1941 it was sold to Germany but was recovered by the Italian government in November of 1948. Subsequently it was placed on deposit in the Palazzo Vecchio, Florence. It has appeared in many exhibitions since the important show of Neapolitan art of 1877 and is the best known of all Cavallino's works, besides being the only one to bear a date.

The Franciscan church and convent of Sant'Antonio da Padova, often called Sant'Antoniello delle Monache, was founded in 1565 under the auspices of a certain Sister Paola Cappellana (or Cappella) of Naples.[2] Although the church itself is no longer in use and was never a major feature in Naples's constellation of superb baroque churches—Cavallino's painting is the one internal decoration consistently mentioned by the seventeenth- and eighteenth-century guidebooks—its location in the city embraces a range of local history from antiquity to the present: situated just above the seventeenth-century Port'Alba (redone in the late eighteenth century and today a lively *allée* lined with student bookstores that gives access to the old quarter of Naples from the present-day via Roma), it adjoins the medieval fabric of the palace of the principi di Conca, purchased by the nuns of the convent in 1637, and today faces recently discovered remnants of the ancient Greek walls of the city.[3] The church's archives, if indeed they exist for the 1640s, have never been examined in the hope of further substantiating the date of Cavallino's painting.

As Cavallino's single identifiable public commission and his only known dated work, standing at the midpoint of his career—he was twenty-nine—this picture has obviously carried considerable weight in the critical history of the artist's oeuvre. Here we see his style at its full maturity. The solid dark backgrounds of the early works have been replaced by complex layers of light and shadow rendered in opaque tones of gray and beige. The saint wears a yellowish-gold dress with a brown veil and blue mantle; the angel, a dull grayish-green with a blue sash. The palette is restricted to grayish beiges, dull green, gray, blue, yellow, and dull red; but it has a cooler and more opaque quality than that of the early works, with their strong reds, blues, and grayish whites against a dominant dark ground. Here the heavy dark shadows of the earlier paintings are replaced by more transparent ones, and whereas the foreground figures are still executed with a rather tight handling of paint, the background ones show a loosening and fluidity of touch that will be developed to a greater degree in the artist's late pictures. The foreground figures are solid, fleshly beings—logical extensions of the naturalistic tradition that was fundamental to Cavallino's work from its beginnings; the sketchier brushwork on the angel at left begins to render its form vibrantly insubstantial, in an adumbration of the treatment of similar background figures in the artist's late pictures [62, 63, 79, 84].   AP

1. For an idea of the circumstances of the removal of well-known paintings from Neapolitan churches and monasteries, see Strazzullo 1962–63. Cavallino's picture was listed as *in situ* in the church by Sigismondo in his guide of 1788–89; it was removed sometime before 1845, when Catalani (1845–53) listed it as no longer in the church; shortly thereafter it was in the marchese di Sant'Angelo's collection (d'Aloë 1847). Galanti 1792, p. 123, mentions the church but does not describe its contents, so one cannot assume that the painting was not there at the time.
2. Caracciolo 1623, p. 222.
3. On the present-day exterior aspect of the church, see Pane 1962–63, pp. 204-8.

Collections

Chiesa di Sant'Antonio da Padova, Naples; marchese di Sant'Angelo, Naples, by 1847; Paolo Wenner, Naples, by 1921; Pericle Roseo, Rome; exported to Germany in 1941; returned to Italy in 1948.

Exhibitions

Naples 1877, cat. no. 120; Florence 1922, cat. no. 263; Rome 1950b, cat. no. 16; Florence 1952, cat. no. 28; Paris 1965, cat. no. 46, repr.; Bucharest 1972, cat. no. 40; Naples 1972, cat. no. 40; London and Washington 1982–83, cat. no. 28, repr.; Paris 1983 cat. no. 13, repr.; Turin 1983, cat. no. 28, repr.

Literature

Celano 1692, 1:26; [1692] 1970, 2:676-77, 747. Parrino 1700, 1:199; 1714, p. 156. Celano 1724, 1:22. De Dominici 1742–43, 3:36. Orlandi 1753, p. 102. Giannone [1773] 1941, p. 107. Sigismondo 1788–89, 1:233. Catalani 1845–53, 2:12 n. 1. D'Aloë 1847, p. 321. Nobile 1855–57, 2:805. Celano 1856–60, 3:47. Polizzi 1872, p. 235. Dalbono 1876, p. 133; 1878, p. 47. De Rinaldis 1909, p. 23, under cat. no. 8; 1911, 2:416; 1920a, p. 6; 1920b, p. 46. Sestieri 1920, pp. 253, 264, 268-69. Musto 1920, p. 180. De Rinaldis 1921, pp. 8, 16, pl. XIII. Sestieri 1921, pp. 184, 188. Ortolani 1922, pp. 191, 194, repr. [Ceci] 1923, pp. 24-25, repr. Nugent 1925–30, 2:573-74, repr. p. 575. Benesch 1926, p. 250. De Rinaldis in Naples 1927, p. 59. Pevsner in Pevsner and Grautoff 1928, pp. 184-85. De Rinaldis in Naples 1928, pp. 60, 431 Costantini 1930, 1:255. McComb 1934, pp. 50-51. C.K.J. 1935, p. 370. Carli 1938, p. 269. Ortolani in Naples 1938, p. 61. Masciotta 1942, p. 147. Salinger 1943, p. 298. Siviero in Rome 1950b, p. 36, pls. CXXXV-CXLI. Camesaca and Galetti 1951, 1:615-16. Montini 1952, p. 35. Milicua 1954, pp. 68-71. Naples 1954b, p. 23. Causa 1957, p. 42. Réau 1955–59, 3:281. Juynboll 1960, pp. 86, 88 n. 6, fig. 4. Percy 1965, pp. 46-47, no. 5. Milan 1967, under no. 31. Moir 1967, 1:175-77, 179, 307, and 2:66, fig. 221. New York 1967b, pp. 28-29. Liebmann 1968, pp. 456, 459. Rosenberg 1968, p. 151 n. 5. Lurie 1969, pp. 136-37, 142-43, fig. 1. *McGraw-Hill Dictionary of Art* 1969, 1:523. Neumann 1969, p. 32 n. 81. Neumann 1971, pp. 239, 241 n. 30. Pée 1971, p. 120 under no. 43, fig. 299. Causa 1972, pp. 942-44. Minicuci in *Dizionario enciclopedico Bolaffi* 3 (1972):207. Ferrari in *Dizionario biografico* 22 (1979):788. Causa in *Larousse Dictionary* 1981, p. 56. Budapest 1981, p. 388. Paris 1984, p. 88.

44

45

45

Judith
with the Head
of Holofernes

Canvas, 101 x 127.5 cm.
Museo di Capodimonte, Naples

Exhibited in Naples only

This picture, executed on coarsely woven canvas, is in extremely poor condition. Except for the figure of Judith, which is similar in its delicate use of impasto and in its transparent shadows to that of Saint Cecilia in the 1645 altarpiece [44], the images have been reduced to a sort of transparent brown underpaint over a background that appears virtually black. Judith, in a blue skirt, white blouse, and gold sandals and with a delicate red ribbon in her hair, appears in her swaying stance and high-waisted, small-headed proportions especially to reflect the influence of Mannerist prints on Cavallino. In particular, one might compare Jacob Matham's *Judith*, from *Old Testament Heroes* after Goltzius (Fig. 18).

The picture is probably near in date to the Florence *Saint Cecilia*.

The Book of Judith is found in the Apocrypha and describes how the Israelite Judith deceived and beheaded the Assyrian general Holofernes, thus delivering her people from capture by the Assyrian army. Cavallino treated the subject twice more, in paintings in London [46] and Stockholm [82]. Along with the subjects of Esther and David, it seems to be one of his favorite themes, perhaps because it allowed him to indulge his highly developed sense of drama in a guise of great refinement and elegance.

This is possibly the picture described by de Dominici as in the collection of the marchese di Grazia at the time of his writing: "In the same house of the above-mentioned marchese one sees also a Judith, who having cut off Holofernes' head, hands it to her old servant . . . ."[1] The dimensions of the Capodimonte picture are close to de Dominici's four by five *palmi* (ca. 106 x 132 cm), and the composition fits the brief description. Although the painting's later ownership is unclear, it seems to have been in the Museum's collection by the latter part of the nineteenth century, as it was included in Capodimonte manuscript inventories of about 1870 (Salazar) and 1930 (Quintavalle).[2]   AP

1. "Nella medesima casa del sopradetto Marchese [di Grazia] vedesi ancora una Giuditta, che avendo reciso il Capo ad Oloferne, lo porge alla vecchia sua serva, e questo quadro è della misura di quattro, e cinque palmi per traverso" (de Dominici 1742–43, 3:39).
2. Information courtesy of Pierluigi Leone de Castris, Museo di Capodimonte.

Collections

Marchese di Grazia (?), Naples; marchese del Vasto; d'Avalos; Museo Reale Borbonico.

Exhibitions

Florence 1922, cat. no. 250.

Literature

De Dominici 1742–43, 3:39. Giannone [1773] 1941, p. 108. De Rinaldis 1909, p. 21, cat. no. 7. Rolfs 1910, p. 277. De Rinaldis 1911, p. 415, no. 392. Hermanin in Thieme-Becker 6 (1912):225. De Rinaldis 1917, p. 182. Sestieri 1920, p. 268. Musto 1920, p. 180. De Rinaldis 1921, p. 16, pl. XXVI. Sestieri 1921, pp. 184, 192, 196, repr. A. Venturi 1921, p. 209. Ortolani 1922, pp. 193, 198. De Rinaldis in Naples 1927, pp. 63-64, pl. 52, fig. 283; in Naples 1928, pp. 63-64, pl. 52, fig. 283. Pevsner in Pevsner and Grautoff 1928, p. 185. De Rinaldis 1929, p. 37. Corna 1930, 1:227. Costantini 1930, 2:152. Nugent 1925–30, 2:579-80, repr. Quintavalle in Naples 1932, p. 22, no. 283, pl. 52. McComb 1934, p. 51. Ortolani in Naples 1938, p. 66. Quintavalle in Naples 1940, pp. 15, 23, no. 283. Molajoli 1948, p. 104. *The Burlington Magazine* 93 (November 1951), suppl. 8, pl. III. Golzio 1955, 1:543. Réau 1955–59, 2 (pt. 1):331. Causa 1957, p. 41, pl. 21. Molajoli in Naples 1957, p. 73; in Naples 1958, p. 56. Zampetti 1960, p. 58. Molajoli in Naples 1961, p. 52; in Naples 1964, p. 54. Percy 1965, p. 53, no. 28. Moir 1967, 1:175, and 2:66, fig. 223. Zampetti 1967, p. 13. Pée 1971, p. 168. Causa 1972, p. 983 n. 111. Minicuci in *Dizionario enciclopedico Bolaffi* 3 (1972):207. London and Washington 1982–83, p. 140. Turin 1983, p. 162. De Maio 1983, pp. 7, 50, 66 n. 53.

46

Judith
with the Head
of Holofernes

Canvas, 88.9 x 76.2 cm.
Brinsley Ford, Esq., London

In catalogue only

Stylistically, this is the second of Cavallino's three identified versions of the subject; it follows the one at Capodimonte [45] in which Judith holds aloft the head of Holofernes, and it precedes the considerably later large-scale single figure of *Judith with the Head of Holofernes* in Stockholm [82]. The present image of Judith slipping Holofernes's severed head into the pouch held open by an old maidservant is based on a widely known Mantegnesque composition[1] known through innumerable prints. The attenuated figures, their swaying stances, and the agitated drapery behind Judith confirm Cavallino's continuous rapport with the graphic work of the Northern late Mannerists.

The painting was once thought to be by Johann Liss (Spinosa in London and Washington 1982–83, cat. no. 27). Undoubtedly, one of the reasons was its Northern Mannerist diction, a feature common to both Cavallino and Liss.[2] For example, the fluttering drapery of the nymph in Liss's *Fall of Phaeton* (collection Denis Mahon, London) resembles that in Cavallino's *Judith*. In both pictures the drapery is at once decorative and expressive of the excitement of the event, and both artists reveal their familiarity with Goltzius's numerous figures with fluttering draperies, such as those in his series of six gods (Hollstein VIII.120-21.367-72). As Cavallino's style matured, however, these agitated pieces of material turned into a convincing flow of billowing drapery giving his figures amplitude, grace, and mobility, as witnessed in Cavallino's triumphant *Galatea* [68].

The old maidservant, reminiscent of ancient sibyls, is a stock figure in Cavallino's paintings as well as those of other Neapolitan contemporaries. She reappears in Cavallino's *Shade of Samuel Invoked by Saul* [85] as the witch of Endor, and she resembles the maidservant in the picture of *Salome* in the Manchester City Art Gallery (there attributed to Stanzione, although Ellis Waterhouse believes it is by Cavallino).

The painting of *Judith* stands out through its predominance of saturated greens and browns, with added touches of rich blue and burgundy red. The reliance on earlier models makes the painting appear somewhat *retardatif*, but Cavallino's sophisticated handling of and emphasis on the drapery relates it to the *Saint Cecilia* in Boston [47], which certainly must date after the two *Saint Cecilias in Ecstasy* of 1645 [43, 44]. Briganti (London 1959, cat. no. 4) had suggested a date of ca. 1645.   ATL

1. See, for example, the *Judith*, workshop of Mantegna, canvas, 46 x 35.5 cm, in the National Gallery of Ireland, Dublin.
   2. See Rüdiger Klessmann in *Johann Liss*, exh. cat. (Augsburg and Cleveland, 1975), pp. 21-31.

Collections

Tryon, 1939; C. Norris, 1945; Clive Pascall, 1951; R. C. Pritchard, 1952; Hazlitt Gallery, London, 1959; Colnaghi & Co., London, 1959.

Exhibitions

London 1950-51, cat. no. 332; London 1952, cat. no. 8; London 1959, cat. no. 4, repr.; London 1960, cat. no. 389; London 1982, cat. no. 27, repr. in color.

Literature

The Burlington Magazine 93, (December 1951): suppl., pl. III. Vernis 1952, pp. 42-43, repr. Faldi et al. in Naples 1963, cat. no. 18. Percy 1965, p. 49, no. 13a. De Maio 1983, fig. 25. London and Washington 1982–83, pp. 140-41, cat. no. 27. Paris 1983, pp. 191, 193. Turin 1983, pp. 161-63, cat. no. 27.

46

47

47

Saint Cecilia

Canvas, 95 x 76 cm.
Museum of Fine Arts, Boston,
The Bigelow Collection

In catalogue only

This picture was first published with a tentative attribution to Stanzione (Constable 1943) but was subsequently recognized as a work by Cavallino. The coloring is rich and strong: brilliant red for the saint's mantle, gold and white for her sleeve. Her flesh has a gray tonality. This half-figure of *Saint Cecilia* appears to date not far from Cavallino's well-known 1645 full-length version with attendant angels. The artist depicted five saints and allegories related to music—three *Saint Cecilias* [43-44, 47], the Capodimonte *Singer* [70], and the Lyon *Clavichordist* [71]—but only one *Allegory of Painting* is known [66].   AP

Collections
Julius Weitzner, New York; acquired by the Museum in 1936.

Exhibitions
None.

Literature
Art Digest 2 (mid-May 1928):29, and (June 1928):23, repr. Constable 1943, pp. 226-27, fig. 8. Percy 1965, p. 46, no. 1. Causa 1966, p. 7, no. XVII and color cover. Fredericksen and Zeri 1972, p. 50. Causa in *Larousse Dictionary* 1981, p. 57. London and Washington 1982–83, p. 135. Paris 1983, p. 189. Turin 1983, p. 158.

48

48

Saint Agatha

Canvas, 68.5 x 58 cm.
The Detroit Institute of Arts

In catalogue only

The picture has been enlarged around all four sides. The three-dimensionality of the figure, the luminous dark brown shadows of the face, the delicate brushstrokes of the transitional passages between light and shadow, the fine impasto highlights edging the folds of the drapery, and the lyrical curves of the contours are all typically Cavallinesque. The tonality is strong and dark: the saint wears a white blouse and holds a beige-brown veil in her fingers; her drapery is golden yellow, shading into orange brown. Textures are treated with the careful observation of lifelike surfaces that Cavallino shared with the Neapolitan followers of Ribera.

The painting can be dated to the latter half of the 1640s; despite the dark tone and the strong chiaroscuro contrasts, it is a relatively mature work. Earlier versions of the same subject are at Naples [14] and York [28].

The intense, emotional lyricism that characterizes all of Cavallino's female half-figures, with their tilted heads, oblique glances, parted lips, and emphasized gestures, is strongly evident in this picture. One might compare it with the *Saint Agatha* at Capodimonte by Cavallino's near-contemporary Francesco Guarino.[1]

AP

1. Repr. in Causa 1957, p. 38.

Collections
Gift of Mrs. Standish Backus to the Institute, 1945.

Exhibitions
Detroit 1965, cat. no. 162, repr.

Literature
Detroit 1946, p. 55. Percy 1965, p. 46, no. 4. Causa 1972, pp. 942, 944. Fredericksen and Zeri 1972, p. 50. Ferrari in *Dizionario biografico* 22 (1979):788. London and Washington 1982–83, p. 143. Paris 1983, p. 195. Turin 1983, p. 164.

49

The Virgin Annunciate

Canvas, 85.1 x 69.2 cm.

National Gallery of Victoria,
Melbourne, Australia

Exhibited in USA only

Jeffrey Daniels (1968, p. 47) praised the Madonna's unself-consciousness and relaxed elegance as a beautiful example "of Cavallino's ingenious fusion of naturalism with profound spiritual content." As a type—in the soft modeling of her profile, the yielding pose, and the preciousness of her costume—the Madonna resembles Saint Catherine in *The Mystical Marriage* [50].

The diagonal cutting of the canvas at four corners indicates that the painting was originally octagonal. The painting of the Archangel Gabriel, which must have accompanied it, is lost. However, an oval canvas of a half-length Gabriel (Fig. 49a), similar in size to the present work and given to "Bernardo Cavallino and Workshop," went through the Parke Bernet sale in New York, 15 March 1945, no. 32; while it is impossible to draw any conclusions from a catalogue illustration alone, it at least provides a hint of what a companion to the Melbourne Madonna may have been like. The unknown artist must have been familiar with the series of Cavallino's half-length female figures dating from 1645 to about 1650, such as *The Singer* [70], *The Clavichordist* [71], *La Pittura* [66], and the female saints, all of which are distinguished by their mannered elegance and delicate gestures.

If the Parke Bernet oval does, indeed, reflect a lost pendant to the Madonna, there are comparisons to be made with an *Annunciation* by Charles Mellin, painted for the church of Santa Maria di Donnaregina Nuova, Naples, in 1646, which shares the delicacy and intimacy of Cavallino's figure of the *Virgin* and other paintings cited above. Charles Sterling, who recognized the subtle stylistic rapport between the two painters, drew special attention to the delicate hands in Mellin's *Annunciation* which he described as "grazia manierata che, par recordando quella del Cavallino, portrebbe essere un eredità del manierismo lorenese."[1] Ferrari has also described the "musicale cadenza lineare" of Mellin's *Annunciation*, which reminded one of the "grazia raffinata delle creazioni cavalliniane."[2]

The stylistic affinities between Cavallino and Mellin are also strikingly evident in two other paintings: Cavallino's *Virgin of the Immaculate Conception* in Milan [51] and Mellin's *Assumption* in the church of Santa Maria di Donnaregina Nuova.[3] (Mellin's work was commissioned for the church at the same time as his *Annunciation*.)

The painting was acquired by Melbourne from the Hazlitt Gallery in 1968, under the terms of the Felton Bequest, on the advice of Dr. M. Woodall, with the assistance of Denis Mahon, Professor Ellis Waterhouse, and Ann Percy.   ATL

1. In Rome 1956, no. 206; (translation) "displaying a graceful manner, which—while equally recalling that of Cavallino—could be [an indication of] his Mannerist heritage of Lorrain."
2. In Naples 1967, p. 34, no. 22.
3. Causa and Ferrari in Naples 1954a, cat. no. 30, fig. 35. Although the painting was entitled "Ascensione," which translates *Assumption* [to Heaven after Her death], Mellin represented the Virgin as the "Second Eve," a sixteenth-century image of the Immacolata. In this role she is depicted standing on a serpent or dragon, an allusion to the words of God to the serpent in the garden of Eden (Genesis 3:15).

Fig. 49a. Attributed to Cavallino and workshop. *The Archangel Gabriel*. Canvas (oval), 91.4 x 73.7 cm. Present whereabouts unknown.

[NUMBER 32]

49

Collections
Private collection, France; Hazlitt Gallery,
London; acquired by the National Gallery in
1968.

Exhibitions
London 1968, cat. no. 6.

Literature
Daniels 1968, pp. 44-45, 47, repr. Lucie-Smith
1968, p. 327. *The Burlington Magazine* 110
(1968):364, 366, fig. 60. *Gazette des Beaux-
Arts* ser. 6, no. 73 (1969):suppl., 38. Victoria
1973, p. 25, fig. 36.

50

50

The Mystical Marriage
of Saint Catherine
of Alexandria

Canvas, 124 x 76 cm.
Private collection, Naples

Exhibited in Naples only

One of the few examples of a mystical subject in Cavallino's oeuvre, this painting represents Saint Catherine's vision of her betrothal to Christ, as told in *The Golden Legend* (1969, p. 712). Its large size, refinement of execution, and the arched top suggest that, like Cavallino's *Saint Cecilia in Ecstasy* [44], it was painted for a church or private chapel.[1]

Even though Cavallino's painting is in the grand manner of lofty baroque visions, the mood is intimate and lyrical. The only spectator, an angel, is kept in shadow. Both the Madonna and Saint Catherine are young and convincingly human, as are all of Cavallino's depictions of women. The saint, whose dress of sumptuous green silk befits her royal birth, bows humbly before the Christ Child, her arms spread in a pose similar to that of Saint Cecilia in the 1645 painting. Also like Cecilia, Saint Catherine is being crowned with a wreath of flowers.

The use of the floral wreath as a wedding symbol rather than the traditional exchange of rings may have been suggested by a painting like Rubens's *Coronation of Saint Catherine* (Toledo Museum of Art, Ohio, originally painted for the church of the Augustines in Malines in 1633), which was engraved by Pieter de Jode II (1606–1674), brother-in-law of Jan Brueghel (1601–1678). Another source for the image of a saint being crowned with a wreath of flowers, particularly in Neapolitan painting at the time of Cavallino, is undoubtedly van Dyck's Sicilian painting of *Saint Rosalie*,[2] which Cavallino may have known through copies or derivations

by Neapolitan artists, such as Paolo Finoglia, whose *Madonna with Putto and Saint Rosa of Viterbo* (church of Saints Cosimo and Damiano, Conversano) also is related compositionally to Cavallino's *Mystical Marriage*.[3]

Cavallino's young Madonna, wearing a red dress and a blue shawl, is seated on a cloud in an opaque orange-pink sky. The ominous storm cloud that moves overhead adds a disquieting note and gives credence to the billowing drapery and the Madonna's windblown hair. Two cherubs emerge from the shadow of the cloud.

Although Refice (1951, p. 268) described the painting as the most beautiful work of Cavallino's early period, its fluent style, accomplished *mise en scène*, and the profound religious sentiment speak for a later date, after the *Saint Cecilia* of 1645. Furthermore, the soft brown shadows on the Madonna's face and the rounded features and humble expression of Saint Catherine's face seem to anticipate the modeling and the tender mood of *Saint Anthony of Padua* [56], a painting that also belongs to Cavallino's maturity. ATL

1. If the painting, formerly owned by Prince Ruffo della Scaletta, actually descended to him through the family of Antonio della Scaletta (1610–1678), son of the famous Sicilian collector Carlo Ruffo (e Spinelli, duca de Baguara), the painting's distinguished early history would be confirmed.
2. Christopher Brown, *Van Dyck* (Ithaca, New York: Cornell University Press, 1983), p. 81, figs. 69, 70.
3. D'Orsi 1938, p. 42, fig. 19. Note that this is one of two altarpieces, the other being the *Madonna, Putto e SS Eligio e Trifone* in the church of Sant'Angelo, Monopoli, and that both date from the mid–1630s. Percy (1965, no. 44) compared them with the present painting and suggested they were evidence that Cavallino traveled and, perhaps, worked more extensively in Apulia than was indicated by the *Pietà* in Molfetta [67].

Collections
Ruffo della Scaletta, Rome; Gilberto Algranti, Milan, 1973.

Exhibitions
Athens 1962–63, cat. no. 17; Naples 1963, cat. no. 17, repr.; Paris 1965, cat. no. 48, repr.; Milan 1973.

Literature
Refice 1951, pp. 263, 265, fig. 4. Paris 1965, p. 103. Percy 1965, p. 57, no. 44. Gonzáles-Palacios 1973, p. 529, fig. 6. Causa in Naples 1975, p. 42. Gregori 1980, p. 298.

51

The Virgin of
the Immaculate Conception

Canvas, 168 x 116 cm.
Pinacoteca di Brera, Milan

Naples, in the ninth century, was one of the first religious centers to celebrate the Feast of the Immaculate Conception. Much later, during the Counter-Reformation, the iconography associated with the worship of the virgin was codified in accordance with the theories and rules of practice set down to comply with the requirements of Counter-Reformatory decorum. Francisco Pacheco, the Spanish painter and artistic advisor to the Inquisition, gave specific instructions to artists who chose to depict the Immaculate Conception.[1] According to Pacheco, the *Immacolata* was to be depicted as a young girl, dressed in white with a blue cloak, with her hands folded on her breasts or held together in prayer.[2] This formula resulted in a distinct family resemblance among *Immacolata* figures by painters of the Spanish artistic milieu, which at that time included the artists of Naples. Therefore, Cavallino's Brera figure, for example, is not very different from Ribera's *Virgin of the Immaculate Conception*, 1637, in the Columbia Museum of Art and Science (Columbia, South Carolina); or Alonso Cano's *Virgin* in the Cathedral at Granada; or Andrea Vaccaro's *Immaculate Conception* in the Fine Arts Museum, Salamanca.

Cavallino depicted the subject several times, although only one other autograph version is known [26]. The canvas at Caen, considerably smaller than the Brera painting and oval in shape, appears to have been especially admired by contemporary artists, since there are at least six copies and variants (see Inv. nos. 42-43, 47-48, 152-53). Another version (Inv. no. 46; Fig. 26a), now known to be a copy, shares certain similarities with the Brera canvas,

151

51

including the billowing folds of the Madonna's robe and the *putti* at her feet who hold flowers and a sprig of olive.

The size of the Brera painting indicates that it was a church commission. Nineteenth-century writers mention a lost *Immacolata* from the church of Santa Maria della Verita, Naples, (see Inv. no. 151), and one in the Chiesa di Spirito Santo.[3] Because of the difference in size, the Brera painting also cannot be identified with an *Immacolata,* measuring 9 x 7 *palmi,* mentioned in a recently discovered document of 16 March 1646.[4]

Opinions vary about the dating of the painting. Spinosa (in London and Washington 1982–83, p. 140) dated it before 1645. Causa, in conversation with this writer, assigned it to a phase in Cavallino's career in the late 1630s that he termed "realism dynamique." Monteverdi (1959, p. 88) and Scavizzi (1963–64, no. 18, p. 28), on the other hand, seemed convinced that the *Immacolata* belonged to Cavallino's maturity, "che si compiace di ricercatezze rare, di raffinate modulazioni de colore, di spiralate eleganze lineari."[5]

The dynamic impact of Cavallino's composition, unprecedented in the earlier works, results in part from the projection of the quietly intense figure of the Virgin, with downcast eyes, immersed in prayer, against a tumultuous sky that approaches the storm-torn skies of El Greco. The dramatic intensity is heightened by Cavallino's juxtaposition of opposites—the sweeping diagonals of the drifting clouds that contrast with the pronounced vertical of the Virgin's attenuated figure. Contributing further to the compositional excitement is the group of lively *putti* encircling the Virgin's feet and carrying flowers of symbolic significance.[6]

It has already been suggested (see discussion under [49]) that Cavallino may have admired Charles Mellin's large *Annunciation* in the church of Santa Maria Donnaregina Nuova, Naples, painted in 1646. It is possible that Mellin's *Immaculate Conception,*[7] also of 1646, in the same church, may have provided the inspiration for Cavallino's unusually dynamic composition in the Brera. Elements from both Mellin altarpieces can be found in Cavallino's painting; Cavallino's group of cherubs, for instance, is similar in type and placement to the cherubim above the Virgin in Mellin's *Annunciation,* and the poses of Cavallino's two *putti* with flowers resemble Mellin's two—one with

a mirror, the other with an olive branch. Cavallino has rendered plant forms in the *Immacolata* with the care and skill of a specialist; his flowers resemble closely those in Stanzione's *Annunciation* of ca. 1655 (Collection Marcianise, Chiesa dell'Annunciata), which Causa and Ferrari[8] believe were painted by Paolo Porpora. ATL

1. In 1615 Pope Paul V formally instituted the office commemorating the Immaculate Conception, and one year later a bull was issued, forbidding anyone to teach or preach a contrary opinion (see Anna Jameson, *Legends of the Madonna* [Boston and New York, 1895], p. 101).
2. Pacheco [1638] 1956, 2:208-12.
3. Catalani 1845–53, 2:26 (see Inv. no. 151); also Galante 1872, p. 355, with reference to the painting in the Chiesa di Santo Spirito. Note, however, that Rolfs 1910, p. 278 (likely relying on Giannone), speaks of it as a "Conception of Mary amidst Disciples" which, therefore, cannot have been an *Immacolata.*
4. Renato Ruotolo kindly brought this document—which also refers to an *Annunciata* of the same size (see Introduction, note 4, and Appendix, no. 2)—to our attention.
5. Translation: " . . . that pleases one because of its exceptional elegance, harmony of color, and graceful spiral movement."
6. The lily is the symbol of the Virgin's purity; the sprig of olive (brought back to the ark by the dove) symbolized to Christians the making of God's peace with man, while the olive branch was also an attribute of the Virgin Mary. The rose is particularly associated with the Virgin, a "rose without thorns," i. e., without sin. See Hall 1979, pp. 192, 228, 268.
7. Causa and Ferrari in Naples 1954a, figs. 28-29.
8. Ibid., p. 35, cat. no. 24.

Collections

Private collection, Rome; acquired by the Gallery in 1955.

Exhibitions

Rome 1957, cat. no. 58; Naples 1963, cat. no. 18.

Literature

Sestieri 1920, p. 260. Ortolani in Naples 1938, p. 66. *Bollettino d'arte* 41 (1956):370. Causa 1957, p. 42. Brugnoli 1959, p. 220. Monteverdi 1959, pp. 88-90, pl. xxxiii. *Kindlers Malerei Lexikon* 1 (1964), unpaginated, repr. Moir 1967, 1:176. *McGraw-Hill Dictionary of Art* 1969, p. 523. Russoli in Milan 1970, pp. 77, 79, repr. Wittkower 1972, p. 232, pl. 140B. Causa 1972, pp. 944, 983 n. 111. Minicuci in *Dizionario enciclopedico Bolaffi* 3 (1972):207. Bonsignori 1974, pl. 16. Ferrari in *Dizionario biografico* 22 (1979):788. Brejon de Lavergnée and Dorival 1979, p. 92. London and Washington 1982–83, p. 140. Turin 1983, p. 162.

52

The Vision
of Saint Dominic

Canvas, 97.2 x 65.6 cm.
National Gallery of Canada, Ottawa

Exhibited in USA only

The painting is unpublished. The author was informed by the present owner (letter of 18 June 1982) that Causa and Spinosa had accepted it into Cavallino's mature oeuvre.

Since the sixteenth century, the Madonna of the Rosary, depicted with Saint Dominic—the founder of the Dominican order in the twelfth century—and often joined by Saint Catherine of Siena, had become a favorite subject in the art of the Counter-Reformation, particularly in Naples, where Caravaggio's *Madonna of the Rosary* (Kunsthistorisches Museum, Vienna) was greatly admired when it was offered for sale in 1607.[1] The veneration of the Rosary Madonna was inspired by her miraculous intervention in the battle of Lepanto in 1571, leading to Admiral Marcantonio Colonna's victory over the Turks.[2] A member of the Colonna family had commissioned Caravaggio's abovementioned painting in 1606.[3] It is of interest that the son of the hero of Lepanto, Cardinal Ascanio Colonna, lived in Naples and was a great patron of Lope de Vega.[4] That Saint Dominic, whose full name was Domingo de Guzman, from Caleruega in Castile, Spain, descended from the same noble family as the two successive Spanish viceroys in Naples—Manuel de Guzman, Conde de Monterrey (1631–37), and Ramiro de Guzman, Duque de Medina de las Torres (1637–44)—may have further contributed to his popularity in Neapolitan painting. Among the numerous examples by the leading artists in that city were Stanzione's *Madonna of the Rosary with Saint Dominic* (Capodimonte), ca. 1643; Francesco

Guarino's two versions—one in the Chiesa di Santa Maria di Materdomini, Nocera Superiore, ca. 1645, and one in San Domenico, Solofra, ca. 1649 (see London 1982, cat. no. 74); Vaccaro's version, painted for the Chiesa della Sacra Famiglia al Rione Luzzatti; and one by Spadaro (Fig. 52a) that is similar to Cavallino's composition. Yet another, anonymous, painting (whereabouts unknown) omits the cherubim under the Madonna's feet, as well as the figure of Saint Catherine, but includes a landscape with a building below.

Stylistically, the painting is close to *The Mystical Marriage of Saint Catherine* in the Ottone collection [50], although its chiaroscuro is not as soft and diffused, and the faces are more portraitlike. The close relationship to the Ambrosio variant by Spadaro, which in Spinosa's opinion cannot date from after 1650 (communicated to this author in a letter from Myron Laskin, 18 June 1982), suggests that Cavallino painted his *Rosary Madonna* in the late 1640s. Laskin (in the same letter) is certain that the garland of flowers (which appears in only one other painting, attributed to Cavallino, now lost; see Inv. no. 152), is not by Cavallino, but is of an

early date. The flowers have been partly cut off in a reduction of the painting and some are concealed by the frame. Causa suggested to Laskin that Giacomo Recco may be responsible for them.　　ATL

1. Wolfgang Prohaska, ''Untersuchungen zur *Rosenkranzmadonna* Caravaggios,'' *Jahrbuch der Kunsthistorischen Sammlungen in Wien* 76 (1980):111-32.
2. Hibbard 1983, pp. 316-17 n. 118.
3. This was Donna Orinzia Colonna's son, Don Marzio, who was Caravaggio's protector during his flight from Rome. However, he went bankrupt and Caravaggio did not complete his painting until after his arrival in Naples.
4. Ezio Levi, *Lope de Vega e L'Italia* (Florence: G.C. Sansoni, 1935), pp. 43, 51.

Collections
Mrs. Waterfield, Nackington House, near Canterbury; Mrs. Waterfield's granddaughter, Mrs. Harriet Green (sale: Christie's, London, 4 April 1978, lot 73).

Exhibitions
None.

Literature
London and Washington 1982–83, p. 135. Paris 1983, p. 189. Turin 1983, p. 158.

Fig. 52a. Domenico Gargiulo, called Micco Spadaro, Naples 1612–ca. 1679. *The Virgin of the Rosary*. Canvas. Collection Ambrosio, Naples.

52

53

Saint Peter and the Centurion Cornelius

Canvas, 102 x 128 cm.

Galleria Nazionale d'Arte Antica,
Palazzo Corsini, Rome

Fig. 53a. Self-portrait. Detail of [53].

The conversion and baptism of the centurion Cornelius by the apostle Peter is related in The Acts of the Apostles (10:1-48). Cornelius, a devout, God-fearing man, was told by an angel to send for Peter, who, enlightened by his vision of unclean beasts,[1] came to Caesarea to meet with Cornelius at his house. With family and friends gathered around him, Cornelius thus became the first Gentile to be baptized.[2] Cavallino depicted the moment when the two men met: Cornelius had fallen to his knees and Peter urged him to rise, saying, "Stand up; I too am a man." (Acts 10:25-26)[3]

The elegant figure in the right foreground, gazing pensively at the spectator, is—we believe—Cavallino himself, assuming his favorite pose, with left hand on his hip (Fig. 53a). He appears considerably younger here than in the self-portrait at the far left in *Mucius Scaevola* [84]. Much like Velázquez, who proudly portrayed himself at the easel in *Las Meninas* (painted 1656), Cavallino places himself in a prominent position directly facing the viewer; this would seem to confirm that he was gaining self-confidence as an artist.

The composition distinctly resembles that of Velázquez's *Surrender of Breda* (1634/35),[4] revealing sources of inspiration that served both masters, including possibly Veronese's *Christ and the Centurion* in the Prado.[5] Cavallino's links with Schönfeld, on the other hand, are more direct. Schönfeld was known to have been in Naples from about 1637 to about 1649,[6] the period during which Cavallino's style matured. It is therefore not surprising that stylistic references to Schönfeld are most apparent in his paintings of that period, as the example of *Peter and Cornelius* shows. One notes the mannered stance of the figure of Cavallino, who parades as a nobleman, as well as the attenuated figure of Peter, his right foot pointing forward, the folds of his heavy drapery gathered in one hand—features that closely resemble Schönfeld's *Diogenes* (Fig. 53b).[7] Other Schönfeldian elements are the hooded philosophers in the crowd, the architectural props stabilizing the horizontal composition, and the *repoussoir* figure on one side of the painting. In turn, as Pée pointed out, Schönfeld absorbed influences from Cavallino's painting, as is evident in his *Solomon Being Anointed King*, painted after Schönfeld's return to Augsburg.[8]

In this author's opinion *Peter and Cornelius* can be dated to the latter part of the 1640s. The slight tilt of the head of the nobleman (Cavallino's presumed self-portrait), the modeling of his face, and the pensive gaze are similar in style to *Saint Lucy* [64] and the *Saint Catherine* in Birmingham [72], both dating from after 1645. The young rider on the left who strains to look over the head of his horse anticipates both the rider in *The Expulsion of Heliodorus* [83] and the young equestrian in the *David and Abigail* painting in Brunswick [80]. ATL

1. Réau 1955–59, 3:1091.
2. Ibid. Réau, citing from A. Loisy, *Traduction et Commentaires des Apôtres* (Paris, 1925), p. 155, points out that this episode involving Peter was invented in order to avoid attributing to Paul the exclusive merit for converting Gentiles.

Fig. 53b. Gabriel Ehinger, Augsburg 1652–1736. After Johann Heinrich Schönfeld, 1609–1684. *Diogenes*. Etching, 39.5 x 31 cm. Städtische Kunstsammlungen Augsburg.

Quæro Homines.

53

3. One of the few other examples, different only in that Cornelius is kneeling, is an engraving by Philipp Galle after Marten van Heemskerck (see Hollstein VII.206-240); it is one of a series of thirty-four devoted to The Acts of the Apostles.

4. López-Rey 1963, cat. no. 80; Lurie 1969, pp. 145-47.

5. López-Rey 1963, p. 65 n. 3.

6. Pée 1971, pp. 27, 36.

7. Ibid., p. 229, cat. no. NS26.

8. Ibid., p. 171, pl. 122.

Collections

Diodati, Naples.

Exhibitions

Florence 1922, cat. no. 253; Paris 1935; Naples 1938; Rome 1958, cat. no. 7; Bucharest 1972, cat. no. 43; Naples 1972, cat. no. 43.

Literature

De Rinaldis 1909, p. 42, cat. no. 14. Hermanin 1910, p. 230, repr. Voss 1911, pp. 249-50, fig. 9. Hermanin 1911, pp. 185, 187, 188; 1912, p. 374. Hermanin in Thieme-Becker 6 (1912):225. De Rinaldis 1917, p. 179. Sestieri 1920, p. 269. Musto 1920, p. 180. De Rinaldis 1920a, p. 3; 1921, p. 17, pl. xx. A. Venturi 1921, p. 211. Ortolani 1922, p. 194. Ojetti, Dami, and Tarchiani 1924, p. 82. Hermanin 1924−25, p. 6. A. Venturi 1925, p. 78. Benesch 1926, pp. 252-53, fig. 177. De Rinaldis 1928, p. 65; 1929, pl. 42. Nugent 1925−30, 2:558-60, 566, repr. Delogu 1931, p. 45, repr. De Rinaldis in Rome 1932, pp. 17, 23, pl. 43. McComb 1934, fig. 49. Ortolani in Naples 1938, p. 66. Masciotta 1942, p. 147. Nebbia 1946, fig. 76. Montini 1952, p. 35. Golzio 1955, 1:543-44, fig. 575. Pigler 1956, 1:388. Réau 1955-59, 3:1092. *Kindlers Malerei Lexikon* 1 (1964), unpaginated. Percy 1965, p. 57, no. 43. Moir 1967, 1:177, and 2:66, fig. 224. Liebmann 1968, p. 459. Lurie 1969, pp. 145-47, figs. 16 and 18. Pée 1971, p. 171. Minicuci in *Dizionario Enciclopedico Bolaffi* 3 (1972):207. London and Washington 1982−83, p. 147. Turin 1983, p. 168.

54

Saint Catherine

Canvas, 68 x 55 cm.
Museum Boymans-van Beuningen,
Rotterdam

Datable to the latter half of the 1640s, this painting is an exquisite example of Cavallino's mature work. The broad, rather visible brushstrokes are similar to the handling of paint in the half-length figures at Naples and Lyon [70, 71], and the cool, opaque coloring—with blues and grays predominating—is close to that of the Moscow *Heliodorus* [83] and the *Saint Lawrence* in Madrid [58]. The ground is red brown, and the background tones vary from dark to pale gray; the ground shows through in places, adding warmth and vitality, as in the Cleveland *Adoration of the Shepherds* [79]. The saint's hair is a luminous red brown, with paler brown highlights; it merges with the background at the left in a typical Cavallinesque fashion. The delicate brushwork around the eyes and brows and the touches of pink around the eyes and nose give the figure a familiar, somewhat vulnerable quality, almost as if Cavallino were recording the features of a woman of his acquaintance. The brushstrokes are broad and sure, despite the delicacy of touch; the tight handling of impasto of Cavallino's earlier years has been abandoned. This is especially apparent in the transitions between the pale flesh and the warm red-brown shadow on the face and at the hairline. The saint's blouse is a hard medium blue, her veil beige brown. The silvery-gray mantle is especially attractive, with its complex folds, its delicate white impasto highlights, and its subtle gradations of gray.

The *Saint Catherine* fits into the mature series of half-length figures by Cavallino [55-58, 64-66], each of which is distinctive in its color relationships and psychological impact.   AP

Collections

Relarte, Milan, 1964; Vitale Bloch, The Hague; Vitale Bloch Bequest 1976.

Exhibitions

Milan 1964; Rotterdam and Paris 1978−79, cat. no. 7, repr.

Literature

Mascherpa 1965, p. 35, repr. p. 34. Percy 1965, p. 48, no. 9. Liebmann 1968, p. 459. Nicolson 1978, pp. 196-97, repr. Ferrari in *Dizionario Biografico* 22 (1979):788. Wright 1980, p. 74. London and Washington 1982−83, pp. 142, 144. Paris 1983, pp. 189, 193. Turin 1983, pp. 158, 163, 165. De Maio 1983, p. 135 n. 72.

54

55

55

A Saint Martyr (Cecilia?)

Canvas, 65 x 77.5 cm.
Museo Poldi Pezzoli, Milan,
Donazione A. Mayer

The identification of the saint as Cecilia, rather than Agatha,[1] was suggested by Natale (in Milan 1982, p. 163). She is shown as the dying martyr rather than in her role as the patron saint of musicians—the role in which Cavallino also painted her [43, 44, 47]. The bloody blade of a knife in her neck alludes to the vandalish means of her execution. According to a fifteenth-century legend,[2] after various attempts to put her to death failed, she was dealt three blows from a sword (the maximum number permitted by Roman law) which half-severed her neck but did not kill her for another three days.

Cavallino's composition was undoubtedly inspired by Caravaggio's lost *Mary Magdalene* of 1606, which Cavallino could have known through numerous copies, the earliest of which was Ludovico Finson's in the Musée des Beaux-Arts in Marseilles.

This *Saint* was first attributed to Cavallino by Marina Betti (1960, p. 17), who referred to the work as "Santa Martire" and related it to the style of the *Saint Cecilia* of 1645 [43]. Natale (in Milan 1982, p. 163) suggested a date of ca. 1640, the period in which Artemisia Gentileschi's influence was particularly strong, as seen in the pronounced painterliness and rich impasto. Spinosa (orally) also agrees with a date before 1645. Indeed, Artemisia's precious raiments of rustling satins, gleaming silks, and velvets continued to impress Cavallino throughout his maturity, as witnessed in this saint's costume as well as that of the *Annunciate Madonna* [49] and *Saint Lawrence* [58], and those of others of Cavallino's pictures dating to the latter part of the 1640s: all share a rich impasto and subtle chiaroscuro that define the textures and tonalities of the fabrics. Moreover, the refined articulation of the saint's slender hands,[3] delicately poised, resemble those of *Saint Anthony of Padua* [56] and Christ's in the *Pietà* [67] dating from the late 1640s—both works with which *Saint Cecilia* (?) shares her fragility and intensely religious sentiment.

ATL

1. See Russoli in Milan 1972, p. 261, fig. 482.
 2. See Réau 1955-59, 3:279.
 3. A pentimento reveals changes in the pose of the saint's hands.

Collections
Serra di Cassano, Naples; Astorre Mayer, until 1960.

Exhibitions
None.

Literature
Betti 1960, pp. 16, 17, fig. 4. Juynboll 1960, p. 85. Mascherpa 1965, p. 35. Percy 1965, p. 50, no. 19. Pée 1971, p. 121 under no. 44. Russoli in Milan 1972, p. 260, fig. 482; in Milan 1978, p. 47. Balboni and Molfino in Milan 1980, p. 198, no. 58. Natale in Milan 1982, p. 163, no. 212, pl. 364. London and Washington 1982–83, p. 135. Paris 1983, p. 189. Turin 1983, p. 158.

56

Saint Anthony of Padua

Canvas, 128 x 103 cm.
Museo di Capodimonte, Naples

Saint Anthony (born Lisbon 1195, died Padua 1231) and Saint Francis of Assisi were the most venerated of the Franciscan saints who were portrayed in the art of the Counter-Reformation. Saint Anthony's vision of the Virgin and Child, like St. Francis's stigmatization, was considered to be the most holy event of his life. Seicento artists often chose to portray the saint alone with the Christ Child; the resultant work was a type of devotional image inspired by Ignatius of Loyola's Spiritual Exercises and intended for private worship.[1] Paintings and sculptures of Saint Anthony with the Child were therefore particularly popular in Spain and, consequently, in Naples as well. Alonso Cano, Murillo, and Ribera[2] were among those artists who treated the subject many times.

Roberto Longhi (1920c, pp. 155-56), seconded by Ettore Sestieri (1921, p. 188), had convincingly assigned this picture to Cavallino as early as 1920, an attribution that has been accepted generally with the exception of Commodo Izzo who gave it to Vaccaro (1951, p. 51).[3] However, the rich tonal variation in describing color, texture, and sheen in the saint's habit and the soft modeling of Saint Anthony's face with brown shadows are typical of Cavallino; so are the slightly bowed mouth and parted lips; the careful delineation of the ear; the delicate rendering of the Christ Child's silken hair; and above all, the distilled sentiment of the scene and Saint Anthony's convincing expression of wonderment—"tanto bello, tenero, dolce" (Causa 1972, p. 944)—are typical of Cavallino, not Vaccaro. Also characteristic of Cavallino is the fondness for elements of still life, here seen in the carefully described open book, with its subtle shades of salmon and ochre offset by the green tablecloth. Typical, too, are Cavallino's small dabs of red—on the Child's toes, on the nose of the saint and the Child, and in the corner of the saint's mouth.

The painting most likely dates from the latter part of the 1640s. Saint Anthony's softly modeled profile anticipates that of King Saul in *The Shade of Samuel Invoked by Saul* [85] and that of the young shepherd in the Cleveland *Adoration* [79]. *Saint Anthony* shares with the latter, as well as with the *Pietà* [67], a sentiment of tenderness and religious surrender that is unprecedented in Cavallino's oeuvre and that most assuredly reflects Cavallino's maturity.   ATL

1. See also *De imaginibus sacris et profanis, illustrissimi et reverendissimi D. D. Gabrielis Paleoti Cardinalis libri quinque* (Ingolstadt, 1594), 1:25.
2. Pérez Sánchez and Spinosa, 1978, pp. 108-9, nos. 101 and 102 a-d.
3. A large, unidentified Saint Anthony of Padua by Andrea Vaccaro was listed in the inventory of Ruffo di Calabria (Ruffo 1916–19, p. 320, no. 327). Commodo Izzo (1951, p. 51) mentions another *Saint Anthony* in the church of San Effremo Nuovo; yet another version is at Capodimonte.

Collections

Giuseppe Sancio, 1846 (sale, 20 April 1846); Museo Reale Borbonico, Naples.

Exhibitions

Florence 1922, cat. no. 1028.

Literature

De Rinaldis 1911, p. 412, no. 389, pl. II. Longhi 1920c, pp. 155-56. Sestieri 1921, p. 188. Ojetti, Dami, and Tarchiani 1924, pl. 295. Nugent 1925–30, 2:34-35, repr. De Rinaldis 1927, pp. 343-44, pl. 49, no. 279. Marangoni 1927, p. 191. De Rinaldis 1928, p. 343, no. 279; 1929, pl. 27. Mâle 1932, p. 179 n. 4. Ortolani in Naples 1938, p. 66. Ortolani in Thieme-Becker 34 (1940): 26, under Vaccaro. Quintavalle in Naples 1940, pp. 15, 33 no. 279. Commdo Izzo 1951, p. 138. Causa 1957, p. 42. Molajoli in Naples 1957, p. 73; in Naples 1958, p. 55; in Naples 1961, p. 51. Longhi 1961, 1:512. *Kindlers Malerei Lexikon* 1 (1964), unpaginated. Molajoli in Naples 1964, p. 54. Percy 1965, pp. 51-52, no. 24. Minicuci in *Dizionario enciclopedico Bolaffi* 3 (1972):207. Causa 1972, pp. 944, 982 n. 110; in Naples 1982, pp. 101, 147, repr. London and Washington 1982–83, pp. 136, 147. Paris 1983, pp. 189, 197. Turin 1983, pp. 159, 166.

56

57

Saint Anthony
of Padua
Holding the
Christ Child

Canvas, 92.7 x 73 cm.
Nelson Shanks,
Andalusia, Pennsylvania

In catalogue only

The painting was offered at Christie's, London, 18 April 1980, lot 62, and again at Christie's, New York, 19 January 1982, lot 93, at which time the present owner acquired it.

Although the painting lacks the intensity of the preceding version [56], it is intimately related to it in both style and subject. In this work, however, Saint Anthony now carries the Christ Child in his arms with the tenderness and apprehension of a father holding his newborn son.

The image closely resembles that in paintings and sculptures by Alonso Cano Fig. 57a).   ATL

Collections
A. de Jouravlev, Leningrad.

Fig. 57a. Alonso Cano, Granada 1601–1667, and Pedro de Meña, Granada 1628–Málaga 1688. *Saint Anthony of Padua and the Infant Christ* (detail). Painted wood, 203 cm high. (After Harold E. Wethey, *Alonso Cano* [Princeton: Princeton Univ. Press, 1955], fig. 126.)

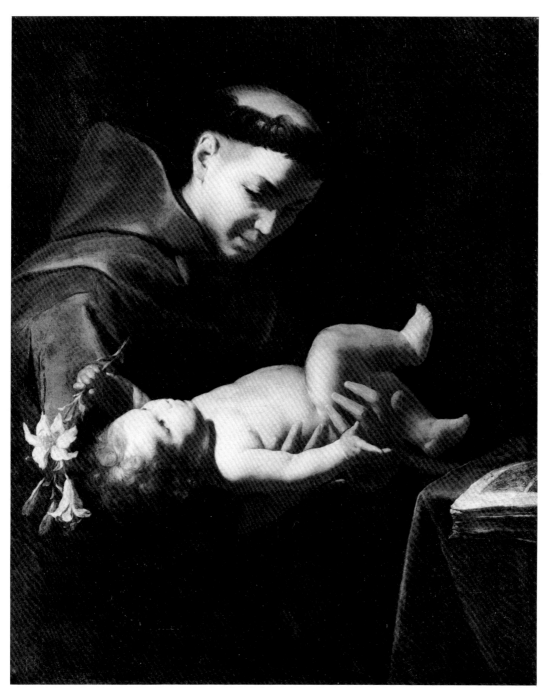

57

58

Saint Lawrence

Canvas, 65.5 x 53.5 cm.
Museo Lázaro Galdiano, Madrid

Exhibited in USA only

It is not known whether Sr. Lázaro acquired the painting in Spain or elsewhere. Camón Aznar, who convincingly identified the figure as the deacon saint Lawrence,[1] first thought the work to be by Francesco Solimena (in Madrid 1951, p. 141); however, three years later (in Madrid 1954, p. 133), both he and Milicua (1954, p. 68) changed the attribution to Cavallino. Milicua accepted the identification of the saint as Lawrence, suggesting that the metal shaft in the saint's left hand could be the handle of the grill on which he was martyred, one of his attributes. Furthermore, Milicua (1954, p. 71) believed that the *Saint Lawrence* belongs to the painter's early period of ca. 1635; Pérez Sánchez, on the other hand (1970, cat. no. 46), thought that the style was characteristic of Cavallino's work of the 1640s. Milicua compared the physiognomy of the saint (the high cheekbones, fleshy lips, slanted eyebrows) to the face of the angel in *Saint Cecilia* , but he expanded his comparison to include faces in paintings now considered to be of a much later date—for example, those of the two maidservants behind the Pharaoh's daughter in the Brunswick *Finding of Moses* [81], which is thought to date from Cavallino's last years. Milicua (1954, p. 69) also suggested that the *Saint Lawrence* and *The Clavichordist* [71] may have been companion paintings. He pointed to certain similarities between them: the way that the saint and the musician incline their heads, as though listening—Lawrence to the voice in his heart, the clavichordist to her music—and the light that plays upon the face of each subject, illuminating the features in high relief and leaving part of the neck in deep shadow.

Causa (1972, p. 944) found that the *Saint Lawrence* and several related paintings—*The Singer* [70], the *Saint Agatha* in Detroit [48] and the *Saint Catherine* in Birmingham [72]—reveal, especially in the use of dense impasto, Cavallino's intimate knowledge of the work of Artemisia Gentileschi.

Because Saint Lawrence has been traditionally associated with another young saint, Stephen, the two have sometimes been portrayed together. It is therefore possible that this painting was originally accompanied by a *Saint Stephen*, who would have faced *Saint Lawrence* from the left.[2]   ATL

1. See Jacobus de Voragine's *Golden Legend* (1969, pp. 437-41). Saint Lawrence was a native of Spain who was brought to Rome in the third century by Saint Sixtus, who ordained him as archdeacon; this took place during the reign of Emperor Philip, who had become a Christian. Philip II of Spain (r. 1556–98) dedicated the Royal Monastery, El Escorial, to Saint Lawrence. According to popular notion, the ground plan represents the gridiron on which the saint died; the Royal Palace is the handle of the gridiron.

2. A *Saint Stephen* and a *Saint Lawrence*, each approximately "2-1/2 x 2 palmi" (66 x 52.8 cm), appeared in an inventory of the collection of Ruffo de Calabria, principe di Scilla (see Inv. nos. 181, 170).

Collections
Don José Lázaro, Madrid.

Exhibitions
Madrid 1970, cat. no. 46, repr.

Literature
Refice 1951, p. 270 n. 2. Camón Aznar in Madrid 1951, p. 141; in Madrid 1954, p. 133. Milicua 1954, pp. 68-72, fig. 1. Causa 1957, p. 42. Bologna 1958, p. 295. Pérez Sánchez 1961, p. 326; 1965, p. 382, pl. 129. Percy 1965, pp. 49-50, no. 15. Causa 1972, p. 944. London and Washington 1982–83, p. 143. Paris 1983, p. 195. Turin 1983, p. 164.

58

59

59

Mattathias
Slaying the Officer
of King Antiochus
on the Altar at Modin

Canvas, 64.5 x 127.6 cm.
Private Collection, USA

This picture is difficult to date because of its worn condition and because the unusual composition—with a row of figures at left and a pair at right, the central action taking place in empty space—does not fall logically into place with others of Cavallino's compositions. It seems to belong to the artist's maturity and is here dated to the latter half of the 1640s, near the Vienna and Rohrau *David* and *Esther* [60-61]. The fourth head from the left is the seventh of the so-called self-portraits. The second and third from the left and the second from the right are likewise highly individualized; yet Cavallino is not known to have painted portraits for their own sakes. (The fifth head from the left is such an apparent afterthought that it is tempting to suggest that it is a later addition, but its condition precludes a final judgment.) The palette ranges from brilliant red and dark blue to a dull gray, blue, mauve, yellow, and orange against a dark ground.

Called "The Sacrifice of the Gentiles" since it was first published in 1951, presumably because de Dominici mentioned a picture of this title in the collection of Nicola Salerno (Appendix, no. 11), the subject is actually from the Apocrypha (1I Maccabees 2:23-25). It concerns the profanation of the temples of Judah under King Antiochus Epiphanes, conqueror of Jerusalem, whose attempts to Hellenize the Jews and repress their religious customs led to the Maccabean rebellion of 167 BC. Mattathias, a descendant of priests, had moved with his five sons from Jerusalem to Modin: they grieved for the repression of the Jewish people, and when the king's officers who were forcing the people to give up their religion came to Modin to make the people offer sacrifice, they called on Mattathias and his sons to set an example by being the first to comply with the king's commands; but Mattathias refused to heed the king's message, to abandon the Law and the ordinances, or to depart in any way from the religion of his forefathers:

As he [Mattathias] ceased to utter these words, a Jew went up before the eyes of all of them to offer sacrifice as the king commanded, on the altar in Modin. And Mattathias saw him and was filled with zeal, and his heart was stirred, and he was very properly roused to anger, and ran up and slaughtered him upon the altar. At the same time he killed the king's officer who was trying to compel them to sacrifice, and he tore down the altar.[2]

Mattathias's sons went on to defeat the armies of Antiochus and to purify the sanctuary on Mount Zion desecrated by the heathen.

If this is the correct interpretation of the subject, the cows in the painting would be the unclean sacrificial cows Antiochus Epiphanes wished to force upon the Jews; the altar with gold utensils is faintly visible in the shadows at the left, and the young men who are not dressed as soldiers would be Mattathias's sons. Either Cavallino or some of his patrons were apparently interested in themes of the cleansing, or sanctity, of temples, as the artist represented related subjects at least three times: in this picture, in the London *Christ Driving the Merchants from the Temple* [42], and in the Moscow *Expulsion of Heliodorus from the Temple* [83]. The unusual subject matter suggests that this could have been a commission like the three late oils on copper [83-85] in which some political or military event related to a patron or an intended recipient may possibly have influenced the choice of theme.

This is the seventh picture to contain an apparent self-portrait of the artist [see also 3, 11, 20, 40, 41, 53, 84] as a figure psychologically isolated from the surrounding action, establishing eye contact with the viewer.   AP

1. It is possible that this picture was once cut in half. The late restorer Antonio de Mata informed me in 1968 that about thirty years previously he came across the left half in Naples and, by coincidence at almost the same time, the right half in Padua.
2. *The Apocrypha* 1959, p. 380.

Collections
Galleria San Marco, Rome, 1951; Manzoni Galleria d'Arte, Milan, 1967; Gilberto Algranti, Milan, 1969.

Exhibitions
Milan 1967, cat. no. 31, repr.

Literature
Refice 1951, pp. 268, 270 n. 4, repr. p. 264, fig. 5.

60

60

David before Saul

Canvas, 65 x 105 cm.

Kunsthistorisches Museum, Vienna

Exhibited in Cleveland only

The painting is a pendant to the *Esther and Ahasuerus* [61] in the collection of Count Harrach, who originally owned both; he donated this painting to the Kunsthistorisches Museum in 1931. Both works, together with a third painting by Cavallino, the *Banquet of Absalom* [17], were probably acquired by Alois Thomas Raimund, Count Harrach, during his viceroyship in Naples from 1728 to 1733.

In 1921 Adolfo Venturi (pp. 212-14) changed the attribution of both paintings from Manfredi to Cavallino. Cavallino painted the subject at least two—possibly three—more times. One version, belonging to the Heim Gallery in London [20], presents Cavallino in the role of King Saul's courtier, standing with his hand on his hip next to the king, a pose and position he will assume again as a much older attendant to King Porsenna in *Mucius Scaevola* [84]. A second version is in Rotterdam [18], and a possible third, now lost, may be one that inspired a painting on loan to Lethbridge University, Alberta, Canada (Fig. 60a); although the latter was for a long time mistitled *The Death of Solomon*, it clearly portrays the silent, brooding Saul, whom David has been summoned to heal with the power of his music. The figure of David in the Lethbridge painting closely resembles his counterpart in the picture in Vienna, and in both he plays a cittern instead of the harp. In the Heim and Rotterdam versions, he plays the harp—the instrument with which he has been traditionally associated.[1]

In the entry for *Tobias Healing His Father* in the Kassel catalogue,[2] compositional comparisons were drawn between the *Tobias* painting and the present paint-

Fig. 60a. Attributed to Cavallino. *David before Saul* (detail). Canvas, 172.7 x 222.8 cm. Anonymous private collection; on loan to Lethbridge University, Alberta, Canada.

ing, with the implication that both paintings may date from the same period—about 1640 to 1645. However, the Kassel painting still lacks the diagonal division of the background into contrasting areas of light and shadow, a device that Cavallino adopted and refined in his mature works and used as a way to bring his main protagonist into prominence; such backgrounds are found in the Harrach *Esther* and even more so in the *David*, which in this last aspect clearly anticipates the *Esther* in the Uffizi [62] dating from the latter part of the 1640s. Moreover, the two old gentlemen conversing in the extreme right of the *David* picture distinctly resemble the (now silent) witnesses in the Uffizi painting. The similarity of background and supporting figures in this *David* and the Uffizi *Esther* would support a date *after*, rather than before, 1645.[3]

ATL

1. The cittern is a sturdier version of the lute with a somewhat concave back and a peg box only slightly at an angle, as in this painting. As early as the Middle Ages, David was often depicted with an instrument called a *citole*, an ancestor of the cittern of the Renaissance and baroque eras. The assumption is made that the word *cetera*, or *cetra*, in turn is the Italian word for the early Greek *kithara*. See David Munroe, *Instruments of the Middle Ages and*

Renaissance (London: Oxford University Press, 1976), p. 26.

2. See Lehmann in Kassel 1980, p. 88.

3. Another Neapolitan painting of the subject, ascribed to Stanzione, passed through an auction sale at Lepke, Berlin, 1 May 1900, lot no. 25B. The pendant (25A) was a *Judith with the Head of Holofernes*. Both measured 124 x 152 cm.; neither one was illustrated.

Collections

Probably Alois Thomas Raimund, Count Harrach, viceroy to Naples (1728–33), and descendants; gift to the Museum in 1931.

Exhibitions

None.

Literature

Vienna 1856. Musto 1921b, p. 160. A. Venturi 1921, pp. 213-14, fig. 5. Ortolani 1922, p. 194. A. Venturi 1925, pp. 78, 80-81, fig. 27. Benesch 1926, pp. 249-52, fig. 174. Harrach cat. 1926, p. 89, no. 229. Delogu 1937, p. 410. Ortolani in Naples 1938, p. 66. Vienna 1938, p. 34, no. 509B. Masciotta 1942, p. 147. London 1949, p. 28. Pigler 1956, 1:133. Juynboll 1960, pp. 88, 91, fig. 6. *Kindlers Malerei Lexikon* 1 (1964), unpaginated. Vienna 1965, p. 37, no. 494. Percy 1965, p. 58, no. 47. Marini 1974, repr., unpaginated. Ferrari in *Dizionario biografico* 22 (1979):788. Lehmann in Kassel 1980, p. 88. London and Washington 1982−83, p. 143. Paris 1983, p. 194. Turin 1983, pp. 164, 168.

61

61

Esther before Ahasuerus

Canvas, 66 x 106 cm.
Graf Harrach'sche Familiensammlung,
Schloss Rohrau, Austria

In catalogue only

This is the third of four known paintings of the subject derived from the Book of Esther [see also 12, 20, 62]. It forms a pair with *David before Saul* [60] and shares its history and former attributions. The subject was misinterpreted in early sources as a scene from the story of the Queen of Sheba and Solomon (I Kings 10:1-13), an error that may have arisen because of the similarity to a painting of that story by Mattia Preti also in the Harrach collection.[1]

The composition resembles that of the later *Esther before Ahasuerus* in the Uffizi [62] but lacks its emotional intensity, coherence of design, and economy of forms. Although Esther's attendants resemble those in the later version, they have not yet faded into the background in order to give their queen the attention she enjoys in the Uffizi painting. The front-most maidservant has a special grace and suggested beauty, and is particularly diverting.

Compared to the Uffizi version with its intensely silent dialogue between the two protagonists, the Harrach painting stresses the narrative and relies on decorative elements. Costumes are described with quick, slashing and curving brushstrokes and delicate impasto, which enhance the impression of rich materials and finery befitting a splendid event at court rather than the deep seriousness of Esther's mission. Unfortunately, the face of the maidservant immediately behind Esther is poorly preserved, and because of its central position in the composition, it inevitably draws attention to the damaged area.   ATL

1. See A. Venturi 1921, pp. 212-13, fig. 4.

Collections
Probably Alois Thomas Raimund, Count Harrach, viceroy to Naples (1728–33), and descendants.

Exhibitions
None.

Literature
Musto 1921b, p. 160. A. Venturi 1921, pp. 212-13, fig. 4. Ortolani 1922, pp. 190, 194, 198. A. Venturi 1925, pp. 78-79, fig. 26. Benesch 1926, pp. 249-53, fig. 173, n. 4. Vienna 1926, p. 94, no. 248. Delogu 1937, p. 410. Ortolani in Naples 1938, p. 66, repr. Pigler 1956, 1:200. Harrach cat. 1960, no. 68. Percy 1965, p. 58, no. 48. Causa 1966, p. 7, color plates x,xi; 1972, pp. 942, 982 n. 108. Florence 1979, p. 212. London and Washington 1982–83, pp. 136, 139, 142, 143. Paris 1983, pp. 189, 194. Turin, 1983, pp. 158, 160, 163, 164.

62

Esther before Ahasuerus

Canvas, 76 x 102 cm.
Galleria degli Uffizi, Florence

In catalogue only

Stylistically, this is the maturest of Cavallino's four autograph versions [see also 12, 21, 61]. In the earliest two, Esther is shown fainting in the presence of King Ahasuerus, who touches her with his scepter as a sign of his pardon for her uninvited appearance. Both of these versions follow the scene described in the Book of Esther (5:1-4), but as Percy points out in [12], Cavallino likely had also read the colorful account of the scene in the Apocrypha. In the last two versions, one at Schloss Rohrau [61], and particularly the one here, Cavallino has sacrificed narrative detail in order to focus on Esther and the seriousness of her mission. The attendants surrounding her in the earlier versions now have receded into the shadow, giving her center stage. The image of Esther's anxious advance towards King Ahasuerus, with both figures extending their hands without touching, recalls Mary Magdalene approaching Christ in the "Noli Me Tangere" paintings. In fact, Tomory in his discussion of these two subjects and their interrelationship with the baroque idea of Sacred and Profane Love, cited Cavallino's present painting of *Esther* as an example of the high seriousness with which artists of that time would treat the present subject.[1]

Since early times the story of Esther and Ahasuerus had special appeal for the theater. Numerous plays were written, both in Italy and in the North, and their characters, settings, and costumes were often reflected in paintings of the subject.[2] It would appear that Cavallino's sustained interest in the subject of Esther before Ahasuerus and the stagelike compositions and studied manner of his characters also came from a particular play performed in Naples in Cavallino's time. The most eminent playwright at that time, Lope de Vega, who was highly esteemed in Naples,[3] actually wrote a *commedia* entitled *La Hermosa Ester*, which included the scene that Cavallino treated four times.[4] In the same year (1610) Lope de Vega also wrote a *commedia* of the *Story of Tobias*, another favorite subject of Cavallino and the painters of his circle (see [24] and Inventory). In these two plays Lope faithfully portrayed the characters and action described in the Bible. In his scene of Esther before Ahasuerus he strives to convey, as Cavallino does in his painting, the beauty of Esther's soul as well as her physical charm.[5] Occasionally Lope would enlarge his cast with what he called *figuras dialoguisticas*, a perfect description for the figures of Cavallino's supporting cast.[6] Although we know that the Teatro dei Fiorentini, built in 1647, performed Lope de Vega's plays, it is not known whether the two mentioned here were among them.

Stylistically, the Uffizi version of *Esther before Ahasuerus* is closest to the one at Schloss Rohrau [61], which must have preceded it. It is closer yet to the latter's pendant, *David before Saul* [60], insofar as Cavallino has placed both Esther and David adjacent to a diagonal shaft of light that gives them prominence over the supporting cast. However, while in the Schloss Rohrau *Esther* and the *David* in Vienna chiaroscuro emphasizes details and texture, in the Uffizi *Esther*, as Spinosa observed (in London and Washington 1982–83, no. 30), a warm light permeates the whole scene, selecting salient points and focusing on the main figure. The fluency of paint—applied more evenly, with zones of pure color—and the restrained elegance in composition and figures, in Spinosa's opinion, revealed influences from van Dyck that are also apparent in Cavallino's *Saint Stephen* [63] and *Saint Lucy* [64]; all three paintings include strident accents of red.

The support for this work is a smooth linen rather than the open-weave canvas that Cavallino mainly used.

Ortolani (1922, p. 193) published a copy of the Uffizi painting, then in the Gigli collection, measuring 64 x 50 cm; however, the copyist added a fluted column near the curtain opening.[7]   ATL

1. Tomory 1967, p. 186.

2. See Oscar Fischel, "Art and the Theatre-II," *Burlington Magazine* 66 (1935):54-67. Albert Heppner, "The Popular Theatre of the Rederijkers in the Work of Jan Steen and His Contemporaries," *Journal of the Warburg Institute* 3 (1939–40):22-48. Lurie 1969, pp. 96-99. Note that Johannes Serwouter's *Hester* or *The Deliverance of the Jews*, which influenced Dutch paintings of the subject, was a free adaption of Lope de Vega's *La Hermosa Ester* of ca. 1610.

3. Croce [1891] 1966, p. 57; see also Ezio Levi, *Lope de Vega e L'Italia* (Florence: G. C. Sansoni, 1935), pp. 43-45.

4. Biblioteca de autores españoles: *Obras de Lope de Vega* VII (Madrid: Consejo Superior de Investigátiones Cientificas, 1965), pp. 280-85. Margarete Baur-Heinhold, *The Baroque Theatre, A Cultural History of the 17th and 18th Centuries* (New York and Toronto: McGraw-Hill, 1967), p. 252.

174

62

5. Edward Glaser, ''Lope de Vega's 'La Hermosa Ester,''' *Sefarad* 20 (1960):117.

6. *Obras de Lope de Vega*, p. 279.

7. A notation on a photograph by Zeri of 25 January 1962, in the Frick Art Reference Library file, led to the assumption that yet another replica existed (Spinosa in London 1982, no. 30), but the photograph undoubtedly is of the Uffizi version.

Collections

Agostino Conte, Naples; acquired in 1917 from Ettore Sestieri.

Exhibitions

Florence 1922, cat. no. 254. Naples 1938. London and Washington 1982–83, cat. no. 30, repr.; Paris 1983, cat. no. 15, repr.; Turin 1983, cat. no. 30, repr.

Literature

De Rinaldis 1917, pp. 179, 180, 182, repr. Sestieri 1920, pp. 253, 263, 266, 268, fig. 18. Musto 1920, p. 180. De Rinaldis 1920a, p. 6. Longhi 1920b , p. 91. De Rinaldis 1921, p. 16, pl. xxi. Sestieri 1921, pp. 188, 194, 198, repr. A. Venturi 1921, pp. 212, 214. Ortolani 1922, pp. 193, 198. Consoli Fiego 1922, p. 107. Nugent 1925–30, 2: 562, 564-66, repr. A. Venturi 1925, p. 78. Benesch 1926, p. 250. Pevsner and Grautoff 1928, pp. 185-86, fig. 143. De Rinaldis 1929, pl. 45. Costantini 1930, 1:255. Corna 1930, 1:227. McComb 1934, pp. 49-51. Goering 1936, p. 21, pl. 20. Masciotta 1942, p. 147. Refice 1951, p. 267. Montini 1952, p. 35. Milicua 1954, p. 72. Juynboll 1960, pp. 89, 90, fig. 5. Waterhouse 1962, p. 182, fig. 157. Percy 1965, p. 47, no. 6. Moir 1967, 1:177, and 2:65, fig. 225. Tomory 1967, pp. 182, 186, pl. xxv, fig. 1. Lurie 1969, pp. 139, 147, fig. 5. Kaufmann 1970, pp. 166, 169, fig. 3. Minicuci in *Dizionario enciclopedico Bolaffi* 3 (1972):207, fig. 186. Causa 1972, pp. 942, 982 n. 108. Marini 1974, pp. 115-16. Ferrari in *Dizionario biografico* 22 (1979):788. Florence 1979, p. 212, no. P395, repr. Causa in *Larousse Dictionary* 1981, p. 56. *Müvészeti Lexikon* 1981 –84, 1:388.

63

The Stoning
of Saint Stephen

Canvas, 71 x 92 cm.
Private collection, Spain

In catalogue only

The painting, attributed to Velázquez, was purchased in Birmingham in 1950 by Ian Appleby, who recognized that it was Neapolitan. The first scholar to attribute it to Cavallino was Xavier de Salas. Pérez Sánchez (1965) included it in his listing of Cavallino's oeuvre and in the exhibition of Italian Seicento art in Madrid in 1970.

To our knowledge, Cavallino painted this scene only once; it is one of his most moving religious paintings. As are most of Cavallino's protagonists, Saint Stephen is young, convincingly human, and vulnerable. He was the first Christian martyr and one of the first seven deacons appointed by the apostles. The subject of his martyrdom (Acts 7:54-60) stirred the imagination of some of the greatest Northern and Southern painters of the sixteenth and seventeenth centuries, among them Giulio Romano (church of Santo Stefano, Genoa), Domenichino (Musée Condé, Chantilly), Elsheimer (National Gallery of Scotland), Rubens (Musée Valenciennes), and lastly, van Dyck (see Fig. 63a). In each of the *Saint Stephens* by these artists, the Heavens are opening up dramatically above the saint in response to his prayer asking forgiveness for his aggressors.

Typically, Cavallino chose to portray Saint Stephen engaged in an internal dialogue. Certain outstanding features in this painting—the saint's spiritual isolation from the crowd surrounding him, the figure bending down to lift up a stone (a female who reminds us of one of Lot's daughters in the Louvre oval [38]), the brilliant red of Stephen's robe of martyrdom, and the all-enveloping diffused light—resemble van Dyck's painting at Tatton Hall dating from that master's Ital-

ian sojourn. Van Dyck executed his work for the church of San Giacomo degli Spagnoli in Rome about 1623. It is not known when or by whom it was sent to Spain, where it was documented in Manuel Godoy's collection in ca. 1803–06, but Rose-de Viejo has proposed that one of the seventeenth-century Spanish viceroys in Naples or a Spanish ambassador to the Vatican could easily have had the power to acquire it for Spain, at which time it could have passed through Naples.[1]

The tender mood of the present painting, its unity of composition created by an over-all haze of warm browns, ochres, mauves, and grays—broken by the vibrant red of Stephen's robe—resembles the last version by Cavallino of *Esther before Abasuerus* [62], in the Uffizi. In 1970 Pérez Sánchez (p. 160) changed his original opinion (1965) about the date of this work (from 1635–40) and suggested instead a

date after that of the *Saint Cecilia* of 1645 [44]. Spinosa (in London and Washington 1982–83) also convincingly assigned *Saint Stephen* a place among Cavallino's half-length saints that are considered to be from his mature period.[2]   ATL

1. I am grateful for the information supplied to me by Isadora Rose-de Viejo, Curator of the Godwin-Ternbach Museum at Queens College, City University of New York, from her unpublished doctoral dissertation "Manuel Godoy, Patron de las Artes y Coleccionista, Madrid; Catálogo Actualizado de la Colección de Manuel Godoy" (Universidad Complutense, 1981), I, no. 141, pp. 121-23.
2. Saint Stephen's face resembles that of the young man appearing in full light in the crowd; he is probably the future Apostle Paul, who is supposed to have been present at the stoning of Saint Stephen—see Réau 1956–59, 3:444.

Fig. 63a. Anthony van Dyck, Antwerp 1599–London 1641. *The Martyrdom of Saint Stephen*. Canvas, 183 x 149.8 cm. Tatton Park, Knutsford, Cheshire, England; courtesy of Cheshire County Council.

63

Collections
Unidentified antique dealer, Birmingham, England, until 1950; Appleby Brothers, London.

Exhibitions
Madrid 1970, cat. no. 45, repr.

Literature
Pérez Sánchez 1965, p. 383, pl. 128. Milicua 1970, p. 5, fig. 4. London and Washington 1982–83, p. 136. Paris 1983, p. 189. Turin 1983, p. 158.

64

Saint Lucy

Canvas, 129.4 x 102.8 cm.
De Vito Collection, Naples

In catalogue only

Saint Lucy was a Sicilian virgin-martyr from Syracuse who became the city's patron saint. She was put to death during the reign of the emperor Diocletian, around AD 304. The legend of the loss of her eyes was told first by Jacobus de Voragine,[1] who claims that Lucy was so beautiful that many men fell in love with her. Indeed, one man would not cease praising the brilliance of her eyes, so, impatiently, she plucked them out, obeying the Biblical admonition, "If your eye offends you, cast it out."

A full-length *Saint Lucy* carrying her eyes in a salver (formerly in the church of San Andrés in Toledo, Spain; present whereabouts unknown) was heavily repainted in the nineteenth century, according to Pérez Sánchez (letters dated 27 July 1982 and 11 May 1984); therefore, it is impossible to confirm Cavallino's authorship on the basis of a photograph alone.

Saint Lucy is Cavallino's first venture into pure portraiture. Its predecessor was the earlier *Saint Martyr* at Capodimonte, wherein Cavallino was still closely bound to the earlier tradition of standing saints, as exemplified in the four engravings attributed to Agostino Carracci.[2] However, *Saint Lucy's* more mundane character is closer to the *ritratti divini*, portraits of virgin-martyrs as imagined in sumptuous contemporary dress, by Francisco Zurbarán, dating ca. 1635–45, as seen in the *Saint Lucy* in the Musée des Beaux-Arts, Chartres, or *Saint Casilda* in the Prado, Madrid. While the subjects in these works openly display their attributes, here Saint Lucy holds a palm frond delicately between her fingers, as a writer would his pen or as Cavallino's *Pittura* [66] holds her brush; a pair of eyes is inconspicuously placed like jewels on a table behind her.[3]

Lucy appears as a young woman dressed in her fineries whom Cavallino portrayed in her chamber, with light—the direction of which is indicated by Cavallino's parallel brushstrokes—streaming in from a concealed source, perhaps a window behind the half-drawn curtain. Obviously, as Spinosa pointed out (in London and Washington 1982–83), Cavallino's *Saint Lucy* reveals influences from van Dyck's Italian portraits. Like van Dyck, Cavallino portrayed his subject standing before a half-drawn curtain of sumptuous velvet, brilliant red in color, with gleaming highlights marking the ridges of the folds.

Lucy's dispassionate stance and the studied ease of her hands also remind one of van Dyck, as does the emphasis on the subject's elegance and modish dress. Unlike van Dyck, however, Cavallino created an area of dazzling light behind the figure, delineated by the contours of the half-drawn curtain and the saint's dress,[4] which gives her greater plasticity and prominence.

Spinosa (ibid., p. 142) suggested a date close to 1645, the date of the *Saint Cecilia* [44]. He pointed to the similarities in the modeling, compactness, and restricted elegance of the *Saint Lucy* to the two paintings of *Saint Catherine*—one in Birmingham [72] and one in Rotterdam [54]—which in this author's mind are both examples of Cavallino's mature style of the second half of the 1640s. ATL

1. *Golden Legend* 1969, pp. 34-37.
2. Diane DeGrazia Bohlin, *Prints and Related Drawings by the Carracci Family* (Washington: National Gallery of Art, 1979), pp. 80-81, figs. 5-8.
3. It is noteworthy that Stanzione's *Madonna of the Rosary* (Capodimonte) included a Saint Lucy who stands out from the other saints through her mundanity and self-conscious gaze at the spectator; Cavallino may have known this work.
4. A faintly visible pentimento of a piece of fluttering drapery shows how important these contours silhouetted against the light were to him.

Collections
Private collection, Milan.

Exhibitions
London and Washington 1982–83, cat. no. 29, repr.; Paris 1983 cat. no. 14, repr.; Turin 1983, cat. no. 29, repr.; Athens, National Gallery, "Il secolo d'oro della pittura napoletana," June–July 1984 (no cat.).

64

65

65

Saint Christina

Canvas, 63.5 x 50.5 cm
The Suida Manning Collection,
New York

In catalogue only

In the 1962 Finch College Museum of Art exhibition (no. 14), the identification of the figure as Saint Christina was made on the basis of the two arrows that she holds in her hand. Christina was a Christian martyr who lived during the reign of Diocletian (AD 284–305). According to *The Golden Legend*, she was condemned to death and subjected to numerous tortures, all of which failed to kill her.[1] Finally, she died after being bound to a pillar and shot through the heart with two arrows.

In the Finch catalogue entry, a compositional relationship to the *Saint Agatha* in York [28] is noted; the paintings are almost identical in size, but Saint Agatha's ecstatic piety is far removed from the more assured, poised, portraitlike manner of Saint Christina. Her gaze toward the spectator, the elegantly poised hand holding her attributes, and the backward tilt of her head link her more intimately with *Pittura* [66], the *Cantatrice* [70], and *Saint Catherine* [72].   ATL

1. *Golden Legend* 1969, pp. 366-68.

Exhibitions
New York 1962, cat. no. 14, repr.

Literature
Neumann 1969, p. 32 n. 77; 1971, pp. 238, 241 n. 27.

66

La Pittura:
An Allegory of Painting

Canvas, 72 x 59 cm.
Collection Novelli, Naples

After 1564, when Battista di Domenico Lorenzi included a female figure representing Painting among the figures of the Liberal Arts on Michelangelo's tomb at Santa Croce, the representation of women in allegories of painting had become increasingly popular.[1] Cesare Ripa's image of Pittura, depicted as a beautiful woman with "drappo cangiante" (garments with broken colors) and various other attributes, in his widely published *Iconologia* (4:386), lent further authority to this practice. At the same time, the growing recognition of Painting as one of the Liberal Arts found immediate expression in the self-portraits that artists included more frequently in their works. Cavallino, for example, appears as a secondary figure in at least eight of his own paintings. It was not surprising, therefore, that the leading woman artist of her time, Artemisia Gentileschi, who was known and admired by Cavallino, took advantage of an opportunity, denied to male artists, to portray herself in an *Allegory of Painting* (Collection of Her Majesty Queen Elizabeth II, Hampton Court).[2]

Artemisia's self-portrait as Pittura and, possibly also, Vaccaro's portrait (Collection Galante, Naples) of another woman painter, Ana Massimo di Rosa,[3] at her easel may have inspired Cavallino's *Allegory of Painting*. Significantly, Cavallino added a personal touch: he crowned his artist with a wreath of laurel, an attribute that Ripa (*Iconologia*, 4:490) had reserved for his Allegory of Poetry. Undoubtedly, this was a subtle yet poignant allusion to the interdependence of painting and poetry—a relationship that is keenly felt and vividly expressed in Cavallino's own art, as well

as a much-debated subject during his period.[4] With his inherent affinity for portraying feminine charm, Cavallino satisfied Ripa's requirement of beauty as an attribute for Pittura, and through his lavish display of color and brushwork he paid tribute to the act of painting itself.

The young artist, represented with the specificity of portraiture, is surrounded by sumptuous fabrics, rich in colors—olive green, white, brilliant red, with touches of blue and gold. The ample folds of her skirt fall into a starlike pattern and encircle the artist's left hand that holds brushes and a palette covered with dabs of the colors used in the painting. Her right hand, delicately poised, holds a fine-pointed brush, loaded with paint as though ready to add the final touches.

The painting seems to have been designed as an independent work, but in style, composition, subject, and size it is related to Cavallino's *Cantatrice* [70]. In each canvas the figure is placed in front of velvet drapery and the right hand is caught in the same delicate gesture, suggesting a closeness in date for the two paintings. Pittura's pensive gaze likewise resembles that of several half-length saints of Cavallino's mid- to late 1640s, among whom *Saint Christina* [65] is the closest, both in the facial type and in the specific gesture of her right hand. Another *Allegorical Figure* with an angel in the background (Fig. 66a) is known to this writer only from a photograph of unknown origin. It suggests that Cavallino may have painted a second *Allegory of Painting*, of which this is a copy. Judging from the type of figure and from the modeling of the face and hands of the copy, the original painting may have come from the period of the *Saint Anthony of Padua* and the *Pietà* in Molfetta.   ATL

Fig. 66a. Copy after Cavallino (?). *An Allegorical Figure*. Present whereabouts unknown.

182

66

1. Kubler 1965, p. 339.

2. Bissell 1968, p. 158; Garrard 1980, p. 97.

3. Ana Massimo di Rosa, also known as Annella, or Aniella di Rosa, was the wife of Stanzione's pupil, Agostino Beltrano; Ortolani in Naples 1938, repr. p. 51.

4. Carducho 1633.

Collections

Private collection, Dijon; Artemis, London; Costantini, Rome; acquired by Novelli in 1979.

Exhibitions

London 1978, cat. no. 12, repr.

67

Pietà

Canvas, 105 x 73.7 cm,
initialed on cross
just above the Virgin's veil:
BC . F
Pinacoteca del Seminario
Vescovile Diocesano,
Molfetta

The painting was formerly in the church of Santa Maria Consolatrice degli Afflitti, or del Purgatorio, in Molfetta (a small town in Apulia on the Adriatic coast, not far from Bari), until about twenty years ago when it was placed on deposit in the Seminario Vescovile during restorations to the church. In the nineteenth century it was attributed to Sebastiano Conca (Salvemini 1878), but by 1938 (Ortolani) it was given to Cavallino, although the artist's initials were not discovered until the picture was cleaned in preparation for the 1964 exhibition of Apulian painting in Bari (D'Elia in Bari 1964).

The Virgin's face, blue mantle, and reddish-orange garment have suffered a loss of glazes, resulting in some rather abrupt transitions between light areas and shadowed ones. A pentimento is visible in her gray-brown veil, which once continued down across her right arm. A nineteenth-century restoration is recorded in an inscription on the back of the canvas: "Nicola Nysio [Nyco ?] Restauro nel 1868/ Rettore Gaetano Lioy Lupis." This information was confirmed by Salvemini in 1878, who stated that the rector Gaetano Lioy-Lupis had recently restored the church and supplied new furnishings.[1]

The overall tonality is limited in range: against a dark background, the blue and reddish orange of the Virgin's garments contrast with the grayish-white impasto of Christ's torso, precisely brushed into the luminous gray-brown shadows on his body to create an image of startling three-dimensionality and surface realism. Christ's lips are blue; he wears the crown of thorns and the cross looms up behind him. The naturalistic depiction of his torso recalls certain of Ribera's works of the late thirties, such as the Christ in the *Pietà* in the Certosa di San Martino in Naples (Fig. 14) or the Marsyas in the *Apollo Flaying Marsyas* in the museum of the Certosa.[2] The simplified composition—with two half-length figures leaning in opposite directions to bisect the canvas diagonally between light and dark, death and life, stillness and gesticulation—allows nonetheless for a sophisticated interrelationship of shapes and contours between the two protagonists.

The church was built at the expense of the *primicerius* and vicar-general don Vespasiano Volpicella (23 June 1591–5 September 1649). It seems to have been begun before 1633 and had not been completed at the time of the donor's death in 1649, although he left funds for this purpose, and the building was consecrated on 6 December 1667.[3] Unfortunately we do not know when Cavallino's painting came to the church, whether it was commissioned for the building or arrived at some later date. By 1878 it was described by Salvemini as located in the left transept.[4] It was placed high over the altar, above another, larger painting, the subject of which was illegible to the present writer in 1968.[5] The decorative enframements for both canvases appeared to be from the eighteenth century.

D'Elia's dating of the canvas to around 1649 (in Bari 1964), which has generally been followed, seems correct. We would certainly want to place the work between the signed *Saint Cecilia* of 1645 [44] and the initialed Cleveland *Adoration of the Shepherds* of the first half of the 1650s [79].   AP

1. Salvemini 1878, pt. 2, pp. 141-42. Members of the Lupis family were heirs of the founder of the church, don Vespasiano Volpicella (d. 1649); don Vespasiano Lupis (d. 1672) was rector in 1654, having inherited the position of patron of the church according to Volpicella's arrangements. The charge eventually passed to Michele Lioy and his last descendant, Caterina Lupis. When Salvemini wrote, Gaetano Lioy-Lupis, as rector, was responsible for a considerable restoration of the church. On the Lupis and Volpicella families, see also a manuscript by the notary Antonio Muti (d. 1750), "Famiglie molfettesi," Biblioteca Comunale, Molfetta, pp. 251, 543.

2. Repr. in London and Washington 1982–83, p. 86, no. 123.

3. Romano 1842, p. 178; Salvemini 1878, pt. 2, pp. 141-42. The date 1633 is part of the inscription over the entrance of the church. An eighteenth-century list of the church's possessions mentions donations from benefactors at least as early as 1633–34; unfortunately no references are made in this list to the decorations of the church or to any of the paintings ("Platea della chiesa di S.ta Maria Consolatrice delli afflitti sott'il Tit. del Purgatorio fondata dal q.m D. Vespasiano Volpicella nell'anno 1649 [A. 1727]"; Biblioteca Comunale, Molfetta, MS 241).

4. "Il quadro del Nazareno morto sul seno della Madre Santissima dipinto dal Cav. Sebastiano Conca" (Salvemini 1878, pt. 2, p. 143).

5. Don Pietro Amato of the Seminario Vescovile kindly informed me that the location of a small Pietà above a larger picture is an iconographical arrangement frequently seen in Apulian churches and chapels. The other paintings listed by Salvemini as located in the left transept of the church were a *Christ Mocked* of the Flemish school and a *Saint Andrea Avellino* by "Calò."

Collections

Chiesa del Purgatorio (Santa Maria Consolatrice degli Afflitti), Molfetta.

Exhibitions

Bari 1964, cat. no. 166; Bucharest 1972, cat. no. 45; Naples 1972, cat. no. 45.

Literature

Salvemini 1878, pt. 2, p. 143. Ortolani in Naples 1938, pp. 66-67. D'Elia in Bari 1964, pp. 168-69, pl. v. Percy 1965, p. 51, no. 21. Liebmann 1968, p. 456. Lurie 1969, pp. 136, 139. Causa 1972, pp. 942, 983 n. 112. Minicuci in *Dizionario enciclopedico Bolaffi* 3 (1972):207. Ferrari in *Dizionario biografico* 22 (1979):787. London and Washington 1982–83, p. 146. Turin 1983, p. 167.

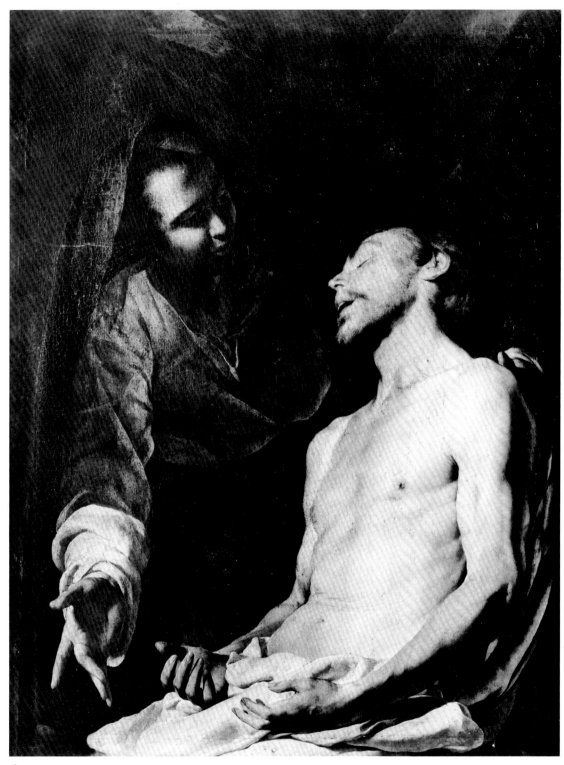

67

68

The Triumph of Galatea

Canvas, 148.5 x 203 cm.
Richard L. Feigen & Company,
New York

Of the fifty Nereids who were children of the sea-god Nereus, Amphitrite and her sister Galatea are the most celebrated in art. Sharing attributes as well as companions, they are often shown riding on their shell chariots drawn by dolphins, in the company of other sea nymphs and tritons blowing their conches or their horns. Poussin painted a Nereid that easily could have played the role of either Galatea or Amphitrite had he not included the sea-god Neptune, the husband of the latter, which clearly turned the scene into a *Triumph of Neptune and Amphitrite*, now in the Philadelphia Museum of Art.[1]

In Cavallino's painting the sea nymph reigns supreme, and she is almost certainly intended to represent Galatea. A number of striking features seem to be directly inspired by Raphael's *Galatea* (Farnesina, Rome), widely known through Marcantonio's engraving. For example, the commanding figure of Galatea encircled with flowing drapery, the delicate manner in which Cavallino has her hold the reins of the dolphins, and the fanfaring triton leading the cortège through the waters were undoubtedly inspired by Raphael's painting.[2]

As a Neapolitan, Cavallino must have been familiar with the Sicilian legend of the nymph Galatea. The story was told by many ancient writers, among them Ovid (*Metamorphoses* 13.735-897), whose works, as we are informed by de Dominici, were required reading for the pupils of Massimo Stanzione. Galatea was loved by the cyclops Polyphemus, who called her "Galatea, whiter than snowy privet-leaves, more blooming than meadows."[3]

But when Galatea rejected his advances, he killed her lover Acis out of jealousy.

The similarity of this painting to the description of a lost *Galatea* by Artemisia Gentileschi strengthens the argument for the identification of the sea nymph as Galatea rather than Amphitrite. Artemisia's painting, ca. 1649, which was commissioned by the famous collector Antonio Ruffo of Sicily, was larger (8x 10 *palmi*, or 211.2 x 264 cm.) than Cavallino's canvas (148.5 x 203 cm), but the composition seems to have been almost exactly the same: "Galatea che siede sopra un granchio, tirata da 2 delfini e accompagnata da 5 tritoni."[4] Although Artemisia included five tritons and Cavallino shows only four, Galatea is the unrivalled female persona in both canvases. She is escorted by male companions only, unlike the more traditional depiction of her entourage that includes her sister-sea nymphs. The wonderful shell on which the Nereid sits is another departure from the imagery traditionally associated with Galatea. Cavallino has substituted the spiky crab shell, the *granchio*, for the scallop shell of earlier images; the *granchio* is the shell named in Artemisia's painting as well.[5]

While the connection with Artemisia's lost work seems undeniable, this painting, like so many of Cavallino's canvases, combines influences from several different sources. The full bodied, long-limbed proportions and the relaxed self-confidence of Galatea recall the female nudes of Orazio Gentileschi (e.g., the *Danaë* in Cleveland and the one at the Feigen Gallery, New York)—a reflection of Orazio's style that may have been transmitted to Cavallino through the agency of Artemisia's *Galatea* .

As is pointed out by Spinosa (in London 1982, no. 33), the *Galatea* reveals Cavallino's continuing fascination with the work of Stanzione, whose large, imposing figures often have fully lighted elliptical faces, as seen in the *Musica* (Galleria Doria Pamphili) and in the *Martyr* (collection of Conte V. Galanti, Naples).

Cavallino's elegantly playful touch is seen throughout the canvas in the form of those stylish passages that must have delighted his patrons: the intricate knot of coral behind Galatea; the silken-tasseled, coral-colored reins; the offhand way in which Galatea grasps the delicate reins—one pair looped over her fingers, the other pair clutched in her fist; a seaweed wreath

tied with a silver bow in the hair of the triton-flutist; the sparkling pearl in Galatea's ear; the bead-bright eyes of the dolphins fixed upon the viewer, and their wet, glistening skin.

Cavallino has created a most convincing nocturnal ambience. Figures rush through dark waters under stormy clouds, and a half-veiled moon spreads its pale light, which reveals an undulating shoreline and transforms Galatea's skin into translucent white, emphasizing her sensuality.

The painting fits easily among the artist's mature works, as Spinosa has noted (in London 1982): "Its compact chromatic structure, its enveloping luminosity, and its elegant classicizing arrangements of form are features shared by Cavallino's other paintings in the mid to late 1640s, culminating in the most classical of his works, the three copper panels [83-85]."

The figure type of the muscular triton-flutist was repeated at least once by Cavallino, in the figure of Heliodorus of the Moscow copper panel [83]. He is seen again, grotesquely parodied as one of the executioners in a lost *Massacre of the Innocents* by an unknown artist (cf. Fig. 34a).   ATL

1. Blunt 1966-67, pp. 120-21, no. 167; Paris 1982, p. 308, cat. no. 89, color plate on p. 95. The painting dates to ca. 1635–36. A number of preparatory drawings rendered at the time he was working on his painting indicates that Poussin was—as he often did—toying with two ideas at once: a Birth of Venus and a Triumph of Galatea. Similarly, Raphael's pictorial idea for Galatea also originated in a sketch for a *Birth of Venus,* which appears on one of the study sheets for the *Disputà* (Oskar Fischel, *Raphael*, Klassiker der Kunst [English ed.; New York: Brentano's, 1948], p. 186).

2. As will be pointed out, it seems that Artemisia Gentileschi may have transmitted these direct impressions from Raphael's painting in Rome.

3. Ovid *Metamorphoses* 13.789-90.

4. Ruffo 1916, p. 315, no. 80: "Galatea who is sitting on a crab shell drawn by two dolphins and accompanied by five tritons."

5. One other artist who turned the traditional smaller shell into a fanciful large shell-chariot was Hendrik Goltzius in his chiaroscuro woodcut *Galatea* (Hollstein VIII.121.368). With Artemisia's *Galatea* in mind, it is interesting that Cavallino's only other mythological subject, *Hercules and Omphale* [22], was also one painted by Artemisia. The description of that painting, which like her *Galatea* is lost, also closely corresponds to Cavallino's *Hercules and*

68

Omphale (see Bissell 1968, p. 165). De Dominici (1742–43, 3:58) mentions that Stanzione sold two paintings with sea nymphs and with Galatea to a Frenchman. Note that according to D'Addosio 1912–13, 38, no. 3:518, the principe di Cardito paid for another large painting (in September 1649) by Andrea Vaccaro. As Percy suggests, it is tempting to identify the present painting of Galatea with the "quatro grande" mentioned in a document of 23 January 1649, concerning payment from the principe di Cardito (see Appendix, no. 2).

Collections

Private collection, Switzerland; Hazlitt, Gooden and Fox, London, 1981/82.

Exhibitions

London and Washington 1982–83, cat. no. 33, repr. in color.

Literature

Spear 1983, p. 128 n. 4. Paris 1983, p. 189. Turin 1983, pp. 159, 165-66, cat. no. 33, repr.

69

69

Saint Mary Magdalene

Canvas, 101 x 127 cm.
Museo di Capodimonte, Naples

In catalogue only

Unfortunately very little remains of Cavallino's original painting, except for the beautifully rendered skull in the right foreground. This Mary Magdalene is close in type to Vouet's figures of the Magdalen, such as the one in the collection of Vicomte René de Vaulchier, Chateau de Savigny-les-Beaune.[1] As in Vouet's paintings, the prostitute is seated in the immediate foreground near the opening of a cave, enveloped in the heavy folds of her dress, and she is as sensual as she is penitent; her heavenward glance, flowing hair, relaxed fleshy hands, and half-modest décolleté are all characteristics shared by Vouet's figure. In turn, the languid, self-assured femininity of both of these figures suggests the influence of the *Repentant Magdalene* paintings of Orazio Gentileschi (e.g., one in the Kunsthistorisches Museum, Vienna), although his figures show a more pronounced classicism than Vouet's or Cavallino's.

The same languid quality and soft modeling are evident, and, in fact, have been greatly exaggerated, in the central figure of the mother protecting her child in the Cavallinesque *Massacre of the Innocents* (cf. Fig. 34a).

Causa (in Naples 1975, p. xxiv) ascribed the painting to Cavallino's full maturity, "nel suo estenuato languore quasi metastasiano." ATL

1. Another *Magdalene* is the lost painting by Vouet that was engraved by Claude Mellan (Bibliothèque Nationale, Cabinet des Estampes, ED 32b, fol. 28); see also Crelly, 1962, cat. nos. 198-200.

Collections
Barone Giuseppe Marzano and Maria Daniele di Bagni, Centurano (Caserta).

Exhibitions
Naples 1975, pp. xxiv, 256, repr.

70

The Singer
(La Cantatrice)

Canvas, 75 x 64 cm.
Museo di Capodimonte, Naples

The painting came to the Museum at the beginning of this century. It was first given to Pacecco de Rosa (Capodimonte Inv. no. S.84368). De Rinaldis (1911, p. 327) listed it as "una giovanetta," measuring 79 x 64 cm, by an anonymous painter whose style reminded him of Pacecco de Rosa and Guarino. Longhi (1920c, p. 156) was the first scholar to attribute it to Cavallino, followed by Sestieri (1920, p. 269; 1921, p. 188). De Rinaldis (in Naples 1927 and 1928 p. 149) suggested that the painting was by a master from the circle of Stanzione and Vaccaro, but since Ortolani's acceptance of the work as a painting by Cavallino in 1938 (p. 66), all scholars have agreed with the attribution to this artist.

After seeing *The Singer* and *The Clavichordist* [71] exhibited together, Bologna (in Naples 1954b, p. 23, no. 24) suggested that they were pendants. A side-by-side comparison in the Neapolitan exhibition at the Louvre was convincing to Rosenberg (in Paris 1983) also, who pointed to the tonal refinement and harmonies of violet and copper browns in both paintings; to the similarities both in the oval shape of the women's faces, framed by brown hair, and their long fingers; and, above all, to the seductive charm and coquettish glance of the two subjects. Spinosa (in London and Washington 1982–83, no. 31), who with Percy rejects the pairing of the two paintings, proposes a date in the late 1640s for the *Singer*, when Cavallino—under the influence of painters from Poussin's circle—moved away from the pronounced painterliness of his earlier style.

The only scholar who referred to the coquettish *Singer* as "Giovine Santa" was Sestieri (1921, p. 188). On the other hand, *The Clavichordist*, whom Cavallino portrayed at her keyboard, was thought to be Saint Cecilia by various scholars.

If the two ovals were intended to be companion pieces, they were probably conceived as personifications of two aspects of Music, which were to be portrayed as young females, in the same way that Ripa had allegorized Painting as a young woman in his *Iconologica*—a work that achieved immediate popularity after its publication in 1593 and became enormously influential as a typological source book for artists. An illustration of a direct copy after *The Singer* in the catalogue of an exhibition of the Collection Rocco-Pagliara held in Naples, May 25–June 15, 1921, was found recently (1983) by Pierre Rosenberg. The caption reads "Esposito G(aetano, 1858–1911) 'Figura' (N. 50)," with an added handwritten notation: "Figura di Donna; dall'antico, dipinto ad olio, cornice dorata."   ATL

Collections
Unidentified private collection, Naples; Museo Reale Borbonico, Naples.

Exhibitions
Naples 1954, cat. no. 23; Paris 1965, cat. no. 47; Bucharest 1972, cat. no. 6; Naples 1972; cat. no. 44; London and Washington 1982–83, cat. no. 31, repr.; Paris 1983, cat. no. 16, repr.; Turin 1983, cat. no. 31, repr.

Literature
De Rinaldis 1911, 2:404, no. 372. Longhi 1920c, p. 156. Sestieri 1920, p. 269; 1921, pp. 188, 195, 198, repr. De Rinaldis in Naples 1927, p. 149, fig. 290; in Naples 1928, p. 149, fig. 290. Ortolani in Naples 1938, p. 66. Commodo Izzo 1951, p. 138. Picone 1955, p. 74. Molajoli in Naples 1957, p. 73. Causa 1957, p. 42, pl. 22. Molajoli in Naples 1958, p. 56; in Naples 1961, fig. 36; in Naples 1964, p. 54, fig. 80. *Kindlers Malerei Lexikon* 1 (1964), unpaginated. Bazin 1965, p. 7, fig. 6. Percy 1965, p. 52, no. 25. Rosenberg 1968, pp. 150, 152, no. 6, fig. 2. Neumann 1969, pp. 31-32; 1971, pp. 237-38, 241, no. 25. Causa 1972, pp. 942, 944. Brejon de Lavergnée and Dorival 1979, p. 92. Causa in *Larousse Dictionary* 1981, p. 57. Causa in Naples 1982, p. 147, repr. p. 100. Ferrari in *Dizionario biografico* 22 (1979):788.

70

71

The Clavichordist

Canvas, 79 x 64 cm.
Musée des Beaux-Arts, Lyon

In catalogue only

This work has been known as *La Clavicembalista* (*The Harpsichordist*); however, Pierre Rosenberg believes that the keyboard instrument is not a harpsichord but a clavichord, which was the more popular instrument in the seventeenth century.[1] Milicua's suggestion (1954, pp. 68-69) that the player represented Saint Cecilia[2] is understandable because numerous Seicento paintings depict her in a similar fashion, for example, Carlo Dolci's *Saint Cecilia* in the Gemäldegalerie (Dresden), and Francesco Guarino's *Cecilia* in an unidentified private collection.[3] He also suggested that *The Clavichordist* may once have been a pendant to the *Saint Lawrence* in Madrid [58], as both figures are modeled similarly and incline their heads—Saint Lawrence "as if listening to the voice of his heart" and the girl in this canvas as if listening to her music.

It is not certain whether Milicua at the time of his publication knew of the closely related *Singer* [70] or whether he, like Spinosa and Percy, did not accept the two musician ovals as pendants. The slightly more textured surface of *The Clavichordist* and the difference in the backgrounds of the two paintings (an undefined space in *The Clavichordist*, sumptuous velvet drapery—similar to that of *La Pittura* [66]—in *The Singer*) supports the argument against the two pictures being companions.

While Bologna (1954), Milicua (1954), and Rosenberg (1983) date the painting close to the *Saint Cecilia* of 1645, Spinosa (1983), Percy, and this writer believe that it dates from the late 1640s.   ATL

1. Rosenberg 1968, p. 150, n. 1.
    2. Ibid., p. 152. Rosenberg also considers the possibility that the Lyon painting may be Saint Cecilia and its pendant in Naples another saint. In this connection it is noteworthy that "Een Ste. Cecilia, uit de Italiaansche School, zeet goedt, op een ovaale doek, hoog 28, breet 25 duimen" was sold from the collection of Muntius Molinari in Wissel-Geld, Brussels, 15 July 1763. The collection included numerous Italian, and specifically Neapolitan, paintings. See Gerard Hoet, *Catalogus of Naamlyst van Schilderyen*, 3 vols. (s'Gravenhage, 1770), 3:346.
    3. Lattuada 1982, p. 59, fig. 12.

Collections
Professor Tito Diodati, Naples; Frederick Mont, New York.

Exhibitions
Naples 1954, cat. no. 24, repr.; Paris 1983, cat. no. 17, repr.

Literature
Milicua 1954, pp. 65-69, fig. 2. Picone 1955, p. 74, repr. Percy 1965, p. 56, no. 39. Rosenberg 1968, pp. 149-56, fig. 1 and color plate; 1972, p. 343, fig. 1. Brejon de Lavergnée and Dorival 1979, p. 92. Besançon 1982, p. 10 n. 67. London and Washington 1982–83, p. 143. Turin 1983, pp. 159, 164.

71

72

72

Saint Catherine
of Alexandria

Canvas, 71.7 x 59 cm.
The Barber Institute of Fine Arts,
The University of Birmingham,
Birmingham, England

In catalogue only

While Saint Catherine shares with her counterpart in Rotterdam [54] a tender grace and subtle chiaroscuro, her demeanor more closely matches that of the *Singer* in Naples [70]. Cavallino has given both figures the same tilt of the head and nearly identical facial features—particularly eyebrows and mouths—yet has made a subtle change in their expressions to reflect their characters: he has exchanged the singer's seductive glance at the spectator for the meditative, unfocused gaze of Catherine. To accentuate for each the integration of external surroundings with inner character, he has made the singer more immediately accessible to the viewer by her placement on the picture plane and a background curtain that both confines and projects her image, but for Saint Catherine he has interposed a line of drapery and a section of an enormous wheel that separates her from the viewer, and has provided her with an undefined background whose glimmer of light evokes a mystical quality.

The neutral gray background of this *Saint Catherine* anticipates the atmospheric space of Cavallino's late paintings. As Spinosa has pointed out (in London and Washington 1982–83, cat. no. 32), the work belongs to the transition from Cavallino's intensely painterly phase to the more classical style of his late paintings that reflect the influence of Poussin and his French followers.   ATL

Collections
Henshaw Skinner Russell; Hazlitt Gallery, London.

Exhibitions
London 1966, cat. no. 16, repr. London 1982, cat. no. 32, repr.

Literature
Percy 1965, p. 49, no. 13. Birmingham 1966. *The Burlington Magazine* 108 (May 1966): fig. 69. Causa 1972, pp. 942, 944, fig. 315. Ferrari in *Dizionario biografico* 22 (1979):788. De Maio 1983, p. 135 n. 72. London and Washington 1982–83, pp. 143-44, cat. no. 32, repr. Paris 1983, pp. 193, 195. Turin 1983, pp. 164-65, cat. no. 32, repr.

73

Nursing Madonna

Canvas, 89 x 71 cm.
Oblastní Galerie,
Olomouc, Czechoslovakia

In catalogue only

The painting reveals a few disturbing blemishes, including a thumbnail damaged area below the Madonna's left eye, where old overpaint is visible, and the Infant's hair, which lacks Cavallino's fine comb-like brush marks—an indication that it may have been in part repainted. A round seal on the back of the canvas that shows a stag within a triangle has not yet been identified: perhaps it was the family motto or emblem of a former owner. A handwritten notation on the stretcher gives the name "de la Hyer" along with the numbers "0 301 791." The attribution to Laurent de La Hyre may have been suggested because of the *Nursing Madonna's*—even if distant—resemblance to a well-known *Charity* (Toledo, Ohio, Museum of Art), until recently given to that master but now believed to be the work by Jacques Blanchard.[1] The points of comparison between Cavallino's and Blanchard's nursing figures are their engaging charm and their oblique look directed at the spectator rather than at their infants, as seen, for example, in Blanchard's *Nursing Madonna* in The J. Paul Getty Museum.

Cavallino's *Nursing Madonna* represents his first large-scale statement in the Caravaggesque idiom; the Madonna joins a host of other young *popolane* portrayed by Italian and Northern Seicento artists in various religious roles, boldly placed into the immediate foreground and raking light, with their gaze directed at the viewer. Cavallino's model, one of his favorite *"bellas madonnas,"*[2] with their dark scintillating eyes, closely resembles the *Judith* in Stockholm [82].

Jaromír Neumann was the first to attribute the painting to Cavallino, convincingly placing it among a group of comparable portraitlike figures of Cavallino's maturity, such as *La Cantatrice* [70], *Saint Christina* [65], and *Judith* [82]. Of these, *Judith* seems closest to the *Nursing Madonna* in composition and in scale. One common feature is the partially lifted curtain that divides an area of luminous space behind the figure and thus creates an intricate contour-pattern. The predominance of clear red, blue, and white in the *Madonna* reminds one more of *La Pittura* [66], however, than of *Judith*, with its dramatic contrast of gold and blue.

The Madonna's dress is cerise and is laced with cuffs similar to those in *La Cantatrice*. A gray headscarf and a white transparent fichu below a blue wrap complete the Madonna's attire. Cavallino has described details with exceptional delicacy: the transparency of skin showing fine, blue veins; the small teeth gleaming between the Madonna's slightly parted lips; the tiny drops of milk pearling from the Infant's mouth; and the tender way in which the Infant is cradled in his Mother's arm. Typical of Cavallino are the tiny dabs of clear red paint (the same he used for the Madonna's lips) in the corner of her eyes, and the few, perhaps involuntary, splatters on her white cuff.

Cavallino has captured the warmth and intimacy of the scene, thereby transforming a nursing *popolana*, with all her natural and coquettish charm, into a moving image of devotion. Although bolder and more assertive in design and spirit, if only for the Madonna's unwavering glance at the spectator, the painting recalls some of the tender rapport between Mother and Child in Aniello Falcone's *Rest on the Flight into Egypt* (Cathedral, Naples), painted for Gaspar Roomer in 1641. By contrast, a small tondo of the same subject, attributed to Pacecco de Rosa (Capodimonte), which in many details is strikingly close to Cavallino's painting, could not be more remote from the profound sentiment of Cavallino's and Falcone's *Nursing Madonnas*. ATL

1. Rosenberg in Paris 1982, cat. no. 5.
2. See Ezio Levi, *Lope de Vega e l'Italia* (Florence: G. C. Sansoni, 1935), p. 40.

Collections
Unidentified private collection.

Exhibitions
Olomouc 1967, cat. no. 10.

Literature
Neumann 1969, pp. 31, 32 n. 74, figs. 17, 19, 20 (detail); 1971, pp. 237-39, 241 n. 24, figs. 7 and 8. Causa 1972, p. 943. Ferrari in *Dizionario biografico* 22 (1979):787.

73

74

74 & 75

Lot and His Daughters

Wood, diam. 38.1 cm.
Silvano Lodi, Campione d'Italia,
Switzerland

The Drunkenness of Noah

Wood, diam. 38.1 cm.
Silvano Lodi, Campione d'Italia,
Switzerland

The subject of Lot and his daughters (Genesis 19:30-35) lent itself well as a counterpart to another Biblical subject, the drunkenness of Noah (Genesis 9:20-23). Both Lot and Noah were chosen by God and given a chance to escape with their families—Noah from the flood (Genesis 7:6-10) and Lot from the burning Sodom. And conversely, both were central figures in degrading situations involving their respective children. During the Counter-Reformation both the Catholic South and the Protestant North recognized the strong moral message inherent in the two subjects, which provided inspiration for numerous representations in the visual arts. For example, the story of Lot and his two daughters, with its intriguing plot and frank display of naturalism, contrasting old age with the charm of the young females, had special appeal to painters with Caravaggesque and classicizing tendencies; hence Neapolitan painters, particularly Cavallino, were especially attracted to the story.

This *Lot and His Daughters* is one of Cavallino's most boisterous and colorful paintings, more so than its more lyrical precedent in the Louvre [38]. Lot, as wretched as the drunken Noah, is being served wine by his young smiling daughter in décolleté. Her slightly dishevelled hair (of Cavallino's favorite chestnut color) is defined in fine brushstrokes, and her delicate white skin offers a striking contrast to her father's ruddy face. She is dressed in blue. Lot's garment becomes moss green in the shadows and Naples yellow in lighter areas, revealing Cavallino's fine comblike brushmarks in the highlights. The laughing daughter on the right wears an ochre skirt and a white blouse. Her sandals are blue, and her foot (with shiny toenails) is unusually sturdy for Cavallino's women. The lips of both girls are bright red. The face of the laughing girl is flushed and her wide face and bulbous nose resemble the physiognomy of the Madonna of the Rosary in the painting in Ottawa [52]. In the background, one sees the reflection of the burning Sodom.

The back of the painting bears two small seals, one of which is clearly legible (see Fig. 74a).[1] The image is in the fashion of a family device; its French inscription points to a one-time French owner of the work.

Cavallino's two tondi of *Lot* and *Noah*, though closely related thematically and in their set of characters to the second pair of

Lot and *Noah* [38-39], appear to be later. Percy and Spinosa suggested a date shortly before 1645 for the latter two; but for the present pair Percy suggested to Rosenberg a date near 1650,[2] with which this author agrees.

In style and theme, *The Drunkenness of Noah* perfectly supplements *Lot and His Daughters*. The episode of Noah's drunkenness (Genesis 9:20-23) occurred after he planted the first vineyard at the end of the flood from which he and his family had been rescued. Cavallino depicts Noah's son Ham pointing mockingly to the source of his amusement, while his brothers Shem and Japheth, deeply embarrassed, try frantically to cover the nakedness of their father. The subject was obviously not considered unsuited to sacred buildings, as Benozzo Gozzoli's frescoes in the Camposanto at Pisa and Michelangelo's in the Sistine ceiling confirm. Maarten van Heemskerck used the scene in his engravings to illustrate the Fourth Commandment as well as the *Story of Noah*.[3] The inscription of Philipp Galle's engraving after Heemskerck, in the Leiden printroom (Hollstein VIII.242.204) showed the artist's faithfulness to the Vulgate: "Dormit in aprico multo Noe victus ridet genitalia Chamus."[4] Like the Mannerist examples, Cavallino's composition is complex, full of tension and of robust naturalism. He has chosen one of the most wretched *lazzaroni* and shows him in unabashed nakedness and drunken stupor,

Fig. 74a. Drawing of the emblem affixed to the back of *Lot and His Daughters*.

199

75

but discreetly places the defenseless Noah facing his family rather than the spectator.[5]

Like its pendant, the painting sings with color. Noah's son to the extreme left wears a yellow tunic, with a blue ribbon on his shoulders and wrists; another son, facing the viewer, wears a dark blue blouse, as does the third son, Ham. The blanket is of rich cinnamon tonality similar to that of Noah's garb. Hidden in the shadow on the right are leaves with purple grapes. A dab of yellow in the foreground surely represents the remnant of Noah's golden drinking cup, the kind Lot drinks from in the companion piece.

The tondo shows Cavallino's gift for turning a scene of robust and commonplace naturalism into an "intermezzo ridanciano, ma scandito in un incastro di rigorosa tensione stilistica."[6]   ATL

1. I am grateful to Marco Grassi, who deciphered the inscription and made the drawing.

2. Paris 1983, cat. no. 12.

3. Thomas Kerrich, *A Catalogue of The Prints, which have been engraved after Martin Heemskerck* (Cambridge: Cambridge University, 1829), p. 4.

4. "Noah is sleeping in broad daylight, overcome by much wine, and Ham [Chamus] laughs at the exposed genitals of his father" (translated by Prof. Charles Reeves, Case Western Reserve University, Cleveland). Heemskerck treated the scene in larger scale in two drawings that are not related to any known engravings (see *Tegninger af Maerten van Heemskerck*, coll. cat. [Copenhagen: Statens Museum for Kunst, 1971], nos. 33 and 55).

5. In contrast, Andrea Sacchi's representations of the *Drunken Noah* (Ann Sutherland Harris, *Andrea Sacchi: Complete Edition of the Paintings with a Critical Catalogue*. [Oxford: Phaidon Press, 1977], p. 95, cat. no. 72, figs. 144-47) recall the frank display of Noah facing front in Heemskerck's compositions.

6. Causa 1972, p. 942.

Exhibitions
Bucharest 1972, cat. nos. 41-42; Naples 1972, cat. nos. 41-42.

Literature
The Burlington Magazine 92, pt. 2 (1975), suppl., pl. xix. Causa 1972, p. 982 n. 108. Ferrari in *Dizionario biografico* 22 (1979):788. London and Washington 1982–83, pp. 135, 140. Paris 1983, pp. 189, 191. Turin 1983, pp. 158, 161, 162. Paris 1984, p. 88, repr.

76

Erminia among the Shepherds

Canvas, 98 x 127 cm.
Museo di Capodimonte, Naples

Torquato Tasso's epic poem *Gerusalemme Liberata* provided the artists of Cavallino's time with rich subject matter and nourished the union between poetry and painting implicit in the Horatian dictum *ut pictura poesis*.[1] The Counter-Reformation Church favored paintings depicting scenes from Tasso's poem because the central idea, the Triumph of Christianity over the Infidels, served the goals of the Church. It is therefore not surprising that Tasso's *Gerusalemme Liberata* was among the "libri di storie" that Massimo Stanzione recommended Cavallino read,[2] and that the seventh canto of "Erminia among the Shepherds," with its pastoral lyricism, especially appealed to Cavallino. Cavallino treated the subject in one other identified version [77] and in two known paintings that are now lost (see Inv. nos. 186-87).

Like his Italian contemporaries, Cavallino revealed his familiarity with the earliest illustrated edition of Tasso's poem, published in Genoa in 1590 and engraved by Agostino Carracci after drawings by Bernardo Castello.[3] In both the engraving and Cavallino's painting of this particular scene, Erminia is similarly dressed—with partial body armor, a helmet, and a billowing skirt—and in both Erminia stands in front of the shepherd and his three sons; however, Agostino's shepherd is older (see Fig. 76a) and, like his children, he is nude.[4] This common source of inspiration resulted in a certain resemblance between versions of *Erminia among the Shepherds*, whether painted in Bologna, Rome, or Naples, including, in particular, Guercino's in the Minneapolis Institute of Arts—believed to be the one painted for Antonio Ruffo in ca. 1648—and Lanfranco's of ca. 1630, now in the Capitoline Museum in Rome. The one most comparable to Cavallino's is the *Erminia among the Shepherds* in the Tyler Art Gallery at Vassar College (Poughkeepsie, New York), given to Mattia Preti, but which in John Spike's opinion, was more likely painted by either Agostino or Giuseppe Beltrano.[5] All three painters portray Erminia in as graceful a pose as her cumbersome armor permits, but Cavallino outshines the other artists. With that beguiling charm of the young women depicted by Cavallino, Erminia steps into the clearing with the grace of a dancer.

In keeping with the spirit of Tasso's poetry, Cavallino has created a convincing ambience of sylvan tranquility "filled with sweet noise, birds, winds and water, of murmuring brooks and whistling winds . . . ./ Thither she went, an old man there she found, at whose right hand and his little flock did feed. . . ./ Beholding one in shiny arms appear, the silly man and his were sore dismayed;/ But sweet Erminia comforted their fear, her vental up, her visage open laid. . . ."[6]

Cavallino's inimitable touches of whimsy are everywhere in the picture: Erminia's squint, as a ray of sunlight shines on her face upon entering the clearing; the red-ribbon reins of her horse, loosely held between her fingers; the ray of sunlight demarcating the muzzle and medallion[7] of her horse hidden in the shade; the loosely bound sash of sumptuous gold-ochre offsetting the cool gray of her armor; the glimpse of sparkling water through the trees (the River Jordan, according to the story); and the contrast of Erminia's small, elegant foot in sandals and the shepherd's large hooflike foot wrapped in rags.

The painting is closely related to works of Cavallino's maturity, therefore suggesting a date near 1650. The seated shepherd is very similar to Joseph in the Cleveland *Adoration of the Shepherds* [79] of ca. 1650. Above all, the pastoral mood of the painting anticipates that of the Brunswick *Finding of Moses* and *David and Abigail* [80-81] of the 1650s in which Cavallino attained that subtle fusion of naturalistic and manneristic elements foreshadowing the pastoral style of the French rococo.

ATL

Fig. 76a. Agostino Carracci, Bologna 1557–Parma 1602. After Bernardo Castello, 1557–1629. *Erminia and the Shepherd* (illustration to canto 7 of *Gerusalemme Liberata*). Engraving, 18.9 x 14.2 cm. Library of Congress, Rosenwald Collection, Washington, D.C.

1. See Clovis Whitfield, "A Programme for 'Erminia and the Shepherds' by G. B. Agucchi," *Storia dell'Arte* 19 (September-December 1973):217. Ellis K. Waterhouse ("Tasso and the Visual Arts," *Italian Studies* 3 [1947–48] :146-47) discusses how poets reversed Horace's dictum of *ut pictura poesis* so as to also embrace the idea of *ut poesis pictura*, namely, that poets and painters in the later sixteenth century believed they were both doing the same thing, with only their medium being different. For example, Agucchi's programme written in 1602 actually served as an aid for translating Tasso's stanza of Erminia among the Shepherds into paint. Agucchi gave the programme to Lodovico Carracci during his visit to Rome in 1602, resulting in Carracci's painting, which he sent to Rome a year later (see Whitfield, cited above). The painting is now considered lost. Note, however, that in the inventory of the Real Palacio de San Idlefonso La Granja of 1774 (Vol. IX, p. 22, no. 17004 [137], preserved in the library of the Museo del Prado, Madrid) a painting by Ludovico Carracci is listed as follows:

"Dos tercias y dos dedos de alto una vara y seis de dos de ancho [ca. 74 x 103.5 cm] Herminia hablano con el pastor un caballo a espaldas de ella bebiendi y otro pastor sentado señalando tres muchachos el otro toca una siringa o flauta de Ludavico Carache en la tercera pieza de azulejon - 4.500."

2. De Dominici 1742–43, 3:34.

3. See Washington 1979, cat. nos. 155-64; see also Mary Newcome, "Drawings by Bernardo Castello in German Collections," *Jahrbuch der Berliner Museen* 21 (1979): 137-51, whose discussion also includes illustrations of some of the engravings of the two later editions of Tasso's *Gerusalemme Liberata* (1604 and 1617).

4. Washington 1979, cat. no. 157. A very similar figure, even more directly resembling Cavallino's Erminia figure, is the figure of *Minerva*, after Hendrik Goltzius (Bartsch III.108.68). Goltzius visited Italy in 1591, i.e., shortly after the first illustrated edition of Tasso's *Gerusalemme Liberata* was published in Genoa.

5. See Arthur McComb, "A Seicento Painting at Vassar College," *Art in America* 15, no. 2 (1926–27):77-80, repr. opp. p. 80.

6. Excerpt from verses 5-7; see Tasso 1901, translation by Edward Fairfax, p. 132.

7. Note that de Dominici describes Erminia's horse in *Erminia among the Shepherds* in the

76

collection of the Signori Caputi (see Inv. no. 186) as "cavallo armata," i.e., an army or cavalry horse. Likely it wore, like the present one, a medallion over its forelock. Another example is Marcus Curtius's horse by Schönfeld (see Pée 1971, p. 140, no. 73).

Collections
Bequest of Francesco Esposito to the Regio Museo Borbonico, Naples.

Exhibitions
None.

Literature
Molajoli in Naples 1957, p. 73; in Naples 1958, p. 56. Naples 1960, p. 111. Molajoli in Naples 1961, fig. 34; in Naples 1964, p. 54, fig. 78. Percy 1965, p. 53, no. 27. Causa 1972, pp. 942, 982 n. 109. Liverpool 1977, p. 42, under no. 2771. Ferrari in *Dizionario biografico* 22 (1979):788. Causa in Naples 1982, p. 75, no. 57, repr. London and Washington 1982–83, pp. 135, 140. Paris 1983, pp. 189, 191. Turin 1983, pp. 158, 161.

77

77 & 78

Erminia
among the Shepherds

Canvas tondo (formerly on oak),
diam. 50.2 cm.
Alte Pinakothek, Munich

In catalogue only

Erminia and
the Wounded Tancred

Canvas tondo (formerly on oak),
diam. 52 cm.
Alte Pinakothek, Munich

In catalogue only

These tondi entered the Residence Gallery in Mannheim in 1756, listed as numbers 232 and 251, as works by Cavallino. By 1885, when they appeared in the inventory of the gallery in Schleissheim and in the catalogue of that gallery in 1905, the attribution had been changed to Domenico Fetti; but in 1911 Hermanin (p. 186) and Voss (p. 250) independently gave the paintings to Cavallino. Hermanin assigned them to the artist's late period; Benesch (1926, p. 253) considered them— together with the Brunswick pendants *The Finding of Moses* and *The Meeting of David and Abigail* [80-81] and the Corsini *Saint Peter and the Centurion Cornelius* [53]—among Cavallino's last works. Both scenes derive from Tasso's 1590 edition (illustrated) of *Gerusalemme Liberata*; the first, from the seventh canto (stanzas 6 and 7),[1] and the second, from the nineteenth canto (stanza 112).[2]

In *Erminia among the Shepherds* the figure of Erminia is much like her counterpart in the earlier painting of the subject in the Capodimonte [76], but here she is divested of her helmet and has taken some steps forward, standing calmly before the shepherd, now an old man as Tasso described him. Although the emotional tonality is also similar to that of the earlier Capodimonte painting, Cavallino's style reveals new classicizing tendencies reminiscent of Poussin's early Roman works, even though Poussin's Tasso subjects did not include this particular scene.[3] In this tondo the air is clearer, colors cooler and more transparent, and the composition shows greater coherence and economy. Cavallino's use of tree trunks behind his figures to enhance the illusion of depth is also found in many of Poussin's early Roman paintings. And the nude shepherd child, like its earlier counterpart wearing a sash around its waist and clinging anxiously to his father's knee, reminds one of Poussin's chubby and lively *putti*.

According to De Dominici, another version of *Erminia among the Shepherds*, with a *Rape of Europa* as its companion, belonged to the Caputi collection in Naples (see Inv. no. 187). Each of the Caputi paintings measured 4 x 3 *palmi*; (105.6 x 79.2); because of the difference in size, however, the Caputi *Erminia among the Shepherds* cannot be identified with either the Munich or the Capodimonte versions.

In *Erminia and the Wounded Tancred* Cavallino has painted the scene where the Christian knight Tancred lies wounded on the ground and is supported by his armor-bearer, Vavrino. Tancred's wounds had been inflicted in combat with Argantes, an Egytian ambassador to Jerusalem, during an assault on that city. Erminia, the daughter of a former Saracen king of Antioch, who had fallen in love with Tancred, was brought to the scene by Vavrino.

More often, artists depicted Erminia rather than Vavrino cradling the wounded Tancred, which was also the way Agostino Carracci illustrated the scene after Castello's drawing in Tasso's Genoese edition of 1590. Instead, Cavallino depicts the moment described in stanza 112 when Erminia cuts off her hair to bind Tancred's wounds:

> From weariness and loss of blood she spied
> His greatest pains and anguish most proceed,
> Naught but her veil amit those deserts wide
> She had to bind his wounds, in so great need,
> But love could other bands, though strange, provide
> And pity wept for joy to see that deed,
> For with her amber locks cut off, each wound
> She tied: O happy man, so cured so bound!

One other notable artist who portrayed Erminia cutting her hair was Nicolas Poussin (one canvas, of ca. 1631–33, is in the Hermitage, Leningrad; another, slightly later version is in the Barber Institute of Fine Arts, Birmingham).[4] However, Cavallino, typical of his intimate spirit, gave Erminia a pair of scissors rather than Poussin's heroic sword; the graceful manner in which Erminia cuts her hair reminds one of the *Singer* [70] braiding hers.

It has been suggested (in Munich 1983, p. 135) that the two tondi may have belonged to a larger cycle of Tasso subjects. There are precedents in the Neapolitan school: a set of "8 quadri con la storia del Tasso" by Antonio Monterosso was mentioned in the inventory of Antonio Ruffo in Messina,[5] and an exten-

78

sive series of subjects taken from Tasso's *Gerusalemme Liberata* was painted by Paolo Finoglia for the Castello in Conversano.[6] ATL

1. Tasso [1590] 1901, p. 132.
  2. Ibid., canto 14, p. 404.
  3. See Washington 1979, p. 278, no. 163.
  4. Cavallino could have become familiar with Poussin's works in Naples—see Blunt 1954, pp. 76-86. Blunt points out the numerous important collectors in Naples, with Roman connections, who owned paintings by Poussin, many of which were early Roman works. One of the most outstanding collectors of Poussin's works was Cardinal Ascanio Filimarino (1583–1666); others in Naples were Gaspar Roomer, Vandeneynden, Carlo and Francesco Garofalo; and Antonio Ruffo in Messina. Blunt 1966–67, 1:142, nos. 206-7.
  5. Ruffo in *Bollettino d'Arte* 10 (1916):41.
  6. D'Orsi 1938, pp. 46-55.

Collections (both paintings)
Gallery Mannheim 1756; Gallery Schleissheim 1799, and again in 1881; Alte Pinakothek 1836-?, and again in 1924, up to the present.

Exhibitions
Wiesbaden 1935, cat. nos. 62 and 63.

Literature (both paintings except where noted)
Schleissheim 1885, p. 84, nos. 1064-65; 1905, p. 134, cat. nos. 636-37. Hermanin 1911, pp. 186-88, pl. 41, figs. 4-5. Voss 1911, pp. 250, 257, fig. 52 (*Erminia and Tancred*), n. 10 (*Erminia among Shepherds*). Hermanin 1912, p. 374. Hermanin in Thieme-Becker 6 (1912):225. Schleissheim 1914, p. 52, no. 3636 (*Erminia among Shepherds*). De Rinaldis 1917, p. 179; 1920a, pp. 2, 4 n. 2; 1921, p. 16. Ortolani 1922, p. 190. Benesch 1926, p. 253. Delogu 1929, pp. 90-92, repr. De Rinaldis 1929, pl. 38. Corna 1930, 1:227. Munich 1930, p. 29. Delogu 1931, p. 45. Munich 1938, pp. 48, 49, nos. 960, 964. Ortolani in Naples 1938, p. 66. Causa 1957, p. 42. Poensgen 1959, pp. 118, 126, pl. v, fig. 23 (*Erminia among Shepherds*). *Kindlers Malerei Lexikon* 1 (1964), unpaginated. Percy 1965, p. 51, nos. 22-23. Causa 1966, p. 7, color pl. XIII (*Erminia among Shepherds*). Moir 1967, 1:177, and 2:65. Liebmann 1968, pp. 457, 459, figs. 52, 53. Lurie 1969, pp. 141-42, fig. 8 (*Erminia and Tancred*). Minicuci in *Dizionario enciclopedico Bolaffi* 3 (1972):207. Causa 1972, p. 944, fig. 317 (*Erminia among Shepherds*); in Naples 1975, p. 42 (*Erminia among Shepherds*). Brejon de Lavergnée and Dorival 1979, p. 92. Ferrari in *Dizionario biografico* 22 (1979):788. Causa in *Larousse Dictionary* 1981, p. 57. De Vito 1982, p. 37. London and Washington 1982–83, pp. 145-47, 250. Munich 1983, pp. 134-35, nos. 960, 964. Turin 1983, pp. 166-67.

79

The Adoration of the Shepherds

Canvas, 126.8 x 148.3 cm, monogrammed.
The Cleveland Museum of Art,
Mr. and Mrs. William Marlatt Fund

Cavallino's monogram, simulating a brand mark (Fig. 79a), appears on the rump of the ox standing behind Mary and the Child; the artist used the same device in *The Expulsion of Heliodorus* [83], in which it appears on the croup of the horse.

Beginning with Giovanni da Nola's large *retable di S. Eustachio* in the church of S. Maria La Nova, representing the *Mistero della Natività* sculpted in 1520, in which a single shepherd timidly approaches the crib, Nativities with adoring shepherds became increasingly popular in Neapolitan art.[1] Shepherds also took on an increasingly important role in the *presepio* groups that were found in great numbers in and around Naples and Sicily at the time of Cavallino.[2] Such crêches included not only the adoring shepherds but also an exotic retinue of the Magi in fanciful costumes, as found, for example, in Cavallino's *Adoration of the Magi* in Vienna [19].

The Cleveland *Adoration*, painted in the artist's full maturity, is one of his most exquisite figural compositions, and reveals his consummate craftsmanship, mastery of design, and tonal orchestration. Cavallino has composed a quiet continuum of movement and gesture, with a subtle crescendo of light leading to the spiritual center—the Madonna and Christ Child, who appear in brilliant light.

The vibrant lapis lazuli of Mary's wrap draped over her left arm, sliding off her right shoulder and cushioning the Infant's head, provides a striking accent for the predominant earth colors of the surrounding figures.[3] Joseph, who bears a noticeable resemblance to the shepherd in the painting of *Erminia among the Shepherds* at Capodimonte [76], looks on alertly. His strongly modeled neck, cheek, and temple give him a heroic thrust. The soft muzzle of an ass emerges from the shadow below his hand. Mary, portrayed in a devout pose, casts her eyes heavenward, where a cluster of swirling angels flaunt a ribbon inscribed "Gloria in Excelsis Deo." The young shepherd looking over Mary's left shoulder is close to several of the youths in Cavallino's late paintings: Vavrino, Tancred's armor-bearer, in the Munich tondo [78], and those in Abigail's retinue in the Brunswick picture [80].

The undulating contours of a large ox provide a backdrop for the main figural group and delineate the area of brilliant light emanating from Heaven. The ingenious use of the ox carries Cavallino's compositional development of patterning backgrounds into light and dark areas to a new height. From 1645 on, the artist began to structure background space into diagonal masses of dark and light, created, for example, by means of the opening in the landscape in *The Stoning of Saint Stephen* [63] or a half-drawn curtain like that in *Saint Cecilia* [44], the Uffizi *Esther before Ahasuerus* [63], the *Nursing Madonna* [73], and the Stockholm *Judith* [82]. Pronounced diagonal shafts of light—as seen in *David before Saul*, Vienna [60]—gradually were diffused by Cavallino into areas of neutral gray with varying intensities of light so as to create the illusion of atmospheric space.

Although the Cleveland *Adoration* differs greatly from the earlier painting of the subject in Brunswick [2], which reveals a far more direct influence from Ribera's surface realism, it may have been Ribera's magnificent *Adoration of the Shepherds* of 1650, in the Louvre, that actually inspired the Cleveland painting. Brigitte Dapra in her discussion of the Micco Spadaro *Adoration* (in London 1982, under cat. no. 45, pp. 249-50) suggested that the Cleveland painting in turn may have provided the inspiration for Spadaro's *Adoration* of ca. 1650-55.

Fig. 79b. Attributed to Cavallino. *The Adoration of the Shepherds*. Canvas, 47 x 92 cm. Present whereabouts unknown. (After *Mostra di Pittura Antica*, exh. cat. [Trieste: Galleria d'Arte al Corso, 1943], cat. no. 30.)

Fig. 79a. Monogram of Bernardo Cavallino.

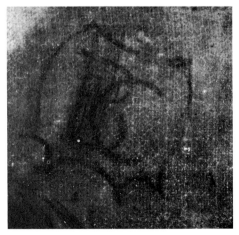

79

An oval *Adoration of the Shepherds* (47 x 92 cm; Fig. 79b) was exhibited in "Mostra di Pittura Antica—XXI" held at the Galleria d'Arte el Corso, Trieste, in 1943 (see Inv. no. 21). It is a smaller, abbreviated version of the Cleveland painting, in which the young shepherd in the center and the shepherd in the far right background of the Cleveland painting are missing. (The omission sheds an interesting light on Cavallino's sketchy handling of the two shepherd-figures in the Cleveland painting, as the Technical Note accompanying this entry points out.) The catalogue for the Trieste exhibition quoted Fiocco's comment on the Castiglionesque style of the Trieste painting. In the Jean Baptiste Angiot sale in Paris in 1875 the Cleveland painting was, in fact, attributed to Castiglione, perhaps partly because his monogram—"BC"—was not only the same as Cavallino's but was also similar in design to Cavallino's.

A drawing for an *Adoration*, in the Gabinetto disegni e stampe degli Uffizi,[4] was published as Cavallino, but more likely it is related to Vaccaro's *Adoration of the Shepherds* in Vienna (Kunsthistorisches Museum). ATL

1. Gennaro Borrelli, *Il Presepe Napoletano* (Rome: De Luca–D'Agostino, 1970), p. 27.
2. Aniello Falcone's nephew, Andrea (ca. 1630–75), sculpted statuettes for such crêches (see Borrelli, *Il Presepe*, p. 206, pl. 12).
3. See technical note.
4. Refice 1951, fig. 7.

Collections
Marquis de Villette, Château de Villette, Oise;
Jean Baptiste Angiot, Paris (sale: Hôtel Drouot,
Paris, 1-2 March 1875, cat. no. 41, as Benedetto
Castiglione); private collection, Buenos Aires;
Frederick Mont, New York; acquired by the
Museum in 1968.

Exhibitions
The Cleveland Museum of Art, January 1969,
The Year in Review, cat. no. 60, repr.; London
and Washington 1982–83, cat. no. 35, color
plate.

Literature
Lurie 1969, pp. 136-150, figs. 4, 10, 12b, and
color plate. Levey 1971, p. 85. Causa 1972, pp.
944, 984 n. 116. Causa in Naples 1975, p. 256.
Meij, Roethlisberger, et al. in Paris 1979, p. 34
under cat. no. 7. Ferrari in *Dizionario biografico* 22 (1979):788. Gregori 1980, p. 298.
Cleveland 1982, cat. no. 145, repr. De Maio
1983, p. 204 n. 67, fig. 29. Paris 1983, p. 196.
Turin 1983, pp. 166-67, 271, cat. no. 36, repr.

Fig. 79c. Photograph of composite X radiograph of the Cleveland painting.

210

Technical Note

Support
The original support is composed of two
pieces of medium-weight, plain-woven
fabric (ca. 11 vertical and 17 horizontal
threads/centimeter), with a stitched
horizontal seam located roughly 54
centimeters from the bottom edge.
Tapelike shadows on either side of the
seam are visible on the X radiograph (Fig.
79c); corresponding to these shadows are
variations in surface texture of the paint
over the seam. These shadows and
textural variations are presumably caused
by strips of paper adhered over the fabric
seam before the ground was applied.[1]

Ground
Because of the abraded paint surface, one
can observe under high magnification the
layer structure of the ground and paint in
virtually every area of the painting. The
ground is an evenly applied red-brown
layer. There is no overall white priming,
but in a few isolated areas a white layer is
present beneath the red ground. This
white layer may be a type of filling
mixture (mentioned by Armenini in 1586)
that was used to patch holes and
irregularities in the canvas.[2]

Paint and Painting Technique
One of the first areas of paint Cavallino
applied over the red ground appears to be
the gray in the ''sky,'' or background.
Instead of using gray to produce a
preliminary modeling of the important
figures (dead coloring), Cavallino has done
the opposite; he has used it to provide a
precisely outlined background for the
figures. (Note in the radiograph how the
gray paint, which appears white in the
radiograph, outlines the *putti* and the
kneeling man's head.) Study of the
abraded edges of the feet of the *putti* at
the far left reveals that some of the pink
flesh tones slightly overlap the gray
background paint, confirming that the
gray was applied first. (Some of the final
contours of the *putti* are outlined with a
second application of gray paint,
however.)

On the shoulder of the second male
figure from the right, an area of similar
gray paint has been penetrated, while still
fluid, by either a stick of charcoal or a
small stiff brush loaded with black paint.
In the process of delineating a fold in the
shepherd's gray tunic, the charcoal, or
brush, swept much of the moist gray paint
off the red ground, leaving the ground
exposed. The fact that Cavallino sketched
into this wet paint is evidence of his rapid
painting technique.

Cavallino's use of gray background
paint can be contrasted to the gray
background on a painting of roughly the
same period, Velázquez's *Portrait of the
Jester Calabazas* (ca. 1632) in the CMA
collection (CMA 65.15). In this work
Velázquez used a fluid paint, which he
applied thinly around the figure and the
stool with long, sweeping brushstrokes
that swirl in many directions, whereas
Cavallino applied his brushstrokes of pasty
gray paint in a meticulous hatching style,
each stroke parallel to the next.[3]

In painting the flesh tones of the
Madonna and Child, Cavallino painted
directly on the red ground with no white
preparation or dead coloring. For the
Child and the Madonna's hand, he
probably started with the pink middle
tone, followed by a more thickly applied

white for the highlights, and a gray/pink tone for the shadows. In the Madonna's face he used a white middle tone, pink highlights, and gray/pink shadow tone. Cavallino appears to have blended together the three tones used to compose the Madonna's flesh, thereby creating a smooth, youthful face and left hand. The Madonna's mouth is slightly open, and the color of this void is, not surprisingly, that of the exposed red ground itself.

The coloration of the flesh tones of the shepherds is considerably different from that of the Child, Madonna, or *putti*. In several of these male figures Cavallino makes extensive use of the ground color in the shadows of the flesh tones, particularly in the face at the far right, which is constructed entirely of thin, transparent glazes and scumbles over the dark red ground. The face of the young shepherd closest to the *putti* is painted over the gray background tone with a few areas of pink and red modeling. As one would expect from the artist's technique, the tonality of this face is pale gray and that of the face at the right is a deep brown. The faces of the older shepherds are painted differently; for these Cavallino used an opaque paste-like paint that retains the brushmarks and offers a textural contrast to the smoother flesh of the Madonna. It appears that Cavallino went to considerable effort to vary the coloration, contrast, and texture of the faces.

The blue pigment used by Cavallino is ultramarine (pulverized lapis lazuli),[4] which was brought to Europe from what is now Afghanistan.[5] In the three samples taken (two from the Madonna's cloak and one from the standing shepherd's sleeve) no other blue pigment was detected. Cavallino even used ultramarine on a secondary figure where one might expect him to have used a less expensive pigment. Another method often used by artists of the sixteenth century to economize was to underpaint the ultramarine with either white, a less expensive blue, or even black or green.[6] Cavallino, however, painted his blue pigment directly on the red ground. There is no intermediary layer of white that would have allowed him to create much the same effect in the light blues with a much thinner and less expensive application of ultramarine.

The other pigments used appear to be mostly earth pigments, although none of these were analyzed. Several factors about Cavallino's pigments are worth noting,

however. The size of the individual pigment particles is often very large, easily seen even under low-power magnification. One also finds unexpected pigments in some of the layers; both green and blue particles can be seen in the red ground, for example.

Numerous pentimenti are evident: the radiograph clearly shows that the position of the ear of Joseph at the far left was shifted forward; the drapery folds of the same figure were altered considerably; the outline of the ox's back and the position of its ear were changed; and the Child's left hand and arm were painted out by Cavallino, who then covered them with the white paint of the Madonna's tunic. Not as easily seen is a change in position of the Madonna's proper right hand and wrist and the hand of the shepherd closest to the Child that has been painted, in part, over the ultramarine of the Madonna's cloak.

Aside from areas of pentimenti, the general paint structure of the painting is simple. Over the red ground, usually only one or two layers of paint were applied. A number of small painted details, such as the straw under the Child and the wicker basket, and parts of the shepherds' costumes, show the mixing of several moist colors with one brushstroke typical of *alla prima* technique. Thus, the simple layer structure, the *alla prima* details, the use of the unaltered red ground in the Madonna's open mouth and elsewhere, the blue paint and the flesh tones painted directly on the red ground, and the pentimenti all suggest that Cavallino painted rapidly and with economy of effort.

Bruce F. Miller, Conservator of Paintings.

1. As seen in the radiograph, there are two large tears in the original fabric: one compound tear at Joseph's face at the far left of the composition, and a long diagonal tear running from the *putti* to the shoulder of the second figure from the right. A number of large losses along the top of the painting have been repaired, and significant portions of the gray sky are inpainted. Much of the paint surface is abraded, but certain areas have been inpainted, especially in the blue and white parts of the Madonna's costume. The Joseph figure at the far left, however, may have been inpainted more broadly due to severe abrasion.

2. See Giovanni Battista Armenini, *On the True Precepts of the Art of Painting*, 1586, trans. Edward J. Olszewski (New York: Burt

Franklin & Co., 1977), p. 192; see also Giambattista Volpato, *Volpato MS*, trans. Mary P. Merrifield, in *Original Treatises on the Arts of Painting*, 2 vols. (London: J. Murray, 1849; New York: Dover, 1967), 2:730-32; Francisco Pacheco, *El Arte de la Pintura* (Seville, 1649), excerpted and trans. Zahira Véliz, ''Francisco Pacheco's Comments on Paintings in Oil,'' *Studies in Conservation* 27, no. 2 (May 1982):50-51; Philip Hendy and Arthur S. Lucas, ''The Ground in Pictures,'' *Museum* 21, no. 4 (1968):266-76 (provides an overview of the types of grounds used in paintings; color photomicrographs of cross-sections by Joyce Plesters illustrate the possible variety of paint layers); Hubert von Sonnenburg, ''Zur Maltechnik Murillos, Part I,'' *Maltechnik Restauro* 86 (July 1980):160-62 (author analyzed five paintings by Murillo in the Alte Pinakothek, Munich, and found that each had a colored ground with no white gesso layer; detailed photographs and radiographs are included, as well as an English summary).

3. Von Sonnenburg, ''Zur Maltechnik Murilos, Part II,'' *Maltechnik Restauro* 88 (January 1982):15, 22 (author describes the brown ground of a sixth painting by Murillo and the light red-brown ground of a portrait by Velázquez, both in the Alte Pinakothek, Munich; in this portrait, Velázquez used a multi-layered, semi-transparent gray background that may not have been completed by the artist; detailed photographs and radiographs are included); José López-Rey, *Velázquez: A Catalogue Raisonné of His Oeuvre* (London: Faber & Faber, 1963), pp. 211-22, 264 (author illustrates fifteen radiographs of paintings by Velázquez in the Prado and comments that the right hand and the background in the Cleveland Velázquez painting appeared to have been repainted; [this overpainting was later removed, in 1965]).

4. The composition of Cavallino's blue pigment was determined to be ultramarine through the use of the Cleveland Museum of Art's polarizing light microscope. Pigment samples from the same three areas were examined in an AMRay 1000 scanning electron microscope using an EDAX energy dispersive X-ray spectrometer. The X-ray data were converted to semi-quantitative elemental weight percents by using oxide stoichiometry and normalizing the values to 100%. The samples were examined in the scanning electron microscope using the backscatter electron imaging mode. The three samples' elemental concentrations of sodium, aluminum, silicon, and sulfur for the most part agreed with those found in a control sample of artificially prepared ultramarine blue pigment. The scanning electron microscope analysis was carried out in 1984 by Dr. Robert H. Duff, Project Leader/Analytical Sciences Laboratory, the Standard Oil Company (Ohio). The initial investigation of Cavallino's use of ultramarine in the *Adoration* was carried out by Sonja L. Sopher, former paintings conservator at the

80

Cleveland Museum.

   5. Joyce Plesters, ''Ultramarine Blue, Natural
and Artificial,'' *Studies in Conservation* 11, no.
2 (May 1966):62-91.

   6. Ibid., pp. 64-65.

80 & 81

The Meeting of David and Abigail

Canvas, 102 x 129 cm.
Herzog Anton Ulrich-Museum,
Brunswick

Exhibited in USA only

The Finding of Moses

Canvas, 102 x 127 cm.
Herzog Anton Ulrich-Museum,
Brunswick

In catalogue only

These two works have always been considered a pair. Although their stories are unrelated—except for their source in the Old Testament—both portray a remarkable woman who through exceptional courage and independent spirit fulfills a divine destiny. It is possible that the two pictures were among those that the duke of Brunswick bought from the marchese Vandeneynden, who had inherited them from Gaspar Roomer (died 1674). This transaction is mentioned in a letter written by Pietro Andrea Andreini to Leopoldo de'Medici on 14 May 1675.[1] The duke, known to have been an amateur poet, was extremely fond of the theater; therefore, the lyrical mood and stagelike setting of the figures would probably have had an immediate appeal for him.[2]

As early as 1710 the two pictures were recorded in the duke's pleasure palace of Salzdahlum as works of Mollo. ''Mollo,'' until now, has been thought to be a pseudonym for Pier Francesco Mola (1612–1666), but it is probably a reference to the French artist Jean Baptiste Mole, a pupil of Vouet and Albani, who was also known as ''Mollo.''[3] He was born in Besançon in 1616 and died in Rome in 1661. In a 1744 inventory of the ducal collection the artist is identified as a disciple of Vouet, a description that would support the assertion that the 1710 inventory referred to the French, not the Italian, artist. In eighteenth- and nineteenth-century inventories the paintings were catalogued consistently as works of another French artist, Jean Boulanger, who studied under Guido Reni and became the head of a school of painting in Modena that was modeled after the Bolognese Academy of the Carracci. P.J. Meier in 1905 (p. 23) was the first to question the Boulanger attribution. In 1911 Voss (pp. 249-50) gave the work to Cavallino, followed since then by other scholars, with the single exception of Pape (in Brunswick 1936, no. 109).

David and Abigail and the *Finding of Moses* are closely related in style and composition, with two groups of confronting figures—one behind David, the other behind Abigail—in a landscape that opens on one side to reveal a sky of the same opaque orange-pink color as is found in the skies of Micco Spadaro and Andrea de Leone. Cavallino has abandoned the strong chiaroscuro effects of his earlier work. In both of these paintings his colors have become lighter, more atmospheric, and range from shimmering mother-of-

pearl to glistening metallic tones. He has lavished striking accents of vibrant blue on the costumes of the main protagonists. Paint is applied fluently, with warm yellow impasto for glistening highlights. The mannered figures are of slightly elongated proportions and strike graceful attitudes. Each is portrayed from a different angle; faces are foreshortened in a manner typical of Cavallino, with eyes slanted and with brows intersecting the line of the nose. Hazy figures in monochrome brown that resemble wash drawings emerge from the shadows in both paintings. As the thinly applied pigment in the backgrounds of the canvases has worn with age, some of the figures have become almost indistinguishable. In both paintings Cavallino has portrayed the young woman with consummate skill, expressive of his own delight in his model's beguiling charm.

The meeting of David and Abigail is recounted in I Samuel 25. During his exile in the Judean desert, David and his men kept themselves supplied with food by ''strong-arm'' methods. When Nabal, a sheep owner, refused to give David's men food after they had agreed to spare his flocks, David threatened to punish him. But Nabal's wife, Abigail, interceded and went out to David with ''two hundred loaves, and two skins of wine, and a hundred clusters of raisins, and two hundred cakes of figs, and laid them on asses.'' David received her offering graciously and blessed her for keeping him from a vengeful act. Soon after this Nabel died, and Abigail later married David.

Abigail's grace and her yielding manner, which is shared by her companions, is a perfect foil for the commanding stance of David and his soldiers. A uniquely Cavallinesque touch is provided by the beautifully rendered bunch of grapes lying on the ground, which the donkey contemplates.

The erect figure-type of the armed David recurs like a stock figure in many Neapolitan paintings of the period. Other examples are the executioner in Stanzione's *Decollation of Saint John*, in the Prado, Madrid, and the Archangel Michael in the *Death of Saint Cayetano* by Andrea Vaccaro, also in the Prado. This type of figure may have been inspired by the numerous warrior figures in Torquato Tasso's 1590 edition of *Gerusalemme Liberata* with illustrations by Agostino Carracci, after drawings by Bernardo

81

Castello.[4] The attendants, with lances, and the horse on the left are similar to a group in Cavallino's *Saint Peter and the Centurion Cornelius* [53], which can be dated somewhat earlier than this painting. For example, the dark-haired youth behind David and the young boy looking up at him are like the two young men in the Corsini painting (left center).

The unknown artist of the Cavallinesque painting of the same subject in the Busiri Vici collection (see Fig. 25a) seems to have been familiar with Cavallino's *David and Abigail* in Brunswick, as well as with the earlier version in the Castello Sforzesco [25], as can be seen by comparing the two main figures in each of the three paintings.

There is a pentimento, barely visible, of a horse's head, between two young men standing behind Abigail. Cavallino must have remembered after he had started on the painting that, according to the Bible, Abigail and her companions traveled on donkeys, not on horses.

The Finding of Moses is the second of the two known versions by Cavallino on the subject (see also [13]). The work complements *David and Abigail* in color and in composition. Both paintings include vivid accents of ultramarine, gold, bright reds, earth tones, and shades of Cavallino's favorite light green. The penetration of space, left background, in *The Finding of Moses* counterbalances a similar opening in the right background of *David and Abigail*. When the paintings are hung side by side, the rhythmic ebb and flow of standing and kneeling figures enhances the compositional harmonies established between the two works.

A comparison with Orazio Gentileschi's *Finding of Moses* (Prado, Madrid) reveals Cavallino's technical mastery of the studied ease and rhetoric of the classical school, as well as his delight in the rich coloristic values borrowed by Gentileschi from Paolo Veronese and the other Venetians. However, the smaller scale of Cavallino's compositions and the fragile grace of his youthful figures transform the grave, grandiloquent scene of his predecessor into an intimate, lyrical passage that is at once highly styled and expressive of a youthful *joie de vivre*.

Causa suggested (1972, p. 944) that the two paintings represent, both in spirit and in form, a "proto-rococo" moment in Cavallino's development. Spinosa remarks (in London and Washington 1982–83, no.

34) that the firmly modeled figures of delicacy and grace almost anticipate the polychrome porcelain figurines of eighteenth-century Naples. ATL

1. Ruotolo 1982, p. 9, notes 21 and 22. According to Andreini, the duke bought these paintings for "rigorous prices."
2. Duke Anton Ulrich's interest in the theater was early awakened by his father, August the Younger, who introduced to his court a theater for amateurs (1636).
3. Thieme-Becker 25 (1931):30.
4. Subsequent editions were published in 1604 and 1607.

Collections (both paintings)
Possibly Gaspar Roomer until 1674, and (through inheritance) marchese Vandeneynden, Naples; dukes of Brunswick, in the ducal gallery at Salzdahlum by 1710.

Exhibitions
Wiesbaden 1935, cat. nos. 60 and 61; London and Washington 1982–83, cat. no. 34, color pl. (*Moses* only); Paris 1983, cat. no. 18, color pl. (*Moses* only).

Literature
Brunswick [1710?], unpaginated. Brunswick 1744, nos. 767 (*Moses*) and 768 (*David and Abigail*). Brunswick 1776, p. 10. In catalogues of the Museum: 1859, nos. 257 and 321; 1867, nos. 191 and 192; 1868, nos. 204 and 205; 1887, nos. 516 and 517. Brunswick 1900, nos. 516 (*Moses*) and 517 (*David and Abigail*). Brunswick 1905, p. 23. Voss 1911, pp. 249-50, figs. 7 and 8. De Rinaldis 1917, p. 179; 1920a, pp. 2-4, 6, figs. 3 and 4; 1921, pp. 16, 21, pls. XVIII and XIX. Sestieri 1921, p. 188. Brunswick 1922, nos. 499a-b. Ortolani 1922, pp. 190, 192. Benesch 1926, p. 253. De Rinaldis in Naples 1927 and 1928, p. 431. Benesch 1928, p. 51. De Rinaldis 1929, pl. 43 (*Moses*). Costantini 1930, 1:254. Nugent 1925–30, 2:560-62. Brunswick 1932, nos. 516 and 517. Brunswick 1936, nos. 97 and 109. Ortolani in Naples 1938, p. 66. Milicua 1954, p. 68. Percy 1965, p. 46, nos. 2 and 3. Causa 1966, p. 6, color pl. XII. Adriani in Brunswick 1969, p. 43, nos. 516 and 517, repr. Lurie 1969, pp. 139-42, fig. 6 (*Moses*), p. 150 n. 7 (*David and Abigail*). Pée 1971, p. 198 (*Moses*). Causa 1972, pp. 942, 944, 982 n. 108. Causa in *Larousse Dictionary* 1981, pp. 56-57 (*Moses* repr.). De Vito 1982, p. 37. London and Washington 1982–83, pp. 145-47. Paris 1983, p. 196. Turin 1983, pp. 166-67 (*Moses* repr.).

82

Judith with the Head of Holofernes

Canvas, 118 x 94 cm, monogrammed on the hilt of the sword.
Nationalmuseum, Stockholm

This is the third of three known versions by Cavallino on the subject (see also [45-46]), and the only one in which Judith is portrayed alone with her victim. As in four other paintings [67, 79, 83, 85] that are believed to date from the artist's last period, the *Judith* is monogrammed. The painting was originally attributed to G. B. Coriolano, and later to G. B. Castiglione.[1] Venturi assigned the work to its rightful author in 1921, some years before Cavallino's monogram was discovered on the hilt of the sword.

The *Judith* is the last in a group of *ritratti divini* executed by Cavallino, which had begun with the full-length *Saint Martyr* [14] painted in the 1630s. The sitters are young *popolane*, thinly disguised as saints, heroines, and allegorical figures, and even as the Madonna [73]. The painting represents a stage in the artist's development that might be described as the threshold of his late style. As Spinosa (in London and Washington 1982–83) pointed out, the composition is more measured and balanced and although *Judith* still retains the imprint of Stanzione and Artemisia Gentileschi, the idiom is distinctly Caravaggesque; yet there is a new compactness of both form and composition that seems to reflect the influence of French artists such as Poussin and Mellin, and will become increasingly important in Cavallino's later works. However, this *Judith* is the artist's boldest statement in the Caravaggesque idiom, which links the canvas to a wide circle of Italian and French Caravaggesque paintings such as Simon Vouet's *Salome* (Fig. 82a),[2] which is a close copy of Artemisia

Gentileschi's painting at Capodimonte.[3] Several others of Vouet's own figures painted during his Italian sojourn may be compared with Cavallino's painting: these include the *Salome* in the Galleria Corsini, Rome; *Judith* in the Alte Pinakothek, Munich; the *Saint Ursula* in the Wadsworth Atheneum, Hartford; and the *Saint William of Aquitaine* in the Musée des Beaux-Arts, Algiers. Like the Stockholm *Judith*, they are all three-quarter figures, of portraitlike specificity, placed close to the picture plane. In each, the figure is turned slightly to the side and is intensely illuminated from above. The head is slightly tilted and the subject gazes directly out towards the viewer, lips parted. But none of these paintings approaches in dramatic impact the effect that is transmitted by Cavallino's *Judith* as a result of his insight into and his sensitive portrayal of the emotionally fatigued state of his subject. This is expressed in her wide-eyed, unseeing gaze; slightly parted lips; and weary hands, one grasping the sword loosely and the other resting limply, almost caressingly, upon the severed head of Holofernes.

In the background Cavallino introduces a compositional element that is almost like a signature in his later works: the definition of a form by using light in such a way as to make an abstract pattern of light and dark, created here by the edge of the half-open curtain meeting the wall. Furthermore, Cavallino has provided dramatic color contrasts between Judith's golden-yellow bodice, the vibrant ultramarine of her skirt, and the green velvet curtain dropped low behind Judith's head—all of which heighten the pallor of her face and bring it into startling focus.

An early copy of this painting (Fig. 82b), slightly smaller in size (112 x 85 cm) and attributed to Giovanni Biliverti (1596–1644),[4] is in the Musée d'Amiens. Two more early *Judiths* of about the same size as the Stockholm painting are recorded. The first is one of four paintings of Old Testament scenes, 4 *palmi* in width, that were sent to Spain by don Pietro Antonio d'Aragona, viceroy to Naples from 1666 to 1672 (see Inv. no. 86); the other appeared in an inventory of 1732 of the Spinelli di Tarsia collections, listed as one entry with a painting of *David*, each 5 x 4 *palmi* (see Inv. no. 84).   ATL

1. Castiglione similarly initialed his paintings with "BC."

2. Bob Jones University, *Catalogue of the Art Collection*, 1: *Italian and French Paintings* (Greenville, South Carolina, 1962), no. 100, repr. Two unpublished opinions favor the attribution to Vouet: William Suida (1958) and Federico Zeri (1959).

3. There called *Judith*.

4. Rosenberg 1968, pp. 151, 153 n. 8, fig. 3.

Collections

Karl XV of Sweden; acquired by the Museum in 1866.

Exhibitions

London and Washington 1982–83, cat. no. 36, color pl.; Paris 1983, cat. no. 19, repr.

Literature

A. Venturi 1921, p. 210. Musto 1921a, p. 64; 1921b, p. 160. Ortolani 1922, pp. 190, 193. A. Venturi 1925, pp. 73, 75, fig. 23. Stockholm 1928, pp. 10-11, cat. no. 80. Sirén in Stockholm 1933, p. 178, pl. 133. Goering 1936, p. 21, pl. 19. *The Burlington Magazine* 93 (December 1951): suppl., pl. III. Ortolani in Naples 1938, p. 66. Réau 1955-59, 2:331. *Kindlers Malerei Lexikon* 1 (1964), unpaginated. Mascherpa 1965, p. 35. Percy 1965, p. 57, no. 45. Causa 1966, p. 7, color pl. IX. Rosenberg 1968, pp. 151, 153 n. 8. Liebmann 1968, pp. 456-57, 459, figs. 50, 51. Lurie 1969, pp. 136-37, 139, 142-43, fig. 2. Neumann 1969, pp. 31-32, fig. 18 and n. 76; 1971, pp. 238, 241 n. 26. Causa 1972, pp. 942, 944, fig. 314. Naples 1975, p. 256. Ferrari in *Dizionario enciclopedico Bolaffi* 3 (1972):788. Causa in *Larousse Dictionary* 1981, p. 57. De Maio 1983, p. 24. Turin 1983, pp. 162, 164, 166-67, cat. no. 35, repr.

Fig. 82a. Simon Vouet, Paris 1590-1649. *Salome with the Head of Saint John the Baptist.* Canvas, 99.1 x 73.3 cm. Bob Jones University, Greenville, South Carolina.

Fig. 82b. Copy after Cavallino. *Judith*. Canvas, 112 x 85 cm. Musée de Picardie, Amiens, France.

82

83

The Expulsion of Heliodorus from the Temple

Copper, 62 x 88 cm, monogrammed.
Pushkin State Museum
of Fine Arts, Moscow

In catalogue only

Fig. 83a. Attributed to Cavallino. *The Expulsion of Heliodorus* (detail). Pencil and black chalk on paper, 27 x 41.6 cm. Art Gallery of Ontario, Toronto. Purchase, Estate of Mrs. Gladdis Joy Tranton, 1970.

Cavallino's monogram appears on the horse's croup; like the one on the ox in the Cleveland *Adoration of the Shepherds* [79], it simulates a brand mark.[1]

The close stylistic links with Cavallino's two copper panels of *Mucius Scaevola* [84] and *The Shade of Samuel* [85]—which belong with a third panel by Andrea Vaccaro (see under [84], Addendum)—suggested to Spinosa (in London and Washington 1982–83), as they do to this writer, the possiblity that the *Heliodorus* belongs with this series.

The scene represented derives from II Maccabees 3: 25-27 and shows how upon entering the temple of Jerusalem, which Heliodorus came to despoil, he was met by a horse with a rider "of terrible aspect." The rearing horse struck Heliodorus with his fore feet, while the rider's "strong, bright, and glorious" companions, who appeared as angels, scourged him without ceasing until Heliodorus fell to the ground. Praising the Lord that had thus glorified the temple, the High Priest Onias succumbed to Heliodorus's plea for help and intervened to save him from death. Onias, in the right background, rushes to the scene with his arms outstretched.

Since medieval times, the story was seen as a prefiguration of Christ's expulsion of the money changers from the temple, a subject also painted by Cavallino [42]. To the Renaissance popes, it also prefigured their liberation from the siege at Castello di Sant'Angelo and explains why Pope Leo X commissioned Raphael to paint the Heliodorus as well as the *Liberation of Saint Peter*—which Cavallino also painted [23] (and see Inv. no. 111) for the private apartments in the Vatican.[2] Both Northern and Italian artists, from Heemskerck to Solimena, who represented the Expulsion of Heliodorus were inspired by Raphael's *Stanza* and faithfully repeated his helmeted rider looking over the head of his light-colored, rearing horse at Heliodorus who lies, face up, in the foreground. A drawing in the Art Gallery of Ontario, Toronto (Fig. 83a), closely related to Cavallino's painting, also follows this Raphaelesque convention. Its former owner Michael Jaffé (in letter of 10 December 1982) tentatively gave it to Biliverti (1576–1644), while Vitzthum assigned it to Cavallino.[3] Existing drawings by Cavallino are too few in number to make convincing comparisons, and none of the accepted ones (see Introduction), as pointed out by Mina Gregori (letter of 20

May 1983), resemble the style of the Toronto drawing, which displays a curious "furinismo fiorentino." Although Cavallino's painting and the Toronto drawing are very close in composition, there are fundamental differences with regard to style and temperament. The angels flogging Heliodorus use both hands to swing their crops and rod; the rider in the drawing, who resembles those in late Mannerist hunting scenes,[4] has turned into a vigorous young angel, who, in turn, resembles Cavallino's youth found in his late works (e.g., Vavrino in *Tancred and Erminia* [78], the young horseman in *Saint Peter and the Centurion* [53] or that in the *David and Abigail* in Brunswick [80]). Both rider and flogging angels have exchanged the boots they wear in the drawing for Cavallino's favorite elegant stringed sandals. Above all, Heliodorus no longer lies spread-eagle on his back as he does in all former representations, including the drawing; instead, he has fallen to his knees, with one arm supporting himself and the other upraised, with fingers spread in spastic agony. His dark hair, tense face, and muscular body recall the fishermen parading as tritons in Cavallino's *Galatea* [68].[5]

The painting was first published by Rosenberg and Liebmann in 1968;[6] they dismissed the old attribution to Sébastien Bourdon and assigned it to Cavallino's mature oeuvre. The discovery of the two additional copper panels in Fort Worth and Los Angeles has confirmed their arguments. All three works stand out through their transparency of light, clarity of colors, and firm plasticity of the foreground figures. In each, additional light streams through an entrance on one side of the composition—in the *Heliodorus* and *Mucius Scaevola* on the right, in *The Shade of Samuel* on the left. Even though the vigorous action and centrifugal composition of the Heliodorus painting contrasts with the calmer, horizontal grouping of figures in the other two copper panels, the three share their pronounced clarity, coherence of design, intricate patterns of light and shadow, and compelling silhouettes.   ATL

83

1. This idea has a precedent, likely many others as well, namely, in Vitale da Bologna's (1330–1361) *Saint George and the Dragon* in the Pinacoteca, Bologna, where it appears on the saint's horse.

2. Réau 1955–59, 3:1092.

3. *Drawings in the Collection of the Art Gallery of Ontario* (Toronto, 1970), cat. no. 8, pl. 5; catalogue notes by Walter Vitzthum.

4. Paintings of Paolo Fiamingo come to mind. Heliodorus and the background scene on the left in the drawing bear distinct resemblance to the *Heliodorus* by Bertholet Flémalle in the Musées royaux des Beaux-Arts de Belgique, Brussels (see *Le Siècle de Rubens*, exh. cat., Musées royaux des Beaux-Arts de Belgique, 1965, no. 82). A copy of the painting by Pierre Paul Prud'hon (1758–1823), 152 x 184 cm, was advertised in *The Burlington Magazine* 115 (April 1973):lii.

5. The collapsing Heliodorus and the rearing horse resemble a similar scene in Andrea de Leone's *Battle between David and Goliath* in the Museo di Capodimonte.

6. Rosenberg 1968, pp. 149-56; Liebmann 1968, pp. 456-59.

Collections

G. M. Feitelberg, Moscow; Rumyanzow Museum, Moscow, 1918–24.

Exhibitions

Moscow 1918, no. 146; Vienna 1981, no. 30, repr.

Literature

Réau 1929, p. 73, no. 448. Pigler 1956, 1:232. Moscow 1948, p. 14; 1957, p. 20; 1961, p. 29. Rosenberg 1968, p. 154 n. 10, fig. 6. Liebmann 1968, p. 456-59, figs. 1,49. Ferrari 1969, p. 217. Lurie 1969, pp. 138-39, fig. 3. Vitzthum 1971, p. 89. Causa 1972, p. 942, fig. 316. Brejon de Lavergnée and Dorival 1979, p. 92. Lehmann in Kassel 1980, p. 88. London and Washington 1982–83, pp. 143, 146. Paris 1983, pp. 194-95. Turin 1983, pp. 164-65, 167-68. De Maio 1983, pp. 5, 17 n. 14, fig. 5.

Introduction
to 84, Addendum, and 85

Coherence of style, sameness in size, and common Spanish ownership of the three panels,[1] all painted on copper, suggest that they belonged to a single commission that Cavallino and Andrea Vaccaro received jointly; according to de Dominici (1742–43, 3:35-36), this was not the first time the two artists worked together. The unusual subjects and the pronounced classicizing style of both Cavallino's and Vaccaro's paintings reveal fresh contacts with the artistic scene in Rome.

Further supporting the argument for a joint commission are the three panels' subjects, which Louise Lippincott of the Getty Museum believes are linked by a common moralizing theme: each is based on a story either from the Old Testament or an ancient Roman legend about a king who receives a prophetic warning of his doom, which he can avert only if he changes his course of action. Lippincott summarizes the stories and their common theme as follows:

In *The Shade of Samuel*, Samuel's spirit warns King Saul that he will be killed if he goes into battle against David and the Philistines. Saul does not fight the battle.

In *Mucius Scaevola* Scaevola warns King Lars Porsenna that he will be killed by one of the 300 young Romans if he continues to wage war against Rome. Porsenna withdraws his troops.

And in *Jonah Preaching at Nineveh* Jonah warns the king and citizens that they will be overthrown if they continue in their corrupt ways. The Ninevites repent and change their ways.[2]

The present author suggests that the preceding *Expulsion of Heliodorus from the Temple* [83] constitutes a fourth panel that could also be fitted into this common theme. Its closeness in style, size, and support—copper, like the other three—strengthens the hypothesis. The painting illustrates the Apocryphal story of Heliodorus (II Maccabees 3:37-40), who was ordered by his king, Seleucus IV of Syria, to despoil the Temple of Solomon. As he enters the temple, Heliodorus is attacked but saved from death by the intervention of the high priest. Heliodorus then returns to warn the king that a mysterious power of God inhabits the temple and terrible punishment awaits any who violate its sanctity; Seleucus took the warning to heart.

Although the painting has been in Russia at least since 1918, nothing is known of its earlier history that would either prove or disprove a Spanish provenance.   ATL

1. A rumor that another copper panel by Cavallino (or Vaccaro?) was sold before the public sale at Subastas Durán opened, has not been confirmed.
2. Louise W. Lippincott at The J. Paul Getty Museum kindly provided the following comments:
"The themes of misguided rulers, conquest, and assassination suggest that the original commission may have been connected with political events in Naples at mid-century. Local opposition to the Spanish viceroys governing the city reached a peak with the Masaniello revolt of 1647–48 when the Spanish were driven out and replaced briefly by a republican government of sorts. The themes of the Cavallino coppers prophesying the overthrow of corrupt rulers and death to the foreign kings who wage war on a virtuous people seem especially appropriate in this context.

"Stylistic evidence, however, points to a later date for the coppers, after the Spanish had indeed invaded and regained control of the city. The repetition of these themes later in the century by other Neapolitan artists, most notably Salvator Rosa, indicate that the Cavallino subjects may not spring directly from the events of 1647–48, but from a generalized 'rhetoric of resistance' to Spain that may have permeated Neapolitan culture after decades of submission to the viceroys. Perhaps similar themes may be found in Neapolitan theatre, which is thought to have influenced Cavallino's style at this time.

"The subject of Heliodorus (which Ann Lurie connects with the three coppers mentioned above) does not depict the moment of prophecy, but shares the theme of resistance to foreign domination. In this case, the issue is not military conquest but legitimate resistance to taxation by foreign rulers, a longstanding grievance between Neapolitans and the Spanish crown. The subject would be repeated on a grander scale by Francesco Solimena as Spanish rule in Naples drew to its end."

84

Mucius Scaevola before King Porsenna

Copper, 60 x 85 cm.
Kimbell Art Museum, Fort Worth, Texas

Like Andrea Vaccaro's painting of *Jonah Preaching to the People of Nineveh* (see Addendum and Figure 84a), *Mucius Scaevola* was sold on the art market in Madrid in 1978. As number 76 in the 14 March 1978 sale at Subastas Durán, it was titled "Escena biblica"—the same title given to Vaccaro's *Jonah* painting at the 22 May 1978 sale—and carried an attribution to Vaccaro as well.[1] The sales catalogue indicated that there appeared in the lower right, alongside some numbers, illegible letters, which Durán believes may have been remnants of a monogram; however, no traces of any letters remain. Nevertheless, the fact that the other two copper panels—[85] and Figure 84a—were monogrammed by Cavallino and Vaccaro, respectively (as well as *The Expulsion of Heliodorus*), makes one suspect that the Kimbell panel was also signed.

Cavallino depicts the dramatic moment in the story told by the ancient writers (Livius II.12; Plutarch VI.17; Valerius Maximus III.3.1) about the young Roman nobleman called Caius Mucius "Scaevola" (meaning "the left-handed"), who during the Etruscan siege of Rome set out to kill Lars Porsenna, king of Clusium, but by mistake killed the royal treasurer instead. Brought before the king for judgment, Mucius demonstrated that he had no less courage to die than to inflict death by thrusting his right hand into the fire; the king, astounded at this surprising sight, leaped from his seat and commanded him to be removed from the altar. Mucius's act of heroism and his warning to King Porsenna that three hundred other Roman soldiers would be prepared to complete his task ended the Etruscan siege of Rome.

84

Fig. 84b. Giovanni Francesco Barbieri, called Guercino, Cento 1591–Bologna 1666. *Mucius Scaevola before King Porsenna* (detail). Canvas, 290 x 282 cm. Marchesa C. Cattaneo Adorno, Palazzo Durazzo Pallavicini, Genoa.

Fig. 84c. Illustration in sales catalogue of Casa de Subastas Durán, Madrid, 14 March 1978, no. 76, showing the figure at the right with outstretched hand.

Cavallino's painting reveals his familiarity with the well-established pictorial tradition of the Mucius story. Throughout the Renaissance it was featured in frescoes, sculpture, paintings, and engravings—among which the most influential example was Polidoro da Caravaggio's in various frescoes painted in Rome between 1520 and 1527. Although nothing remains of these, Cristofano Gherardi borrowed from them in his frescoes painted between 1537 and 1555. The most reliable reproductions of Polidoro's original frescoes were drawings and prints of the sixteenth and early seventeenth centuries;[2] among these, Andrea Andreani's chiaroscuro woodcut of 1608[3] appears to have been widely known. Nearly all artists, including Cavallino, repeated the traditional pose of Mucius stemming his left hand on his hip while thrusting his right into the fire in a manner that enhanced his proud, assertive stance. It was, in fact, Cavallino's own favorite pose for himself, judging from the presumed self-portraits in eight of his paintings, including *Mucius Scaevola*. Parading as a noble counsellor who takes his place at the right of King Porsenna and diagonally across from Mucius, he not only mirrors the latter's pose but also the unwavering gaze that Mucius directs at the king; Cavallino's gaze, however, is directed at the spectator.

Artists who painted the scene in which Mucius puts his hand into the fire chose between a heavy stone altar, like the one Rubens chose for his *Mucius Scaevola* (Museum of Fine Arts, Budapest),[4] or a portable pan (as Plutarch's text suggests),[5] such as the one seen in Poussin's study (Hermitage, Leningrad)[6] for a now-lost painting. Cavallino's tripod burner is obviously a homespun version of Poussin's type; both are based on Cartari's tripod[7] symbolizing heroic virtues. Ripa used the brazier as an attribute for the figure of Constancy.[8]

Most painters who included the body of Porsenna's treasurer were Northerners—for example, Rubens in the above-cited example and Terbrugghen in his painting in Lausanne.[9] Few painters included the secretarial table with the inkwell and quill and money bags below as Cavallino did and as it is suggested in Livy's text,[10] implying that the treasurer had been engaged in paying soldiers their dues when Mucius came to kill the king. One notable exception among Italian painters was Guercino. His painting in the Palazzo Durazzo Pallavicini, Genoa,[11] had been commissioned by a French patron between 1646 and 1649, but it was apparently never delivered. It was included in Malvasia's list of paintings left in Guercino's studio when he died in 1666.[12] Whether Cavallino had actually seen Guercino's painting in person cannot be verified, since there is no documentation of his travel outside of Naples. However, one almost suspects that he had seen all or parts of the composition, considering the close resemblance between Cavallino's helmetless Mucius, dressed, as Livy recounts, in the disguise of an Etruscan soldier, and Guercino's young Etruscan soldier in similar attire standing by the table with inkwell and quill (Fig. 84b).

Pillsbury (1982, fig. 5) and Spinosa (in London and Washington 1982–83, no. 37) both confidently assigned the work to Cavallino's late period, given the obvious stylistic resemblance to paintings like the Munich tondi [77-78], the two Brunswick pendants [80-81], the signed *Adoration of the Shepherds* in Cleveland [79], and particularly, of course, the painting in the J. Paul Getty Museum [85]. Pillsbury (p.v) pointed to the panel's typical Cavallinesque features, such as the "refined coloristic and luministic effects and the placement of the figures close to the picture plane in a stage-like setting flanked by curtains drawn at the sides, leaving a ground of light, neutral tones to serve as a backdrop for the action with additional light flooding into the scene from the left illuminating the central protagonist and creating a complicated, abstract shadow pattern on the floor.''

Similar to those in *The Shade of Samuel*, Cavallino's bystanders in *Mucius Scaevola*, almost monochrome in color and thinly painted, offer a striking contrast to the insistent plasticity of his main protagonists. These background figures have suffered over time and in some cases have either partly vanished or have been restored (e. g., the male with staff standing in the doorway in the right background). For that reason it is also difficult to decide whether the man on the extreme right, looking down, originally may have extended one hand in a gesture of dismay over the dead treasurer at his feet—a gesture that is at least suggested in the illustration of the abovementioned Madrid sales catalogue (Fig.84c) in which a spidery hand is extended. Similar gestures of hands silhouetted against the light for expression and for marking space are often found in Cavallino's paintings, as can be seen particularly in the two other copper panels—e.g., Samuel in *The Shade of Samuel* extends his hand in an eloquent gesture, and the High Priest Onias in the Moscow picture [83], though removed to the background, rushes to the rescue of Heliodorus with his hands anxiously reaching out.

Spinosa (ibid.) ventured a guess at the age of Cavallino in the role of King Porsenna's counsellor, suggesting that he might be over forty, which would not only date the painting very late but also jeopardize Cavallino's assumed year of death—1656. Although Cavallino looks distinctly older here than in his self-portrait in *Saint Peter and the Centurion Cornelius* [53], self-portraits can be particularly deceiving with regard to the age of the sitter.   ATL

1. It makes one wonder how many other paintings by Vaccaro in Spain may be by Cavallino instead. See Pérez Sánchez 1965, pp. 462-76.

2. Avraham Ronen, ''Storie de'fatti de'romani: Cristofano Gherardi and Polidoro da Caravaggio,'' *Storia dell'arte* 20 (1974):5-16 Alessandro Marabottini, *Polidoro da Caravaggio*, 2 vols. (Rome: Edizioni dell'Elefante, 1969). Note that Celano (1692, 1:188-89) in his description of the palace built for don Diomede Carafa, first count of Maddaloni, mentions that in one of the arches leading to the atrium there stood a full-length antique statue of Mucius Scaevola.

3. Ronen 1974, fig. 19.

4. Max Rooses, *L'Oeuvre de P. P Rubens* (Antwerp, 1890), 4:222, pl. 256.

5. *Plutarch's Lives*, English translation by Sir Thomas North (London, 1898–99), 1:370.

6. Blunt 1966-67, 2:160-61.

7. Cartari [1647] 1963, p. 185.

8. Ripa [1758–60] 1971, no. 139.

9. Benedict Nicolson in *Album Amicorum J. G. Van Gelder* (The Hague: Martinus Nijhoff, 1973), pp. 238-39, pl. 7.

10. *Livy's Roman History*, trans. J. H. Freese, A. J. Church, and W. J. Brodribb (New York: P. Appleton and Co., 1898), p. 86.

11. Torriti in Genoa 1967, fig. 202.

12. As Denis Mahon kindly informed me, the reason for the failure of this commission is still not known, although Malvasia states (*Felsina Pittrice. Vite de'pittori bolognesi del Conte Carlo Cesare Malvasia*, with additions and corrections by Giampietro Zanotti, et al. [Bologna: Tipografia Guidi all' Ancora, 1841] 273, 1st column) that a large picture with the story of Mucius Scaevola executed for ''Monsu Auriliere, primo segretario de Cristianissimo,'' because of the death of the latter, was kept by Guercino ''come fatto di tutto genio, e mirabilissimo.''

Collections

Private collection, Madrid; Subastas Durán, Madrid (sale: 14 March 1978, no. 76); Somerville & Simpson, London.

Exhibitions

London and Washington 1982–83, cat. no. 37, repr.

Literature

Pillsbury 1982, pp. i-viii, fig. 5. Turin 1983, pp. 167, 271, cat. no. 37, repr.

Author's note: A painting described as ''Un soldado que se está quemando la mano con diferentes figuras de soldados'' was listed in an inventory taken after the death of Señor don José Francisco Sarmiento, conde de Salvatierra in 1728 (Mercedes Agulló y Cobo, *Mas noticias sobre pintores madrileños de los siglos XVI al XVIII* [Madrid, 1981], p. 73). Undoubtedly this was a representation of Mucius Scaevola burning his right hand in the presence of King Porsenna. Unfortunately, neither the name of the artist nor measurements were given, nor did the inventory include any of the other subjects represented in the other coppers by Cavallino and Vaccaro.

I am grateful to William Jordan of the Kimbell Art Museum for bringing this reference to my attention.

Fig. 84a. Andrea Vaccaro, Naples 1605–1670. *Jonah Preaching to the People at Nineveh*. Copper, 61 x 85 cm. Private collection, London (?)

Addendum

Jonah Preaching to the People at Nineveh
by Andrea Vaccaro
(Naples 1605–1670)

The painting appeared in two sales at Subastas Durán in Madrid, the first on 22 May 1978 (no. 24, repr. p. 33, as "Escena biblica" by Andrea Vaccaro), and in sale number 168 of March 1983 (no. 24). The subject represents Jonah—after his rescue from the whale, which can be seen in the distant background—preaching, as God had commanded him, to the citizens of Nineveh (Jonah 3:1-5). He warned them to change their wicked ways or suffer the destruction of their city within forty days. The people accepted Jonah's message; they proclaimed a feast, and the king and all the people put on sackcloth as a sign of their repentance. The Jonah cycle was popular in Northern art,[1] but it is rarely depicted by Italian artists. One notable exception, in addition to Vaccaro, was Salvator Rosa, whose *Jonah Preaching at Nineveh* is now at the Statens Museum for Kunst, Copenhagen. Both Vaccaro's and Rosa's compositions closely resemble Bernard Salomon's woodcut illustrating the event in numerous publications of the Bible in France that appeared in several languages from 1553 on.[2] Salomon's woodcut, in turn, inspired Maarten van Heemskerck's engraving, one of his four illustrations for the *Story of Noah*.[3]

Vaccaro's classical style in this painting pays a kind of heavy-handed tribute to Poussin; his Jonah paraphrases that master's type of Moses—e. g., in the *Israelites Gathering Manna* (Louvre) of the late 1630s. Within Vaccaro's own oeuvre, his painting is stylistically close to his *Sacrifice of Noah* (Escorial), which joins a host of other contemporary paintings paying homage to Poussin's lost work.[4] It was preserved in an engraving by I. Frey.[5] Heemskerck in his *Story of Noah* series had pai. ed *Noah's Sacrifice* with *The Drunkenness of Noah* (see Hollstein V.40.8 and VIII.241.190; see also fn. 2 below, p. 226).

This author has not seen Vaccaro's painting. On the basis of the photograph (reproduced here), it appears to be in poor condition. ATL

1. B. Knipping, *De Iconografie van de Contra-Reformatie in de Nederlanden* (Hilversum: N. V. Paul Brand's Uitgeversbedrijf, 1939), 1:258.

2. See Eleanor A. Saunders, "Old Testament Subjects in the Prints of Maarten van Heemskerck: 'als een claere Spiegele der Tegenwoordige Tijden'" (Ph.D. diss., Yale University, 1978; University Microfilms, Ann Arbor, 1981), pp. 98-99. Salomon's woodcut is reproduced in *The Holy Bible* [The Authorized or King James Version of 1611 Reprinted with the Apocrypha], 3 vols. (London: Nonesuch Press; New York: Random House, 1963), p. 762.

3. Thomas Kerrich, *A Catalogue of The Prints, Which Have Been Engraved after Martin Heemskerck* (Cambridge: Cambridge University, 1829), p. 33.

4. Blunt 1966-67, 1:158, no. L2.

5. Blunt, "La première période romaine de Poussin," *Actes* 1 (1960):165, fig. 134.

85

The Shade of Samuel Invoked by Saul

Copper, 61 x 85 cm, monogrammed.
The J. Paul Getty Museum,
Malibu, California

Exhibited in USA only

Cavallino's monogram appears on the stone base in the lower left near some scattered objects that may represent the necromancer's tools. The painting is one of the two known panels by Cavallino from the commission he shared with Andrea Vaccaro (see also Addendum to [84], and Figure 84a). Like *Mucius Scaevola* [84]—as well as the *Heliodorus* [83]—*The Shade of Samuel* is painted on hammered copper. The masterful adaptation of brushwork and coloration to the copper ground is described in the J. Paul Getty Museum's announcement of its acquisition: "[Cavallino applied his paint] with rapid, sketchy strokes and emphasized the translucency of his medium," [allowing] "the warm tones of the copper itself to glow through the thinly brushed paint in sections of the drapery and background."[1]

Cavallino depicts the moment of confrontation between the spirit of Samuel, the prophet who had died recently, and Saul, the first king of Israel (I Samuel 28: 7-25). Fearing defeat, Saul had disguised himself on the eve of the battle against the Philistines and went to find a necromancer at Endor to invoke the spirit of Samuel for counsel. Samuel then told Saul that the next day Israel would be lost to the Philistines and he and his sons would die. Only an understanding of the characters makes it possible to appreciate fully the profound insights and sensitivity of Cavallino's portrayal of this event. Samuel is silhouetted against the dazzling light that emanates from the doorway on the left. His ancient figure, bearing a shroud that partly covers his pale skin and ashen

face (tinged with green), leans toward Saul with a penetrating gaze that expresses troubled concern. His ghostly pallor is in direct contrast to the ruddy coarseness of the medium's face, which reflects the combination of amazement and fear that she is experiencing: in recognizing King Saul, she knows that her own fate lies in the balance because she had defied the king's earlier condemnation and banishment of mediums and wizards and had remained secretly in Israel.

The main focus is on the kneeling King Saul: though he was inevitably doomed, Cavallino portrays him with great sympathy as a mature, deeply troubled man who at the same time appears young and vulnerable. His soft features recall the sensitive young face of Cavallino's *Saint Anthony* [56]; the treatment of his hair— silken texture with deep waves—is like that of the angel in the foreground of the *Heliodorus* [83]. Shown as a king in full royal attire and diadem, he wears a sparkling breastplate with a cloak of vibrant red draped over it;[2] his robe is of green-gold tonality.

Both the subject of this painting and that of Vaccaro's *Jonah Preaching at Nineveh*, from the same commission, are almost unknown in Italian art, although they were popular subjects in the North. Salvator Rosa's *Witch of Endor* (Nationalmuseum, Copenhagen) is the only important other example found in Italy. And, it is interesting to note, Rosa is also the only other major Italian artist who painted the Jonah subject. Rosa's *Jonah* is generally dated in the 1650s,[3] and his *Witch of Endor* is dated in the late 1660s, undoubtedly because it was exhibited at San Giovanni Decollato in Rome in 1668;[4] both paintings draw upon his earlier witchcraft scenes painted in Florence in the 1640s. Rosa left Florence to return to Rome in 1649. An argument for dating his *Witch of Endor* in the 1650s, however, like *Jonah Preaching*, is Schönfeld's print of the same subject—though dating from twenty years later—that evokes memories of Rosa's painting.[5] Like Rosa's, it is a macabre witchcraft scene, with a sepulchral skeleton and a devastated King Saul, who has violently thrown himself to the ground; it even includes Rosa's two soldiers who witness the invocation of Samuel's spirit. These direct echoes would at least make one suspect that Schönfeld had seen Rosa's painting during his sojourn in Rome in the early 1650s[6] before returning to Germany.

Regardless of whether Rosa's *Jonah Preaching at Nineveh* and *Witch of Endor* preceded or followed Vaccaro's and Cavallino's paintings, the choice of these particular themes, so unusual in Italian art, was probably not a coincidence. As Lippincott (see Introduction to [84] and Addendum, note 2) suggested, the subjects chosen by the three native Neapolitan artists may reflect their awareness of the general climate of resistance against the Spanish overlordship of Naples that led to the Masaniello Revolt in that city in 1647–48.[7]

Cavallino's three main characters are restrained in their actions; their subtle, physical gestures are carefully balanced and are chosen to convey an interaction of emotional response. Their dialogue is silent but eloquent. In particular, Cavallino's deeply worried necromancer is a far cry from Rosa's screaming counterpart, and Cavallino's Samuel reminds one of a Schönfeld philospher (e. g., the *Diogenes* in his etching—see under [53]) rather than Rosa's figure of a warlock.

The technical and coloristic refinement, the compositional clarity, and the psychological penetration of Cavallino's figures speak for a very late date; the work epitomizes his late style.   ATL

1. "Recent Acquisitions: Two Italian Seventeenth-Century Paintings on Copper," *The J. Paul Getty Museum Calendar* (February 1984), reproduced without number.

2. Some areas of the red drapery suffered losses, which have now been restored.

3. The painting was sold to King Christian IV of Denmark in 1661 (Salerno 1963, p. 112; Voss 1924, p. 569).

4. Salerno 1963, p. 113.

5. Pée, 1971, p. 219, cat. no. NS45.

6. Schönfeld returned to Augsburg in 1651. See Helen C. M. Marres-Schretlen, "Schönfeld-Ehinger en de heks van Endor," *Bulletin van het Rijksmuseum* 24 (1974):100-104.

7. An interesting parallel to Lippincott's hypothesis is suggested by the art of the North at the time of the Netherlandish revolt against Spain from 1568–1609. Netherlandish artists and, as Saunders (see Addendum, note 2, pp. 224-94) demonstrates, particularly Maarten van Heemskerck in his series of the *Clades Judaeae Gentis* (*Disasters of the Jewish Nation*) chose subjects both for their didactic potential in general and their relevance to contemporary misfortunes. Two of Heemskerck's Old Testament scenes included in the *Clades* series were also treated by Cavallino, namely, the *Drunkenness of Noah* [39, 75] and *Lot and His Daughters* [29, 38, 74]. Heemskerck also did engravings of *Jonah Preaching at Nineveh* (Hollstein VIII. 243.270) and the *Heliodorus*

85

(Hollstein VIII. 247.544), although they were
not part of the *Clades* series.

Collections
Private collection, Madrid; Somerville & Simpson, London; private collection, New York (on
loan to The Metropolitan Museum of Art,
1982/83); acquired by the Museum in 1983.

Exhibitions
None.

Literature
London and Washington 1982—83, pp. 146-47.
Turin 1983, pp. 167-68.

Inventory

Compiled by Grace G. Fowler

This inventory is divided into two sections:

Existing works are those whose locations are known to us today; they have been published at one time or another as by Bernardo Cavallino but are now questioned or dismissed as autograph works by the artist.

Lost works are those whose present whereabouts are unknown; they have either been published as by Cavallino or mentioned in unpublished documents. This section includes known paintings that are considered to have been executed by Cavallino, as well as those now under question as autograph works, and others that have never been identified.

The designations appearing at the end of each entry reflect, in the considered opinion of the authors of the present catalogue, the merits of an attribution to Cavallino, and in the case of reattributed works take into account recent scholarship. These designations are abbreviated as follows:

Pr = probably autograph
Po = possibly autograph
D = doubtfully attributed
W = wrongly attributed
R = reattributed
U = unidentified

Unpublished paintings, and drawings, do not appear in the inventory. Works listed in the inventory that are recorded in private collections in seventeenth- or eighteenth-century sources also appear in the Appendix.

Both sections of the inventory are arranged, with works listed alphabetically, under these categories:

Old Testament and Apocryphal Subjects
New Testament Subjects
Devotional Images of Christ and the Virgin Mary
Saints
Miscellaneous Subjects Derived from History, Literature, and Mythology

Existing Works

Old Testament and Apocryphal Subjects

1   The Curing of Tobit

104 x 125.5 cm, Museo Correale, Sorrento. *References*: de Rinaldis 1917, p. 180, and 1921, p. 17; Nugent 1925–30, 2:564; Carli 1938, p. 256 (copy); Causa 1953, p. 91 (workshop copy); Milicua 1954, p. 72 (copy); Percy 1965, p. 71, no. 110 (rejected attribution; derives from follower of Ribera, such as Fracanzano); Causa 1972, p. 983 n. 111 (17th-century copy). *Remarks*: This is a pendant to Inv. no. 16.   W

2   The Curing of Tobit

109 x 122 cm, Rebuffat Collection, Naples (Fig. 24e). *Collections*: Buffardi, Naples. *References*: Percy 1965, p. 61, no. 66 (copy); Spinosa, in conversation 1983 (copy).   W

3   The Curing of Tobit

82.5 x 104.6 cm, David E. Rust Collection, Washington, DC, acquired 1963. *Collections*: Julius Weitzner, London. *References*: *Architectural Digest*, October 1984, p. 175. *Remarks*: Although the composition closely resembles that of the Prado version (Inv. no. 6), this work is by a different hand. Another closely related version, by an unidentified artist, belongs to the collection of Dr. Alfred Bader, Milwaukee.   W

4   The Curing of Tobit

76 x 101.5 cm, Seattle Art Museum, Gift of the Seattle Art Museum Guild, no. 51.124, acquired 1951 (Fig. 24f). *Collections*: Olivetti, Rome, through 1938; Corsi, Florence. *References*: Sestieri 1921, pp. 181-82, repr.; Ortolani 1922, p. 192; Ortolani in Naples 1938, p. 65; Percy 1965, p. 63, no. 76 (copy); Causa 1972, p. 982 n. 110 (copy).   W

5   The Curing of Tobit

100 x 130 cm, Museo Nazionale d'Abruzzo, L'Aquila. *Collections*: Cappelli, San Demetrio dei Vestini, L'Aquila, through 1938. *References*: Carli 1938, pp. 256-61, fig. 2 (as *Return of Tobias*, excellent copy after Cavallino, exhibited at "Mostra della pittura napoletana dell' '600, '700 e '800" as original work by Cavallino); Naples 1938, p. 319; Oertel 1938, p. 230; Percy 1965, p. 64, no. 78 (rejected attribution to Cavallino; copy after Fracanzano?). *Remarks*: This is a pendant to Inv. no. 17.   W

6 The Curing of Tobit

76 x 103 cm, Museo del Prado, Madrid, no. 3151, acquired 1969 (Fig. 24c). *Collections*: Salvatore Romano, Naples. *References*: Nugent 1925–30, 2:564 (variant of painting at Museo Correale [Inv. no. 1]); Madrid 1970, no. 47, and 1972, p. 866, no. 3151; de Salas 1976, pp. 70-71, and 1978, pp. 51, 53, repr. p. 52. *Remarks*: This is a pendant to Inv. no. 18. W

7 David Playing the Harp before Saul

112.5 x 155 cm, Národní Galerie, Prague, no. D0204. *References*: In Gallery catalogues 1936, no. 278, and 1938, no. 338; Schleier 1971, p. 101 (as Giovanni Battista Spinelli); Spinosa in London and Washington 1982–83, p. 255, no. 152 (as Spinelli, perhaps the preparatory study for the larger painting now in the Uffizi). *Remarks*: The Gallery also possesses a copy of this painting, no. D04978, formerly attributed to Stanzione. R

8 The Death of Abel

102 x 129.5 cm, Museo di Capodimonte, Naples (Fig. 39). *Collections*: Don Francesco d'Avalos, marchese del Vasto, Naples. *References*: de Rinaldis 1909, p. 14, no. 3, and 1911, p. 416; Hermanin in Thieme-Becker 6 (1912):225; de Rinaldis 1920a, p. 5, and 1921, p. 16, and 1927, p. 58; Corna 1930, 1:227; Naples 1932, p. 22, no. 523, and 1938, pp. 64, 320; Ortolani 1938, p. 178, repr. p. 182; Refice 1951, p. 263; Causa 1957, p. 40 (rejects attribution to Cavallino); Naples 1957, p. 74, no. 523 (17th-century Neapolitan school), and 1964, p. 55, no. [523] (follower of Cavallino); Percy 1965, p. 68, no. 97 (reattributed at Capodimonte to the Cain and Abel Master). *Remarks*: The handling of paint in this work is so close to Cavallino's manner that it must be by a close follower of the artist, known at present as the Cain and Abel Master. R

9 The Departure of Tobias

78 x 100 cm, Galleria Nazionale d'Arte Antica, Palazzo Corsini, Rome, no. 1484, acquired 1909 (Fig. 24a). *Collections*: P. Tesorone, Naples, through 1877. *References*: Naples 1877, no. 18; de Rinaldis 1909, p. 27, no. 9; Hermanin 1910, p. 230; Rolfs 1910, p. 278 n. 1; *Kunstchronik* n. f. 21 (1910), col. 14; Hermanin 1911, p. 183, pl. 40, fig. 1, and 1912, p. 374, and in Thieme-Becker 6 (1912):225; de Rinaldis 1917, p. 182; Longhi 1920b, p. 91; de Rinaldis 1920a, pp. 3-4 n. 2; Sestieri 1920, p. 260; de Rinaldis 1921, p. 17, pl. vi; Sestieri 1921, pp. 181-83, 188; Florence 1922, no. 252; Consoli Fiego 1922, p. 108 (may be replica on canvas, by Cavallino, of version mentioned by de Dominici in house of Francesco Valletta); Hermanin 1924–25, p. 6; Ojetti, Dami, and Tarchiani 1924, pl. 84; Nugent 1925–30, 2:562, repr. p. 563; Benesch 1926, p. 248; Pevsner in Pevsner and Grautoff 1928, p. 186; de Rinaldis 1929, pl. 39; London 1930, no. 758, and 1931, 1:167, no. 489 (758), 2:pl. clxxxii; de Rinaldis 1932, pp. 17, 23, pl. 43; McComb 1934, pp. 49-51; Carli 1938, p. 262; Naples 1938, p. 319; Masciotta 1942, p. 147; Montini 1952, p. 35; Golzio 1955, 1:543, fig. 467; Carpegna in Rome 1958, no. 9 (notes that Longhi suggested in conversation that the work is an 18th-century copy); Percy 1965, pp. 62-63, no. 74 (considered to be a copy by Longhi, Causa, and Bologna); Causa 1972, p. 983 n. 111 (18th-century copy; Longhi attributed to Giacinto Diana). *Remarks*: This is probably an 18th-century copy after a lost

original by Cavallino, described by de Dominici as painted on copper (Inv. no. 80). A related drawing attributed to Corrado Giaquinto was sold at Sotheby's, London, 4 July 1977, lot 135, as attributed to Cavallino, and a damaged rough copy was recently on the Italian art market—known only from a photograph. W

10 The Finding of Moses

91.5 x 131 cm, The National Gallery, London, no. 6297, acquired 1959, as Cavallino (Fig. 38). *Collections*: Lord Darnley, Cobham Hall, Kent, where apparently the same picture recorded 1808 as by Salvator Rosa; sale, Cobham Hall, 23 July 1957, lot 377 (unattributed); sale, Sotheby's, London, 30 April 1958, lot 159 (as Salvator Rosa), to Appleby; Julius Weitzner, London. *References*: Juynboll 1960, p. 85 (questions attributions to Cavallino); Ellis in Barnard Castle 1962, no. 36; Crombie 1962, p. 397 (a Flemish-Spadaresque work); Nicolson 1962, p. 317 (attribution to Cavallino has been questioned); Waterhouse 1962, p. 183, fig. 158; London 1963, p. 14, no. 6297 (as Cavallino, with doubts); Nicolson 1963, p. 295 (National Gallery acknowledges painting may not be by Cavallino); Percy 1965, p. 65, no. 81 (rejected attribution to Cavallino; suggests a collaboration of hands between landscape and figures); London 1971, pp. 107-8, no. 6297 (as Gargiulo?); Causa 1972, p. 983 n. 111 (manner of Gargiulo); London 1973b, p. 254, no. 6297 (as Gargiulo?); De Vito 1982, p. 45, fig. 37 (as Antonio de Bellis). R

11 Jacob at the Well

92 x 118 cm, Museo del Prado, Madrid, no. 2324. *Collections*: Queen Elizabetta Farnese, Palacio de la Granja, 1746 inventory, no. 970, as Cavallino. *References*: Madrid 1920, p. 455, no. 2324 (as school of Poussin); Pérez Sánchez 1965, p. 383 (catalogued at Prado as school of Poussin, but undoubtedly Neapolitan). *Remarks*: Juan Luna, in letter of 15 September 1983, states that, following Pérez Sánchez, the Prado now catalogues the picture as anonymous, 17th-century Neapolitan school. W

12 Judith with the Head of Holofernes

71 x 96.5 cm, Museo di Capodimonte, Naples, no. 551, gift of Giuseppe Cenzato, 1957. *Collections*: Giuseppe Cenzato, Naples, by 1938. *References*: Naples 1938, p. 319; Molajoli 1948, p. 104; *The Burlington Magazine* 93 (December 1951), adv. suppl., note to pl. III; Naples 1957, p. 73 (attributed to Cavallino), and 1964, p. 54 (attributed to Cavallino); Percy 1965, p. 69, no. 102 (rejected attribution to Cavallino; Causa suggests unknown artist influenced by Falcone); Moir 1967, 2:66, no. 5b (attributed to Cavallino); Pée 1971, p. 168; Causa 1972, p. 983 n. 111 (17th-century copy after Cavallino). *Remarks*: This work is considered now by Capodimonte to be by an unknown artist in the circle of Cavallino. W

13 Lot and His Daughters

Principessa Vittoria Alliata de Villafranca, Palermo. *Collections*: Astarita, Naples, through 1951. *References*: Ortolani 1938, p. 178, repr. p. 183; Ortolani in Naples 1938, p. 65, repr.; Refice 1951, p. 268; Percy 1965, p. 73, no. 130 (lost); Causa 1972, p. 982 n. 110 (copy). *Remarks*: This is considered by Spinosa (orally, 1983) to be a contemporary copy. In Percy's opinion, based on a photograph and without firsthand acquaintance with the picture, it could be an original. A copy apparently once existed in a Roman private collection (Gabinetto Fotografico Nazionale, Rome, D 7314). D

14 The Marriage of Tobias
101.6 x 129.5 cm, The Chrysler Museum, Norfolk (Virginia), gift of Walter P. Chrysler, Jr., no. 71.531, acquired 1954 (Fig. 24d). *Collections*: Ilo Nunes Mauri, Rome, ca. 1945–53, no. 22. *References*: Refice 1951, p. 268; Chamberlain 1956, p. 46, repr.; B. S. Manning 1956, p. 32; Sarasota 1961, p. 30, no. 27, repr.; Percy 1965, p. 62, no. 72 (copy); Causa 1972, p. 983 n. 111 (17th-century copy). W

15 The Marriage of Tobias
De Biase Collection, Naples. *Collections*: Geri, Naples; Gualtieri, Naples, before 1938. *References*: Consoli Fiego 1922, pp. 107-8 (poor variant of Sorrento composition); Carli 1938, p. 262 (very weak copy with angel almost touching Tobias, as in Romano version); Percy 1965, p. 67, no. 93 (rejected attribution to Cavallino). W

16 The Marriage of Tobias
104 x 125.5 cm, Museo Correale, Sorrento. *References*: de Rinaldis 1917, p. 180, and 1921, p. 17; Consoli Fiego 1922, p. 107 (copy of painting in Salvatore Romano collection [Inv. no. 18, now Prado], may be by Cavallino); Nugent 1925–30, 2:564; Carli 1938, pp. 256, 262 (copy); Causa 1953, p. 91 (workshop copy); Milicua 1954, p. 72 (copy); Percy 1965, p. 71, no. 111 (rejected attribution to Cavallino; derives from follower of Ribera, such as Fracanzano); Causa 1972, p. 983 n. 111 (17th-century copy). *Remarks*: This is a pendant to Inv. no. 1. W

17 The Marriage of Tobias
104 x 130 cm, Museo Nazionale d'Abruzzo, L'Aquila. *Collections*: Cappelli, San Demetrio dei Vestini, L'Aquila, through 1938. *References*: Carli 1938, pp. 256, 261-62, fig. 1 (excellent copy after Cavallino); Percy 1965, p. 64, no. 79 (rejected attribution to Cavallino; copy after Fracanzano?). *Remarks*: This is a pendant to Inv. no. 5. W

18 The Marriage of Tobias
76 x 103 cm, Museo del Prado, Madrid, no. 3152; acquired 1969 (Fig. 24b). *Collections*: Salvatore Romano, Naples. *References*: de Rinaldis 1909, p. 38, no. 13; Hermanin 1911, p. 185, pl. 40, fig. 2; Hermanin in Thieme-Becker 6 (1912):225; de Rinaldis 1917, p. 180 n. 1 (replica of painting in Sorrento [Inv. no. 16]), and 1920a, p. 3, and 1921, p. 17; Consoli Fiego 1922, p. 107 (identical with painting, 3 x 4 *palmi*, seen by de Dominici in the house of Francesco Valletta); Nugent 1925–30, 2:564 (variant of the painting in Sorrento); Corna 1930, 1:227; Madrid 1970, no. 48, and 1972, p. 866, no. 3152; de Salas 1976, p. 70, and in Madrid 1978, pp. 51, 53, repr. p. 52. *Remarks*: This is a pendant to Inv. no. 6. W

19 The Sacrifice of Noah
101 x 127.8 cm, Museum of Fine Arts, Houston, Samuel H. Kress Collection, no. 61.63, acquired 1961. *Collections*: Maurice Kann, Paris; Alphonse Kann, Paris; sale, American Art Association,

New York, 7 January 1927, pl. 71 (as *Abraham Sacrificing the Sheep* by Nicolas Poussin); Findlay Galleries, New York; Julius Weitzner, New York, 1937; Kress acquisition, 1945; given in 1961 to the Museum of Fine Arts, Houston. *References*: H. Voss, in letter of 15 June 1937 to Weitzner (now in Museum file), attributes to Cavallino and reinterprets subject; Frankfurter 1946, p. 68, repr.; Houston 1953, pl. 21; Bologna 1958, p. 31 (as Bartolomeo Passante); Juynboll 1960, p. 85; Ferrari 1962, p. 236 (as Passante); Percy 1965, p. 64, no. 80 (rejected attribution to Cavallino; suggests a painter of Riberesque naturalist persuasion, possibly from the school of Falcone, close to Spadaro); Shapley 1973, p. 96, fig. 172; Marini 1974, p. 118 (as Passante); Houston 1981, p. 54, no. 98; De Vito 1982, p. 45, fig. 34 (as Antonio de Bellis); De Vito in London and Washington 1982–83, p. 49 (as de Bellis). *Remarks*: In Spinosa's opinion also, the work is by Antonio de Bellis. R

20 The Triumph of David
82.6 x 115.6 cm, The John and Mable Ringling Museum of Art, Sarasota, Florida, no. 155, acquired between 1926 and 1931. *References*: de Rinaldis in Naples 1927, p. 28 (as Giovanni Battista Quagliata); Sarasota 1949, p. 137, no. 155; Hartford 1958, p. 17; Gilbert in Sarasota 1961, no. 17, repr. (as Domenico Gargiulo); Percy 1965, p. 70, no. 109 (rejected attribution to Cavallino); Sarasota 1976, p. 148, no. 155, repr. (as Gargiulo). *Remarks*: Reattributed to Domenico Gargiulo. R

21 The Triumph of David
115 x 207 cm, Staatliche Kunsthalle, Karlsruhe, no. 2473. *Collections*: Salvatore Romano, Florence or Naples, through 1938. *References*: de Rinaldis 1917, p. 181, and 1921, p. 17; Oertel 1938, p. 231, repr. p. 228 (as Schönfeld); Ortolani in Naples 1938, pp. 82, 321 (as J. H. Schönfeld); Pée 1971, pp. 115-16, no. 37, pls. 43-44 with bibliography (as Schönfeld). *Remarks*: Reattributed to Johann Heinrich Schönfeld. R

New Testament Subjects

22 The Adoration of the Shepherds
105 x 130 cm, Museo Nazionale d'Abruzzo, L'Aquila. *Collections*: Cappelli, San Demetrio dei Vestini, L'Aquila, through 1960. *References*: Carli 1938, p. 269, fig. 3 (detail); Naples 1938, pp. 64, 319; Oertel 1938, p. 230; Ortolani 1938, p. 178; Juynboll 1960, p. 88 n. 6; Percy 1965, p. 60, no. 60 (in the opinion of Causa, a copy). *Remarks*: The authenticity of this work is difficult to assess from a photograph; unfortunately it has not been possible to see the work at the time of writing. Possibly it is a copy after a lost original. D

23 The Angel Liberating Saint Peter from Prison
147 x 190 cm, Galleria degli Uffizi, Florence, no. 578 (P1455). *References*: Borea in Florence 1970, no. 17, repr. (unknown follower of Caravaggio); Volpe 1970, pp. 113-14, pl. 54 (young Cavallino?); Schleier 1971, p. 94, fig. 1c (young Vouet?); Spear 1971, p. 109 (Northern painter, influenced by Saraceni); Paris 1974, no. 75; Rome 1974, no. 75 (unknown French follower of Caravaggio); Volpe 1974, p. 31 (young Cavallino copying older master?); Florence 1979, p. 480, P1455 (school of Caravaggio, 17th century). W

24 The Angel Liberating Saint Peter from Prison

75.8 x 52.4 cm, private collection, Switzerland. *Collections*: Tatafiore, Naples, through 1921; Mario Lanfranchi and Anna Moffo, Rome, early 1970s; Silvano Lodi, Munich, in 1973; Gilberto Algranti, Milan, 1981. *References*: de Rinaldis 1920a, p. 56, repr.; Longhi 1920b, p. 153; de Rinaldis 1921, p. 16; Sestieri 1921, p. 184; Percy 1965, p. 74, no. 138 (lost); *The Burlington Magazine* 115 (October 1973):lxiv (Silvano Lodi); New York 1981, no. 13, repr. *Remarks*: Although the composition and handling of paint seem to derive from a close association with Cavallino's work, a certain crudeness of execution suggests that the picture is by an imitator.   W

25 The Annunciation to the Shepherds

Octagonal, 67 x 64 cm, Galleria Falanga, Naples (Fig. 15a). *Collections*: Ospedale abbruzzese pro orfani dei contadini morti in guerra, Naples, 1920; Alberto Gualtieri, 1921; de Biase, Naples, 1938; Galleria Falanga, Milan, by about 1958. *References*: de Rinaldis 1920a, p. 57, repr.; Longhi 1920c, p. 153; de Rinaldis 1921, p. 16, pl. XXIII; Sestieri 1921, p. 184; Ortolani 1922, p. 193; Naples 1938, p. 318; Hernández Perera 1957, p. 219, pl. IV (as the Master of the Annunciations to the Shepherds; location wrongly given as Capodimonte); Bologna 1958, p. 31 n. 7 (attributed to the Master of the Annunciations); Pérez Sánchez 1961, p. 327 (attributed to the Master of the Annunciations); Percy 1965, p. 65, no. 85 (rejected attribution to Cavallino); Causa 1972, p. 982 n. 110 (typical of the work of the Master of the Annunciations). *Remarks*: Reattributed to the Master of the Annunciations to the Shepherds. The canvas appears to have been cut down at some time into its present octagonal shape in order to appear to be a pendant to [15], now in the same Neapolitan collection.   R

26 Christ and the Adulteress

121 x 142 cm, Civico Museo d'Arte, Castelvecchio, Verona, acquired 1871. *Collections*: Bernasconi, Verona. *References*: Hermanin in Thieme-Becker 6 (1912):225; Longhi 1916a, p. 308; de Rinaldis 1917, p. 179, repr. p. 181, and 1920a, p. 5; Sestieri 1920, p. 253 (doubts attribution to Cavallino); de Rinaldis 1921, p. 18, pl. XVI; Consoli Fiego 1922, p. 108; Ortolani 1922, p. 190; Corna 1930, 1:227, repr. p. 226; Causa 1957, p. 40 (rejects attribution to Cavallino); Sutton 1957, p. 110 n. 4 (rejects attribution to Cavallino); Longhi 1959, pp. 33-34, pl. 8 (attributes to Spadarino); Zampetti 1960, p. 55 (questions attribution to Cavallino); Percy 1965, p. 71, no. 112 (rejected attribution to Cavallino; Longhi gives to Spadarino); Moir 1967, 1:95 n. 85 (as Spadarino); Causa 1972, p. 983 n. 111 (Longhi gives to Spadarino). *Remarks*: Reattributed to Giacomo Galli, called Lo Spadarino.   R

27 Christ Driving the Merchants from the Temple

101 x 135 cm, Museo del Prado, Madrid, no. 94. *Collections*: Queen Elizabetta Farnese, Palacio de la Granja, 1746 inventory, no. 971 (as Cavallino). *References*: Eusebius in Museum catalogues 1818–43; Madrid 1945, p. 129, no. 94 (Castiglione?; according to Voss, by Aniello Falcone), and 1963, p. 207, no. 94 (as Falcone); Pérez Sánchez 1965, p. 390, pl. 134 (as Falcone); Madrid 1972, p. 207, no. 94 (as Falcone). *Remarks*: Reattributed to Aniello Falcone.   R

28 Christ on the Cross, with Mary Magdalene

35 x 25 cm, Borbon y Braganza Collection, Madrid. *References*: Catalogue Abrégé de la Galerie de Feu S.A.R. L'Enfant Don Sebastian, 1876, p. 56, no. 499 (as Ferdinand Cavallino); Colegio Notarial de Madrid, 1887 [Testimonio de particulares de la testamentaria de S.A.R. Don Sebastian Gabriel de Borbon y Braganza], no. 1020 (as Bernardo Cavallino).   U

29 The Dead Christ with Two Attendant Figures

Oil on paper (?) laid on canvas, 34.5 x 43 cm, Musée de Peinture et de Sculpture, Grenoble, gift of Jules Murzonne fils, 1835. *References*: Rosenberg 1972, p. 343, fig. 2 (attributed to the school of the Carracci, Tintoretto, and Guarino in the various 19th-century museum inventories); London and Washington 1982–83, p. 140; Paris 1983, pp. 191, 195; Turin 1983, p. 161. *Remarks*: It is very difficult to ascertain whether this is a copy or a very ruined original, given the picture's present state. The composition and the approach to the handling of paint are typical of Cavallino; the work corresponds closely to de Dominici's description of a small picture (Inv. no. 124) in the Valletta collection, "un quadretto di due palmi [ca. 53 cm; in which one sees] la figura di un Cristo morto in positura difficile, poicchè stà colla testa, e col petto avanti inscorcio per cui si perde la veduta delle gambe, e de'piedi, e questo si scorge esser dipinto ul naturale" (de Dominici 1742–43, 3:38). Although the Grenoble picture must record a composition by Cavallino himself, it is nearly impossible to find any trace of the artist's hand in the picture as it now appears.   D

30 The Denial of Saint Peter

66 x 105 cm, Graf Harrach'sche Familiensammlung, Schloss Rohrau, acquired by Alois Thomas Raimund, Count Harrach, Viceroy to Naples 1728–33; in inventories of 1745 and 1749 attributed to Domenico Fetti; later attributed to Bartolomeo Manfredi. *References*: Harrach cat. 1856, p. 81, no. 352 (as Manfredi); A. Venturi 1921, pp. 209-11, fig. 2; Musto 1921a, p. 160 (as copy of original in Torre del Greco, collection marchese di Campolattaro); Ortolani 1922, p. 191; Consoli Fiego 1922, p. 108 (copy); A. Venturi 1925, p. 74, fig. 24; Harrach cat. 1926, p. 90, no. 231 (352); Benesch 1926, p. 250 n. 4 (copy); Ortolani in Naples 1938, p. 65 (copy); Harrach cat. 1960, p. 25, no. 67; Percy 1965, p. 63, no. 77 (copy). *Remarks*: This is a copy of the painting of the subject formerly in a private collection in Torre del Greco, now in a private collection in Bologna [9].   W

31 The Dream of Saint Joseph

102 x 75 cm, Herzog Anton Ulrich-Museum, Brunswick, no. 789, acquired 1963. *Collections*: Probably Ugo Jandolo, Rome, through 1909; Ludovico Pollak, Rome, by 1921, through 1938; Studio d'Arte Palma, Rome, 1944–45; sale, Sotheby's, London, 4 April 1962, lot 54; G. Kramer, Oude Kunst, The Hague, 1962. *References*: de Rinaldis 1909, p. 48, no. 17 (Jandolo collection, flat handling of paint and rigid folds of drapery suggest that it is repainted or by another hand); de Rinaldis 1920a, p. 4 n. 2 (private collection, Rome), and 1921, p. 17, pl. I; Sestieri 1921, p. 184 (as *Rest on the Flight into Egypt*); Benesch 1926, p. 248, fig. 172; Carli 1938, p. 264; Ortolani in Naples 1938, p. 65; Rome 1944–45, no. 21; Refice 1951, p. 262; Białostocki and Walicki 1957, p. 511; *The Burlington Magazine* 104 (June 1962), note to

pl. IV; Percy 1965, p. 61, no. 62 (copy). *Remarks*: This is an old copy of *The Dream of Saint Joseph* in the Muzeum Narodowe, Warsaw [37]. At least one other copy of the picture existed (Inv. no. 133).   W

32 Ecce Homo

151 x 206 cm, Bayerische Staatsgemäldesammlungen, Munich, no. 13399, acquired 1963, as J. H. Schönfeld. *Collections*: Duca di Corigliano-Saluzzo, Naples, through 1922; principessa di Gerace, Naples, through 1938. *References*: Ortolani 1922, p. 195, fig. 8; Voss 1927, pp. 64-65, 76 (as Schönfeld); Naples 1938, p. 321 (as Schönfeld); Oertel 1938, p. 230 (as Schönfeld); Voss 1964, pp. 15, 33 (as Schönfeld); Percy 1965, p. 66, no. 87 (reattributed to Schönfeld); Ulm 1967, no. 43 (as Schönfeld); Adriani 1967, p. 794 (as Schönfeld); Dussler 1967, p. 377 (as Schönfeld); Pée 1971, pp. 124-25, no. 49, figs. 56-57 (as Schönfeld). *Remarks*: Reattributed to Johann Heinrich Schönfeld.   R

33 Ecce Homo

81 x 62 cm, Chigi-Saracini, Monte dei Paschi di Siena. *References*: Salmi 1967, pp. 207, 210, fig. 150 (as Cavallino?).   W

34 The Good Samaritan

96 x 118.5 cm, Museo di Capodimonte, Naples, no. 567, acquired 1882. *Collections*: Don Francesco d'Avalos, marchese del Vasto. *References*: de Rinaldis 1909, p. 13, no. 2 (an early work), and 1911, p. 416; Hermanin in Thieme-Becker 6 (1912):225; de Rinaldis 1920a, p. 5, and 1921, p. 16, and 1927, p. 58; Corna 1930, 1:227; Naples 1932, p. 22, no. 522; Ortolani 1938, p. 178, and in Naples 1938, p. 64; Naples 1957, p. 74, no. 528 (Neapolitan school, first half 17th century), and 1964, p. 55, no. [522] (follower of Cavallino); Percy 1965, p. 68, no. 98 (reattributed at Capodimonte to the Cain and Abel Master); Causa 1972, p. 982 n. 110 (rejects attribution to Cavallino; by another strongly naturalist painter). *Remarks*: This picture, the Capodimonte *Death of Abel* (Inv. no. 8), and the Rome *Saint Sebastian Cured by Saint Irene* (Inv. no. 63) present the interesting possibility of a Cavallino pupil or close follower: the naturalistic observation of materials and the handling of paint are very close to Cavallino's own work, although the pictures do not seem to be by his hand.   W

35 The Incredulity of Saint Thomas

37 x 33.5 cm, private collection, Naples. *Remarks*: This is a smaller version of the canvas at the Pio Monte della Misericordia (Inv. no. 36), but without the architecture. Considered by Percy, in conversation 1983, to be a contemporary copy of a lost composition by Cavallino or a work by another hand in his manner.   W

36 The Incredulity of Saint Thomas

48 x 36 cm, Pinacoteca del Pio Monte della Misericordia, Naples. *References:* Causa 1970, p. 90, no. 11 (figures by Cavallino, architecture by another hand — perhaps Filippo Gagliardi); de Maio 1983, p. 136. *Remarks*: Causa, in conversation 1983, indicated his current belief that the work is a copy. Another version, without the architecture, is in a private collection, Naples (Inv. no. 35).   W

37 The Nativity

153.3 x 134 cm, The National Gallery, London, no. 1157, gift of Woodford Pilkington, 1884. *References*: London 1901, p. 120, no. 1157, and 1915, p. 49, no. 1157, and 1925, p. 162, no. 1157 (Italian school, 17th century); Longhi 1969, pp. 42-43 (as G. B. Spinelli); Levey in London 1971, p. 209, no. 1157 (Spinelli?); Spinosa in London and Washington 1982–83, pp. 254-55 (as Spinelli). *Remarks*: Reattributed to Giovanni Battista Spinelli.   R

38 The Visitation of Mary and Elizabeth

Private collection, Naples. *Collections*: A. Carbone, Tortona, through 1938. *References*: Naples 1938, p. 319; Ortolani 1938, p. 178, repr. p. 172 (attributed to Cavallino by Venturi); Percy 1965, p. 74, no. 146 (lost). *Remarks*: Causa, in conversation 1983, called the work, which is in a ruined state, a copy. The present writers have not seen the picture and must reserve judgment. If a copy, it must record a lost original by Cavallino.   D

Devotional Images of Christ and the Virgin Mary

39 The Assumption of the Virgin

Oil on copper, 41 x 32.5 cm, Fondazione Roberto Longhi, Florence. *References*: Florence 1980, p. 298, no. 131, fig. 152 (attributed to Bernardo Cavallino, following suggestion of Carlo Volpe and Giuliano Briganti; Zeri, on the other hand, suggests Bartolomeo Passante). *Remarks*: Judging from the reproduction, the painting is not by Cavallino; the Virgin and *putti* bear scant resemblance to his usual figural types.   W

40 Head of Christ

50 x 38 cm, private collection, Rome. *Collections*: Francesco Romano, Rome; Mario Colucci, Rome, until late 1970s. *References*: Marini 1974, pp. 115-16, no. 13, repr. *Remarks*: Causa, in letter to Cleveland Museum of Art 5 January 1984, rejects the attribution to Cavallino. In Percy's opinion the work, known only from a photograph, may be an original.   D

41 The Presentation of the Virgin in the Temple

Chiesa di Santa Maria degli Angeli a Pizzofalcone, Naples. *References*: Dalbono 1876, p. 302. *Remarks*: Reattributed to Francesco Maria Caselli.   R

42 The Virgin of the Immaculate Conception

Arcivescovado, Caserta. *Remarks*: This appears, from a photograph, to be a copy of the painting at Caen [26].   W

43 The Virgin of the Immaculate Conception

75.6 x 55.3 cm, The Bowes Museum, Barnard Castle, Durham, England. *Collections*: Conde de Quinto sale, 1862, no. 38 (as Eugenio Caxés); bought by John Bowes. *References*: Soria 1961, pp. 33, 37, fig. 1; Ellis in Barnard Castle 1962, no. 37; Crombie 1962, p. 396; Percy 1965, p. 60, no. 61 (copy); Pérez Sánchez 1965, p. 383; Barnard Castle 1970, p. 84, no. 580, pl. 50 (as studio of Cavallino); Causa 1972, p. 983 n. 111 (old copy). *Remarks*: This is a copy of the canvas at Caen [26]; there are three other known versions deriving from the Caen picture (Inv. nos. 42, 47, 152).   W

44   The Virgin of the Immaculate Conception

249 x 110 cm, Chiesa di San Lorenzo Maggiore, Naples (sacristy). *References*: Catalani 1845–53, 1:95 (some attribute to Massimo Stanzione or Cavallino; may be by Andrea Malinconico); Nobile 1855–57, 2:826; Celano 1856–60, 3:175; Galante 1872, p. 186 (some attribute to Stanzione, some to Cavallino, some to Malinconico); Dalbono 1876, p. 84 (some paintings in the sacristy, including an *Immaculate Conception* by Marullo); Filangieri 1883, p. 91 (considered to be Cavallino), and 1883–91, 2:151 (considered to be Cavallino); Müller and Singer 1895–1901, 1:240; Longhi 1920c, p. 156; Sestieri 1920, pp. 254-56, fig. 9, and 1921, p. 196; D'Orsi 1938, pp. 29-30, fig. 12 (painting is signed by Paolo Finoglia); Ortolani 1938, p. 178, repr. p. 181 (as Finoglia), and in Naples 1938, p. 62, repr. p. 59 (formerly attributed to Cavallino, but a signed work by Finoglia); Naples 1954a, no. 35 (as Finoglia); Percy 1965, p. 66, no. 88 (as Finoglia); Causa 1972, pp. 935, 977 n. 81 (dated 1629–30); V. Pacelli in De Vito et al. 1983, p. 124, fig. 42 (as Finoglia). *Remarks*: An attribution to Cavallino, originating in 19th-century guidebooks to Naples, continued to be accepted until D'Orsi discovered Finoglia's signature at the bottom of the canvas in 1938. Causa (1972) refers to Strazzullo's publication of documents dating Finoglia's two versions of *The Immaculate Conception* in San Lorenzo to 1629–30 (see Strazzullo 1955, p. 40). The other *Immaculate Conception* by Finoglia in the church was in the Buonaiuti Chapel.   R

45   The Virgin of the Immaculate Conception

100 x 77 cm, Museo di Capodimonte, Naples, acquired ca. 1938. *Collections*: Cominelli, Sicily. *References*: Ortolani 1938, p. 178, and in Naples 1938, p. 66; Naples 1957, p. 73, no. 1706, and 1964, p. 54, no. 1706; Percy 1965, p. 61, no. 68 (Bologna and Causa consider the work to be a copy); Causa 1972, p. 982 n. 110 (copy).   W

46   The Virgin of the Immaculate Conception

230 x 120 cm, Museo di Capodimonte, Naples (Fig. 26a). *Collections*: Chiesa di San Giovanni Battista delle Monache, Naples (first chapel right). *References*: Catalani 1845–53, 2:11 (as Finoglia or school of Stanzione); Dalbono 1871, p. 107; Galante 1872, p. 104 (as school of Stanzione); Dalbono 1876, p. 133; Naples 1877, p. 133 (without title); de Rinaldis 1909, p. 11, no. 1; Rolfs 1910, p. 275; Hermanin in Thieme-Becker 6 (1912): 225; de Rinaldis 1920a, p. 2; Sestieri 1920, p. 255; de Rinaldis 1921, p. 16; Sestieri 1921, p. 196; Corna 1930, 1:227; Ortolani in Naples 1938, p. 62 (questions attribution to Cavallino); Percy 1965, p. 56, no. 37; Causa 1972, p. 982 n. 110 (not by Cavallino; may derive from a type like the Brera *Immacolata* by an artist close to Finoglia and Artemisia Gentileschi). *Remarks*: As a result of examination during recent restoration at Capodimonte, the canvas is now concluded to be a contemporary work by another hand, much influenced by Cavallino. The work is very Cavallinesque but falls short of the essential refinement of the artist's autograph works. It is inscribed on the verso on an old relining canvas: ''Orig¹ᵉ di Bernardo/ Cavallino/ Ristaurato dal/ Pittor Ferdinando/ G[?]i[?]sih[?]glia nel/ 1801.''   W

47   The Virgin of the Immaculate Conception

59 x 38 cm, private collection, Italy. *Collections*: Adolph Loewi, Los Angeles, 1965; sale, Sotheby's, London, 29 June 1966, lot 28; Julius Weitzner, London; Gilberto Algranti, Milan, 1969. *References*: Causa 1972, p. 983 n. 111 (as copy). *Remarks*: This is a variant copy of *The Virgin of the Immaculate Conception* at Caen [26].   W

48   The Virgin of the Immaculate Conception

74 x 54 cm, private collection, Italy. *Collections*: Gilberto Algranti, Milan, 1978; sale, Finarte, Milan, 5 December 1978, lot 80.   U

Saints

49   The Death of Saint Joseph

180 x 204 cm, Museo di Capodimonte, Naples, no. 499, acquired 1917. *Collections*: Felice de Santi, Naples. *References*: de Rinaldis 1917, p. 182, repr. pp. 184, 185 (detail); Longhi 1918b, p. 142 (as Vaccaro); Gamba 1919, pp. 30-31, repr. p. 30; de Rinaldis 1920a, pp. 2, 4, 57; Longhi 1920a, p. 89 (as Vaccaro), and 1920c, p. 156 (as Vaccaro); Sestieri 1920, p. 246 (as Vaccaro); de Rinaldis 1921, p. 16, pl. xiv; Voss 1922–23, p. 511 (as Vaccaro); Borenius 1923, pp. 37-38, fig. A; de Rinaldis 1927, pp. 61-62, no. 282, pl. 53; Nugent 1925–30, 2:567, 569; Marangoni 1927, p. 191 (as Vaccaro); Naples 1932, p. 22, no. 282 (attributed to Cavallino); Carli 1938, p. 261 (as Vaccaro); Ortolani in Naples 1938, p. 50 (as Vaccaro); Golzio 1950, p. 539; Commodo Izzo 1951, p. 59, figs. 12, 13 (as Vaccaro); Naples 1957, p. 72, no. 282 (as Vaccaro), and 1964, p. 53, no. 282 (as Vaccaro); Percy 1965, p. 68, no. 99 (rejected attribution to Cavallino; clearly by Vaccaro); Leone de Castris in Naples 1982, p. 71 (as Vaccaro). *Remarks*: Reattributed to Andrea Vaccaro.   R

50   The Death of Saint Joseph

43.5 x 33 cm, Museo di Capodimonte, Naples, Banco di Napoli Collection, BN12, acquired 1942; exh. Museo Filangieri, 1948–51; on loan to Capodimonte since 1960. *References*: Molajoli 1948, p. 103; Montini 1952, p. 35; Naples 1953, p. 45, pls. ii, 50, and 1961, p. 53, and 1964, p. 59; Percy 1965, p. 55, no. 33; de Filippis 1970, pl. iv; Lattuada 1982, p. 66, fig. 30. *Remarks*: Causa (orally, 1983) rejected attribution to Cavallino; Spinosa and Percy (in conversation, 1984) agreed. Although the picture is very Cavallinesque, a rather hard and labored quality in its execution suggests that it is a copy, or the work of a contemporary imitator. It surely records a composition by Cavallino, nevertheless.   W

51   The Death of Saint Joseph

113 x 92 cm, private collection, Italy. *Collections*: Limoncelli, Naples; Sinigaglia, Naples, through 1938; Gilberto Algranti, Milan, 1969. *References*: de Rinaldis 1920a, p. 2; Sestieri 1920, pp. 254, 263, fig. 13; de Rinaldis 1921, p. 17; Sestieri 1921, p. 181; Florence 1922, no. 264; Ortolani 1922, p. 193; Nugent 1925–30, 2:567; Benesch 1926, p. 248; de Rinaldis 1929, pp. 25, 28-29; Carli 1938, p. 264; Ortolani in Naples 1938, pp. 65, 319, repr.; Commodo Izzo 1951, p. 102 (doubts attribution to Cavallino); Percy 1965, p. 56, no. 40; Pée 1971, pp. 120-21. *Remarks*: Although the painting has a long history of attributions to

Cavallino, the quality of execution suggests that it may be a copy of a lost original.   D

52 The Martyrdom of Saint Lawrence

59 x 83 cm, Galleria dell'Accademia di Belle Arti "Tadini," Lovere, no. 322. *References*: Sestieri 1920, p. 251, fig. 6; de Rinaldis 1921, p. 16; Sestieri 1921, p. 184; Ortolani 1922, p. 193; de Rinaldis in Naples 1927, p. 58, and 1929, p. 32; Ortolani in Naples 1938, p. 64; Percy 1965, p. 61, no. 64 (copy); Causa 1972, p. 982 n. 110 (old copy). *Remarks*: This is a pendant to Inv. no. 62, probably an old copy or imitation of a lost composition by Cavallino.   W

53 Saint Agatha

77 x 64 cm, private collection, Italy, since 1972. *Collections*: Gilberto Algranti, Milan, in 1967. *References*: Milan 1967, no. 30, repr. *Remarks*: Possibly by or near Francesco Guarino.   W

54 Saint Catherine of Alexandria

127.7 x 102 cm, Metropolitan Museum of Art, New York, Rogers Fund Purchase, no. 43.23, acquired 1943. *Collections*: Alessandro Laliccia, Naples, through 1938; Samuel Untermeyer; sale, Parke-Bernet, New York, 16 May 1940, lot 539; to Arnold Seligmann, Rey & Co. *References*: de Rinaldis 1921, p. 17, pl. xv; Sestieri 1921, pp. 188, 196, repr. p. 191; Nugent 1925–30, 2:573; Ortolani in Naples 1938, p. 66; Salinger 1943, pp. 296-99, repr.; Percy 1965, p. 56, no. 41; Causa 1972, p. 984 n. 116 (questions attribution, but has not seen painting); Baetjer in New York 1983, 1:25, repr. in 2:101. *Remarks*: Whereas the type of female figure and the blue and gold of the palette are very Cavallinesque, the flat, wooden handling of paint and the clumsy contours of draperies make it impossible to accept this work as autograph. It appears, however, to be by an artist intimately acquainted with Cavallino's manner.   W

55 Saint Cecilia

96.5 x 75 cm, John Winter, Milan. *Collections*: Marquess of Abercorn, Bentley Priory, Stanmore, before 1868 (attributed to Honthorst); sale, Christie's, London, 27 November 1970, lot 55; sale, Sotheby's, London, 9 March 1983, 19t 40, repr. *Remarks*: Possibly by or near Francesco Guarino.   W

56 Saint George

130.5 x 102 cm, Museo di Capodimonte, Naples, Banco di Napoli Collection, BN33; exh. Museo Filangieri, 1948–51. *Collections*: Alberto Gualtieri, Naples, through 1924; Baronessa Maria de Biase, Naples, 1938. *References*: de Rinaldis 1920a, p. 6, and 1921, p. 16, pl. xvii; [Ceci] 1923, p. 24; Ojetti, Dami, and Tarchiani 1924, p. 86, repr.; Nugent 1925–30, 2: 577, repr. 578; Naples 1938, p. 319; Nebbia 1946, pl. 1; Naples 1951, no. 33 (as Francesco Guarino); Bologna in Salerno 1954–55, no. 1 (as Guarino); Grieco 1963, pp. 105-6, no. 11, pl. xxvi (attributed to Guarino); Naples 1964, p. 60, BN33 (as Guarino); Percy 1965, p. 69, no. 100 (rejected attribution to Cavallino; attributes to Guarino); Causa 1972, p. 983 n. 111 (as Guarino); Lattuada in London and Washington 1982–83, no. 75, repr. (as Guarino). *Remarks*: Reattributed to Francesco Guarino.   R

57 Saint Helena Discovering the True Cross

103 x 154 cm, Museo di Capodimonte, Naples, no. 281. *Collections*: Accademia di Belle Arti, Naples. *References*: de Rinaldis 1921, p. 16; Musto 1921a, p. 64; Ortolani 1922, p. 195; de Rinaldis 1927, pp. 64-65, no. 281, pl. 52; Voss 1927, p. 76 (as J. H. Schönfeld); Naples 1932, p. 22, no. 281 (attributed to Cavallino); Ortolani in Naples 1938, p. 82 (as Schönfeld); Commodo Izzo 1951, p. 16 n. 9 (as Schönfeld); Voss 1964, p. 33 (as Schönfeld); Percy 1965, p. 69, no. 101 (rejected attribution to Cavallino; attributed to Schönfeld); Ulm 1967, no. 39 (as Schönfeld); Pée 1971, pp. 119-20, no. 42, fig. 49 (as Schönfeld). *Remarks*: Reattributed to Johann Heinrich Schönfeld.   R

58 Saint John the Evangelist

128 x 101 cm, P & D Colnaghi & Co., London (Fig. 40). *Collections*: Conti, Naples (as unknown painter, Neapolitan school, 17th century). *References*: London 1979, no. 10, repr.; Spinosa in London and Washington 1982–83, no. 21, repr.; Spear 1983, pp. 128 n. 4, 135, fig. 6 (attribution to Cavallino acceptable, although questioned by several scholars in London). *Remarks*: Although the face of the saint is Cavallinesque in type and brushwork, the relatively open and broad handling of paint on the hands and the brushwork of the sleeves and drapery are unlike Cavallino's usual refinement of touch. The author of this picture must, however, have been closely influenced by the artist.   W

59 Saint Lucy

Signed by Girolamo de Magistris, Chiesa di Santa Maria della Sanità, Naples (fourth chapel left). *References*: Dalbono 1876, pp. 498-99 (as school of Stanzione); Longhi 1920c, p. 156; Sestieri 1920, p. 257, and 1921, p. 196; Ortolani in Naples 1938, p. 62 (not by Cavallino, could be work of pupil); Causa 1957, p. 40 (signed by Girolamo de Magistris); Percy 1965, p. 67, no. 90 (as de Magistris); Causa 1972, p. 982 n. 110 (as de Magistris, with signature). *Remarks*: Reattributed to Girolamo de Magistris.   R

60 Saint Mary Magdalene

75 x 62 cm, Banco di Napoli Collection, Museo di Capodimonte, Naples; exh. Museo Filangieri, 1948–51; on loan to Capodimonte since 1960 (deposit). *References*: Ortolani in Naples 1938, p. 32; Molajoli 1948, p. 103; Percy 1965, p. 55, no. 36. *Remarks*: This is probably a copy.   W

61 Saint Peter Penitent

Oval, 90 x 71 cm, private collection, Italy. *Collections*: London art market; Gilberto Algranti, Milan, 1969. *References*: Milan 1969(?), repr.; Pérez Sánchez and Spinosa 1978, p. 93, no. 15, repr. (as Jusepe de Ribera; attribution first made by F. Bologna in conversation). *Remarks*: Reattributed to Jusepe de Ribera.   R

62 Saint Sebastian Cured by Saint Irene

59 x 83 cm, Galleria dell'Accademia di Belle Arti "Tadini," Lovere, no. 324. *References*: Sestieri 1920, p. 251, fig. 5 (attribution by Longhi); de Rinaldis 1921, p. 16; Sestieri 1921, p. 184; Ortolani 1922, p. 193; de Rinaldis 1927, p. 58, and 1929, p. 32; Ortolani in Naples 1938, p. 64; Refice 1951, p. 263; Percy 1965, p. 61, no. 65 (copy); Causa 1972, p. 982 n. 110 (copy). *Remarks*: This is a pendant to *The Martyrdom of Saint Lawrence* (Inv. no.

52) also at Lovere; both are old copies after, or imitations of, Cavallino. A vertical version is at Capodimonte, also a copy or imitation (Inv. no. 64). W

63 Saint Sebastian Cured by Saint Irene

100 x 127.5 cm, Galleria Nazionale d'Arte Antica, Palazzo Corsini, Rome, no. 1524, acquired 1911; on loan since 1967 to the Pinacoteca Provinciale, Bari. *Collections*: Enrico Frascione, Naples. *References*: Hermanin 1912, p. 374; Hermanin in Thieme-Becker 6 (1912):225; Hermanin 1924–25, p. 6, repr. p. 9; de Rinaldis 1932, p. 23, and 1936, p. 28; Naples 1938, p. 320; di Carpegna in Rome 1958, no. 8 (possibly by a member of Ribera's circle); Percy 1965, p. 70, no. 105 (rejected attribution to Cavallino); Causa 1972, p. 983 n. 111 (rejects attribution to Cavallino; same hand as Capodimonte *Martyrdom of Saint Lawrence* [*Death of Abel* ? (Inv. no. 8); or Lovere *Martyrdom of Saint Lawrence* ? (Inv. no. 52)] and *The Good Samaritan* (Inv. no. 34). W

64 Saint Sebastian Cured by Saint Irene

69 x 55 cm, Museo di Capodimonte, Naples, inv. no. 1369. *References*: Naples 1846, p. 243, no. 230; Dalbono 1876, pp. 470-71; de Rinaldis 1909, p. 15, no. 4; Rolfs 1910, p. 277 (no. 84381); Hermanin 1911, p. 185; de Rinaldis 1911, p. 415, no. 391; Hermanin in Thieme-Becker 6 (1912):255; de Rinaldis 1917, p. 179, and 1920a, p. 5; Sestieri 1920, p. 251, fig. 4; de Rinaldis 1921, p. 16; Sestieri 1921, p. 184; de Rinaldis 1927, p. 58, no. 284; Corna 1930, 1:227; Naples 1932, p. 22, no. 284; McComb 1934, p. 50; Ortolani in Naples 1938, p. 64; Percy 1965, p. 61, no. 69 (Causa and Bologna judge work to be a copy); Causa 1972, p. 982 n. 110 (copy). *Remarks*: The same composition appears in a painting of different proportions wrongly attributed to Cavallino in Lovere (Inv. no. 62). Both works may be copies of a lost painting by Cavallino. W

65 Saint Thomas

100 x 80 cm, initialled "BC" at lower right center, Maurizio Marini, Rome. *References*: Marini 1974, p. 116 n. 1. *Remarks*: It has not been possible to see this picture, which is currently undergoing restoration. The handling of paint on flesh and drapery and the figure's face and hands appears (from a photograph) untypical of Cavallino's work, and suggests another hand, despite the BC monogram. Spinosa, in conversation 1984, suggests Andrea de Leone as the author. W

Miscellaneous Subjects Derived from History, Literature, and Mythology

66 Bacchanal

27 x 54.5 cm, Museo di Capodimonte, Naples, no. 305. *Collections*: Bourbon, Naples, inv. no. 84535. *References*: Rolfs 1910, p. 277; Voss 1927, p. 76 (as J. H. Schönfeld); de Rinaldis 1928, p. 7 (as Schönfeld), and 1929, p. 30 (as Schönfeld, signed "Gio. Anzeric"); Naples 1957, p. 73, no. 305 (as Schönfeld), and 1964, p. 54, no. 305 (as Schönfeld); Voss 1964, pp. 14, 20, 33 (as Schönfeld); Berlin 1966, no. 87 (as Schönfeld); Ulm 1967, no. 29 (as Schönfeld); Pée 1971, p. 113, no. 34 (as Schönfeld). *Remarks*: Reattributed to Johann Heinrich Schönfeld., R

67 A Concert

109 x 127 cm, Museo del Prado, Madrid, no. 87. *Collections*: Royal collections, Palacio Nuevo, 1772 inventory, as Stanzione. *References*: In Museum catalogues 1823–24 and 1828; Madrid 1945, p. 128, no. 87, and 1949, p. 124, no. 87 (as Giovanni Benedetto Castiglione); Soria 1954, pp. 10-13, fig. 9 (as Aniello Falcone); Pérez Sánchez 1965, pp. 389-90, pl. 134 (as Falcone), and 1971, p. 389 (as Falcone); Madrid 1972, p. 870, no. 87 (as Falcone). *Remarks*: The painting was given to Cavallino by Eusebius in early-19th-century Prado catalogues, subsequently to Castiglione, until the 1972 catalogue. The correct attribution to Falcone was made by Hermann Voss before 1933. R

68 Daedalus and Icarus

135 x 98 cm, Wadsworth Atheneum, Hartford (Connecticut), no. 44.38, acquired 1944. *Collections*: Mrs. Anne Douglas Hamilton, Oakley House, Norfolk, England. *References*: San Francisco 1941, no. 21, repr. p. 47; Howe 1941, p. 29; Dayton 1954, no. 137, pl. 5; Percy 1965, p. 64, no. 79 (rejected attribution to Cavallino); Gregori 1972, pl. 61 (as Orazio Riminaldi); Mahoney and Cadogan [1985] (as Orazio Riminaldi). *Remarks*: Reattributed to Orazio Riminaldi. R

69 A Dead Soldier

104.8 x 167 cm, inscribed "A" at center right, The National Gallery, London, no. 741, acquired 1865. *Collections*: Anonymous sale, Duparc de la Rue and Veuve Laforest, Paris, 20 August & following days 1821, lot 104 (as Velázquez); M. de Saint Rémy; sale, Paris, 3 February 1841, lot 16; Pourtalès-Gorgier, 1841, where thought to have come from a Spanish royal palace; sale, Paris, 27 March 1865, lot 205, to National Gallery. *References*: Zampetti 1967, p. 13, figs. 30-30a (as Cavallino ?); London 1971, pp. 148-49, no. 741 with bibliography; Causa 1972, p. 983 n. 111 (as Salvator Rosa); London 1973b, p. 339, no. 741, repr. (Italian [?], 17th century [?]); Whitfield in London and Washington 1982–83, p. 197, no. 88 (as Neapolitan school). W

70 The Death of Cleopatra

120 x 100 cm, Palazzo Durazzo Giustiniani, Genoa. *References*: Zampetti 1967, pp. 14-15, fig. 32; Genoa 1967, pp. 263, 268, figs. 236-38 (as Stanzione); Causa 1972, pp. 932, 975 n. 60, 983 n. 111, fig. 290 (as Guarino). *Remarks*: Reattributed to Francesco Guarino. R

71   Head of a Girl

39 x 36.5 cm, private collection, London. *Collections*: Heim Gallery, London, through 1970. *References*: London 1970, no. 6, repr.; Nicolson in *The Burlington Magazine* 112 (December 1970):838 (not by Cavallino). *Remarks*: Andrew S. Ciechanowiecki of the Heim Gallery, in letter of 11 April 1984, informs us that following the opinions of Denis Mahon, Benedict Nicolson, and Stephen Pepper, the painting has been reattributed to Simone Cantarini.   R

72   The Rape of Europa

100 x 128 cm, Museo Nazionale Pepoli, Trapani, Sicily, no. 334, gift of Giovanni Battista Fardella, 1830. *Collections*: Fardella, Naples. *References*: F.N.A. 1968, p. 160, fig. 53; Negri Arnoldi in Trapani 1969, pp. 14-15, no. 5, fig. 7. *Remarks*: The work, which has suffered considerable damage, shows the influence of both Cavallino and Vaccaro.   W

Lost Works

Old Testament and Apocryphal Subjects

73   Abraham and the Three Angels

115.9 x 144.8 cm. *Collections*: Quentin Crewe, London, through 1962. *References*: Ellis in Barnard Castle 1962, no. 38 (tentative attribution to Cavallino); Nicolson 1962, p. 317 (rejects attribution to Cavallino).   W

74   Adam and Eve Lamenting the Death of Abel

Collections: Duca di San Severina, Naples, recorded in 1742–43. *References*: de Dominici 1742–43, 3:43. *Remarks*: See Appendix, no. 12.   U

75   The Banquet of Absalom

Collections: Tesorone, Naples, until 1919; Galleria Diodati, Naples, 1919. *References*: Musto 1921b, p. 160 (exhibited in Tesorone sale of 1919 as Cavallino; variant by the same hand of painting in the Harrach collection [17]); Spinosa in London and Washington 1982–83, p. 139 (recorded in Tesorone sale, wrongly ascribed to Cavallino).   W

76   Cain Slaying Abel

Collections: Duca di San Severina, Naples, recorded in 1742–43. *References*: See Appendix, no. 12.   U

77   The Curing of Tobit

Collections: Ciardiello, Naples, through 1938. *References*: Carli 1938, p. 256 (copy, inferior version of same subject in Cappelli collection [now L'Aquila; see Inv. no. 5]); Percy 1965, p. 73, no. 124 (lost).   U

78   David

5 x 4 *palmi* (ca. 132 x 105 cm). *Collections*: Spinelli di Tarsia, Naples, 1734 inventory. *References*: See Appendix, no. 9.   U

79   Deborah and Barak

4 *palmi* across (ca. 105 cm). *References*: de Dominici 1742–43, 3:37. *Remarks*: One of four canvases, each measuring "4 *palmi* across," reported by de Dominici to have been sent to Spain by don Pedro Antonio de Aragón, viceroy in Naples from 1666–72 (see also Inv. nos. 83, 86, 105).   U

80   The Departure of Tobias

Copper, 2 x 2-1/2 *palmi* (ca. 53 x 66 cm). *Collections*: Francesco Valletta, Naples, recorded in 1742–43. *References*: See Appendix, no. 13. *Remarks*: This is a pendant to *The Marriage of Tobias* in the de Grazia collection, Naples (Inv. no. 94).   U

81   Esther before Ahasuerus

3 x 5 *palmi* (ca. 79 x 132 cm). *Collections*: Francesco Valletta, Naples, recorded in 1742–43. *References*: See Appendix, no. 13.   U

82 Esther before Ahasuerus

99.8 x 154 cm, private collection, Milan. *Collections*: E. Moratilla, Paris, in 1974. *References*: Marini 1974, p. 115, no. 13, repr.; Spinosa in London and Washington 1982–83, p. 143. *Remarks*: This is a copy of the picture now in a Swiss private collection [21].   W

83 Jael Slaying Sisera

4 palmi across (ca. 105 cm). *References*: de Dominici 1742–43, 3:37. *Remarks*: See Inv. no. 79.   U

84 Judith

5 x 4 *palmi* (ca. 132 x 105 cm). *Collections*: Spinelli di Tarsia, Naples, 1734 inventory. *References*: See Appendix, no. 9.   U

85 Judith with the Head of Holofernes

4 x 5 *palmi* (ca. 105 x 132 cm). *Collections*: Marchese di Grazia, Naples, recorded in 1742–43. *References*: See Appendix, no. 14.
U

86 Judith with the Head of Holofernes

4 palmi across. (ca. 105 cm). *References*: de Dominici 1742–43, 3:37. *Remarks*: See Inv. no. 79.   U

87 Lot

1 x 1-1/2 *palmi* (ca. 26 x 40 cm). *Collections*: Don Francesco Emanuele Pinto, principe di Ischitella, Naples, 1767 inventory. *References*: See Appendix, no. 17.   U

88 Lot and His Daughters

Oval, *4 palmi* high (ca. 105 cm). *References*: de Dominici 1742–43, 3:37 *Remarks*: According to de Dominici, a pendant to Inv. no. 92; both pictures were exported to Germany.   U

89 Lot and His Daughters

Collections: Antonio Lucchesi-Palli, principe di Campofranco, Palermo, 1838. *References*: Vaccaro 1838, pp. 7-10, 21-23.   U

90 Lot and His Daughters

Collections: Private collection, Rome, 1938. *References*: Naples 1938, p. 319. *Remarks*: Perhaps identical to a painting in a private collection in Rome, known through a photograph preserved in the Gabinetto Fotografico Nazionale, Rome, D-7314; if so, it is a copy of the painting in the Alliata de Villafranca collection, Palermo (Inv. no. 13).   W

91 Lot and His Daughters

94 x 123 cm. *Collections*: sale, Christie's, London, 21 April 1967, lot 66, repr. (probably the picture in the collection of Charles, Lord Halifax, sale, 10 March 1740, lot 82); Julius Weitzner, London, ca. 1970. *Remarks*: Note accompanying lot 66 in Christie's catalogue, 21 April 1967, p. 24, refers reader to M. Davies, *National Gallery Catalogues: The British School* (London, 1949 ed.), pp. 54, 65 n. 74, for a similar composition in the background of Hogarth's *The Countess's Morning Levée* from the *Marriage à la Mode* series. There seems to be no reason, on the basis of the composition, figural types, or handling of paint to attribute the picture, known only from the illustration, to Cavallino.   W

92 Lot and His Family Fleeing Sodom

Oval, *4 palmi* high (ca. 105 cm). *References*: de Dominici 1742–43, 3:37. *Remarks*: According to de Dominici, a pendant to Inv. no. 88; both pictures were exported to Germany.   U

93 The Marriage of Tobias

3 x 4 *palmi* (ca. 79 x 105 cm). *Collections*: Francesco Valletta, Naples, recorded in 1742–43. *References*: See Appendix, no. 13; Consoli Fiego 1922, p. 107 (identifies this painting with one in the Salvatore Romano collection).   U

94 The Marriage of Tobias

Copper, 2 x 2-1/2 *palmi* (ca. 53 x 66 cm). *Collections*: Marchese di Grazia, Naples, recorded in 1742–43. *References*: See Appendix, no. 14.   U

95 The Marriage of Tobias

47 x 71 cm. *Collections*: Giuseppe Cimaglia, Naples, through 1877. *References*: Naples 1877, no. 117; de Rinaldis 1909, p. 69, no. 46 (lost).   U

96 The Marriage of Tobias

Collections: Iaccarino, Naples, 1938. *References*: Carli 1938, p. 262 (copy or variant of the same subject now in L'Aquila; Inv. no. 17).   U

97 The Marriage of Tobias

Collections: Postiglione, Naples. *References*: Consoli Fiego 1922, p. 107 (replica, perhaps by another hand, of the same subject in the Salvatore Romano collection, Florence or Naples [now Prado; see Inv. no. 18)].   U

98 Moses and the Brazen Serpent

Collections: Roseo, Naples, through 1920. *References*: Sestieri 1920, pp. 253-54; Percy 1965, p. 73, no. 137 (lost). *Remarks*: Judging from Sestieri's description, this is probably identical with the version formerly in the Gigli collection, Naples (Inv. no. 99).   U

99 Moses and the Brazen Serpent

Collections: Roberto Gigli, Naples, through 1922; private collection, Milan, 1938. *References*: de Rinaldis 1920a, p. 5, fig. 1; Longhi 1920b, p. 91 (attribution to Cavallino made by Sestieri); de Rinaldis 1921, p. 17, pl. II; Sestieri 1921, p. 184; Ortolani 1922, p. 192, fig. 2; Nugent 1925–30, 2:562 (remarks on relationship to Domenico Gargiulo in landscape and that subject not congenial to Cavallino); Ortolani in Naples 1938, p. 64; Percy 1965, p. 66, no. 86 (as Gargiulo, premised on small proportions of figures and their relationship to landscape). *Remarks*: Probably identical with Inv. no. 98, formerly in the Roseo collection, Naples, recorded by Sestieri in 1920.   W

100 Moses Striking the Rock
Collections: Antonio Lucchesi-Palli, principe di Campofranco, Palermo, 1838. *References*: Vaccaro 1838, pp. 7-10, 21-23. U

101 Moses Striking the Rock
Collections: Sbordone, Naples, through 1938. *References*: Ortolani 1922, p. 192, fig. 1; Ortolani in Naples 1938, p. 65; Percy 1965, p. 68, no. 95 (rejected attribution to Cavallino; Causa attributes to Domenico Gargiulo); Causa 1972, p. 983 n. 111 (copy of Cavallino by Gargiulo). *Remarks*: Reattributed to Domenico Gargiulo. R

102 Rebecca and Eleazer
Collections: Ghezzi, Naples, through 1871. *References*: Dalbono 1871, p. 107; de Rinaldis 1909, p. 69, no. 38 (lost). U

103 Rebecca and Eleazer
180.2 x 253.9 cm. *Collections*: Private collection, Rome; sale, Christie's, London, 26 March 1971, lot 13, repr.; private collection, Milan, 1974. *References*: Marini 1974, p. 103, no. 8, repr. (as Juan Dò). W

104 The Sacrifice of Noah
Collections: Antonio Lucchesi-Palli, principe de Campofranco, Palermo, 1838. *References*: Vaccaro 1838, pp. 7-10, 21-23. U

105 Samson among the Philistines
4 palmi across (ca. 105 cm). *References*: de Dominici 1742-43, 3:37. *Remarks*: See Inv. no. 79. U

New Testament Subjects

106 The Adoration of the Magi
Collections: Gaetano Zir, Naples, recorded in 1874. *References*: de Rinaldis 1909, p. 69, no. 39 (lost, cites source as G. Carelli, *Collezione di Quadri . . . Gaetano Zir* [Naples, 1874], p. 11: "Nascita con la presentazione de' magi, quadro di figure terzine sopra tela, con cornice dorata, di palmi 5, 80, opera pregiatissima di Bernardo Cavallino"). U

107 The Adoration of the Magi
88 x 135 cm. *Collections*: Filippo Rocco, Naples, through 1878. *References*: Naples 1877, no. 121; Dalbono 1878, p. 47 (indicates that this is sharpest and liveliest in color of works by Cavallino exhibited; notes that Cavallino was not usually a proponent of brilliant enamel-like color, but of chiaroscuro); de Rinaldis 1909, p. 69, no. 45 (lost). U

108 The Adoration of the Magi
Collections: Galleria Corona, Naples, through 1921. *References*: di Rinaldis 1920a, p. 5 n. 2 (perhaps identifiable with painting formerly in Zir collection [Inv. no. 106]), and 1921, p. 17; Percy 1965, p. 73, no. 125 (lost). U

109 The Adoration of the Shepherds
Oval, 47 x 92 cm. *Collections*: Private collection, Trieste, through 1943. *References*: Trieste 1943, no. 30, repr. *Remarks*: This is a smaller version, possibly autograph, of the Cleveland painting [79]. Po

110 The Angel Liberating Saint Peter from Prison
Collections: Duca di San Severina, Naples, recorded in 1742-43. *References*: See Appendix, no. 12. U

111 The Angel Liberating Saint Peter from Prison
60 x 90 cm (originally 54 x 76 cm) (Fig. 23b). *Collections*: Chiesa dei Gerolamini, Naples (Cappella di San Filippo Neri), through 1934; in the Gerolamini *quadreria* from ca. 1938; stolen in 1982. *References*: Catalani 1845-53, 1:74; Biancale 1920, p. 13 n. 1; de Rinaldis 1920a, p. 56; Longhi 1920c, p. 156; Sestieri 1920, pp. 264-66, fig. 15; de Rinaldis 1921, p. 16, pl. IV; Sestieri 1921, pp. 184, 188, 194; Consoli Fiego 1922, p. 108; Florence 1922, no. 255; Ortolani 1922, p. 193; A. Venturi 1925, pp. 73-74; Nugent 1925-30, 2:562, 567, repr. 568; Benesch 1926, p. 248; Pevsner in Pevsner and Grautoff 1928, pp. 184-85, fig. 142; de Rinaldis 1929, pp. 25, 28 [pp. 29, 32 in English ed.]; McComb 1934, p. 49, fig. 47; Carli 1938, p. 264; Naples 1938, p. 319; Oertel 1938, p. 230; Masciotta 1942, p. 147; Refice 1951, p. 263; Naples 1953-54, no. 19; Percy 1965, p. 62, no. 71 (as a copy after Cavallino; recognized as such by Causa); Moir 1967, 1:175 n. 77, and 2:66, no. 10; de Filippis 1970, pl. 71 (attributed to Cavallino); Causa 1972, p. 982 n. 110 (copy). *Remarks*: This is a pendant to Inv. no. 130. A crudeness of execution evident in photographs indicate that the work is a copy, although the original is not known. W

112 The Angel Waking Saint Peter to Liberate Him from Prison
Collections: Duca di San Severina, Naples, recorded in 1742-43. *References*: See Appendix, no. 12. U

113 The Annunciation
9 x 7 *palmi* (ca. 237 x 185 cm). *Collections*: Carlo Cioli (?), Naples, documented in 1646. *References*: See Appendix, no. 1. U

114 The Annunciation to the Shepherds
Collections: Casciaro, Naples, through 1951. *References*: Refice 1951, p. 263; Percy 1965, p. 73, no. 132 (lost). U

115 The Archangel Gabriel
Oval, 91.4 x 73.7 cm. *Collections*: Edwin Fricke; sale, Parke Bernet, New York, 15 March 1945, lot 32, repr. (as Cavallino and atelier). W

116 The Baptism of the Infidels
Collections: Calcagno, Naples, through 1921. *References*: de Rinaldis 1921, p. 7; Percy 1965, p. 73, no. 131 (lost). U

117 Christ and the Adulteress
3 x 4 *palmi* (ca. 79 x 105 cm). *Collections*: Francesco Valletta, Naples, recorded in 1742-43. *References*: See Appendix, no. 13. U

118   Christ and the Adulteress

4 x 5 *palmi* (ca. 105 x 132 cm). *Collections*: Francesco Valletta, Naples, recorded in 1742–43. *References*: See Appendix, no. 13.
                                                                                                          U

119   Christ and the Adulteress

Collections: Salvatore Romano, Florence or Naples, through 1938. *References*: Naples 1938, p. 319; Percy 1965, p. 61, no. 67 (copy). *Remarks*: Appears, from a photograph, too coarse in quality to be an original by Cavallino; the composition seems to derive from Cavallino, however, and probably records a lost original.   W

120   Christ and the Woman of Samaria

128 x 100 cm. *Collections*: Salvatore Romano, Florence or Naples, through 1938. *References*: de Rinaldis 1909, p. 47, no. 16; Hermanin in Thieme-Becker 6 (1912):225; de Rinaldis 1921, p. 17; Corna 1930, 1:227; Naples 1938, p. 319; Percy 1965, p. 73, no. 127 (lost); Abbate 1970, p. 61, pl. 59 (reattributed to G. B. Spinelli). *Remarks*: The reattribution to Giovanni Battista Spinelli is convincing, on the basis of a photograph.   R

121   Christ at Calvary

Collections: Francesco Romano, Naples, 1920. *References*: de Rinaldis 1920a, p. 5; Sestieri 1920, p. 254; Percy 1965, p. 73, no. 126 (lost).   U

122   Christ Crowned with Thorns

Collections: Ciardiello, Naples, through 1921. *References*: de Rinaldis 1920a, p. 5; Sestieri 1920, p. 254; de Rinaldis 1921, p. 17; Percy 1965, p. 72, no. 122 (lost).   U

123   Christ Driving the Merchants from the Temple

105 x 157 cm. *Collections*: Roberto Gigli, Naples, through 1922. Ortolani 1922, pp. 194-95, fig. 5; Voss 1927, p. 76 (as Schön-feld), and 1964, p. 33 (as Schönfeld); Pée 1971, p. 206 (definitive attribution impossible without being able to look at painting).   W

124   The Dead Christ

2 *palmi* (ca. 53 cm). *Collections*: Francesco Valletta, Naples, recorded in 1742–43. *References*: See Appendix, no. 13. *Remarks*: A composition very similar to de Dominici's description is known through the probable copy in Grenoble (Inv. no. 29).   U

125   The Denial of Saint Peter

3 *palmi* across (ca. 79 cm). *Collections*: Nicola Salerno, Naples, recorded in 1742–43. *References*: See Appendix, no. 11.   U

126   The Denial of Saint Peter

Collections: Duca di San Severina, Naples, recorded in 1742–43. *References*: See Appendix, no. 12.   U

127   The Denial of Saint Peter

3 x 2-1/2 *palmi* (ca. 79 x 66 cm). *Collections*: Francesco Valletta, Naples, recorded in 1742–43. *References*: See Appendix, no. 13.   U

128   The Denial of Saint Peter

Collections: Ferdinando Russo, Naples, through 1877. *References*: Naples 1877, no. 119; de Rinaldis 1909, p. 69, no. 47 (lost).   U

129   The Denial of Saint Peter

Collections: Vincenzo Torelli, Naples. *References*: Naples 1877, no. 122; Dalbono 1878, p. 47; de Rinaldis 1909, p. 69, no. 43 (lost).   U

130   The Denial of Saint Peter

60 x 90 cm (originally 54 x 76 cm) (Fig. 23a). *Collections*: Chiesa dei Gerolamini, Naples (Cappella di San Filippo Neri, Naples), through 1934; in the Gerolamini *quadreria* from ca. 1938; stolen in 1982. *References*: Catalani 1845–53, 1:74; Biancale 1920, p. 13 n. 1; Longhi 1920c, p. 156; de Rinaldis 1920a, p. 56; Sestieri 1920, pp. 264-65; de Rinaldis 1921, p. 16, pl. III; Sestieri 1921, pp. 184, 194; Ortolani 1922, p. 193; Consoli Fiego 1922, p. 108; A. Venturi 1925, pp. 73-74; Benesch 1926, p. 248; Pevsner in Pevsner and Grautoff 1928, pp. 184-85; de Rinaldis 1929, pp. 25, 28 [pp. 29, 32 in English ed.]; McComb 1934, p. 50; Carli 1938, p. 264; Naples 1938, p. 319; Oertel 1938, p. 230; Masciotta 1942, p. 147; Refice 1951, p. 263; Naples 1953-54, no. 18, fig. 25; Percy 1965, p. 62, no. 70 (as a copy after Cavallino; recognized as such by Causa); de Filippis 1970, pl. 20 (as attributed to Cavallino); Causa 1972, p. 982 n. 110 (copy). *Remarks*: This is a pendant to Inv. no. 111. The possible original of which this work is a copy, now lost, was published by Refice in 1951 (Inv. no. 131).   W

131   The Denial of Saint Peter

Collections: Sabadini, Rome. *References*: Refice 1951, pp. 263-64, fig. 3 (as an autograph copy of the Gerolamini painting). *Remarks*: This is probably the original, of which the painting in the Chiesa dei Gerolamini (Inv. no. 130) is a copy. Pr

132   The Denial of Saint Peter

References: Montini 1952, p. 35 (formerly in deposit at Museo Filangieri). *Remarks*: Perhaps identical with *The Payment of the Tribute*, formerly Cenzato collection, Naples, now Museo di Capodimonte [16].   U

133   The Dream of Saint Joseph

Collections: Ciardiello, Naples, through 1921. *References*: Sestieri 1920, p. 264, fig. 14 (as *Holy Family with Angel*), and 1921, p. 184 (as *Rest on the Flight into Egypt*); de Rinaldis 1921, p. 17 (as copy of the Pollak picture now in Brunswick [Inv. no. 31]); Ortolani in Naples 1938, p. 65 (as copy of the Pollak picture); Percy 1965, p. 73, no. 124 (lost); Causa 1972, p. 983 n. 111 (17th-century copy of the painting in Warsaw [37]).   W

134 The Flagellation of Christ

(Fragment?), 59 x 47 cm. *Collections*: Casciaro, Naples; sale, Finarte, Milan, 23 November 1972, lot 76. *References*: de Rinaldis 1920a, p. 59, repr.; Longhi 1920c, p. 153 (rejects attribution to Cavallino); de Rinaldis 1921, p. 16, pl. xxii; Ortolani in Naples 1938, p. 66; Percy 1965, p. 73, no. 133 (lost); Causa 1972, p. 982 n. 110 (not by Cavallino).　　D

135 The Good Samaritan

Collections: Antonio Lucchesi-Palli, principe di Campofranco, Palermo, through 1838. *References*: Vaccaro 1838, pp. 7-10, 21-23.　　U

136 The Marriage at Cana

105 x 157 cm. *Collections*: Roberto Gigli, Naples, through 1927; private collection, Milan, 1938. *References*: Ortolani 1922, p. 194, fig. 4; Voss 1927, pp. 64, 76 (as J. H. Schönfeld); Ortolani in Naples 1938, p. 82 (as Schönfeld); Voss 1964, pp. 15, 33 (as Schönfeld); Pée 1971, p. 123, no. 47, fig. 54 (as Schönfeld). *Remarks*: Reattributed to Johann Heinrich Schönfeld.　　R

137 The Massacre of the Innocents

109 x 260 cm. *Collections*: Almodóvar, Madrid, through 1965. *References*: Milicua 1954, p. 71, fig. 5 (doubtful attribution to Cavallino); Percy 1965, p. 72, no. 116 (lost); Pérez Sánchez 1965, p. 383 (as Vaccaro). *Remarks*: Although apparently influenced by Cavallino's facial types and dramatic compositions, this work does not appear, from a photograph, to be by his hand.　W

138 The Preparation for the Crucifixion

Collections: Carlos IV, casita del Principe, El Escorial, recorded last third of 18th century. *References*: Zarco Cuevas 1934, p. 17, no. 104 (a canvas representing Christ seated at the cross); Pérez Sánchez 1965, p. 384. *Remarks*: The depiction of Christ seated on or beside the cross while being prepared for the crucifixion occurs infrequently in Italy but often in Spain. Francisco Ribalta (1565–1628) and Alonso Cano (1601–1667) each painted several versions of the subject. An example of the type, executed by Ribera, that may have been known to Cavallino was inventoried in the collection of don Fernándo Afán Enriquez de Ribera, viceroy of Naples from 1629 to 1631 (see Pérez Sánchez and Spinosa 1978, p. 98, no. 37, repr.).　　U

139 The Prodigal Son

Collections: Museo Reale Borbonico, Naples, 1846. *References*: Naples 1846, p. 146, no. 243.　　U

140 The Raising of Lazarus

Collections: Galleria Corona, Naples, through 1921; conte Giuseppe Matarazzo di Licosa, Naples, by 1938, through 1950. *References*: de Rinaldis 1920a, p. 5 (heavily repainted); Sestieri 1920, p. 252, fig. 7 (copy after Cavallino), and 1921, p. 181 (copy); Naples 1938, p. 320; Parlat 1950, pp. 62-63, repr. p. 63; Percy 1965, p. 67, no. 94 (copy after Fracanzano?). *Remarks*: This work appears, from a photograph, to be a copy after a lost original by Cavallino.　　W

141 The Road to Emmaus

Collections: Borromeo, Isola Bella, through 1921. *References*: Longhi 1916a, p. 309 (an early work influenced by Artemisia Gentileschi, incorrectly labelled Caravaggio); de Rinaldis 1920a, p. 5, and 1921, p. 18; Percy 1965, p. 72, no. 115 (lost).　　U

142 The Sacrifice of the Gentiles

3 *palmi* across (ca. 79 cm). *Collections*: Nicola Salerno, Naples, recorded in 1742–43. *References*: See Appendix, no. 11.　　U

**143 Saint Paul Destroying the Viper
    after Landing on Malta**

48.2 x 74.2 cm. *Collections*: Heim Gallery, London, in 1967. *References*: London 1967, no. 9, repr.　　W

144 Saint Paul Shipwrecked on Malta

99.5 x 152 cm. *Collections*: Diodati, Naples, through 1922; private collection, Rome, by 1971. *References*: Ortolani 1922, p. 195, fig. 9; Voss 1927, p. 76 (as Schönfeld), and 1964, p. 33 (as Schönfeld); Percy 1965, p. 67, no. 91 (Cavallino attribution rejected; better attributed to Schönfeld); Pée 1971, p. 207, no. F3 (as Schönfeld). *Remarks*: Reattributed to Johann Heinrich Schönfeld.　　R

145 Supper in Bethany

Collections: Paolo Wenner, Naples, through 1920. *References*: de Rinaldis 1920a, p. 6, fig. 5; note in *Napoli Nobilissima* n. s. 1, no. 3 (1920):47 (*bozzetto* by Bernardo Strozzi for painting in R. Gallerie [Accademia], Venice; information from Giuseppe Fiocco); Longhi 1920b, p. 91 (*bozzetto* for painting by Strozzi in the Accademia, Venice); Percy 1965, p. 68, no. 96 (rejected attribution to Cavallino; reattributed to Strozzi). *Remarks*: Reattributed to Bernardo Strozzi.　　R

Devotional Images of Christ and the Virgin Mary

**146 The Holy Trinity
    or The Immmaculate Conception**

Collections: Chiesa dello Spirito Santo, Naples (second chapel right), through 1894. *References*: Catalani 1845–53, 2:35 (*Immaculate Conception*, period of Stanzione, perhaps by Cavallino); Galante 1872, p. 355 (*Immaculate Conception*, school of Stanzione, perhaps by Cavallino); Carafa 1894, p. 180 (the *Immaculate Conception* by Francesco Curia, the *Holy Trinity* by Cavallino); de Rinaldis 1909, p. 68, no. 36 (*Holy Trinity*, lost); Rolfs 1910, p. 278 (*Immaculate Conception with Apostles*, which people give to Cavallino but hard vivid colors and conventional composition resemble the school of Marco da Siena; *Holy Trinity* in the Chapel of the Brothers of the Holy Ghost, not known); Percy 1965, p. 72, no. 120 (*Holy Trinity*, lost).　　U

147 The Marriage of the Virgin

Collections: Achille Minozzi, Naples, through 1921. *References*: de Rinaldis 1920a, p. 5, and 1921, p. 17; Percy 1965, p. 73, no. 136 (lost).　　U

148 Pietà

Collections: Chiesa di Santa Maria della Sapienza, Naples (third chapel left), through 1902. *References*: Catalani 1845–53, 2:7 (as school of Stanzione, perhaps by Cavallino); Galante 1872, p. 107 (as school of Stanzione, perhaps by Cavallino); Naples 1877, p. 133 (without title); Colombo 1902, p. 69 (suggested attribution to Cavallino by not-always-accurate sources); Percy 1965, p. 72, no. 119 (lost).   U

149 The Virgin and Child with Four Crowned Saints

Collections: Chiesa di Santa Chiara, Naples (first chapel right). *References*: Catalani 1845–53, 2:101 (some attribute the work to Massimo Stanzione); Nobile 1855–57, 1:175 (supposed to be by Stanzione but does not appear to be his work); Dalbono 1876, p. 21; Percy 1965, p. 72, no. 118 (lost).   U

150 The Virgin of the Immaculate Conception

9 x 7 *palmi* (ca. 237 x 185 cm). *Collections*: Carlo Cioli (?), Naples, documented in 1646. *References*: See Appendix, no. 1.   U

151 The Virgin of the Immaculate Conception

Collections: Chiesa di Santa Maria della Verità, Naples. *References*: Catalani 1845–53, 2:26; Percy 1965, p. 50 (lost).   U

152 The Virgin of the Immaculate Conception

72 x 56 cm. *Collections*: Sestieri, Rome; sale, Rome, 24 March 1931, lot 154. *References*: Sestieri 1920, pp. 260-61, fig. 12 (as *The Assumption of the Virgin*; figure is by Cavallino, the garland of flowers by another hand); Ortolani in Naples 1938, p. 66; Percy 1965, p. 74, no. 145 (lost); Causa 1972, p. 983 n. 111 (old copy). *Remarks*: This work is similar to the composition at Caen [26], but the canvas is rectangular and the figure of the Virgin is surrounded by a garland of flowers.   D

153 The Virgin of the Immaculate Conception

Collections: Private collection, Palermo, through 1938 (Fig. 26b). *References*: Sestieri 1920, p. 269, fig. 22, and 1921, p. 188; de Rinaldis 1921, p. 18 (probably by Cavallino); Ortolani in Naples 1938, p. 66 (in Sicily); Percy 1965, p. 74, no. 141 (lost). *Remarks*: A chalk drawing, formerly in the János Scholz collection, now in the Pierpont Morgan Library (Fig. 28), appears to be a study for this work (see Introduction, note 78).   Pr

154 A Virgin Saint
     or The Blessed Virgin

1 x 1-1/2 *palmi* (ca. 26 x 40 cm). *Collections*: Don Francesco Emanuele Pinto, principe di Ischitella, Naples, 1767 inventory. *References*: See Appendix, no. 17.   U

Saints

155 The Death of Saint Mary Magdalene

Collections: Paolo Wenner, Naples, through 1921. *References*: de Rinaldis 1921, p. 16; Percy 1965, p. 74, no. 140 (lost).   U

156 Head of a Saint

Collections: Aldo Briganti, Rome, through 1922. *References*: Florence 1922, no. 266; Nugent 1925–30, 2:577 (probably by Cavallino); Percy 1965, p. 74, no. 143 (lost).   U

157 The Martyrdom of Franciscan Saints

Collections: Chiesa di San Diego all' Ospedaletto, Naples (ceiling), recorded in 1742–43. *References*: de Dominici 1742–43, 3:36; Giannone [1773] 1941, p. 107. *Remarks*: Cavallino is recorded by de Dominici as a participant in this decorative work, which was destroyed in an earthquake in 1784 (see Introduction, note 23).   U

158 The Martyrdom of Saint Cecilia, with Angels

Collections: Francesco Santangelo; Marchese Santangelo(?). *References*: Celano [1692] 1970, 2:1124-26. *Remarks*: This painting, together with an *Erminia among the Shepherds* (Inv. no. 186), is mentioned in the old palace formerly of don Diomede Carafa, first count of Maddaloni. The palace later belonged to the principe de Columbrano, also of the Carafa family, and in 1813 it was acquired by the jurist and poet Francesco Santangelo and his family. The picture hung in the first hall and is described as ''S. Cecilia corteggiata dagli Angeli nel momento del martirio'' (Celano [1692] 1970, 2:1126). Although the painting is likely identical with the *Saint Cecilia in Ecstasy* in the Palazzo Vecchio [44], its description is sufficiently at variance to warrant its inclusion here.   U

159 The Martyrdom of Saint Januarius

Collections: Tesorone, Naples; Marino, Naples, through 1922. *References*: Ortolani 1922, p. 195.   U

160 The Martyrdom of Saint Lawrence

Collections: Carlo Tito Dalbono, Naples, 1871. *References*: Dalbono 1871, p. 107; de Rinaldis 1909, p. 68, no. 37 (lost).   U

161 The Martyrdom of Saint Lawrence

100x 129 cm. *Collections*: Sale, Aste-Vendite Internazionali, Rome, 17-26 May 1969, repr.; Julius Weitzner, London. *Remarks*: This is probably a copy of a lost composition by Cavallino. The figure at the far right appears to record one of the artist's self-portraits.   W

162 The Martyrdom of Saint Lawrence

180 x 90 cm. *Collections*: Sale, Palais Galliera, Paris, 11 June 1977, no. 53, repr. *Remarks*: Note in sale catalogue credits Hermann Voss with attribution to Cavallino. Spinosa, in conversation 1983, rejects attribution to Cavallino, suggests Antonio de Bellis.   W

163 A Praying Saint

Octagonal, 95 x 75 cm. (Fig. 30-31b). *Collections*: Gilberto Algranti, Milan, 1969; private collection, Milan, 1970s. *References*: *Arte Illustrata*, nos. 5-6 (May-June 1968), repr.; Milan 1969, repr. *Remarks*: This is one of four octagonal half-figures of male saints or apostles, now lost, that appear to be originals by Cavallino (see also Figs. 30-31a, c, d).   Pr

164   Saint Agnes Beheaded

Collections: Private collection, Recanati, through 1967. *References*: Zampetti 1967, p. 15, fig. 34 (as questionable attribution to Cavallino). *Remarks*: Judging from the 1967 illustration, the work has nothing to do with Cavallino.   W

165   Saint Alexis

5 x 6 *palmi* (ca. 132 x 158 cm). *Collections*: Paolo Francone, marchese di Salcito, Naples, 1718 inventory. *References*: See Appendix, no. 8. *Remarks*: This is a pendant to a *Saint Roch* recorded in the same collection (Inv. no. 179).   U

166   Saint Cecilia

Collections: Ciardiello, Naples, through 1921. *References*: de Rinaldis 1921, p. 17; Percy 1965, p. 72, no. 121 (lost).   U

167   Saint Cecilia

References: A. Venturi 1938, p. 77, fig. 13.   W

168   Saint Dorothea

125 x 89 cm. *Collections*: Duchessa Proto d'Albaneta, Naples, by 1909; Rothmann, Berlin, by 1927; Carlo Sestieri, Rome, ca. 1950; Galleria Francesco Romano, Rome, ca. 1960. *References*: de Rinaldis 1909, p. 46, no. 15; Hermanin in Thieme-Becker 6 (1912):225; de Rinaldis 1920a, p. 4, and 1921, p. 16; Bloch 1927, pp. 176-77, fig. 4; Ortolani in Naples 1938, p. 65; Percy 1965, p. 72, no. 114 (lost). *Remarks*: This painting, identified from the photograph as a lost original, has sometimes been called *Saint Rosa*, but the presence of the young angel beside the figure, holding a basket of apples and roses, identifies the figure as Saint Dorothea.   Pr

169   Saint Jerome

Collections: Ettore Sestieri, Rome, through 1922. *References*: Florence 1922, no. 257; Nugent 1925–30, 2:571 (dubious attribution to Cavallino); Percy 1965, p. 70 (rejected attribution to Cavallino).   W

170   Saint Lawrence

2-1/2 x 2 *palmi* (ca. 66 x 53 cm). *Collections*: Guglielmo Ruffo, principe di Scilla, Naples, 1747 inventory. *References*: See Appendix, no. 16.   U

171   Saint Lawrence

Collections: Moretti, Rome, through 1951. *References*: Refice 1951, p. 270 n. 2.   U

172   Saint Lucy

51 x 32 cm. *Collections*: Iglesia de San Andrés, Toledo (Spain) through 1965; private collection. *References*: Pérez Sánchez 1965, p. 382 (associates this painting with Cavallino's "virgin saints" mentioned by de Dominici as having been sent to Spain). *Remarks*: Although this work is known to the authors only by photograph, the graceless proportions and stance of the figure make the attribution to Cavallino impossible to accept. Even if it is overpainted, the clumsy brushwork is nothing like Cavallino's manner.   W

173   Saint Margaret and the Dragon

4 x 5 *palmi* (ca. 105 x 132 cm). *Collections*: Ferdinand Vandeneynden, Naples; don Giuliano Colonna, principe di Galatro, Naples, 1688 inventory by Luca Giordano. *References*: See Appendix, no. 4.   U

174   A Saint Martyr

77 x 64 cm. *Collections*: Private collection, Sweden, through 1935. *References*: Wiesbaden 1935, no. 64.   U

175   A Saint Martyr

Collections: Enrico Frascione, Naples, through 1938. *References*: de Rinaldis 1920a, p. 6, fig. 6, and 1921, p. 17, repr. pl. XI; Ortolani in Naples 1938, p. 66 (as Saint Catherine); Percy 1965, p. 48. *Remarks*: This appears to be a copy of the autograph painting by Cavallino of the same subject in the Palazzo Doria, Genoa [27], although it cannot be securely determined at this point that they are not the same painting.   U

176   Saint Paul

Octagonal (Fig. 30-31a). *Collections*: Conde de Muguiro, Madrid, through 1965. *References*: Milicua 1954, p. 72, fig. 6; Percy 1965, p. 72, no. 117 (lost); Pérez Sánchez 1965, p. 382; Spinosa in London and Washington 1982–83, p. 137 (early work). *Remarks*: Another version of the subject, by Cavallino, is in London [31]; the picture is one of four lost half-figures of male saints or apostles by Cavallino (Figs. 30-31b-d).   Pr

177   Saint Peter and the Apostles

Collections: Giuseppe Cenzato, Naples. *References*: Naples 1938, pp. 178, 319; Ortolani 1938, p. 178.   U

178   Saint Peter and the Apostles

Collections: Salvatore Romano, Florence or Naples, 1938. *References*: Ortolani 1938, p. 178.   U

179   Saint Roch

5 x 6 *palmi* (ca. 132 x 158 cm). *Collections*: Paolo Francone, marchese di Salcito, Naples, 1718 inventory. *References*: See Appendix, no. 8. *Remarks*: This is a pendant to a *Saint Alexis* recorded in the same collection (Inv. no. 165).   U

180   Saint Sebastian

67 x 47 cm. *Collections*: Grzimek, Ravensburg, West Germany, through 1966. *References*: Grzimek 1966. *Remarks*: A drawing in the Ashmolean Museum, Oxford, apparently related to the Grzimek painting, is one of the few sheets attributed to Cavallino (see Introduction, note 77, and Fig. 27).   Po

181   Saint Stephen

2-1/2 x 2 *palmi* (ca. 66 x 53 cm). *Collections*, Guglielmo Ruffo, principe di Scilla, Naples, 1747 inventory. *References*: See Appendix, no. 16.   U

182   Saints Catherine and Clara

Collections: Augusto Jandolo, Rome, through 1951. *References*: Sestieri 1920, p. 253, fig. 8; Refice 1951, p. 265 (Cavallinesque figures); Percy 1965, p. 70, no. 107 (rejected attribution to

Cavallino). *Remarks*: Although this work is known to the authors only by photograph, the composition and the figure types are very unlike Cavallino's work.　W

Miscellaneous Subjects Derived from History, Literature, and Mythology

183　An Allegorical Figure

Collections: Guido Mascheri [Marchesi?], Rome, through 1922. *References*: Florence 1922, no. 264; Nugent, 1925-30, 2:571 (probably Neapolitan school, questionable attribution to Cavallino); Percy 1965, p. 70 (rejected attribution to Cavallino).　U

184　Blind Belisarius

Collections: L. de B. Spiridon, Rome, through 1922. *References*: Florence 1922, no. 260; Nugent 1925–30, 2:571 (attribution to Cavallino dubious; nearer to Ribera).　U

185　"La divina pastorella"

Collections: Conte M. Piscicelli, Rome, through 1938. *References*: Naples 1938, p. 319; Percy 1965, p. 74, no. 144 (lost).　U

186　Erminia among the Shepherds

Collections: Francesco Santangelo; Marchese Santangelo(?). *References*: De Rinaldis 1921, p. 18 (not known to him personally); Celano [1692] 1970, 2:1126. *Remarks*: This painting comes from the same collection as that in Inv. no. 158; it is described as "Erminia che scovre il viso a' pastori" (ibid.).　U

187　Erminia among the Shepherds

4 x 3 *palmi* (ca. 105 x 79 cm). *Collections*: Caputi, Naples, recorded in 1742–43. *References*: See Appendix, no. 10.　U

188　A Goatherd and His Flock

90 x 70 cm. *Collections*: Galleria d'Arte Accademia, Milan, in 1970. *References*: *The Burlington Magazine* 112 (June 1970):cxv, repr.　W

189　Portrait of a Lady (Justice ?)

70.5 x 58.4 cm. *Collections*: Sale, Christie's, London, 14 December 1928, lot 85, to Jarvis; sale, Christie's, London, 14 June 1929, lot 69, to Leger.　U

190　The Rape of Europa

4 x 3 *palmi* (ca. 105 x 79 cm). *Collections*: Caputi, Naples, recorded in 1742–43. *References*: See Appendix, no. 10.　U

191　Sleeping Venus Surrounded by Cupids

Recorded in 1742–43. *References*: de Dominici 1742–43, 3:42 (copy by Cavallino of a *Sleeping Venus Surrounded by Cupids* by Titian, said by de Dominici to have been owned by the principe di Conca).　U

Note

The question of the many scenes from the Apocryphal story of Tobit attributed to Cavallino is complicated enough to require some explanation. Numerous versions of these subjects, often done in pairs and described by de Dominici, seem (1) to derive from original works by Cavallino that are now considered lost or in unknown locations, or (2) to be the work of a close follower. For example, an original painting by Cavallino of *The Departure of Tobias* (now lost) is known through a copy in Rome (Inv. no. 9).

The Marriage of Tobias exists in five locatable versions — in Norfolk (Virginia), Naples, Sorrento, L'Aquila, and Madrid (Inv. nos. 14-18) — and in three versions (all in Naples; Inv. nos. 95-97) that are considered lost. Of these eight works, none are believed to be autograph works of Cavallino; those in Sorrento, L'Aquila, and Madrid have companion pieces entitled *The Curing of Tobit*. The Norfolk *Marriage of Tobias* shows figures of graceful, slender proportions that are nearer to Cavallino's works than do the Naples, L'Aquila, and Madrid versions, wherein the figures have large heads and rather stocky bodies that are untypical of Cavallino.

The Curing of Tobit is known through one lost work (Inv. no. 77) and six existing, published versions: in Sorrento, Naples, Washington, Seattle, L'Aquila, and Madrid (Inv. nos. 1-6) — those in Sorrento, L'Aquila, and Madrid are companion pieces to the abovementioned versions of *The Marriage of Tobias*. The compositions of *The Curing of Tobit* in Washington, L'Aquila, and Madrid are quite similar and contain the stocky, heavily proportioned figures that bespeak a follower of Cavallino, although the pictures are clearly related to the artist's work. The paintings in Naples and Seattle, however, have different compositions — especially the latter, which is close to the one known original picture by Cavallino of the subject [24] and definitely seems to derive from a prototype by the artist himself.

It is impossible to assess how many separate hands are involved in this problem, whether the many versions indicate a possible studio or pupils, and why there are so few surviving original paintings of subjects that must have been highly popular with Cavallino.

Appendix

Listed here are works by Bernardo Cavallino—now lost or lacking specific identification—that were recorded as being in seventeenth- and eighteenth-century private collections. In each instance, the earliest-known documentary source is cited, and in some instances the verbatim excerpt is given.

1 Presumably in the collection of Carlo Cioli, Naples, an *Annunciation* and an *Immaculate Conception*, each nine *palmi* high and seven wide (ca. 237 x 186 cm), for which Cioli paid Cavallino forty-seven ducats in March of 1646 (see Introduction, note 4). *Remarks*: The pictures are so large that they may have been commissioned for a church rather than for Cioli's private collection. Unfortunately nothing is known about Cioli.

2 Presumably in the collection of the principe di Cardito, Naples, a large painting whose subject is not known, for which the principe paid Cavallino forty ducats on account in January of 1649 (see Introduction, note 5).

3 Presumably in the collection of Cardinal Leopoldo de'Medici, Florence, an unnamed drawing included by Filippo Baldinucci in a collection list of 1673 (with additions of 1675?; see Introduction, note 7).

4 In the collection of don Giuliano Colonna, principe di Galatro (husband of the eldest daughter of Ferdinand Vandeneynden, the son of Gaspar Roomer's business associate and compatriot, the Flemish merchant Jan Vandeneynden), Naples, one work listed in an inventory completed by Luca Giordano on 17 November 1688: "no. 62. Un [quadro] di palmi 4 e 5 [ca. 105 x 132 cm] con cornice ind.ta una S.ta Margarita, con il drago, m.o di Bernardo Cavallino . . . [L.] 30" (Colonna di Stigliano 1895, p. 31; de Rinaldis 1909, p. 69, no. 40; Ruotolo 1982, p. 34). *Remarks*: The painting is lost; the collection was gradually dispersed in the eighteenth century and the palace on via Toledo was sacked in 1799. Ruotolo points out (1982, p. 12) that the Colonna inventory of 1688 represents that part of the Vandeneynden collection inherited by Giovanna Vandeneynden, Ferdinand Vandeneynden's daughter who married Giuliano Colonna in that year.

5 In the collection of the principe di Tarsia, Naples, an unnamed painting or paintings (Celano [1692] 1970, 3:1616). *Remarks*: The artist is mistakenly called Francesco Cavallino; see also no. 9 below.

6 In the collection of Domenico di Martino, Naples, an unnamed painting or paintings (Celano [1692] 1970, 3:1617; Parrino 1714, p. 342).

7 In the collection of the maestro di Campo Martino de Castrocon, Naples, three paintings listed in an inventory of 1700: "due quadri con cornice di pero nere con stragalli d'oro mano di Bernardo Cavallini con istorie; . . . S. Apollonia della scola di Cavallino di l palmo e mezzo et l in circa [ca. 40 x 26 cm]" (information courtesy of Renato Ruotolo; the inventory, in course of publication by Gérard Labrot in an article entitled "Deux collectionneurs étrangers à Naples" in the forthcoming *Ricerche sul Seicento napoletano*, is in the Archivio di Stato di Napoli, notaio Pier Angelo Volpe, sec. XVII, scheda 1277, prot. 23).

8 In the collection of Paolo Francone, marchese di Salcito (1688–ca. 1771), Naples, two paintings listed in an inventory of 22 September 1718: "13. un S. Alessio di palmi 5 e 6 [ca. 132 x 158 cm] originale di Bernardino Cavallino di prezzo ducati centocinquanta; 14. un S. Rocco di palmi 5 e 6 originale del medesimo Cavallino di prezzo ducati centocinquanta." *Remarks*: The inventory also lists works by Giuseppe Marullo, Domenico Gargiulo, Artemisia Gentileschi, Giacinto de Popolis, Paolo Finoglia, as well as some older masters and four attributions to Caravaggio; the collection was dispersed by the early nineteenth century (Caracciolo 1959, pp. 32, 35-36, 50).

9 In the estate of Francesco Carlo Spinelli, principe di Tarsia, Naples, two works recorded in an inventory of 4 March 1734: "due quadri, uno di David e l'altro di Giuditta di palmi 5 e 4 [ca. 132 x 105 cm], mano di Bernardo Cavallino, cornice liscia indorata" (Mormone 1961–62, p. 223; see also no. 5 above).

10 In the Caputi collection, Naples, two works, each 4 x 3 *palmi* (ca. 105 x 79 cm): a *Rape of Europa* and an *Erminia among the Shepherds* (de Dominici 1742–43, 3:40; Giannone [1773] 1941, p. 108).

11 In the collection of Nicola Salerno, Naples, two works: a *Denial of Saint Peter* and a *Sacrifice of the Gentiles*, each ca. 3 *palmi* (ca. 79 cm) across (de Dominici 1742–43, 3:39-40).

12 In the collection of the duca di San Severina, Naples, two scenes from the story of Tobit, each ca. 5 x 4 *palmi* (ca. 132 x 105 cm); two versions of the *Liberation of Saint Peter*; a *Denial of Saint Peter*; and a *Cain Slaying Abel* and an *Adam and Eve Lamenting the Death of Abel* (ibid., p. 43). *Remarks*: The latter two subjects could be one picture, as the subject is not completely clear in de Dominici's description.

13 In the collection of don Francesco Valletta, Naples, an *Esther before Ahasuerus* (3 x 5 *palmi* [ca. 79 x 132 cm] — tentatively identified with cat. no. 21); a *Marriage of Tobias* (3 x 4 *palmi* [ca. 79 x 105 cm]); two versions of *Christ and the Adulteress* (one 3 x 4 *palmi* [ca. 79 x 105 cm], the other 4 x 5 *palmi* [ca. 105 x 132 cm] — the latter tentatively identified with cat. no. 40); a *Denial of Saint Peter* (3 x 2-1/2 *palmi* [ca. 79 x 66 cm]); a *Dead Christ* (2 *palmi* [ca. 53 cm]); and a *Departure of Tobias* (copper, 2 x 2-1/2 *palmi* [ca. 53 x 66 cm], known through a copy in the Palazzo Corsini, Rome [Inv. no. 9]; ibid., pp. 38-39).

14 In the collection of the marchese di Grazia, Naples, a *Marriage of Tobias* (copper, 2 x 2-1/2 *palmi* [ca. 53 x 66 cm], pendant to the *Departure of Tobias* in the Valletta collection [see no. 13 above]), and a *Judith with the Head of Holofernes*, (4 x 5 *palmi* [ca. 105 x 132 cm])—tentatively identified with cat. no. 45) (ibid., p. 39; Giannone [1773] 1941, p. 108).

15 In the collection of Gennaro Marotta, Naples, four half-figures of female saints, bought by Jean Charpin to send to England in 1722 (ibid., p. 37; see Introduction, note 90).

16 In the estate of don Guglielmo Ruffo, principe di Scilla, Naples, two paintings listed in an inventory of 27 March 1747: "due quadri originali di Bernardo Cavallino, uno rappresentante S. Lorenzo e l'altro S. Stefano con la cornice nera a tre ordini d'oro di palmi 2-1/2 e 2 [ca. 66 x 53 cm]" (Rogadeo di Torrequadra 1898, p. 73). *Remarks*: For a painting of *Saint Lawrence* of about the same dimensions, see cat. no. 58.

17 In the estate of don Francesco Emanuele Pinto, principe di Ischitella, Naples (d. 24 October 1767), two paintings listed in an inventory of 1767: "Di Bernardo Cavallino due quadri di palmi 1 e 1-1/2 [ca. 26 x 40 cm] con cornice intagliata indorata, in uno l'Istoria di Lot, e nell'altro una Vergine" (Pacelli 1979a, p. 175).

18 In the collection of the French amateur and writer on the arts Pierre Jean Mariette, Paris (1694–1774), two drawings: "359. Deux Sujets de l'Histoire de David, largement touchés, au bistre et à la plume" (Basan 1775, p. 58). *Remarks*: On Mariette's collection, see Paris 1967a.

Bibliography

Abbate, Francesco. 1970. "Giovan Battista Spinelli: La 'Samaritana al Pozzo'." *Paragone* 21 (January):61-62.

Adriani, Götz, 1969: see Brunswick 1969.

Algranti, Gilberto, 1967: see Milan 1967.

Algranti 1969(?): see Milan 1969(?).

Algranti 1973: see Milan 1973.

A. M. F. 1938. "Art in Naples over 300 Years: A Neapolitan Exhibition of Native Painters: 1600–1900." *Art News* 36, no. 35 (May):9-10, 21.

The Apocrypha: An American Translation. 1959. Translated by Edgar J. Goodspeed. New York and Toronto: Random House.

L'Arte 1899. [Note] "Antonio van Dyck da Palermo a Napoli" 2:502.

Athens 1962–63: see Naples 1963.

Austin [Texas] 1963: see Fort Worth 1962.

Baetjer, Katharine, 1980: see New York 1980.

Baglione, Giovanni. 1733. *Le vite de' pittori, scultori, architetti, ed intagliatori, dal pontificato di Gregorio XIII del 1572 fino a' tempi di papa Urbano VIII nel 1642. Scritte da Gio. Baglione romano. Con la vita di Salvator Rosa napoletano, pittore, e poeta, scritta da Gio. Batista Passari, nuovamente aggiunta.* Naples: n. publ.

Balboni, M. T., 1980: see Milan 1980.

Baldinucci, Filippo. [1845–47] 1974–75. *Notizie dei professori del disegno da Cimabue in qua.* Reprint, edited by Paola Barocchi. 7 vols. Florence: Edizioni S. P. E. S.

Bari 1964. Pinacoteca Provinciale. *Mostra dell'arte in Puglia dal tardo antico al rococo.* Exh. cat. by Michele D'Elia.

Barnard Castle [County Durham, England] 1962. Bowes Museum. *Neapolitan Baroque and Rococo Painting.* Exh. cat. by Tony Ellis.

Barnard Castle 1970. *Catalogue of Spanish and Italian Paintings. The Bowes Museum, Barnard Castle, County Durham* [England]. Coll. cat. by Tony Ellis and Eric Young.

Basan, F. 1775. *Catalogue raisonné des différens objets de curiosités dans les sciences et arts, qui composoient le Cabinet de feu M.r Mariette Controleur général de la Grande Chancellerie de France, honoraire amateur de l'Académie R.le de Peinture, et de celle de Florence, par F. Basan, Graveur.* Paris: F. Basan and G. Desprez.

Battisti, Eugenio. 1961–63. "La data di morte di Artemisia Gentileschi." *Mitteilungen des Kunsthistorischen Institutes in Florenz* 10, nos. 1-4:297.

Baxandall, David, 1957: see Edinburgh 1957.

Bazin, Germain. 1965. "Le Caravage et la peinture italienne au XVIIe siècle." *Revue du Louvre et des Musées de France* 15:1-8.

Bean, Jacob, 1967: see New York 1967a.

Bean 1979: see New York 1979.

Benesch, Otto. 1926. "Seicentostudien, I. Zu Bernardo Cavallinos Werdegang." *Jahrbuch der Kunsthistorischen Sammlungen in Wien*, n.s. 1:245-68.

Benesch 1928. "Wien." *Pantheon* 1:46-51.

Bénézit, E. 1976. *Dictionnaire critique et documentaire des Peintres, Sculpteurs, Dessinateurs et Graveurs*, n.s. 10 vols. Paris: Librairie Gründ.

Berlin 1966. Orangerie des Schlosses Charlottenburg. *Deutsche Maler und Zeichner des 17. Jahrhunderts.* Exh. cat.

Besançon. 1982. Musée des Beaux-Arts et d'Archéologie Besançon. *Collections du Musée.* Part 3: *Peintures napolitaines.* Coll. cat.

Bessone-Aureli, Antonietta Maria. 1915. *Dizionario dei pittori italiani.* Città di Castello: Casa Editrice S. Lapi.

Betti, Marina. 1960. "Arricchito di una tela di Bernardo Cavallino il rinnovato Museo Poldi Pezzoli." *Arte Figurativa Antica e Moderna* 8 (November-December):14-17.

Białostocki, Jan, and M. Walicki. 1957. *Europäische Malerei in polnischen Sammlungen 1300–1800.* Warsaw: Państwowy Instytut Wydawniczy.

Biancale, Michele. 1920. "Attribuzioni caravaggesche." *Bollettino d'Arte* 14:7-16.

Birmingham [England] 1966. *Barber Institute Director's Report.*

Bissell, R. Ward. 1968. "Artemisia Gentileschi - A New Documented Chronology." *The Art Bulletin* 50 (June):153-68.

Blasius, J. J., 1867 and 1868: see Brunswick 1867 and 1868.

Bloch, Vitale. 1927. "La pittura italiana a Berlino." *Vita Artistica* 2, nos. 8-9:174-80.

Bloch 1968. *Michael Sweerts.* The Hague: L. J. C. Boucher.

Blunt, Anthony. 1939–40. "A Poussin-Castiglione Problem. Classicism and the Picturesque in 17th-Century Rome." *Journal of the Warburg and Courtauld Institutes* 3:142-47.

Blunt 1958. "Poussin Studies VII: Poussins in Neapolitan and Sicilian Collections." *The Burlington Magazine* 100:76-86.

Blunt 1966–67. *The Paintings of Nicolas Poussin. A Critical Catalogue.* 3 vols. London: Phaidon Press, 1966; New York: Bollingen Foundation, 1967.

Blunt 1969. "A Frescoed Ceiling by Aniello Falcone." *The Burlington Magazine* 111:215.

Blunt 1974. "Naples as Seen by French Travellers 1630–1780." In *The Artist and the Writer in France: Essays in Honour of Jean Seznec.* Edited by Francis Haskell, Anthony Levi, and Robert Shackleton. Oxford: Clarendon Press.

Bohlin, Diane DeGrazia, 1979: see Washington 1979.

Bologna, Ferdinando. 1952. "A proposito dei 'Ribera' del Museo di Bruxelles." *Musées Royaux des Beaux-Arts Bulletin* 1 (June):47-56.

Bologna, F., 1954: see Naples 1954b.

Bologna, F., 1955: see Salerno [Italy] 1955.

Bologna, F., 1958. *Francesco Solimena.* Naples: L'Arte Tipografica.

Bonsignori, Filippo. 1974. *La Pittura nel '600.* Milan: Silvana Editoriale d'Arte.

Bordeaux 1959. Galerie des Beaux-Arts. *La découverte de la lumière des primitifs aux impressionistes.* Exh. cat. by Gilberte Martin-Méry.

Borenius, Tancred. 1923. "Vermeer's Master." *The Burlington Magazine* 42:37-38.

Borenius 1935. "London. Aus den Museen." *Pantheon* 16:319.

Borsook, Eve. 1954. "Documents Concerning the Artistic Associates of Santa Maria della Scala in Rome." *The Burlington Magazine* 96:270-75.

Borzelli, Angelo. 1900. "L'Accademia del disegno a Napoli nella seconda metà del secolo XVIII." *Napoli Nobilissima* 9, no. 5:71-76.

Boston 1955. Museum of Fine Arts. *Summary Catalogue of European Paintings in Oil, Tempera, and Pastel.* Coll. cat.

Bottari, Stefano. 1966. "Una ipotesi per Aniello Falcone." *Arte Antica e Moderna* 33 (January-March):141-43.

Braham, Allan, 1970: see London 1952b.

Brejon de Lavergnée, Arnauld, 1974: see Paris 1974.

Brejon de Lavergnée, Arnauld, and Bernard Dorival. 1979. *Baroque et classicisme au XVIIe siècle en Italie et en France.* Histoire Universelle de la Peinture. Geneva: Famot.

Bridgeport [Connecticut] 1962. Museum of Art, Science, and Industry. *Twenty Top Treasures from Connecticut Museums.* Exh. cat.

Briganti, Giuliano. 1950. "Pieter van Laer e Michelangelo Cerquozzi." *Proporzioni* 3:185-98.

Brigstocke, Hugh. 1980. "Castiglione: Two Recently Discovered Paintings and New Thoughts on His Development." *The Burlington Magazine* 122:293-98.

Brown, Jonathan, 1973: see Princeton 1973.

Brugnoli, Maria Vittoria, ed. 1959. *Ragguaglio delle arti: Incremento del patrimonio artistico italiano.* Rome: Editalia.

Brulliot, François. 1832. *Dictionnaire des monogrammes, marques figurées, lettres initiales, noms abrégés, etc. avec lesquels les peintres, dessinateurs, graveurs et sculpteurs ont désigné leurs noms.* Munich: J. G. Cotta.

Brunswick [1710?]. *Kurtze Beschreibung des Fürstlichen Lustschlosses Saltzdahlum.* Coll. cat. by Tobias Querfurt. N.p.

Brunswick 1744. Handwritten Inventory of the Ducal Gallery near Saltzdahlum. N.p., n. publ.

Brunswick 1776. *Verzeichnis der Herzoglichen Bilder-Gallerie zu Saltzdahlum.* Coll. cat. by C. N. Eberlein.

Brunswick 1867 and 1868. *Verzeichnis der Gemäldesammlung des Herzoglichen Museums in Braunschweig.* Coll. cats. by J. J. Blasius.

Brunswick 1900. *Verzeichnis der Gemäldesammlung, Herzogliches Museum, Braunschweig.* Coll. cat. by H. Riegel.

Brunswick 1905. *Nachtrag zum Führer durch die Sammlungen des Herzoglichen Museums zu Braunschweig, 1902.* Coll. cat. by P. J. Meier.

Brunswick 1922. *Verzeichnis der Gemäldesammlung im Landesmuseum zu Braunschweig.* Coll. cat. by Eduard Flechsig.

Brunswick 1932. *Kurzes Verzeichnis der Gemäldesammlung im Herzog Anton Ulrich-Museum zu Braunschweig.* Coll. cat. by August Fink.

Brunswick 1936. *Verzeichnis der Gemäldesammlung des Herzoglichen Museums zu Braunschweig.* Coll. cat. by L. Pape.

Brunswick 1969. *Herzog Anton Ulrich-Museum. Verzeichnis der Gemälde.* Coll. cat. by Götz Adriani.

Brunswick 1976. *Herzog Anton Ulrich-Museum: Verzeichnis der Gemälde vor 1800.* Coll. cat.

Bryan's Dictionary of Painters and Engravers. 1903–5. Rev. and enl. ed. 5 vols. New York: MacMillan Co.; London: George Bell and Sons.

Bucharest 1972. Muzeul de Artă al Republicii Socialiste România. *Secolul de aur al picturii napolitane.* Exh. cat. by Nicola Spinosa. Intro. by Raffaello Causa.

Budapest 1883. *Landes-Gemäldegalerie Budapest.* Coll. cat. by H. Tschudi and K. Pulszky.

Budapest 1904. *Katalog der Gemäldegalerie Alter Meister.* Coll. cat. by G. de Térey.

Budapest 1906. *Tableaux anciens du Musée des Beaux-Arts de Budapest.* Coll. cat. by G. de Térey.

Budapest 1913. *Katalog der Gemäldegalerie Alter Meister.* Coll. cat. by G. de Térey.

Budapest 1916. *Die Gemäldegalerie des Museums für Bildende-Künste* in Budapest. Coll. cat. by G. de Térey.

Budapest 1937, 1954. *A Régi Képtár Katalógusa* [Old Picture Gallery]. 2 vols. Coll. cats. by A. Pigler.

Budapest 1968. *Katalog der Galerie Alter Meister.* 2 vols. Coll. cat. by A. Pigler.

Bulletin of the [Detroit] Institute of Arts. 1946. Vol. 25, no. 3:55.

Burchard, Ludwig. 1953. "Rubens' 'Feast of Herod' at Port Sunlight." *The Burlington Magazine* 95:383-87.

Caen 1980. Musée des Beaux-Arts de Caen. *Dix ans d'enrichessement du Musée des Beaux-Arts et de la collection Mancel.*

Camón Aznar, José, 1951 and 1954: see Madrid 1951 and 1954.

Capaccio, Giulio Cesare. 1634. *Il Forastiero: dialogi di Giulio Cesare Capaccio.* Naples: Gio. Domenico Roncagliolo.

Caracciolo, Ambrogino. 1959. "Alcune notizie sulla famiglia Francone e l'arredamento di una casa patrizia napoletana al principio del sec. XVIII" (3:29-50). In *Studi in onore di Riccardo Filangieri.* 3 vols. Naples: L'Arte Tipografica.

Caracciolo, Cesare d'Engenio. 1623. *Napoli sacra di D. Cesare d'Engenio Caracciolo napolitano.* Naples: Ottavio Beltrano.

Carafa, duca d'Andria. 1894. "Di alcune opere d'arte conservate negli Ospedali, Orfanotrofii ed Ospizii di mendicità di Napoli." *Napoli Nobilissima* 3, no. 12: 180-82.

Carducho, Vicencio [1633] 1865. *Diálogos de la pintura, su defensa . . ., definición modos y diferencias . . . .*, Facsimile edition, edited by G. Cruzada Villaamil. Madrid: n. publ.

Carletti, Niccolò. 1776. *Topografia universale della città di Napoli in campagna felice e note enciclopediche storiografe di Niccolò Carletti*. Naples: Stamperia Raimondiana.

Carli, Enzo. 1938. "Segnalazioni di pittura napoletana." *L'Arte* n.s. 41:255-79.

Carritt, David. 1957. "Pictures from Gosford House." *The Burlington Magazine* 99:343-44.

Cartari, Vicenzo [1647] 1963. *Imagini delli dei de gl'Antichi*. Reprint. Graz: Akademische Druck u. Verlagsanstalt.

Catalani, Luigi [1845] 1969. *I palazzi di Napoli. Ristampa dell'unica e rara edizione del 1845*. Reprint. Naples: Gaetano Colonnese Editore.

Catalani. 1845-53. *Le chiese di Napoli, descrizione storica ed artistica*. 2 vols. Naples: Tipografia fu Migliaccio.

Causa, Raffaello. 1949. "Restauri nella quadreria del Museo di S. Martino." *Bollettino d'Arte* 34:274-78.

Causa 1953. "Il riordinamento del Museo Correale di Sorrento." *Bollettino d'Arte* 38:90-93.

Causa 1953-54: see Naples 1953-54.

Causa 1954: see Naples 1954a.

Causa 1957. *Pittura napoletana dal XV al XIX secolo*. Bergamo: Istituto Italiano d'Arti Grafiche.

Causa 1960: see Naples 1960.

Causa 1963: see Naples 1963.

Causa 1966. *I Seguaci del Caravaggio a Napoli*. I Maestri del Colore, no. 222. Milan: Fratelli Fabbri.

Causa 1969-70: see Rome 1969-70.

Causa 1970. *Opere d'arte nel Pio Monte della Misericordia a Napoli*. Naples: Di Mauro Editore.

Causa 1972. *La Pittura del Seicento a Napoli dal naturalismo al barocco*. In Vol. 5, pt. 2 of *Storia di Napoli*. Naples: Società Editrice Storia di Napoli.

Causa 1973. *L'Arte nella Certosa di San Martino a Napoli*. Naples: Di Mauro Editore.

Causa 1982: see Naples 1982.

Causid, Simon, 1783: see Kassel 1783.

Ceci, Giuseppe. 1893. "Il più antico teatro di Napoli, il Teatro dei Fiorentini." *Napoli Nobilissima* 2, no. 6:81-85.

Ceci 1898a. "La Corporazione dei pittori." *Napoli Nobilissima* 7, no. 1:8-13.

Ceci 1898b. "Scrittori della storia dell'arte napoletana anteriori al De Dominici." *Napoli Nobilissima* 8, no. 11:163-68. (Editor's note: Correct year for this reference is *1899*.)

Ceci 1902. *Domenico Gargiulo detto Micco Spadaro. Memoria letta all'Accademia Pontiana nella tornata del 16 Febbrario 1902*. Naples: A Tessitore e Figlio.

Ceci 1905. "Domenico Gargiulo, detto Micco Spadaro." *Napoli Nobilissima* 14, no. 5: 65-68; no. 7:104-8.

Ceci 1908. "Il primo critico del De Dominici." *Archivio Storico per le province napoletane* 33, no. 4:618-36.

Ceci 1911. *Saggio di una bibliografia per la storia delle arti figurative nell'Italia meridionale*. Bari: Gius. Laterza & Figli.

Ceci 1913. "La Compagnia della Morte in Napoli." *Archivio storico per le province napoletane* 38, no. 1:145-62.

Ceci 1920. "Un mercante mecenate del secolo XVII, Gaspare Roomer." *Napoli Nobilissima*, n.s. 1, nos. 11-12:160-64.

[Ceci] 1923. "La pittura napoletana all' esposizione di Firenze." *Napoli Nobilissima*, n.s. 3, nos. 1-2:24-26. (Editor's note: The year 1923 [MCMXXIII] is imprinted on the title page of the issue, but the correct year is 1922 for new series 3; Ceci is bracketed because he did not actually sign the article.)

Ceci 1937. *Bibliografia per la storia delle arti figurative nell'Italia meridionale*. 2 vols. Naples: R. Deputazione Napoletana di Storia Patria.

Celano, Carlo [1692] 1970. *Notizie del bello dell'antico e del curioso della città di Napoli divise dall'autore in dieci giornate per guida e comodo de' viaggiatori*. 10 vols. in 3. Reprint, with additions by Giovan Battista Chiarini; edited by Atanasio Mozzillo, Alfredo Profeta, and Francesco Paolo Macchia. Naples: Edizioni Scientifiche Italiane.

Celano 1724. *Delle notizie del bello, dell'antico, e del curioso della citta di Napoli, per i signori forastieri*. 3 vols. Naples: Giovanni Francesco Paci.

Celano [1856-60] 1972. *Notizie del bello, dell'antico e del curioso della città di Napoli*. 5 vols. Reprint, edited by Giovanni Battista Chiarini. Naples: Stamperia Floriana.

Chamberlain, Betty. 1956. "The Extraordinary Taste of Mr. Chrysler." *Art News* 55, no. 4:44-47.

Chiarelli, Renzo. 1954. "Mostra della Galleria del Banco di Napoli all 'Strozzina'." *Emporium* 119:220-21.

Chiarini, Marco. 1972. "Filippo Napoletano, Poelenburgh, Breenbergh e la nascita del paesaggio realistico in Italia." *Paragone* 23, no. 269:18-34.

Chimirri, B., and A. Frangipane. 1914. *Mattia Preti, detto Il Cavalier Calabrese*. Milan: Alfieri & Lacroix.

C. K. J. 1935. "The New Cavallino at the National Gallery." *Apollo* 22 (1935):370.

Clark, Kenneth, 1931: see London 1931.

Cleveland 1971. The Cleveland Museum of Art. *Caravaggio and His Followers*. Exh. cat. by Richard E. Spear.

Cleveland 1982. The Cleveland Museum of Art. *Catalogue of Paintings. Part 3: European Paintings of the 16th, 17th, and 18th Centuries*. Coll. cat. by Ann Tzeutschler Lurie, et al.

Colletta, Teresa. 1974. "La villa Sanseverino di Bisignano e il casale napoletano della Barra." *Napoli Nobilissima* 13, no. 4:121-40.

Colombo, Antonio. 1895. "La Strada di Toledo, v. altri palazzi signorili, i ministeri di stato." *Napoli Nobilissima* 4, no. 8:124-27.

Colombo 1900. "Il palazzo dei principi di Conca alla strada di S. Maria di Costantinopoli." *Napoli Nobilissima* 9, no. 9:129-32; no. 11:172-75; no. 12:185-90.

Colombo 1902. "Il monastero e la chiesa di Santa Maria della Sapienza." *Napoli Nobilissima* 11, no. 5:67-73.

Colonna di Stigliano, Ferdinando. 1895. "Inventario dei quadri di Casa Colonna fatto da Luca Giordano." *Napoli Nobilissima* 4, no. 2:29-32.

Commodo Izzo, Maria. 1951. *Andrea Vaccaro Pittore (1604-1670)*. Naples: Conte Editore.

Comolli, Angelo. 1788-92. *Bibliografia storico-critica dell'architettura civile ed arti subalterne*. 4 vols. Rome: Luigi Perego Salvioni (Stamperia Vaticana).

Consoli Fiego, G. 1922. "Il museo Valletta." *Napoli Nobilissima*, n.s. 3, nos. 7-8:105-10; nos. 11-12:172-75.

Constable, W. G. 1943. "Some Unpublished Baroque Paintings." *Gazette des Beaux-Arts* 23:219-36.

Cook, Herbert. 1907-8. "Pacheco, the Master of Velázquez." *The Burlington Magazine* 12:299-300 and pls. 1,2.

Corna, P. A. 1930. *Dizionario della storia dell'arte in Italia*. 2 vols. Piacenza: Carlo Tarantola Editore.

Costamagna, Alba, 1981: see Rome 1981.

Costantini, Vincenzo. 1930. *La Pittura italiana del Seicento*. 2 vols. Milan: Casa Editrice Ceschina.

Costello, Jane. 1950. "The Twelve Pictures 'Ordered by Velázquez' and the Trial of Valguarnera." *Journal of the Warburg and Courtauld Institutes* 13:237-84.

Crelly, William R. 1962. *The Painting of Simon Vouet*. New Haven and London: Yale University Press.

Croce, Benedetto. 1889-90. "I Teatri di Napoli, secolo XV-XVIII." *Archivio storico per le province napoletane* 14, nos. 3-4:556-684; 15, no. 1:126-80, no. 2:233-352, no. 3:472-564.

Croce [1891] 1926 or 1966. *I Teatri di Napoli dal rinascimento alla fine del secolo decimottavo*. Reprints, 3rd and 5th eds. Bari: Giuseppe Laterza & Figli.

Croce 1892. "Sommario critico della storia dell'arte nel napoletano, I. Il Falsario." *Napoli Nobilissima* 1, no. 8:122-26; no. 9:140-44.

Croce 1893. "Un innamorato di Napoli, Carlo Celano." *Napoli Nobilissima* 2, no. 4:66-70.

Croce 1898a. "Scrittori della storia dell'arte napoletana anteriori al De Dominici." *Napoli Nobilissima* 7, no. 2:17-20.

Croce 1898b. "Il manoscritto di Camillo Tutini sulla storia dell'arte napoletana." *Napoli Nobilissima* 7, no. 8:121-24.

Croce 1898c. "Pulcinella e il personaggio del napoletano in commedia, ricerche ed osservazioni." *Archivio storico per le province napoletane* 23, no. 3:605-68; no. 4:702-42.

Crombie, Theodore. 1962. "Naples in the North." *Apollo*, n.s. 77 (July):395-99.

Cropper, Elizabeth. 1983. "Naples at the Royal Academy." *The Burlington Magazine* 125:104-6.

Cuzin, Jean-Pierre, 1974: see Paris 1974.

D'Addosio, Giambattista. 1912-13. "Documenti inediti di artisti napoletani del XVI e XVII secolo." *Archivio storico per le province napoletane* 37, no. 4:593-616; 38, no. 1:36-72, no. 2:232-59, no. 3:483-524, no. 4:578-610.

Dalbono, Carlo Tito. 1871. *Massimo, i suoi tempi e la sua scuola*. 3rd ed. Naples: Tipografia S. Pietro a Majella 31.

Dalbono 1876. *Nuova guida di Napoli e dintorni*. Naples: Vincenzo Morano.

Dalbono 1878. *Ritorni sull'arte antica napolitana*. Naples: Tipografia de' Classici Italiani.

D'Aloë, Stanislas. 1847. *Naples ses monuments et ses curiosités*. Naples: Imprimerie Virgile.

Daniels, Jeffrey. 1968. "Baroque Rat Race." *Art and Artists* 3, no. 3:44-48.

D'Argaville, Brian T. 1972. "Neapolitan Seicento Painting: Additions and Revisions." *The Burlington Magazine* 114:808-10.

Dargent, Georgette, and Jacques Thuillier. 1965. "Simon Vouet en Italie: Essai de catalogue critique." *Saggi e Memorie di Storia dell'Arte* 4:27-63.

Dayton [Ohio] 1953-54. *Flight*. Exhibition cosponsored by the Dayton Chamber of Commerce and the Dayton Art Institute.

De Blasiis, Giuseppe. 1876. "Relazione della pestilenza accaduta in Napoli l'anno 1656." *Archivio storico per le province napoletane* 1, no. 2:323-57.

De Dominici, Bernardo. 1742–43. *Vite de' pittori, scultori, ed architetti napoletani*. 3 vols. Naples: Stamperia del Ricciardi.

Dee, Elaine Evans, 1970: see New York 1970.

De Filippis, Felice. 1970. *Vite de' pittori, scultori ed architetti napoletani scritte da Bernardo de Dominici, pagine scelte ed annotate da Felice de Filippis*. Naples: E. D. A. R. T.

De la Tourette, Gilles, 1935: see Paris 1935.

De la Ville sur-Yllon, Ludovico. 1904. "Il palazzo dei duchi di Maddaloni alla Stella." *Napoli Nobilissima* 13, no. 10:145-47.

De Lellis, Carlo. 1654. *Parte seconda o'vero supplimento a Napoli sacra di D. Cesare d'Engenio Caracciolo*. Naples: Roberto Mollo.

De Lellis [1654-88] 1977. *Aggiunta alla Napoli Sacra del d'Engenio*. Edited by Francesco Aceto. Naples: Fiorentino Editrice S.p.A.

Di Liphart, E. 1910. *Les anciennes Ecoles de Peinture dans les Palais et Collections privées Russes*. Brussels: n. publ.

Delogu, Giuseppe. 1929. "Pittori italiani al Castello di Schleissheim." *Emporium* 69, no. 410:81-95.

Delogu 1931. *La pittura italiana del seicento*. Florence: Novissima Enciclopedia Monografica Illustrata.

Delogu 1937. "Le grandi collezioni, II: La Galleria Harrach a Vienna." *Emporium* 86, no. 513:405-14.

De Maio, Romeo. 1983. *Pittura e Controriforma a Napoli*. Rome-Bari: Editori Laterza.

De'Pietri, Francesco. 1634. *Dell'historia napoletana, scritta dal Signor Francesco de'Pietri*. Naples: Gio. Domenico Montanaro.

De'Pietri 1642. *I problemi accademici del signor Francesco de'Pietri l'impedito accademico otioso ove le più famose quistioni proposte nell'illustrissima accademia de gli otiosi di Napoli si spiegano*. Naples: Francesco Savio.

De Rinaldis, Aldo, 1909. *Bernardo Cavallino*. Naples: n. publ.

De Rinaldis 1911. *Guida Illustrata del Museo Nazionale di Napoli*. 2 vols. Naples: Richter & Co.

De Rinaldis 1917. "Bernardo Cavallino ed alcuni suoi nuovi quadri." *Rassegna d'Arte* 17:179-86.

De Rinaldis 1920a. "Bernardo Cavallino ed alcuni suoi quadri inediti." *Napoli Nobilissima*, n.s. 1, no. 1:1-7; no. 4:56-59.

De Rinaldis 1920b. "Massimo Stanzione al Prado." *Napoli Nobilissima*, n.s. 1, no. 3:44-46.

De Rinaldis 1921. *Bernardo Cavallino*. Rome: Società Editrice della Biblioteca d'Arte Illustrata.

De Rinaldis 1927 and 1928: see Naples 1927 and 1928.

De Rinaldis 1929. *La Pittura del Seicento dell'Italia meridionale*. Verona: Casa Editrice Apollo. (English ed.: *Neapolitan Painting of the Seicento*. New York: Harcourt, Brace and Co.)

De Rinaldis 1932. "Caravaggio and the Evolution of Neapolitan Painting in the Seventeenth Century." *Formes*, no. 30:324-26.

De Rinaldis 1932: see Rome 1932.

De Salas, Xavier. 1976. "Ultimas Adquisiciones del Museo del Prado, II - Otras Escuelas." *Goya*, no. 134:70.

De Salas 1978: see Madrid 1978.

Destito, Caterina. 1925. "Giambattista Vico nella vita domestica, la moglie - i figli - la casa, appunti e documenti." *Archivio storico per le province napoletane*, n.s. 11:227-98.

De Térey 1904: see Budapest 1904.

De Térey 1906: see Budapest 1906.

De Térey 1913: see Budapest 1913.

De Térey 1916: see Budapest 1916.

Detroit 1965. The Detroit Institute of Arts. *Art in Italy 1600-1700.* Exh. cat. by Robert Enggass, Bertina Suida Manning, Robert Manning, et al.

DeVito, Giuseppe. 1982. *Ricerche sul 600 napoletano: A. Falcone, B. Cavallino, A. de Bellis, M. Stanzione, N. Rossi.* Milan: privately published.

De Vito 1983. "The Author of the 'Duns Scotus' at Hampton Court." *The Burlington Magazine* 125:685.

De Vito et al. 1983. *Ricerche sul 600 napoletano. Saggi vari.* Milan: privately published.

De Vito 1984. *Ricerche sul 600 napoletano. Saggi vari in memoria di R. Causa.* Milan: forthcoming.

Di Carpegna, Nolfo, 1958: see Rome 1958.

Dizionario biografico degli italiani. 1960–. 25 vols. to date. Rome: Istituto della Enciclopedia Italiana.

Dizionario enciclopedico Bolaffi dei pittori e degli incisori italiani dall' XI al XX secolo. 1972–76. 11 vols. Turin: Giulio Bolaffi Editore.

Doria, Gino, 1954: see Naples 1954b.

Dorival, Bernard, 1979: see Brejon de Lavergnée 1979.

Dörnhofer, Friedrich, 1930: see Munich 1930.

D'Orsi, Mario. 1938. *Paolo Finoglio, pittore napoletano.* Bari: Alfredo Cressati Editore.

D'Ossat, Guglielmo de Angelis. 1949. "Nuovi acquisti delle gallerie dello stato; Bernardo Cavallino: Strage degli Innocenti." *Bollettino d'Arte* 34:191-92.

Dussler, Leopold. 1967. "Besprechung der Ulmer Schönfeld-Ausstellung." *Pantheon* 25:375-77.

Eberlein, C. N., 1776: see Brunswick 1776.

Edinburgh 1957. National Gallery of Scotland. *Pictures from Gosford House Lent by The Earl of Wemyss and March.* Exh. cat. by David Baxandall.

Eisenmann, Oscar, 1888: see Kassel 1888.

Ellis, Tony, 1962: see Barnard Castle 1962.

Ellis 1970: see Barnard Castle 1970.

Enciclopedia della pittura italiana. 1951. 3 vols. Edited by Ettore Camesaca and Ugo Galetti. Milan: Aldo Garzanti Editore.

Enggass, Robert. 1961. "Neapolitan Seicento in Sarasota." *The Burlington Magazine* 103:199-200.

Enggass 1965: see Detroit 1965.

Esterházy cat. 1835. *Catalog der Gemälde-Gallerie Seiner Durchlaucht des Fürsten Paul Esterházy von Galantha in Wien.* Vienna: n. publ.

Faldi, Italo, 1963: see Naples 1963.

Faraglia, Nunzio Federigo. 1882–83. "Le Memorie degli artisti napoletani pubblicate da Bernardo de Dominici, storico critico." *Archivio storico per le province napoletane* 7, no. 2:329-64; 8, no. 1:83-110, and no. 2:259-86.

Faraglia 1892. "Notizie di alcuni artisti che lavorarono nella chiesa di S. Martino sopra Napoli." *Archivio storico per le province napoletane* 17, no. 3:657-78.

Faraglia 1905. "Il testamento di Aniello Falcone." *Napoli Nobilissima* 14, no. 2:17-20.

Fastidio, Don. 1898. "Il pittore Bartolomeo Passante." *Napoli Nobilissima* 7, no. 6:96.

Fastidio 1906. "La quadreria del principe di Salerno." *Napoli Nobilissima* 15, no. 6:92-94.

Felton, Craig, 1982–83: see Fort Worth 1982–83.

Ferrari, Oreste, 1954: see Naples 1954a.

Ferrari 1960: see Naples 1960.

Ferrari 1961–62. "Seicento napoletano a Sarasota." *Napoli Nobilissima* 1, no. 6:235-38.

Ferrari 1963. Review of Luigi Salerno, *Salvator Rosa.* In *Napoli Nobilissima* 3, no. 4:162-64.

Ferrari 1969. "Pittura napoletana del Seicento e Settecento." *Storia dell'Arte,* 1-2:217.

Ferrari 1970. "Le arti figurative." *Storia di Napoli* 6, pt. 2:1223-1363.

Ferrari 1979. "Considerazioni sulle vicende artistiche a Napoli durante il viceregno austriaco (1707–1734)." *Storia dell'Arte* 35:11-27.

Ferrari, Oreste, and Giuseppe Scavizzi. 1966. *Luca Giordano.* 2 vols. Naples: Edizioni Scientifiche Italiane.

Filangieri, Gaetano. 1883. *Chiesa e convento di S. Lorenzo Maggiore in Napoli.* Naples: Tipografia dell'Accademia Reale delle Scienze.

Filangieri 1883–91. *Documenti per la storia, le arti e le industrie delle provincie napoletane.* 6 vols. Naples: Tipografia dell'Accademia Reale delle Scienze.

Filangieri di Candida, A. 1902. "La Galleria Nazionale di Napoli (documenti e ricerche)." *Le Gallerie nazionali italiane, notizie e documenti* 5:208-354.

Fink, August, 1932: see Brunswick 1932.

Fiorillo, J. D. 1801. *Geschichte der Künste und Wissenschaften.* 2 vols. Göttingen: F. G. Rosenbusch.

Flechsig, Eduard, 1922: see Brunswick 1922.

Florence 1922. Palazzo Pitti. *Mostra della pittura italiana del seicento e del settecento.* Exh. cat.

Florence 1952. Palazzo Vecchio. *Seconda Mostra nazionale delle opere d'arte recuperate.* Exh. cat. by Rodolfo Siviero.

Florence 1967. Gabinetto Disegni e Stampe degli Uffizi. *Cento disegni napoletani sec. XVI-XVIII.* Exh. cat. by Walter Vitzthum.

Florence 1970. Palazzo Pitti. *Caravaggio e Caravaggeschi nelle Gallerie di Firenze.* Exh. cat. edited by E. Borea.

Florence 1979. *Gli Uffizi. Catalogo Generale.* Coll. cat. Florence: Centro Di.

Florence 1980. *La Fondazione Roberto Longhi.* Coll. cat. Milan: Editoriale Electa.

Florence 1983. Gabinetto Disegni e Stampe degli Uffizi. *Disegni di Giovanni Lanfranco (1582–1647).* Exh. cat. by Erich Schleier.

F. N. A. 1968. "Bernardo Cavallino: 'Ratto d'Europa.'" *Bollettino d'Arte* 53:160.

Fort Worth [Texas] 1962. Fort Worth Art Center. *1550–1660: A Century of Masters from the Collection of Walter P. Chrysler Jr.* (Also at Philbrook Art Center, Tulsa, 1962–63, and University of Texas, Austin, 1963.) Exh. cat.

Fort Worth 1982–83. Kimbell Art Museum. *Jusepe de Ribera, lo Spagnoletto, 1591–1652.* Exh. cat. by Craig Felton and William B. Jordan.

Frangipane, A., 1914: see Chimirri 1914.

Frankfurter, Alfred M. 1946. "Supplement to the Kress Collection." *Art News* 44, no. 20:23-84.

Fredericksen, Burton B., and Federico Zeri. 1972. *Census of Pre-Nineteenth-Century Italian Paintings in North American Public Collections.* Cambridge, Mass.: Harvard University Press.

Galante, Gennaro Aspreno. 1872. *Guida sacra della città di Napoli*. Naples: Stamperia del Fibreno.

Galante, Lucio. 1975. "Giovanni Andrea Coppola, Francesco Fracanzano e altri fatti di pittura in Puglia (nella prima metà del Seicento)." *Annali della Scuola Normale Superiore di Pisa. Classe di lettere e filosofia* 5, no. 4:1491-1510.

Galanti, Giuseppe Maria. 1792. *Breve descrizione della città di Napoli e del suo contorno*. Naples: Società del Gabinetto Letterario.

Galanti 1829. *Napoli e contorni*. Naples: Borel & Co.

Gamba, Carlo. 1919. "Sur un dipinto di Bernardo Cavallino." *Bollettino d'Arte* 13, suppl. 6, no. 1:30-31.

Gamulin, Grgo. 1972. "Contributo ai napoletani." *Commentari* n. s. 23:292-98.

Garrard, Mary D. 1980. "Artemisia Gentileschi's Self-Portrait as the Allegory of Painting." *The Art Bulletin* 62:97-112.

Gaya Nuño, J. A. 1958. *La Pintura española fuera de España*. Madrid: Espasa-Calpe.

Genoa 1967. *La Galleria del Palazzo Durazzo Pallavicini a Genova*. Coll. cat. by Piero Torriti.

Giannone, Onofrio [1773] 1941. *Giunte sulle vite de'pittori napoletani*. Edited by Ottavio Morisani. Naples: R. Deputazione di Storia Patria.

Giglioli, Odoardo H. 1922. "Le Mostre d'arte antica a Firenze." *Rassegna d'arte antica e moderna* 9:201-31.

Gilbert, Creighton, 1961: see Sarasota 1961.

Goering, Max. 1936. *Italienische Malerei des siebzehnten und achtzehnten Jahrhunderts*. Berlin: Kurt Wolff Verlag.

The Golden Legend of Jacobus de Voragine. 1969. Translated by Granger Ryan and Helmut Ripperger. New York: Arno Press.

Golzio, Vincenzo. 1955. *Il Seicento e il Settecento*. 2 vols. Storia Universale dell'Arte, vol. 5. Turin: Unione Tipografico, Editrice Torinese.

González-Palacios, Alvar. 1973. "Letter from Italy: New Pleasures at the Pitti." *Apollo* 97:528-29.

Grautoff, Otto, 1928: see Pevsner, Nikolaus, 1928.

Gregori, Mina. 1972. "Note su Orazio Riminaldi e i suoi rapporti con l'ambiente romano." *Paragone* 23, no. 269:35-66.

Gregori 1980. *La Fondazione Roberto Longhi a Firenze*. Milan: Gruppo Editoriale Electa.

Grieco, Michele. 1963. *Francesco Guarini da Solofra nella pittura napoletana del '600*. Avellino: Tipografia Pergola.

Gronau, Georg, 1913: see Kassel 1913.

Gronau 1929: see Kassel 1929.

Gronau 1969: see Kassel 1969.

Grossi, Giovanni Battista Gennaro, et al. 1813. *Biografia degli uomini illustri del regno di Napoli*. Naples: Nicola Gerrasi Calcografo.

Grzimek, Günther. 1966. *Katalog der Sammlung der Familie Grzimek*. Ravensburg: n. publ.

Hall, James. 1979. *Dictionary of Subjects and Symbols in Art*. Rev. ed. New York and London: Harper & Row.

Harrach cat. 1856. *Verzeichniss der Gräflich Harrach'schen Gemälde Gallerie zu Wien*. Coll. cat. by Anton Gruss.

Harrach cat. 1897. *Paintings Gallery Count Harrach*. Vienna: n. publ.

Harrach cat. 1926. *Katalog der Erlaucht Gräflich Harrach'schen Gemäldegalerie in Wien*. Coll. cat. by Hermann Ritschl.

Harrach cat. 1960. *Katalog der Graf Harrach'schen Gemäldegalerie*. Coll. cat. by Günther Heinz.

Harris, Enriqueta. 1982. *Velázquez*. Oxford: Phaidon Press; Ithaca, NY: Cornell University Press.

Hartford [Connecticut] 1958. Wadsworth Atheneum. *A. Everett Austin Jr., a Director's Taste and Achievement*. (Also at John and Mable Ringling Museum of Art, Sarasota, Fla.) Exh. cat.

Haskell, Francis. 1963 *or* 1971. *Patrons and Painters*. London: Chatto & Windus, 1963. Reprint. New York, Evanston, San Francisco, London: Harper & Row, 1971.

Heinz, Günther, 1960: see Harrach cat. 1960.

Hermanin, Federico. 1910. "Gli acquisti della Galleria Nazionale d'Arte Antica in Roma." *Bollettino d'Arte* 4:225-35.

Hermanin 1911. "Uber einige unedierte Bilder des neapolitaner Malers Bernardo Cavallino." *Monatshefte für Kunstwissenschaft* 4:183-88.

Hermanin 1912. "Nuovi acquisti della Galleria Nazionale d'Arte Antica a Palazzo Corsini in Roma." *Bollettino d'Arte* 6:369-82.

Hermanin 1924–25. "Acquisti della Regia Galleria d'Arte Antica in Roma." *Bollettino d'Arte*, n. s. 4:3-10.

Hernández Perera, Jesús. 1955. "En Torno a Bartolomé Passante." *Archivo Español de Arte* 28:266-73.

Hernández Perera 1957. "Bartolomé Bassante y el 'Maestro del Anuncio a los Pastores'." *Archivo Español de Arte* 30:211-22.

Herzog, Erich, 1969: see Kassel 1969.

Hibbard, Howard. 1983. *Caravaggio*. New York: Harper & Row.

Hibbard, Howard, and Milton Lewine. 1965. "Seicento at Detroit." *The Burlington Magazine* 107:370-72.

Hollstein, F. W. H. 1949-83. *Dutch and Flemish Etchings, Engravings, and Woodcuts ca. 1450–1700*. 27 vols. Amsterdam: Menno Hertzberger.

Houston [Texas] 1953. *The Samuel H. Kress Collection at the Museum of Fine Arts, Houston*. Coll. cat. by Wilhelm Suida.

Houston 1981. *The Museum of Fine Arts, Houston: A Guide to the Collection*.

Howe, Thomas Carr. 1941. "San Francisco Explores an Era Rediscovered by Modern Taste." *Art News* 40:28-29.

The Illustrated Bartsch. 1978–. Vol. 1–. Edited by Walter L. Strauss. New York: Abaris Books.

Ivanoff, Nicola. 1959. *I disegni italiani del Seicento: scuole veneta, lombarda, ligure, napoletana*. Venice: Sodalizio del Libro.

Jordan, William B., 1982–83: see Fort Worth 1982–83.

Juynboll, W. R. 1960. "Bernardo Cavallino." *Bulletin Museum Boymans-van Beuningen* 11, no. 3:82-91.

Kassel 1783. *Verzeichnis der Hochfürstlich-Hessischen Gemähldesammlung in Cassel*. Coll. cat. by Simon Causid.

Kassel 1819. *Versuch eines Verzeichnisses der Kurfürstlich Hessischen Gemäldesammlung*. Coll. cat. by Ernst Friedrich Ferdinand Robert.

Kassel 1830. *Verzeichniss der Kurfürstlichen Gemähde-Sammlung*. Coll. cat. by Ernst Friedrich Ferdinand Robert.

Kassel 1888. *Katalog der Königlichen Gemähde-Galerie zu Cassel, mit einem Nachwort von C. Alhard von Drach*. Coll. cat. by Oscar Eisenmann.

Kassel 1913. *Katalog der Königlichen Gemäldegalerie zu Cassel*. Coll. cat. by Georg Gronau.

Kassel 1929. *Katalog der Staatlichen Gemäldegalerie zu Kassel.* 2d ed. Coll. cat. by Georg Gronau and Kurt Luthmer.

Kassel 1958. *Katalog der Staatlichen Gemäldegalerie zu Kassel.* Coll. cat. by Hans Vogel.

Kassel 1969. *Die Gemäldegalerie der Staatlichen Kunstsammlungen Kassel.* Coll. cat. by Erich Herzog and Georg Gronau.

Kassel 1975. *Staatliche Kunstsammlungen Kassel. Gemäldegalerie Alte Meister, Schloss Wilhelmshöhe.* Coll. cat. by Jürgen Lehmann.

Kassel 1980. *Staatliche Kunstsammlungen Kassel: Italienische, französische und spanische Gemälde des 16. bis 18. Jahrhunderts.* Coll. cat. by Jürgen Lehmann.

Kaufmann, Thomas DaCosta. 1970. "Esther before Ahasuerus." *The Metropolitan Museum of The Art Bulletin*, n. s. 29, no. 4:165-69.

Kindlers Malerei Lexikon. 1964–71. 6 vols. Zurich: Kindler Verlag.

Kubler, George. 1965. "Vicente Carducho's Allegories of Painting." *The Art Bulletin* 47:339-445.

Kubler, George, and Martin Soria. 1959. *Art and Architecture in Spain and Portugal and Their American Dominions 1500–1800.* The Pelican History of Art. Edited by Nikolaus Pevsner. Baltimore: Penguin Books.

Labrot, Gérard. 1979. *Baroni in città: residenze e comportamenti dell'aristocrazia napoletana, 1530–1734.* Translated by Renato Ruotolo. Naples: Società Editrice Napoletana.

Labrot, Gérard, and Renato Ruotolo. 1980. "Pour une étude historique de la commande aristocratique dans le royaume de Naples espagnol." *Revue historique* 264, no. 1:25-48.

Langdon, Helen, 1973: see London 1973.

Lanzi, Luigi. 1792. *La storia pittorica della Italia inferiore, o sia delle scuole fiorentina, senese, romana, napoletana.* 2 vols. Florence: Antonio Giuseppe Pagani.

Larousse Dictionary of Painters. 1981. London and New York: Hamlyn.

Lattuada, Riccardo. 1982. "Opere di Francesco Guarino a Campobasso." *Prospettiva*, no. 31 (October):50-69.

Lee, Rensselaer W. [1940] 1967. *Ut pictura poesis: The Humanistic Theory of Painting.* Reprint. New York: W. W. Norton.

Lehmann, Jürgen, 1975: see Kassel 1975.

Lehmann 1980: see Kassel 1980.

Levey, Michael, 1971: see London 1971.

Lewine, Milton, 1965: see Hibbard, Howard, 1965.

Liebmann, Michael J. 1968. "A Signed Picture by Bernardo Cavallino in the Pushkin Museum, Moscow." *The Burlington Magazine* 110:456-59.

Lindsay, David, 1931: see London 1931.

Liverpool 1885. Walker Art Gallery. *Descriptive Catalogue of the Permanent Collection of Pictures.*

Liverpool 1955. Walker Art Gallery. *Cleaned Pictures. An Exhibition of Pictures from the Walker Art Gallery Liverpool.* Exh. cat.

Liverpool 1977. Walker Art Gallery. *Foreign Catalogue.* 2 vols. Coll. cat.

London 1901. National Gallery Catalogues. *Descriptive and Historical Catalogue of the Pictures in The National Gallery. Foreign Schools.* Coll. cat.

London 1929. National Gallery Catalogues. *Italian Schools.* Coll. cat.

London 1930. Royal Academy of Arts, Burlington House. *Exhibition of Italian Art 1200-1900.* Exh. cat.

London 1931. *A Commemorative Catalogue of the Exhibition of Italian Art Held in the Galleries of the Royal Academy, Burlington House, London, January-March 1930.* 2 vols. Cat. by David Lindsay and Kenneth Clark, with Ettore Modigliani. Oxford: Oxford University Press; London: Humphrey Milford.

London 1937. National Gallery Catalogues. *Italian Schools* [Supplement]. Coll. cat.

London 1938. Royal Academy of Arts, Burlington House. *Exhibition of 17th-Century Art in Europe.* Exh. cat.

London 1949. The Tate Gallery. *Art Treasures from Vienna.* Exh. cat.

London 1950–51. Royal Academy of Arts. *Exhibition of Works by Holbein and Other Masters.* Exh. cat.

London 1952a. Hazlitt Gallery. *Vasari to Tiepolo.* Exh. cat.

London 1952b, 1970. National Gallery Catalogues. *The Spanish School.* Coll. cat. by Neil MacLaren; 2d ed., 1970, revised by Allan Braham.

London 1958. National Gallery Catalogues. *Summary Catalogue.* Coll. cat.

London 1959. Colnaghi & Co. *Paintings by Old Masters.* Exh. cat.

London 1960. Royal Academy of Arts. *Italian Art and Britain.* Exh. cat. by Denis Mahon, et al.

London 1963. National Gallery. *Acquisitions, 1953–62.* Exh. cat.

London 1966. Hazlitt Gallery. *Italian and the Italianate.* Exh. cat.

London 1967. Heim Gallery. *Baroque Sketches, Drawings, and Sculptures.* Exh. cat.

London 1968. Hazlitt Gallery. *17th- and 18th-Century Paintings: 18 Paintings.* Exh. cat.

London 1970. Heim Gallery. *Paintings and Sculptures of the Baroque.* Exh. cat.

London 1971. National Gallery Catalogues. *The Seventeenth- and Eighteenth-Century Italian Schools.* Coll. cat. by Michael Levey.

London 1973a. Hayward Gallery. *Salvator Rosa.* Exh. cat. by Helen Langdon et al.

London 1973b. National Gallery. *The National Gallery, London. Illustrated General Catalogue.* Coll. cat.

London 1978. Artemis Fine Arts, Ltd. *Selections of Italian Paintings 15th–18th Century.* Exh. cat.

London 1979. Colnaghi & Co. *Old Master Paintings and Drawings.* Exh. cat.

London 1982. Royal Academy of Arts. *Painting in Naples 1606–1705: From Caravaggio to Giordano.* Exh. cat. edited by Clovis Whitfield and Jane Martineau.

London and Washington 1982–83: see London 1982.

Longhi, Roberto. 1914. Review of Mayer, *Geschichte der Spanischen Malerei.* In *L'Arte* 17:317-19.

Longhi 1915. "Battistello." *L'Arte* 18:58-75, 120-37.

Longhi 1916a. "Gentileschi, padre e figlia," *L'Arte* 19:245-314.

Longhi 1916b. Review of Chimirri and Frangipane, *Mattia Preti.* In *L'Arte* 19:370-71.

Longhi 1918a. Review of Ruffo, "Galleria Ruffo . . ." In *L'Arte* 21: 140-41.

Longhi 1918b. Review of de Rinaldis, "Bernardo Cavallino ed alcuni suoi nuovi quadri." In *L'Arte* 21:142.

Longhi 1920a. Review of Gamba, "Sur un dipinto di Bernardo Cavallino." In *L'Arte* 23:89-90.

Longhi 1920b. Review of de Rinaldis, "Bernardo Cavallino ed alcuni suoi quadri inediti." In *L'Arte* 23:90-91, 153.

Longhi 1920c. "Una Mosca 'Cavallina'." *L'Arte* 23:155-56.

Longhi 1927. "Di Gaspare Traversi." *Vita Artistica* 2, nos. 8-9:145-67.

Longhi 1943. "Ultimi studi sul Caravaggio e la sua cerchia." *Proporzioni* 1:5-63.

Longhi 1950. "Velázquez 1630: 'La rissa all'ambasciata di Spagna'." *Paragone* 1, no. 1:28-34.

Longhi 1959. "Presenze alla Sala Regia." *Paragone* 9, no. 117:29-38.

Longhi 1961. *Scritti Giovanili 1912–1922*. 2 vols. Florence: Sansoni.

Longhi 1969. "G. B. Spinelli e i naturalisti napoletani del Seicento." *Paragone* 20, no. 227:42-52.

Longhi 1979. *Disegno della pittura italiana*. 2 vols. Edited by Carlo Volpe. Florence: Sansoni.

López-Rey, José. 1963. *Velázquez: A Catalogue Raisonné of His Oeuvre*. London: Faber & Faber.

Lublin [Poland] 1921. *Muzeum Lubelskie Wystawa sztuki i starożytności w Lublinie* [Exhibition of Art and Antiquities in Lublin].

Lucie-Smith, E. 1968. "17th & 18th Century Paintings." *Arts Review* 20, no. 11:323-30.

Lurie, Ann Tzeutschler. 1969. "Bernardo Cavallino: Adoration of the Shepherds." *The Cleveland Museum of Art Bulletin* 56 (April):136-50.

Luthmer, Kurt, 1929: see Kassel 1929.

MacLaren, Neil, 1952: see London 1952b.

Madrid 1945. *Museo del Prado. Catalogo de los Cuadros*. Coll. cat.

Madrid 1951. *Guia del Museo Lázaro Galdiano*. Guide by José Camón Aznar. Madrid: Fundacion "Lázaro Galdiano."

Madrid 1954. *Guia del Museo Lázaro Galdiano*. 2d ed. Guide by José Camón Aznar.

Madrid 1963. *Museo del Prado. Catalogo de las Pinturas*. Coll. cat.

Madrid 1970. Casón del Buen Retiro. *Pintura italiana del siglo XVII*. Exh. cat. by Alfonso E. Pérez Sánchez.

Madrid 1972. *Museo del Prado. Catalogo de las Pinturas*. Coll. cat.

Madrid 1978. *Museo del Prado: Adquisiciones de 1969 a 1977*. Cat. by Xavier de Salas. Madrid: Patronato Nacional de Museos.

Mahon, Denis, 1960: see London 1960.

Mâle, Emile. 1932. *L'Art Religieux après de Concile de Trent*. Paris: Librairie Armand Colin.

Manning, Bertina S., 1956: see Portland 1956.

Manning, Bertina Suida, 1965: see Suida Manning.

Manning, Robert L., 1962: see New York 1962.

Manning, R., 1965: see Detroit 1965.

Manning, R., 1969: see New York 1969.

Manning, R., 1970: see New York 1970.

Marabottini, Alessandro, 1956: see Rome 1956.

Marangoni, Matteo. 1927. "Un Domenichino di meno e un Vaccaro di più." In *Arte barocca: revisioni critiche*. Florence: Vallecchi Editore.

Marcheix, Lucien [1897?]. *Un Parisien à Rome et à Naples en 1632, d'après un manuscrit inédit de J.-J. Bouchard*. Paris: Ernest Leroux.

Mariani, Valerio. 1956. *La raccolta d'arte*. Naples: Istituto Suor Orsola Benincasa. Fondazione Pagliara.

Mariette, Pierre Jean. 1853–62. *Abecedario de P. J. Mariette et autres notes inédites de cet amateur sur les arts et les artistes*. Archives de l'art français, vols. 2, 4, 6, 8, 10, 12. Paris: J.-B. Dumoulin.

Marini, Maurizio. 1974. *Pittori a Napoli 1610–1656. Contributi e schede*. Rome: Bulzoni Editore S. R. L.

Martineau, Jane, 1982: see London 1982.

Martin-Méry, Gilberte, 1959: see Bordeaux 1959.

Mascherpa, Giorgio. 1965. "Maestri italiani del '600 e '700: una mostra nella nuova sede della Relarte." *Arte Figurativa Antica e Moderna* 13:27-37.

Masciotta, Michelangelo. 1942. "La bella maniera del Cavallino." *Primato* 3:147-48.

Mauceri, Enrico. 1921-22. "Giovan Battista Quagliata." *Bollettino d'Arte*, n.s. 1:381-85.

Mayer, August L. 1908. "Die spanischen Gemälde im Museum der schönen Künste zu Budapest." *Monatshefte für Kunstwissenschaft* 1, pt. 1:517-22.

Mayer 1910. "Pablo Legote." *Repertorium für Kunstwissenschaft* 33:398-99.

Mayer 1911. *Die Sevillaner Malerschule*. Leipzig: Klinkhardt & Biermann.

Mayer [1913] 1922. *Geschichte der spanischen Malerei*. 2d ed. Leipzig: Klinkhardt & Biermann.

Mayer 1923. *Jusepe de Ribera (Lo Spagnoletto)*. 2d ed. Leipzig: K. W. Hiersemann.

McComb, Arthur Kilgore. 1934. *The Baroque Painters of Italy*. Cambridge, Mass.: Harvard University Press.

McGraw-Hill Dictionary of Art. 1969. 5 vols. Edited by Bernard S. Myers. London: McGraw-Hill.

McTavish, David, 1981–82: see Toronto 1981–82.

Meier, P. J., 1902: see Brunswick 1902.

Milan 1959. *Tesori della Pinacoteca di Brera*. Coll. cat. by Mario Monteverdi.

Milan 1964. Relarte. *Maestri italiani del '600 e '700*. Exh. cat.

Milan 1967. Manzoni Galleria d'Arte. *33 Opere del Seicento*. Exh. cat. by Gilberto Algranti and Giovanni Testori.

Milan 1969 (?). *Seicento: Arte "moderna," arte di domani*. Exh. cat. by Gilberto Algranti.

Milan 1970. *Pinacoteca di Brera*. Musei del mondo. Milan: Arnoldo Mondadori.

Milan 1972. *Il Museo Poldi Pezzoli*. Coll. cat. by Guida Gregorietti, et al. *Pittura e Scultura* section by Franco Russoli. Milan: Cassa di risparmio delle provincie Lombardie.

Milan 1973. Palazzo Vigoni-Mainoni. *Selezione 1973*. Exh. cat. by Gilberto Algranti.

Milan 1977. Pinacoteca di Brera. *Catalogo della Pinacoteca di Brera*. Coll. cat. by Ettore Modigliani.

Milan 1978. *Il Museo Poldi Pezzoli in Milano. Guida per il Visitatore*. Guide by Franco Russoli.

Milan 1980. *Donazioni al Museo Poldi Pezzoli*. Coll. cat. by M. T. Balboni and A. Mottola Molfino.

Milan 1982. *Museo Poldi Pezzoli.* I: *Dipinti.* Coll. cat. Milan: Gruppo Editoriale Electa.

Milicua, José. 1954 . "Inéditos de Bernardo Cavallino." *Goya,* no. 2:68-73.

Milicua 1970. "Pintura italiana del siglo XVII en el Casón del Buen Retiro." *Goya,* no. 97:2-10.

Minieri Riccio, Camillo. 1844. *Memorie storiche degli scrittori nati nel regno di Napoli.* Naples: n. publ.

Minieri Riccio 1879–80. "Cenno storico delle accademie fiorite nella città di Napoli." *Archivio storico per le province napoletane* 4, no. 1:163-78; no. 2:379-94; no. 3:519-36; vol. 5 (1880), no. 1:131-57; no. 2:349-73; no. 3:578-612.

Mitidieri, Salvatore. 1913. "Mattia Preti detto il 'Cavalier Calabresi.' " *L'Arte* 16:428-50.

Modigliani, Ettore, 1977: see Milan 1977.

Moir, Alfred. 1967. *The Italian Followers of Caravaggio.* 2 vols. Cambridge, Mass.: Harvard University Press.

Moir 1974: see Santa Barbara 1974.

Moir 1976. *Caravaggio and His Copyists.* New York: New York University Press.

Molajoli, Bruno. 1948. *Musei ed opere d'arte di Napoli attraverso la guerra.* Naples: Soprintendenza alle Gallerie, ed. Stab. Tip. G. Montanino.

Molajoli 1953: see Naples 1953.

Molajoli 1957: see Naples 1957.

Molajoli 1958: see Naples 1958.

Molajoli 1961: see Naples 1961.

Molajoli 1964: see Naples 1964.

Monbeig-Goguel, Catherine, 1967: see Paris 1967b.

Monteverdi, Mario, 1959: see Milan 1959.

Montini, Renzo U. 1952. *Profilo storico dell'arte in Campania.* Naples: Fausto Fiorentino Libraio.

Morisani, Ottavio. 1941. "L'Edizione napoletana dell'Abecedario dell'Orlandi e l'aggiunta di Antonio Roviglione." *Rassegna Storica Napoletana,* n.s. 2, no. 1:19-56.

Mormone, Raffaele. 1961–62. "Domenico Antonio Vaccaro architetto, II: Il palazzo Tarsia." *Napoli Nobilissima* 1, no. 6:216-27.

Moschini, Vittorio. 1922. "La pittura italiana del Seicento e del Settecento alla mostra di Firenze." *La Cultura* 1, no. 10:448-54.

Moscow 1918. *Catalogue of the First Exhibition of the National Museum Fund.* Exh. location unknown.

Moscow 1948, 1957, 1961. *Catalogues of the Pushkin Museum.* Coll. cats.

Mottola Molfino, A., 1980: see Milan 1980.

Müller, Hermann Alexander, and Hans Wolfgang Singer. 1895–1901. *Allgemeines Künstlerlexicon.* 5 vols. Frankfurt: Rütten and Loening.

Munich 1930. *Katalog der Alteren Pinakothek zu München.* Coll. cat. by Friedrich Dörnhofer.

Munich 1938. *Alte Pinakothek.* 19th ed. Coll. cat. Munich: Bayerische Staatsgemäldesammlungen.

Munich 1983. *Alte Pinakothek München. Erläuterungen zu den ausgestellten Gemälden.* Munich: Bayerische Staatsgemäldesammlungen.

Musto, Adolfo. 1920. Review of Sestieri, "Cenni sullo svolgimento dell'arte di Bernardo Cavallino." In *Napoli Nobilissima,* n. s. 1, nos. 11-12:180.

Musto 1921a. "Un quadro di Bernardo Cavallino." *Napoli Nobilissima,* n. s. 2, nos. 3-4:64.

Musto 1921b. Review of Venturi, "Bernardo Cavallino nella Galleria Nazionale di Stoccolma e nella raccolta Harrach di Vienna." In *Napoli Nobilissima,* n. s. 2, nos. 9-10:160.

Müvészeti Lexikon. 1981-84. 4 vols. 3d ed. Edited by Anna Zádor and Istvan Genthon. Budapest: Akadémiai Kiadó.

Nagler, G. K. 1835–52. *Neues allgemeines Künstlerlexicon.* 22 vols. Munich: E. A. Fleischmann.

Nagler 1858–79. *Die Monogrammisten.* 5 vols. Munich and Leipzig: G. Hirth.

Naples 1846. *Le Mystagogue: Guide Général du Musée Royal Bourbon.* Guide by Bernard Quaranta. Naples: Nicolas Fabricatore.

Naples 1877. *Esposizione nazionale di belle arti in Napoli.* Exh. cat. by Demetrio Salazaro, et al.

Naples 1927 and 1928. *Pinacoteca del Museo Nazionale di Napoli.* Coll. cats. by Aldo de Rinaldis.

Naples 1932. *La pinacoteca del Museo Nazionale di Napoli.* Coll. cat. by A. O. Quintavalle.

Naples 1938. Castel Nuovo. *La mostra della pittura napoletana dei secoli XVII - XVIII - XIX.* Exh. cat. by Sergio Ortolani, et al.

Naples 1940. *La Pinacothèque du Musée Nationale de Naples.* Coll. cat. by A. O. Quintavalle. Translated by Isis C. Labate.

Naples 1953. Banco di Napoli. *Opere d'arte del Banco di Napoli.* Coll. cat.

Naples 1953–54. Museo di San Martino. *III Mostra di restauri.* Exh. cat. by Raffaello Causa.

Naples 1954a. Castel Nuovo. *La Madonna nella pittura del '600 a Napoli.* Exh. cat. by Raffaello Causa and Oreste Ferrari.

Naples 1954b. Palazzo Reale. *Mostra del ritratto storico napoletano.* Exh. cat. by Gino Doria and Ferdinando Bologna.

Naples 1957. *Notizie su Capodimonte.* Coll. cat. by Bruno Molajoli.

Naples 1958. *Notizie su Capodimonte.* Coll. cat. by Bruno Molajoli.

Naples 1960. Palazzo Reale. *IV Mostra di restauri.* Exh. cat. by Raffaello Causa, Oreste Ferrari, and Marina Picone.

Naples 1961. *Il Museo di Capodimonte.* Coll. cat. by Bruno Molajoli.

Naples 1963. Palazzo Reale. *Caravaggio e Caravaggeschi.* (Also at Athens, 1962-63.) Exh. cat. by Italo Faldi, Raffaello Causa, and Giuseppe Scavizzi.

Naples 1964. *Notizie su Capodimonte.* Coll. cat. by Bruno Molajoli.

Naples 1966-67. Museo di Capodimonte. *Disegni napoletani del Sei e del Settecento nel Museo di Capodimonte.* Exh. cat. by Walter Vitzthum.

Naples 1967. Palazzo Reale. *Arte Francese a Napoli.* (Also at University of Grenoble, France.) Exh. cat.

Naples 1972. *Il secolo d'oro della pittura napoletana.* Exh. cat. by Raffaello Causa and Nicola Spinosa.

Naples 1975. Museo Pignatelli Cortes. *Acquisitioni 1960–1975.* Exh. cat. edited by Nicola Spinosa. Intro. by Raffaello Causa.

Naples 1977. Museo di Capodimonte. *Mostra didattica di Carlo Sellitto, primo caravaggesco napoletano.* Exh. cat. edited by Ferdinando Bologna and Raffaello Causa.

Naples 1982. *Le Collezioni del Museo di Capodimonte*. Coll. cat. by Raffaello Causa. Milan: Touring Club Italiano.

Nappi, Eduardo. 1980. *Aspetti della società e dell'economia napoletana durante la peste del 1656 dai documenti dell'Archivio Storico del Banco di Napoli*. Naples: Banco di Napoli.

Nebbia, Ugo. 1946. *La Pittura italiana del Seicento*. Novara: Istituto Geografico de Agostini.

Negri Arnoldi, F., 1969: see Trapani 1969.

Neumann, Jaromír, 1967: see Olomouc 1967.

Neumann 1969. "Neznámá díla Italských mistrů v olomouci" [Unknown works of Italian masters in Olomouc]. *Uměni* 18, no. 1: 1-49.

Neumann 1971. "Unbekannte Werke italienischer Barockmeister in Olomouc." Pp. 233-41 in *Studi di Storia dell'Arte in onore di Antonio Morassi*. Venice: Alfieri.

Newcome, Mary. 1978. "A Castiglione-Leone Problem." *Master Drawings* 16, no. 2:163-72.

New York 1940. The Museum of Modern Art. *Italian Masters, Lent by the Royal Italian Government*. Exh. cat.

New York 1946. Durlacher Brothers. *Caravaggio and the Caravaggisti*. Exh. cat.

New York 1962. Finch College Museum of Art. *A Loan Exhibition of Neapolitan Masters of the Seventeenth and Eighteenth Centuries*. Exh. cat. by Robert L. Manning.

New York 1967a. The Metropolitan Museum of Art and The Pierpont Morgan Library. *Drawings from New York Collections II: The Seventeenth Century in Italy*. Exh. cat. by Felice Stampfle and Jacob Bean.

New York 1967b. M. Knoedler and Company. *Masters of the Loaded Brush: Oil Sketches from Rubens to Tiepolo*. Exh. cat.

New York 1969. Finch College Museum of Art. *In the Shadow of Vesuvius: Neapolitan Drawings from the Collection of János Scholz*. Exh. cat. by Robert L. Manning and János Scholz.

New York 1970. Finch College Museum of Art. *The Two Sicilies: Drawings from the Cooper-Hewitt Museum*. Exh. cat. by Robert L. Manning and Elaine Evans Dee.

New York 1979. The Metropolitan Museum of Art. *17th-Century Drawings in the Metropolitan Museum of Art*. Coll. cat. by Jacob Bean.

New York 1980. The Metropolitan Museum of Art. *European Paintings in the Metropolitan Museum of Art by Artists Born in or before 1865: A Summary Catalogue*. 3 vols. Coll. cat. by Katharine Baetjer.

New York 1981. Fine Arts International in collaboration with Knoedler Gallery. *Exhibition of Old Masters*.

Nicolson, Benedict. 1962. "Neapolitan Art at the Bowes Museum." *The Burlington Magazine* 104:317.

Nicolson 1963. "New National Gallery Acquisitions." *The Burlington Magazine* 105:295.

Nicolson 1978. "The Vitale Bloch Bequest to Rotterdam." *The Burlington Magazine* 120:197.

Nicolson 1979. *The International Caravaggesque Movement: Lists of Pictures by Caravaggio and His Followers throughout Europe from 1590 to 1650*. Oxford: Phaidon Press.

Nobile, Gaetano. 1855-57. *Un mese a Napoli. Descrizione della città di Napoli e delle sue vicinanze divisa in XXX giornate*. 3 vols. Naples: Stabilimento Tipografico di Gaetano Nobile.

Norfolk [Virginia] 1967-68. The Chrysler Museum. *Italian Renaissance and Baroque Paintings from the Collections of Walter P. Chrysler, Jr*. Exh. cat.

Norfolk 1982. The Chrysler Museum. *Selections from the Permanent Collection*. Coll. cat.

Northampton [Massachusetts] 1947. Smith College Museum of Art. *Italian Baroque Painting*. (Mimeographed checklist.)

Novelli, Magda. 1974. "Agostino Beltrano, uno 'stanzionesco' da riabilitare." *Paragone* 25, no. 287:67-82.

Novelli Radice, Magda. 1974. "Precisazioni cronologiche su Massimo Stanzione." *Campania Sacra*, no. 5:98-103.

Novelli Radice 1976. "Contributi alla conoscenza di Andrea e Onofrio de Lione." *Napoli Nobilissima* 15, nos. 5-6:162-69.

Novelli Radice 1978. "Appunti per il pittore Nicolò de Simone." *Napoli Nobilissima* 17, no. 1:21-29.

Novelli Radice 1980. "Inediti di Nunzio Russo." *Napoli Nobilissima* 19, nos. 5-6:185-98.

Nugent, Margherita. 1925-30. *Alla mostra della pittura italiana del '600 e '700: note e impressioni*. 2 vols. San Casciano Val di Pesa: Società Editrice Toscana.

Oertel, Robert. 1938. "Neapolitanische Malerei des 17.-19. Jahrhunderts: Ausstellung im Castel Nuovo in Neapel." *Pantheon* 22:225-32.

Ojetti, Ugo. 1930. *Bello e Brutto*. Milan: Fratelli Treves.

Ojetti, Ugo, Luigi Dami, and Nello Tarchiani. 1924. *La Pittura italiana del Seicento e del Settecento alla mostra di Palazzo Pitti*. Milan and Rome: Casa Editrice d'Arte Bestetti e Tumminelli.

Olomouc [Czechoslovakia] 1967. Oblastní Galerie. *Mistrovská díla starého umění v Olomoucí*. Exh. cat. by Jaromír Neumann and Eduard Safařík.

Orlandi, Pellegrino Antonio. 1734. *L'Abecedario pittorico dall'autore ristampato, corretto, ed accresciuto di molti professori, e di altre notizie*. Reissued by Niccolò Parrino. Naples: n. publ.

Orlandi 1753. *Abecedario pittorico del M. R. P. Pellegrino Antonio Orlandi bolognese contenente le notizie de' professori di pittura, scoltura, ed architettura in questa edizione corretto e notabilmente di nuove notizie accresciuto da Pietro Guarienti*. Venice: Giambattista Pasquali.

Ortolani, Sergio. 1922. "Cavalliniana (10 Dicembre 1622-10 Dicembre 1922)." *L'Arte* 25:190-99.

Ortolani 1938. "La Pittura napoletana dal Seicento all'Ottocento." *Emporium* 87, no. 520:173-92.

Oxford 1956. *Catalogue of the Collection of Drawings in the Ashmolean Museum*. Vol. 2, *Italian Schools*. Coll. cat. by K. T. Parker.

Pacelli, Vincenzo. 1979a. "La collezione di Francesco Emanuele Pinto, principe di Ischitella." *Storia dell'Arte* 36-37:165-204.

Pacelli 1979b. "Processo tra Ribera e un committente." *Napoli Nobilissima* 18, no. 1:28-36.

Pacheco, Francisco [1638] 1956. *Arte de la Pintura*. Reprint, with intro., notes, and indexes by F. J. Sánchez Cantón.

Pane, Giulio. 1970. "Napoli seicentesca nella veduta di A. Baratta, I." *Napoli Nobilissima* 9, nos. 4-6:118-59.

Pane, Roberto. 1962-63. "I monasteri napoletani del centro antico. La zona di S. Maria di Costantinopoli." *Napoli Nobilissima* 2, no. 6:203-13.

Pape, L., 1936: see Brunswick 1936.

Paris 1935. Petit Palais. *Exposition de l'art italien de Cimabue à Tiepolo.* Exh. cat.

Paris 1965. Musée du Louvre. *Le Caravage et la peinture italienne du XVIIe siècle.* Exh. cat. edited by Germain Bazin and J. Châtelain.

Paris 1967a. Musée du Louvre, Galerie Mollien. *Le Cabinet d'un Grand Amateur P.-J. Mariette 1694-1774: Dessins du XVe siècle au XVIIIe siècle.* Exh. cat. by Roseline Bacou, et al.

Paris 1967b. Musée du Louvre, Cabinet des Dessins. *Le dessin à Naples du XVIe siècle au XVIIIe siècle.* Exh. cat. by Catherine Monbeig-Goguel and Walter Vitzthum.

Paris 1974. Grand Palais. *Valentin et les Caravagesques français.* Exh. cat. by Arnauld Brejon de Lavergnée and Jean-Pierre Cuzin. Intro. by Jacques Thuillier.

Paris 1979. Institut Néerlandais. *Le choix d'un amateur éclairé. Oeuvres de la collection Vitale Bloch provenant du musée Boymans-van Beuningen avec quelques apports de la Fondation Custodia.* Exh. cat. edited by A. W. F. M. Meij, Marcel Roethlisberger, et al.

Paris 1982. Grand Palais. *La Peinture française du XVIIe siècle dans les collections américaines.* Exh. cat. by Pierre Rosenberg.

Paris 1983. Grand Palais. *La peinture napolitaine de Caravage à Giordano.* (Also at London, Turin, Washington, 1982–83.) Exh. cat. by Clovis Whitfield et al.

Paris (*Dessins*) 1983. Ecole nationale supérieure des Beaux-Arts. *Dessins napolitains XVIIe et XVIIIe siècles: Collections des musées de Naples.* Exh. cat.

Paris 1984. Musée du Louvre. *Catalogue de la donation Othon Kaufmann et François Schlageter au Département des peintures.* Exh. cat. by Pierre Rosenberg.

Parker, K. T., 1956: see Oxford 1956.

Parlat, Felice. 1950. *La collezione del Conte Giuseppe Matarazzo di Licosa.* Naples: privately printed.

Parrino, Domenico Antonio. 1700. *Napoli Città Nobilissima.* N. p.: n. publ.

Parrino 1714. *Nuova guida de' forestieri per osservare, e godere le curiosità più vaghe, e più rare della real fedelissima gran Napoli.* Naples: Presso il Parrino.

Parthey, Gustav. 1863–64. *Deutscher Bildersaal. Verzeichniss der in Deutschland vorhandenen Oelbilder verstorbener Maler aller Schulen.* 2 vols. Berlin: Nicolaische Verlagsbuchhandlung.

Pée, Herbert. 1971. *Johann Heinrich Schönfeld.* Berlin: Deutscher Verlag für Kunstwissenschaft.

Percy, Ann. 1965. "Bernardo Cavallino." Master's thesis, Pennsylvania State University.

Percy 1971: see Philadelphia 1971.

Pérez Sánchez, Alfonso E. 1961. "Una nueva obra del 'Maestro del Anuncio a los pastores.'" *Archivo Español de Arte* 34:325-27.

Pérez Sánchez 1965. *Pintura italiana del s. XVII en España.* Madrid: Universidad de Madrid (Fundación Valdecilla).

Pérez Sánchez 1970: see Madrid 1970.

Pérez Sánchez 1971. "Caravaggio e Caravaggeschi a Firenze." *Arte Illustra* 4:85-89.

Pérez Sánchez, Alfonso E., and Nicola Spinosa. 1978. *L'Opera completa di Ribera.* Milan: Rizzoli Editore.

Pevsner, Nikolaus, and Otto Grautoff. 1928. *Barockmalerei in den romanischen Ländern.* 2 parts: pt. 1 by Pevsner, pt. 2 by Grautoff. Wildpark-Potsdam: Akademische Verlagsgesellschaft Athenaion.

Philadelphia 1971. Philadelphia Museum of Art. *Giovanni Benedetto Castiglione: Master Draughtsman of the Italian Baroque.* Exh. cat. by Ann Percy. Foreword by Anthony Blunt.

Picone, Marina. 1955. "La mostra del ritratto storico napoletano." *Emporium* 122, no. 728:70-77.

Picone 1960: see Naples 1960.

Pigler, Andor. 1931. "Pacecco de Rosa Müvészetéhez." *Archaeologiai Ertesitö* 45:148-67.

Pigler 1937: see Budapest 1937.

Pigler 1954: see Budapest 1954.

Pigler 1956. *Barockthemen.* 2 vols. Budapest: Verlag der ungarischen Akademie der Wissenschaften.

Pilkington, Matthew. 1824. *A General Dictionary of Painters, Containing Memoirs of the Lives and Works of the Most Eminent Professors of the Art of Painting, from Its Revival by Cimabue, in the Year 1250, to the Present Time.* 2 vols. London: Thomas McLean.

Pillsbury, Edmund. 1982. "Recent Painting Acquisitions: The Kimbell Art Museum." *The Burlington Magazine* 124 (January), suppl.:i-viii.

Poensgen, Georg. 1959. "Die Ausstellung 'Ausklang des Barock. Kunst und Künstler des 18. Jahrhunderts in der Pfalz und ihre ideelle Ergänzung.'" In *Ruperto Carola* [University of Heidelberg] 26:107-26.

Polizzi, Lorenzo. 1872. *Guida della città di Napoli e contorni.* Naples: Gabriele Regina Librajo-Editore.

Ponnau, Dominique. 1976. "Principales acquisitions des musées de province 1973–1976." *Revue du Louvre et des Musées de France* 26, nos. 5-6:322-462.

Portland [Oregon] 1956. Portland Art Museum. *Paintings from the Collection of Walter P. Chrysler, Jr.* Exh. cat. by Bertina S. Manning.

Posner, Donald. 1977. "Jacques Callot and the Dances Called *Sfessania.*" *The Art Bulletin* 59, no. 2:203-16.

Princeton 1973. The Art Museum, Princeton University. *Jusepe de Ribera: Prints and Drawings.* (Also at Cambridge, Fogg Art Museum, Harvard University, 1973–74.) Exh. cat. by Jonathan Brown.

Prohaska, Wolfgang. 1975. "Carlo Sellitto." *The Burlington Magazine* 117:3-11.

Prohaska 1978. "Beiträge zu Giovanni Battista Caracciolo." *Jahrbuch der Kunsthistorischen Sammlungen in Wien* 74:153-278.

Prota-Giurleo, Ulisse. 1929. *La famiglia e la giovinezza di Salvator Rosa.* Naples: privately published.

Prota-Giurleo 1952. "Breve storia del teatro di corte e della musica a Napoli nei secoli XVII-XVIII": 19-146. In Felice de Filippis and Ulisse Prota-Giurleo, *Il Teatro di Corte del Palazzo Reale di Napoli.* Naples: L'Arte Tipografica.

Prota-Giurleo 1953. *Pittori napoletani del seicento.* Naples: Fausto Fiorentino Libraio.

Prota-Giurleo 1955. "Notizie su Massimo Stanzione e sul presunto suo manoscritto falsificato dal de Dominici." *Napoli-Rivista Municipale* 81 (November):17-32.

Prota-Giurleo 1962. *I Teatri di Napoli nel '600: La commedia e le maschere*. Naples: Fausto Fiorentino Editore.

Provincetown [Massachusetts] 1958. Chrysler Art Museum of Provincetown. *Inaugural Exhibition*. Exh. cat.

Pulszky, K., 1883: see Budapest 1883.

Putaturo Murano, Antonella. 1976. "Filippo Napoletano incisore." *Archivio storico per le province napoletane* 14:185-209.

Quintavalle, A. O., 1932: see Naples 1932.

Quintavalle 1940: see Naples 1940.

Querfurt, Tobias [1710?]: see Brunswick [1710?].

Ranalli, Ferdinando. 1845. *Storia delle belle arti in Italia*. Florence: Società Editrice Fiorentina.

Réau, Louis. 1929. *Catalogue de l'art français dans les musées russes*. Paris: Librairie Armand Colin.

Réau 1955–59. *Iconographie de L'Art Chrétien*. 3 vols. Paris: Presses universitaires de France.

Redford, George. 1888. *Art Sales. A History of Sales of Pictures and Other Works of Art*. 2 vols. London: Whitefriars Press.

Refice, Claudia. 1951. "Ancora del pittore Bernardo Cavallino." *Emporium* 113, no. 678:259-70.

Regina and Montreal 1970. Norman MacKenzie Art Gallery, University of Saskatchewan, Regina. *A Selection of Italian Drawings from North American Collections*. (Also at Montreal Museum of Fine Arts.) Exh. cat. by Walter Vitzthum.

Riegel, H., 1900: see Brunswick 1900.

Ripa, Cesare. 1764–67. *Iconologia del cavaliere Cesare Ripa*. 5 vols. Perugia: Piergiovanni Costantini.

Ripa [1758–60] 1971. *Baroque and Rococo Pictorial Imagery*. Reprint, with intro., translations, and 200 commentaries by Edward A. Maser. New York: Dover Publications.

Ritschl 1926: see Harrach cat. 1926.

Rivosecchi, Mario. 1959. "I 'bamboccianti' e Michael Sweerts." *Bollettino della Capitole* 34:24, 26.

Robert, Ernst F. F., 1819: see Kassel 1819.

Robert 1830: see Kassel 1830.

Rogadeo di Torrequadra, Eustachio. 1898. "La quadreria del principe di Scilla." *Napoli Nobilissima* 7, no. 5:72-75, and no. 7:107-10.

Rolfs, Wilhelm. 1910. *Geschichte der Malerei Neapels*. Leipzig: Verlag E. A. Seemann.

Romano, Michele. 1842. *Saggio sulla storia di Molfetta dall'epoca dell'antica respa sino al 1840*. Naples: Fratelli de Bonis.

Rome 1932. *La Galleria Nazionale d'Arte Antica in Roma*. Coll. cat. by Aldo de Rinaldis.

Rome 1944-45. Studio d'Arte Palma. *Mostra di pittori italiani del Seicento*. Exh. cat. edited by Giuliano Briganti.

Rome 1950a. Palazzo Massimo alle Colonne. *I Bamboccianti: pittori della vita popolare nel seicento*. Exh. cat. edited by Giuliano Briganti.

Rome 1950b. Palazzo Venezia. *Seconda mostra nazionale delle opere d'arte recuperate in Germania*. Exh. cat. by Rodolfo Siviero.

Rome 1956. Palazzo delle Esposizioni. *Il Seicento Europeo: realismo, classicismo, barocco*. Exh. cat. edited by Luigi Salerno and Alessandro Marabottini.

Rome 1958. Palazzo Barberini. *Pittori napoletani del '600 e del '700*. Exh. cat. by Nolfo di Carpegna.

Rome 1969–70. Palazzo Barberini. *Disegni napoletani del sei e del settecento*. Exh. cat. by Walter Vitzthum and Raffaello Causa.

Rome 1973. Accademia di Francia, Villa Medici. *I Caravaggeschi Francesi*. Exh. cat. edited by Arnauld Brejon de Lavergnée and Jean-Pierre Cuzin.

Rome 1981. Villa Farnesina, Istituto Nazionale per la Grafica, Gabinetto Nazionale delle Stampe. *Incisori napoletani del '600*. Exh. cat. by Alba Costamagna et al.

Ronci, Gilberto, 1954: see São Paulo [Brazil] 1954.

Rosenberg, Pierre. 1968. "Une toile de Bernardo Cavallino au Musée des Beaux-Arts." *Bulletin des Musées et Monuments Lyonnais* 4, no. 4:149-57.

Rosenberg 1972. "Acquisitions de tableaux italiens des XVIIe et XVIIIe siècles." *La Revue du Louvre et des Musées de France* 22:343-48.

Rosenberg 1982: see Paris 1982.

Rosenberg 1984: see Paris 1984.

Rosini, Giovanni. 1839–47. *Storia della pittura italiana esposta coi monumenti*. 7 vols. Pisa: Niccolò Capurro.

Rotterdam 1978. Museum Boymans-van Beuningen. *Legaat Vitale Bloch*. Coll. cat.

Ruffo, Vincenzo. 1916–19. "Galleria Ruffo nel secolo XVII in Messina (con lettere di pittori ed altri documenti inediti)." *Bollettino d'Arte* 10:21-64, 95-128, 165-92, 237-56, 284-320, 369-88; vol. 13 (1919):43-56.

Ruotolo, Renato. 1973. "Collezioni e mecenati napoletani del XVII secolo." *Napoli Nobilissima* 12, no. 3:118-19; no. 4, 145-53.

Ruotolo 1974. "La raccolta Carafa di S. Lorenzo." *Napoli Nobilissima* 13, no. 5:161-68.

Ruotolo 1977. "Aspetti del collezionismo napoletano: il Cardinale Filomarino." *Antologia di Belle Arti* 1, no. 1:71-82.

Ruotolo 1979. "Brevi note sul collezionismo aristocratico napoletano fra sei e settecento." *Storia dell'Arte* 35:29-38.

Ruotolo 1980: see Labrot, Gérard, 1980.

Ruotolo 1982. *Ricerche sul '600 napoletano: Mercanti-collezionisti fiamminghi a Napoli, Gaspare Roomer e i Vandeneynden*. Massa Lubrense (Naples): Tipografia G. Scarpati.

Russell, H. Diane, 1975: see Washington 1975.

Russoli, Franco, 1972: see Milan 1972.

Russoli 1978: see Milan 1978.

Salazar, Lorenzo. 1895–98. "Documenti inediti intorno ad artisti napoletani del secolo XVII." *Napoli Nobilissima* 4, no. 12: 185-87; vol. 5, no. 8 (1896):123-25; vol. 6, no. 9 (1897):129-32; vol. 7, no. 6 (1898):90-92.

Salazar 1903. "Salvator Rosa ed i Fracanzani (nuovi documenti)." *Napoli Nobilissima* 12, no. 8:119-23.

Salazar 1904. "Marco del Pino da Siena ed altri artisti dei secoli XVI e XVII (nuovi documenti)." *Napoli Nobilissima* 13, no. 2: 17-22.

Salazaro, Demetrio, 1877: see Naples 1877.

Salerno [Italy] 1954-55. Salerno Cathedral. *Opere d'arte nel salernitano dal XII al XVIII secolo*. Exh. cat. by Ferdinando Bologna.

Salerno, Luigi, 1956: see Rome 1956.

Salerno, L., 1963. *Salvator Rosa*. Florence: G. Barbèra Editore; Milan: Edizioni per il Club del Libro.

Salerno, L. 1970. "Il dissenso nella pittura: intorno a Filippo Napoletano, Caroselli, Salvator Rosa e altri." *Storia dell'Arte* 5:34-65.

Salinger, Margaretta. 1943. "A Baroque Painting of Saint Catherine." *The Metropolitan Museum of Art Bulletin*, n. s. 1:296-99.

Salmi, Mario. 1967. *Il Palazzo e la collezione Chigi-Saracini.* Siena: Monte dei Paschi.

Salvemini, Antonio. 1878. *Saggio storico della città di Molfetta.* Naples: Tipografia dell'Accademia Reale delle Scienze.

San Francisco 1939. San Francisco Bay Exposition Co. *Masterworks of Five Centuries.* Official cat., Dept. of Fine Arts, Division of European Art, Golden Gate International Exposition. San Francisco: Schwabacher-Frey.

San Francisco 1941. California Palace of the Legion of Honor. *Exhibition of Italian Baroque Painting, 17th and 18th Centuries.* Exh. cat.

Santa Barbara [California] 1974. University of California at Santa Barbara, Art Gallery. *Drawings by Seventeenth-Century Italian Masters from the Collection of János Scholz.* (Also at Fine Arts Gallery of San Diego; University of Michigan Museum of Art, Ann Arbor; and Stanford University Museum of Art.) Exh. cat. edited by Alfred Moir.

Santangelo, A. 1955. "Bernardo Cavallino: 'Il figliuol prodigo.'" *Bollettino d'Arte* 40:374.

São Paulo [Brazil] 1954. *Da Caravaggio a Tiepolo: Pittura italiana del XVII e XVIII secolo.* Exh. cat. by Gilberto Ronci.

Sarasota [Florida] 1949. *A Catalogue of Paintings in the John and Mable Ringling Museum of Art.* By Wilhelm Suida.

Sarasota 1961. John and Mable Ringling Museum of Art. *Baroque Painters of Naples.* Exh. cat. by Creighton Gilbert.

Sarasota 1976. John and Mable Ringling Museum of Art. *The Italian Paintings before 1800.* Coll. cat. by Peter A. Tomory.

Sarnelli, Pompeo. 1697. *Guida de'forestieri, curiosi di vedere, e d'intendere le cose più notabili della regal città di Napoli, e del suo amenissimo distretto.* Naples: Giuseppe Roselli.

Sarnelli 1791. *Nuova guida de'forestieri, e dell'istoria di Napoli.* Naples: n. publ.

Saxl, F. 1939-40. "The Battle Scene Without a Hero. Aniello Falcone and His Patrons." *Journal of the Warburg and Courtauld Institutes* 3, nos. 1-2:70-87.

Scaramuccia, Luigi [1674] 1965. *Le Finezze de'pennelli italiani ammirate, e studiate da Girupeno sotto la scorta, e disciplina del genio di Raffaello d'Urbino.* Gli storici della letteratura artistica italiana, vol. 16. Facsimile ed. Milan: Edizioni Labor.

Scavizzi, Giuseppe, 1963: see Naples 1963.

Scavizzi 1963-64. "Disegni di Luca Giordano a Capodimonte e a San Martino." *Napoli Nobilissima* 3, no. 3:41-49.

Scavizzi 1966: see Ferrari, Oreste, 1966.

Schipa, M. 1901. "Il Muratori e la coltura napoletana del suo tempo." *Archivio storico per le province napoletane* 26, no. 4:553-649.

Schleier, Erich. 1971. "Caravaggio e Caravaggeschi nelle Gallerie di Firenze. Zur Ausstellung im Palazzo Pitti." *Kunstchronik* 24, no. 4:85-102.

Schleier 1975. "Unbekanntes von Francesco Guarino: Beiträge zur neapolitanischen Seicentomalerei." *Pantheon* 33:27-33.

Schleier 1983: see Florence 1983.

Schleissheim [West Germany] 1885. *Verzeichniss der in der königlichen Gallerie zu Schleissheim aufgestellten Gemälde.* Coll. cat. Munich: Knorr & Hirth.

Schleissheim 1905. *Katalog der Gemäldegalerie im königlichen Schlosse zu Schleissheim.* Coll. cat. Munich: Knorr & Hirth.

Schleissheim 1914. *Katalog der königlichen Gemäldegalerie zu Schleissheim.* Coll. cat. Munich: n. publ.

Schlosser, Julius [1964] 1977. *La letteratura artistica: Manuale delle fonti della storia dell'arte moderna.* 3d ed. updated by Otto Kurz and translated by Filippo Rossi. Florence: "La Nuova Italia" Editrice.

Scholz, János. 1960. Sei- and Settecento Drawings in Venice: Notes on Two Exhibitions and a Publication." *The Art Quarterly* 23(Spring):52-68.

Scholz 1969: see New York 1969.

Scholz 1976. *Italian Master Drawings 1350-1800 from the János Scholz Collection.* New York: Dover Publications.

Schwanenberg, Hanns. 1937. *Leben und Werk des Massimo Stanzioni; ein Beitrag zur Geschichte der neapolitanischen Malerei des XVII. Jahrhunderts.* Bonn: Verlag Gebr. Scheur. Bonner Universitäts-Buchdruckerei.

Seattle 1954. Seattle Art Museum. *Caravaggio and the Tenebrosi.* Exh. checklist.

Serra, Luigi. 1937-38. "La mostra della pittura napoletana dal Seicento all'Ottocento." *Bollettino d'Arte* 31:522-28.

Sestieri, Ettore. 1920. "Cenni sullo svolgimento dell'Arte di Bernardo Cavallino." *L'Arte* 23:245-69.

Sestieri 1921. "Ricerche su Cavallino." *Dedalo* 2:181-98.

Shapley, Fern Rusk. 1973. *Paintings from the Samuel H. Kress Collection: Italian Schools, XVI-XVIII Century.* London: Phaidon Press.

Sigismondo, Giuseppe. 1788-89. *Descrizione della città di Napoli e suoi borghi.* 3 vols. N. p.: Fratelli Terres.

Sirén, Osvald, 1933: see Stockholm 1933.

Siret, Adolphe. 1848. *Dictionnaire historique des peintres de toutes les écoles depuis les temps les plus reculés jusqu'a nos jours.* Brussels: Librairie Encyclopédique de Périchon.

Siviero, Rodolfo, 1950: see Rome 1950b.

Siviero 1952: see Florence 1952.

Soria, Martin. 1954. "Some Paintings by Aniello Falcone." *The Art Quarterly* 17 (Spring):3-15.

Soria 1959: see Kubler, George, 1959.

Soria 1960. "Andrea de Leone, a Master of the Bucolic Scene." *The Art Quarterly* 23(Spring):23-35.

Soria 1961. "Notes on the Spanish Paintings in the Bowes Museum." *The Connoisseur* 148:30-37.

Spear, Richard, 1971: see Cleveland 1971.

Spear 1982. *Domenichino.* 2 vols. New Haven and London: Yale Univeristy Press.

Spear 1983. "Notes on Naples in the Seicento." *Storia dell'Arte* 48:127-37.

Spinosa, Nicola. 1967. "Domenico Mondo e il rococo napoletano." *Napoli Nobilissima* 6, no. 5-6:204-16.

Spinosa 1972: see Bucharest 1972.

Spinosa 1978: see Pérez Sánchez 1978.

Spinosa 1982. "Un tableau de Charles Mellin retrouvé au Mont-Cassin." *Revue de l'Art* 57:79-84.

Stampfle, Felice, 1967: see New York 1967a.

Standring, Timothy. 1982. "Genium io: Benedicti Castlionis Ianuen. The Paintings of Giovanni Benedetto Castiglione (1609–1663/65)." 2 vols. Ph.D. diss., University of Chicago.

Starzyński, J., 1938: see Warsaw 1938.

Stockholm 1928. Nationalmuseum. *Catalogue descriptif des collection des peintures du Musée National.* Coll. cat.

Stockholm 1933. *Italienska tavlor och Teckningar in Nationalmuseum och andra Svenska och Finska Samlingar.* Coll. cat. by Osvald Sirén.

Stockholm 1958. Nationalmuseum. *Aldre Utländska Malningar och Skulturer.* Coll. cat.

Storia di Napoli. 1967–74. 10 vols. Edited by Ernesto Pontieri, Salvatore Battaglia, et al. Naples: Società Editrice Storia di Napoli.

Strazzullo, Franco. 1955. *Documenti inediti per la storia dell'arte a Napoli (Pittori).* Naples: Il Fuidoro.

Strazzullo 1962a. *La corporazione dei pittori napoletani.* Naples: Tipografia Gennaro D'Agostino.

Strazzullo 1962b. "Postille alla 'Guida sacra della città di Napoli' del Galante." [Extract from *Asprenas* 9]. Naples: Tipografia Gennaro D'Agostino.

Strazzullo 1962–63. "Un progetto di Murat per una galleria di pittori napoletani." *Napoli Nobilissima* 2:29-39.

Suida, Wilhelm, 1949: see Sarasota 1949.

Suida 1953: see Houston 1953.

Suida Manning, Bertina, 1965: see Detroit 1965.

Sutton, Denys. 1957. "Seventeenth-Century Art in Rome." *The Burlington Magazine* 99:109-15.

Tasso, Torquato [1581, 1590] 1901. *Gerusalemme Liberata* [Jerusalem Delivered]. Reprint, translated by Edward Fairfax; edited by Henry Morley. London and New York: Colonial Press.

Testori, Giovanni, 1967: see Milan 1967.

Thieme, Ulrich, and Felix Becker. 1907–50. *Allgemeines Lexikon der Bildenden Künstler von der Antike bis zur Gegenwart.* 37 vols. Leipzig: Verlag E. A. Seemann.

Thuillier, Jacques, 1965: see Dargent, Georgette, 1965.

Ticozzi, Stefano. 1818. *Dizionario dei pittori dal rinnovamento delle belle arti fino al 1800.* 2 vols. Milan: Vincenzo Ferrario.

Toesca, Ilaria. 1971. "Versi in lode di Artemisia Gentileschi." *Paragone* 22, no. 251:89-92.

Tomory, Peter. 1967. "Profane Love in Italian Early and High Baroque Painting." In *Essays in the History of Art Presented to Rudolf Wittkower.* London: Phaidon Press.

Tomory 1976: see Sarasota 1976.

Toronto 1981–82. Art Gallery of Ontario, Toronto. *The Arts of Italy in Toronto Collections, 1300–1800, Based on the Holdings of the Art Gallery of Ontario, the Royal Ontario Museum, and Private Collections.* Exh. cat. by David McTavish et al.

Torriti, Piero, 1967: see Genoa 1967.

Torriti 1971. *Tesori di Strada Nuova la Via Aurea dei Genovesi.* Genoa: Sagep Editrice.

Trapani 1969. Museo Pepoli. *IV mostra di opere d'arte restaurate.* Exh. cat. by F. Negri Arnoldi.

Trieste 1943. Galleria d'Arte al Corso. *Mostra di Pittura Antica.* Exh. cat.

Tschudi, H., 1883: see Budapest 1883.

Turin 1983. Fondazione Agnelli. *La pittura napoletana dal Caravaggio a Luca Giordano.* (Also at London, Paris, Washington 1982–83.) Italian edition, exh. cat.

Ulm [West Germany] 1967. Museum Ulm. *Johann Heinrich Schönfeld.* Exh. cat.

Vaccaro, Emmanuele. 1838. *La galleria de'quadri del palazzo di Palermo di S. E. D. Antonio Lucchesi-Palli, principe di Campofranco.* Palermo: Filippo Solli.

Vaes, Maurice. 1924. "Le Séjour de van Dyck en Italie (Mi-Novembre 1621–Automne 1627)." *Bulletin de l'Institut Historique Belge de Rome* 4:163-234.

Vaes 1925. "Corneille De Wael 1592–1667." *Bulletin de l'Institut Historique Belge de Rome* 5:137-247.

Venturi, Adolfo. 1921. "Bernardo Cavallino nella Galleria Nazionale di Stoccolma e nella raccolta Harrach di Vienna." *L'Arte* 24:209-14.

Venturi, A., 1925. *Grandi artisti italiani.* Bologna: Nicola Zanichelli.

Venturi, A., 1938. "Gruppo di cose inedite." *L'Arte*, n. s. 41:44-78.

Venturi, Lionello. 1956–57. *La pittura italiana.* 3 vols. Geneva: Albert Skira.

Vernis 1952. *International Studio.* In *Connoisseur* 130:42-43.

Victoria [Australia] 1973. National Gallery of Victoria. *European Painting and Sculpture before 1800.* 3d ed. Coll. cat.

Vienna 1928, 1938. Kunsthistorisches Museum. *Katalog der Gemäldegalerie.* Coll. cats.

Vienna 1965. Kunsthistorisches Museum. *Katalog der Gemäldegalerie, I: Italiener, Spanier, Franzosen, Engländer.* Coll. cat.

Vienna 1981. Kunsthistorisches Museum. *Gemälde aus der Eremitage und dem Pushkin Museum.* Exh. cat.

Vitzthum, Walter. 1961. "Neapolitan Seicento Drawings in Florida." *The Burlington Magazine* 103:313-17.

Vitzthum 1966: see Naples 1966.

Vitzthum 1967: see Florence 1967.

Vitzthum 1968. "Jacques Callot et Filippo Napoletano." *L'Oeil*, no. 159 (March):25-27.

Vitzthum 1969–70: see Rome 1969–70.

Vitzthum 1970: see Regina and Montreal 1970.

Vitzthum 1971. *Il Barocco a Napoli e nell'Italia meridionale.* I disegni dei Maestri, 9. Milan: Fratelli Fabbri.

Vogel, Hans, 1958: see Kassel 1958.

Volpe, Carlo. 1970. "Caravaggio e caravaggeschi nelle Gallerie di Firenze." *Paragone* 21, no. 249:106-18.

Volpe 1974a. "I Caravaggeschi francesi alla mostra di Roma." *Paragone* 25, no. 287:29-44.

Volpe 1974b. "Un'altra opera firmata di Agostino Beltrano." *Paragone* 25, no. 287:82-85.

Von Loga, Valerian. 1923. *Malerei in Spanien vom XIV bis XVIII Jahrhundert.* Berlin: G. Grote.

Voss, Hermann. 1911. "Spätitalienische Bilder in der Gemäldesammlung des Herzoglichen Museums zu Braunschweig." *Münchner Jahrbuch der Bildenden Kunst* 6:235-55.

Voss 1922–23. "Forschungen über italienische Malerei des 16.-18. Jahrhunderts in ausländischen Zeitschriften." *Kunstchronik*, n. s. 34:509-12.

Voss 1924. *Malerei des Barock in Rom*. Berlin: Propyläen-Verlag.

Voss 1927. "Johann Heinrich Schönfeld." *Das schwäbische Museum* 3:57-67.

Voss 1964. *Johann Heinrich Schönfeld, ein schwäbischer Maler des 17. Jahrhunderts*. Biberach: Biberacher Verlagsdruckerei.

Walicki, M., 1938: see Warsaw 1938.

Walicki 1957: see Białostocki, Jan, 1957.

Warsaw [n. d.]. National Museum. *Catalogue of Paintings. Foreign Schools*. Coll. cat.

Warsaw 1901. *Wystawa obrazow wielkich mistrzów szkoly wloskiej i flamandzkiej ze zbiorów nieborowskich ks. M. Radziwilla* [Exhibition of Paintings of Great Masters of the Flemish and Italian Schools from the Collection of Prince Radziwill]. Exh. cat.

Warsaw 1938. *Katalog Galerii Marlarstwa Obcego Muzeum Narodowe w Warszawie*. [Catalogue of Paintings of the Foreign Schools in the National Museum]. Coll. cat. by J. Starzýnski and M. Walicki.

Warsaw 1956. National Museum. *Wystawa malarstwa wloskiego w zbiorach polskich XVII-XVIII w.* [Exhibition of Italian Paintings of the 17th and 18th Centuries from Polish Collections]. Exh. cat.

Washington 1975. National Gallery of Art. *Jacques Callot: Prints and Related Drawings*. Exh. cat. by H. Diane Russell.

Washington 1979. National Gallery of Art. *Prints and Drawings by the Carracci Family: A Catalogue Raisonné*. Exh. cat. by Diane DeGrazia Bohlin.

Washington 1983: see London 1982.

Waterhouse, Ellis. 1962. *Italian Baroque Painting*. London: Phaidon Press.

Whitfield, Clovis, 1982: see London 1982.

Whitfield 1983: see Paris 1983.

Wiesbaden. 1935. Nassauisches Landesmuseum. *Italienische Malerei des 17. and 18. Jahrhunderts*. Coll. cat.

Wittkower, Rudolf. 1972. *Art and Architecture in Italy 1600–1750*. 3d rev. ed. Harmondsworth, Middlesex; Baltimore, Maryland; Victoria, Australia: Penguin Books.

Wright, Christopher. 1980. *Paintings in Dutch Museums: An Index of Oil Paintings in Public Collections in the Netherlands by Artists Born before 1870*. London: Sotheby Parke Bernet.

York [England] 1955. City of York Art Gallery. *Inaugural Exhibition: The Lycett Green Collection*. Exh. cat.

York 1961. *Catalogue of Paintings. City of York Art Gallery*. Coll. cat.

Young, Eric, 1970: see Barnard Castle 1970.

Zafran, Eric. 1978. "From the Renaissance to the Grand Tour." *Apollo* 107:242-53.

Zampetti, Pietro. 1960. *Pittura italiana del Seicento*. Bergamo: Istituto Italiano d'Arti Grafiche.

Zampetti 1967. *Note sparse sul '600*. Venice: Fantoni.

Zani, Pietro. 1819–24. *Enciclopedia metodica critico-ragionata delle belle arti*. 28 vols. Parma: Tipografia Ducale.

Zeri, Federico, 1972: see Fredericksen, Burton, 1972.

Z. V. 1956. "Varsavia: Una mostra del ritratto veneto e una mostra d'arte italiana." *Emporium* 124, no. 743:231-33.

Index of Subjects

Photograph Credits

Joachim Blauel, Artothek, Munich: 77
Foto Boccardi, Rome: 13
Bullaty-Lomeo Photographers, New York, NY: Fig. 33
Courtauld Institute of Art, London: Figs. 1c, 1d
Prudence Cuming Associates Ltd., London: 20, 30, 31, 32, 68;
    Figs. 30, 40
Ali Elai, New York, NY: 29
Frequin-Photos, Voorburg, Netherlands: 18
Gabinetto Fotografico Nazionale, Rome: Figs. 13, 21
Galerie Heim, Paris: 5
Instituto Amatller de Arte Hispanico, Barcelona: Fig. 8
Bob Jones University ("Unusual Films"), Greenville, South
    Carolina: Fig. 80a
Bruce C. Jones, Fine Art Photography, Rocky Point, NY: 74,
    75
Jaroslav Juryšek, Olomouc, Czechoslovakia: 73
MAS, Barcelona: 57a
John Mills, Ltd., Liverpool: 35
Museumfoto B. P. Keiser, Brunswick, West Germany: 2, 80, 81
Pedicini, Naples: 43, 50, 56, 66
Mario Perotti, Milan: 9
Photographic Archives, National Gallery of Art, Washington,
    DC: Fig. 76a
Tom Scott, Edinburgh